Learn Clip Studio P

Fourth Edition

A beginner's guide to creating compelling art in manga, comics, and animation

Inko Ai Takita

Liz Staley

Learn Clip Studio Paint
Fourth Edition

Senior Publishing Product Manager: Larissa Pinto
Acquisition Editor – Peer Reviews: Jane Dsouza
Project Editor: Amisha Vathare
Content Development Editor: Matthew Davies
Copy Editor: Safis Editing
Technical Editor: Kushal Sharma
Proofreader: Safis Editing
Indexer: Manju Arasan
Presentation Designers: Pranit Padwal & Rajesh Shirsath
Developer Relations Marketing Executive: Sohini Ghosh

First published: April 2014
Second Edition: December 2018
Third Edition: July 2021
Fourth Edition: July 2024

Production reference: 1240724

Published by Packt Publishing Ltd.
Grosvenor House
11 St Paul's Square
Birmingham
B3 1RB, UK.

ISBN 978-1-83588-658-8

www.packt.com

This book is dedicated to all comic and manga lovers.

– Inko Ai Takita

Contributors

About the author

Inko Ai Takita is a distinguished manga artist from Kyoto, Japan, who currently resides in the UK after honing her craft at Kyoto Zokei University of Art & Design and Central Saint Martin's College of Art & Design. Since joining the illustrator agency illo in 2023, she has collaborated on artwork posters for *Alpha Tauri* and created advert animation art for *Intel*.

In the past, Inko has created illustrations for notable media campaigns, such as Sony Entertainment Japan's campaign for the Netflix drama series *The Crown*. She has also published manga collaborating with Scottish comic writer Séan Michael Wilson, including the critically acclaimed titles *Manga Yokai Stories* (Tuttle), *Lady Murasaki's Tale of Genji: The Manga Edition* (Tuttle), and the award-winning *Portrait of Violence* (New International). Furthermore, her illustrative contributions to the online theatre *Flight Paths* earned recognition at the Superfest Disability Film Festival in 2021. She has also submitted character designs for the *Kamigawa* set of *Magic: The Gathering* (Wizards of the Coast) and worked on 2D game art for *Promise Mascot Agency* (Kaizen Gameworks).

Outside of creating artwork, Inko has delivered manga workshops with the esteemed British Museum and the Victoria and Albert Museum. She has also collaborated with British artist David Blandy on manga posters for the London Underground's Embankment station. Her online tutorial "How to Draw Chibi Manga Characters" (The Guardian, Children's books) inspires young manga lovers.

I wish to thank to my dearest family, Miyako, Kazuo, Kumi, and Fumio, as well as my friends, relatives, and boyfriend, and the Packt staff for their magnificent support.

Liz Staley *is a visual artist and blogger who loves horses, animation, comics, and true crime. She began her digital art journey using Adobe Photoshop and then learned how to use Clip Studio Paint. She currently writes a weekly blog for Graphixly with art and Clip Studio Paint tips. Although she still loves the medium of comics and animation, her personal art now mostly consists of animal portraits that combine education with conservation. Liz loves horses, dogs, horror movies, anime, and learning the Japanese language.*

About the reviewer

Steven Dai is a 2D artist working on projects in comics, concept art, storyboarding, and illustration. He is academically trained in fine arts from the Complutense University of Madrid, from which he later specialized in comics and concept art. He is also trained in comic art and narratives from Escola Joso in Barcelona and Academia C10.

In the past, Steven has worked for clients on projects related to comics and manga, music cover illustrations, book covers, posters, and advertising. You can find a folio of his work on Behance, as well as on his own website, stevendai.org.

Me gustaría dar las gracias a mi familia y amigos por apoyarme en mi aventura en el mundo de las artes. Y al equipo de Packt por darme de oportunidad de aportar mi visión en este libro.

Join us on Discord!

Read this book alongside other users. Ask questions, provide solutions to other readers, and much more.

Scan the QR code or visit the link to join the community.

https://packt.link/clipstudiopaint

Table of Contents

Chapter 6: Erasers, Selections, and the Sub View Palette   109

Chapter 16: Using Clip Studio Paint to Color Your Manga 307

Chapter 17: Auto Actions and Your Workflow 335

Preface

Clip Studio Paint was previously called *Manga Studio*, and is today used by more than 15 million artists around the world to create manga artwork. It is one of the most loved software among illustrators, manga artists, and comic writers due to its special features for drawing manga and comics. With just this software, a computer, and a graphics tablet, you can create black and white comics, fully colored comics, illustrations, and short animations.

This book is for Clip Studio Paint users at all levels, but I want you to be able to easily follow along as a beginner. To that end, I have tried to give tons of guidance and visual examples, and even a few beginner tips for drawing manga. I hope that, by the end of this book, you'll be comfortable with Clip Studio Paint and be well on your way to being a manga art master!

Who this book is for

If you have just started working on your art digitally or are trying to shift your creation process from analog to digital, this book is for you, as well as for people who want to brush up their knowledge and skills on using Clip Studio Paint.

What this book covers

Chapter 1, Image Gallery of Manga and Illustrations Created by Clip Studio Paint, showcases a few examples of Clip Studio Paint artwork, to get you thinking about what styles and tools will be interesting to you.

Chapter 2, Installing Clip Studio Paint Pro and Interface Basics, walks you through the work of installing Clip Studio Paint and picking the right graphics tablet. It then guides you through the software preferences, the default interface, and how to make workspaces.

Chapter 3, Penciling: Layer and Layer Property Palettes, gets you started on the first stage in making digital art, penciling. Along the way, you will be introduced to the important concept of layers, layer menu options, and the Layer palette icons.

Chapter 4, Introducing Clip Studio Paint Brushes, gets you started with a few different brushes and what sort of marks they make. You'll also learn how to edit your brushes by customizing the brush engine and configuring the tool properties. Finally, you'll learn how to save and restore brush configurations.

Chapter 5, Pages and Panels to Shape Manga, revisits the concept of layers and applies it to an integral part of writing comics: how to make comic pages and panels.

Chapter 6, Erasers, Selections, and the Sub View Palette, teaches you about the various erasers and selection tools and how to use the Sub View palette. You'll learn how to use these erasers and selection tools for artistic effect as well as to correct mistakes.

Chapter 7, Using Text and Balloon Tools, aids comic writers by teaching you how to add text and speech bubbles to your comics.

Chapter 8, Getting Started with Inking Tools, goes over the next stage in making digital art after penciling: inking. You'll learn a few artistic techniques, as well as encountering a few inking pens, brushes, and markers that come included in Clip Studio Paint.

Chapter 9, Material Palette and Inking Special Effects, shows you how to create special effect brushes, textured brushes, and brushes with patterns such as foliage, as well as how to use the Material palette.

Chapter 10, Exploring Vector Layers, steps into geometric art by exploring how to create vector images, edit vector lines, and use the Material palette to add a design created by a vector.

Chapter 11, Creating Your Own Sound Effects, covers creating specialized text, adding strokes and gradient to text, and how to use Mesh Transformation to morph text into punchy sound effects and manga titles.

Chapter 12, Making Layer Masks and Screentones, covers the use and creation of layer masks, how to apply screentones to black and white manga by using selections and layer masks, and how to use the clipping layer function.

Chapter 13, All About Rulers, covers the myriad ruler tools in Clip Studio Paint. We will cover basic rulers, as well as symmetry rulers, focus and parallel line rulers, and perspective rulers.

Chapter 14, Using 3D Figures and Objects, teaches you how to use the 3D materials in Clip Studio Paint. Placing characters, posing them, customizing poses, importing poses from photos, and importing poses from Posemaniacs are all topics covered in this chapter.

Chapter 15, Color Palette, covers color selection and mixing palettes such as the Color Wheel, Color Set, Intermediate Color, Approximate Color, Color History, and Color Mixing. Creating a color palette from the Sub View palette is also covered.

Chapter 16, Using Clip Studio Paint to Color Your Manga, discusses the use of reference layers, how to create a flat color layer, the use of layer blending modes, and changing the line art color. It also covers how to use Shading Assist, Color Match, some great filters, and the Liquify tool to edit your art.

Chapter 17, Auto Actions and Your Workflow, covers auto actions and how to use them to make recurring parts of your setup process easier.

Chapter 18, Exploring the Clip Studio Assets and Animation, covers how to download new assets and materials using the Clip Studio Assets. You'll also take your first steps into creating simple animations in Clip Studio Paint, looking at how to create animation timelines and cels.

Chapter 19, Exporting, Printing, and Uploading Your Manga, covers how to use the print preview and print settings to create a physical copy of your manga. It also looks at exporting your work in various formats: for printing, display on the web, Webtoon exports, and Clip Studio SHARE.

To get the most out of this book

Having a graphics tablet or a tablet computer with a stylus and pressure sensitivity is highly recommended for using this software. Drawing with a stylus is much more natural than drawing with a mouse or trackpad. For more information on graphics tablets, see *Chapter 2, Installing Clip Studio Paint Pro and Interface Basics*.

Chapter 2 will also explain system requirements in much more detail. In short, the requirements are as follows:

Software covered in the book	OS requirements
Clip Studio Paint version 3.0.0	Windows 10 or 11, or macOS 12, 13, or 14

Disclaimer

There might be some differences in the option naming, placement, and availability depending on what version of Clip Studio Paint you are currently using. If needed, earlier versions of Clip Studio Paint can run on older OSes.

Download the color images

We also provide a PDF file that has color images of the screenshots/diagrams used in this book. You can download it here: https://packt.link/gbp/9781835886588.

Conventions used

There are a few text conventions used throughout this book.

`Code in text`: Indicates filenames, URLs, user input, and Twitter handles. Here is an example: "Export the `Manga page 1.jpg` image file to an internet-friendly file."

Bold: Indicates a new term, an important word, or words that you see onscreen. For example, words in menus or dialog boxes appear in the text like this. Here is an example: "Select **G-Pen** from the **Pen sub tool** palette."

Tips

Appear like this.

Important notes

Appear like this.

Get in touch

Feedback from our readers is always welcome.

General feedback: If you have questions about any aspect of this book, email us at `customercare@packtpub.com` and mention the book title in the subject of your message.

Errata: Although we have taken every care to ensure the accuracy of our content, mistakes do happen. If you have found a mistake in this book, we would be grateful if you would report this to us. Please visit `www.packtpub.com/support/errata` and fill in the form.

Piracy: If you come across any illegal copies of our works in any form on the internet, we would be grateful if you would provide us with the location address or website name. Please contact us at `copyright@packt.com` with a link to the material.

If you are interested in becoming an author: If there is a topic that you have expertise in and you are interested in either writing or contributing to a book, please visit `authors.packtpub.com`.

Share your thoughts

Once you've read *Learn Clip Studio Paint, Fourth Edition*, we'd love to hear your thoughts! Scan the QR code below to go straight to the Amazon review page for this book and share your feedback.

`https://packt.link/r/1835886590`

Your review is important to us and the tech community and will help us make sure we're delivering excellent quality content.

Download a free PDF copy of this book

Thanks for purchasing this book!

Do you like to read on the go but are unable to carry your print books everywhere?

Is your eBook purchase not compatible with the device of your choice?

Don't worry, now with every Packt book you get a DRM-free PDF version of that book at no cost.

Read anywhere, any place, on any device. Search, copy, and paste code from your favorite technical books directly into your application.

The perks don't stop there, you can get exclusive access to discounts, newsletters, and great free content in your inbox daily.

Follow these simple steps to get the benefits:

1. Scan the QR code or visit the link below:

https://packt.link/free-ebook/9781835886588

2. Submit your proof of purchase.
3. That's it! We'll send your free PDF and other benefits to your email directly.

1

Image Gallery of Manga and Illustrations Created by Clip Studio Paint

Hello everyone! A warm welcome to the fun world of **Clip Studio Paint.** Whether you want to start your creative journey or simply brush up on your skills, you've come to the right place. You will find great freedom in controlling digital tools for your manga creations by going through this book. Some chapters might even inspire you to try different types of art and effects that you never before imagined you could utilize! Whenever you feel stuck or unsure, you can always come back to this book to check how to use certain tools. It's going to be a fun ride, building your ability to express your manga story. So, let's start our adventure.

To begin with, this chapter is dedicated to showing you visual examples of Clip Studio Paint creations. Just a glance at this chapter's pages tells us exactly what features and capabilities Clip Studio Paint has. You can also see this as an early window into what creative ideas you can start to develop over the course of this book.

Don't worry – these tools and techniques will be explained step by step as we progress. In this chapter, you will find pointers to the parts of the book that introduce each tool, so you can jump to the places where the precise techniques you would like to learn are set out in detail. Of course, feel free to skip topics you are already familiar with.

This chapter will cover the following main topics:

- Illustration gallery
- What tools are used

Illustration gallery

In the following sections, we will preview each Clip Studio Paint tool you'll learn how to use in this book. If there's a style in particular that calls to you, consider jumping straight to that chapter to learn the techniques.

Pencil tools

Figure 1.1 shows examples of pencils that are available in this set of tools. You can use pencils for sketching and expressing warm, crafty art. Yes, you can use pencil tools to complete an entire full-colour manga illustration! Details of how to use pencils can be found in *Chapter 3, Penciling: Layer and Layer Property Palettes.*

Figure 1.1: A pencil tools sample image

Figure 1.2: An Inking tools sample image

Inking tools

Figure 1.2 shows examples of pens that are available in this set of tools. These are the most popular tools for manga. They produce clean and crisp manga drawings that make it easy to see what's going on in the scene and are still clear even when printed on colored or bad-quality paper. Details of how to use the pens can be found in *Chapter 8, Getting Started with Inking Tools.*

Brush tools

Figure 1.3 shows examples of brushes that are available in this set of tools. Yes, just like physical brushes, we can mix and blend colors with the brush tools in the latest version of Clip Studio Paint! Oil, water, and calligraphic...there are so many good brushes there. Details of how to use brushes can be found in *Chapter 4, Introducing Clip Studio Paint Brushes.*

Figure 1.3: A brush tools sample image

Figure 1.4: A shape tools sample image

Shape tools

Figure 1.4 shows an example of a shape tool drawing. These tools free you from wobbly, shaky lines. Instead, you can create accurate, precise objects, buildings, and décor shapes with shape tools! Learn more in *Chapter 11, Exploring Vector Layers*.

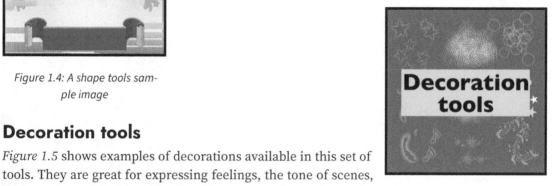

Figure 1.5: A decoration tools sample image

Decoration tools

Figure 1.5 shows examples of decorations available in this set of tools. They are great for expressing feelings, the tone of scenes, and patterns of clothing! Details of how to use decoration tools can be found in *Chapter 4, Introducing Clip Studio Paint Brushes*.

Figure 1.6: Textures sample

Textures

Figure 1.6 shows a sample image with and without a texture. If you want to add a paper/scratched/decayed texture to your art, you can always add extra effects by creating or downloading texture images.

You can simply add an extra layer with the texture image and change the layer blending mode. You can learn more in *Chapter 16, Using Clip Studio Paint to Color Your Manga*.

Text and balloon tools

Figure 1.7 shows examples of text and balloon tools. Manga creation involves several stages, including panel sketching, inking, coloring (if it's color manga), adding tones and effects, and adding text. So, you can add dialogue to tell your story. You can learn how to add text and speech balloons in *Chapter 7, Using Text and Balloon Tools*.

Figure 1.7: Text and balloon tools sample

Figure 1.8: 3D figures sample

3D figures

Figure 1.8 shows an example of using 3D figures as a pose reference. You can refer to or trace over 3D models to draw characters. It comes in handy especially when you want to draw accurate posture or objects/bodies from unusual angles. Learn more about using 3D models in *Chapter 14, Using 3D Figures and Objects*.

Layer blending modes

Figure 1.9 shows an example of a drawing with and without layer blending modes. After completing the basic coloring of your drawing, you might want to add shade, lighting, or light reflection, or even change the overall impression. It is possible to do this using layer blending mode. You can see the entirety of the effects available in *Chapter 16, Using Clip Studio Paint to Color Your Manga*.

Figure 1.9: Layer blending mode sample

Figure 1.10: Shading Assist sample

Shading Assist

Figure 1.10 shows an example of a drawing with and without **Shading Assist**. After completing the basic coloring of your drawing, you might want to give it an effective shade. You can choose what type of shading to add, such as **Simple shade** or **Evening shade**. The sample image shows **Evening shade**. You can see the entirety of the effects available in *Chapter 16, Using Clip Studio Paint to Color Your Manga*.

Color jitter

Figure 1.11 shows an example of a drawing using color jitter. The latest version of Clip Studio Paint has made very vibrant and realistic color mixing possible. Just turn **Change brush tip** on for your brush, and you can enjoy how the colors are mixed as you draw. Find out more in *Chapter 4, Introducing Clip Studio Paint Brushes*.

Figure 1.11: Color mixing sample

Figure 1.12: Liquify tools sample

Liquify tools

Figure 1.12 shows an example of a drawing before and after it is retouched with **Liquify tools**. Notice how the character's face expands a little, like a fish-eye effect. As you can see, you can change the shape and size of a specific part of an image by tracing it with a pen. It's so handy when you want to make a minor adjustment to a shape. More details can be found in *Chapter 16, Using Clip Studio Paint to Color Your Manga*.

Summary

Now that you have seen some actual art created by using Clip Studio Paint, I hope you have a better idea of what tools and functions the program offers. It is fine if you don't know the exact details of how this is achieved at this point, because you don't have to be an expert to use them all, but it is always good to know the tools and functions that are available.

You will have also noticed that some analog effects, such as scratching or bleeding, can be made digitally. This will give you the opportunity to illustrate mishaps, smudges, or accidental merges of color, which might add interesting effects to your creations!

If you have some images already scanned onto your device, you can add these effects as an extra bit of detail. It would be great if you could find an effect or two that appeals to you. After reading this chapter, installing the program, and obtaining a graphic tablet, you can ignore the order of the rest of the chapters and jump to a specific chapter that details the techniques you want to learn about.

But, most of all, enjoy Clip Studio Paint!

Join us on Discord!

Read this book alongside other users. Ask questions, provide solutions to other readers, and much more.

Scan the QR code or visit the link to join the community.

https://packt.link/clipstudiopaint

2

Installing Clip Studio Paint Pro and Interface Basics

In this chapter, we're going to dive right into the thick of it and start getting to know Clip Studio Paint. First, we'll look at the recommended system specifications for running Clip Studio Paint and how to install the program. We'll also talk about graphics tablets, their importance, and how to obtain one.

Once we have installed Clip Studio Paint, we'll get to know the interface. First, we'll go over the parts of the default interface. Then, we'll learn how to customize and change the interface to suit our needs, as well as how to select tools, and learn about the various palettes that comprise the Clip Studio Paint interface and their properties.

By the end of this chapter, you will be able to install Clip Studio Paint and identify the different parts of its interface. Although installation and navigation may sound a bit dull, it's important to know. Once we understand the different navigation sections, the door is opened to a whole world of artistic creation. It's like taking the first tour of a new home!

In this chapter, we will learn about the following topics:

- System specs, installation, and your activation number
- About graphics tablets
- The default user interface
- Moving, collapsing, and stacking palettes
- Using the tool palette
- Using the command bar

System specs, installation, and your serial number

Before installing Clip Studio Paint, we need to ensure that our computer hardware is capable of running the program. Graphics software can be taxing on system resources, so it is important to ensure that your computer is up to the task!

Clip Studio Paint is made for both Windows PCs as well as Mac operating systems; you pay by one-time purchase for a perpetual license. As well as Macs and PCs, it is also available on iPad, iPhone, Galaxy, Android, and Chromebook in monthly and annual usage plans. You can use the free trial version for all hardware mentioned. Once we have ensured that we can run the program on our computer, we can then download and install the software and run it for the first time.

System requirements

To run Clip Studio Paint effectively, our computer must meet certain system requirements. These requirements are slightly different for PCs than for Macs, so please check the system requirements carefully against the computer that you will be installing the software on to ensure that Clip Studio Paint will run properly.

Both PC and Mac computers have the following requirements for use of the program:

- **Storage space:** At least 3 GB of storage space available on the hard drive.
- **Monitor:** XGA (1,024 x 768) or higher, and high color (16-bit, 65,536 colors) or higher required.
- **Internet access:** An internet connection will be necessary for license authentication.

Windows system requirements

The following are the requirements to run Clip Studio Paint version 2 on Windows:

- **Operating system:**
  - Microsoft Windows English operating system
  - Windows 10 (64-bit)
  - Windows 11 (64-bit)
- **Main computer/CPU:**
  - Intel processors compatible with SSE2 or an AMD CPU.
  - GPUs compatible with OpenGL 2.1.
  - 2 GB of memory or more is required; 8 GB or more is recommended.

Important note

Memory space and CPU capability are required for top software performance regarding the image size, number of layers, and so on. Generally, the larger the image size and the number of layers, the more memory and the faster the CPU required.

- **Tablet:**

    - Tablets compatible with the Windows Ink platform.

    - A pen tablet or tablet monitor that supports a pressure-sensitive stylus (compatible with Wintab).

    - WACOM, XPPen, and Huion devices are recommended as tablets compatible with Wintab.

macOS requirements

If you are using a macOS computer, you will need to meet the following system requirements to run Clip Studio Paint version 3:

- **Operating system:**

    - macOS English operating systems 12, 13, and 14.

- **Main computer/CPU:**

    - Apple M series chips or Intel processor.

    - GPUs compatible with OpenGL 2.1.

    - 2 GB of memory or more is required; 8 GB or more is recommended.

We'll go into tablets in more detail in the *About graphics tablets* section. If your computer system meets or exceeds the requirements listed, then it's time to install the program!

Installing the program

To purchase and download the Clip Studio Paint program, you will need an internet connection. The program is available through the Clip Studio website. To access the English version of the website, you will need to visit the URL http://www.clipstudio.net/en in your internet browser.

Clip Studio does have a free trial of the program, which is very handy if you want to try the program to make sure your computer system can run it, or if you want to explore the program and ensure that it will meet your needs before buying it. At the time of writing, the Clip Studio Paint free trial lasts for up to 3 months on most devices, and 6 months on Galaxy. You can try both the Clip Studio Paint Pro and Clip Studio Paint EX versions of the program. Also, when using the trial version of the software, you will need to register for a free Clip Studio account.

We will discuss the Clip Studio account further in *Chapter 18, Exploring the Clip Studio Assets and Animation*.

Important note

Clip Studio Paint Pro or Clip Studio Paint EX? Which version should you choose? There are very few differences between the Pro and EX versions of the software. The Pro version is the standard version, and EX is the full-featured version. Clip Studio Paint Pro is less expensive than the EX version. The biggest difference between the two versions of the program is that the EX version allows you to create multi-page files (files with multiple pages in them that can be viewed and edited all at once) and that the EX version has no limit regarding the number of animation frames in a file, while the Pro version limits animation frames to a total of 24. If you will be creating long animations, chapters of a comic or manga, or other works where viewing multiple pages is needed, it is highly recommended to get the EX version of Clip Studio Paint.

Downloading the trial version

Once we're on the Clip Studio website, we'll need to download the trial version or buy the software. To download the trial version, complete the following steps:

1. On the ClipStudio.net/en website, click on the green button labeled **Free Trial**.
2. Choose the version of the software compatible with your operating system (Windows or macOS) and click on the corresponding **Download Trial** button.
3. Click **Sign up to get your first 3 months free** for Windows and mac OS if you haven't signed up yet, or log in with your Clip Studio account if you already have one.
4. On the next window, click **Get 30 days free!** to register your Clip Studio account and get 30 days free. Click **3 month free trial** to get 3 months free when you apply for a monthly plan.
5. The program installation file will be saved to your computer.

Purchasing Clip Studio Paint

Clip Studio offers two different types of purchase: One-time purchase and Annual/Monthly plans. One-time purchase means, as the name says, you only pay once to use Clip Studio, and Annual/Monthly plans mean you can choose to either pay once a year or monthly to use Clip Studio. Let's have a look at the following chart to get to know the difference and see which is the best option for you!

	One-time purchase	Annual/Monthly plans
Supported device	Windows and MacOS	Windows, macOS, iPad, iPhone, Galaxy, Android, and Chromebook
Issues activation code and serial number	Yes	No
Number of devices	1 unit	1–4 units
Updated items	Stability update	Stability and feature updates
Payment methods	Credit cards and PayPal	Varies depending on the store you order from
Clip Studio account	Registration required	Created upon purchase
Purchase/contract information	It will show in your Clip Studio account after it's authenticated.	It will show in your Clip Studio account once signed up.

Important note

There are some exceptions and conditions on top of the information in the above chart. For example, One-time purchase software can be updated with new features by subscribing to the Update Pass. Additionally, Apple Pay and Google Pay allow you to buy One-time Purchase software from smartphones. It's always best to check the details again on your purchase!

If you are ready to purchase Clip Studio Paint, follow these steps:

1. On the ClipStudio.net/en website, click on the button in the upper-right-hand corner labeled **Buy**.
2. The price list for the Perpetual license Pro and EX Annual/Monthly plans and the 12-month license (a single payment) will appear. Select your currency from the drop-down menu next to the price, and then click on the **Buy Now** button beneath the version of the software that you wish to purchase.
3. On the next screen, fill in your valid email address to receive your activation code.
4. Select the payment method on the next screen and fill in your payment information.
5. Complete the necessary fields and click on the button marked **Pay**.

When registering a purchased version, we will enter the activation code (and serial number for one-time purchase) for the software while launching the application for the first time. Your activation code and serial number will be sent to the email address that you registered with when purchasing the program. The email will be sent from no-reply@clip-studio.com, with the title **[CLIP STUDIO PAINT] Here is your Clip Studio Paint activation code.**

The following image is a screenshot of the email contents:

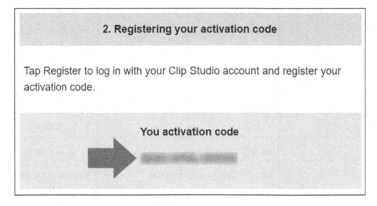

Figure 2.1: Screenshot of the email contents for an activation code

With your activation code ready, let's install the Clip Studio launcher!

Follow these steps to install your Clip Studio launcher:

Go to the web browser `https://ec.clip-studio.com/en-us/activation-codes/` and enter your activation code in the box, as shown in the following screenshot:

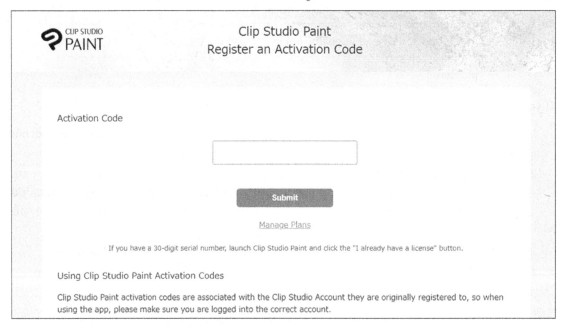

Figure 2.2: Screenshot of the register page

Click **Apply** on the next page, as shown in the following screenshot:

Your Activation Code

CLIP STUDIO PAINT EX Ver. 3.0 for Windows/macOS (One-Time Purchase)

Use it for an unlimited amount of time on one Windows or macOS device.

This activation code has yet to be used.

Cancel   Apply

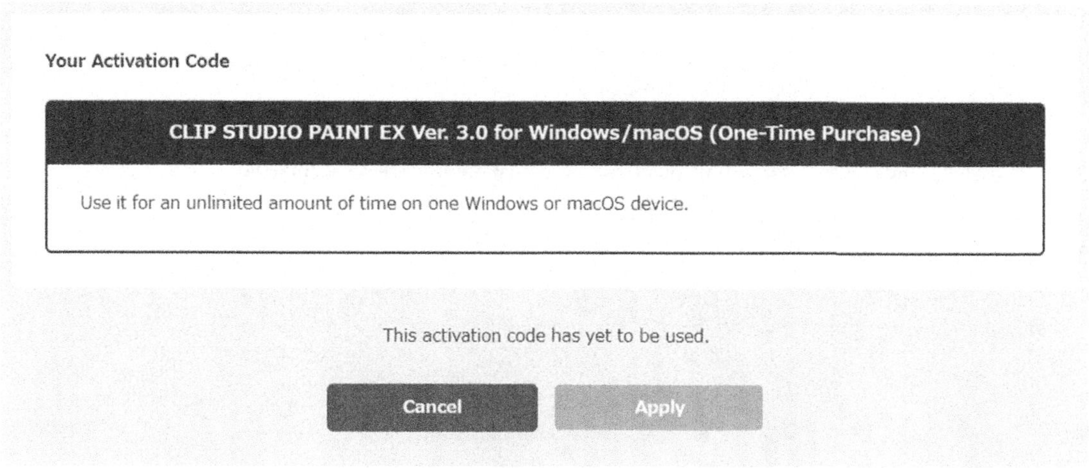

Figure 2.3: Screenshot of the type of purchase

Click **Confirm** on the next page, as shown in the following screenshot:

Can be used with the following

Clip Studio Paint EX Ver. 3.0 One-time purchase, perpetual license (Windows/macOS)

Use it for an unlimited amount of time on one Windows or macOS device.

Tap "Confirm" to apply the activation code.

Cancel   Confirm

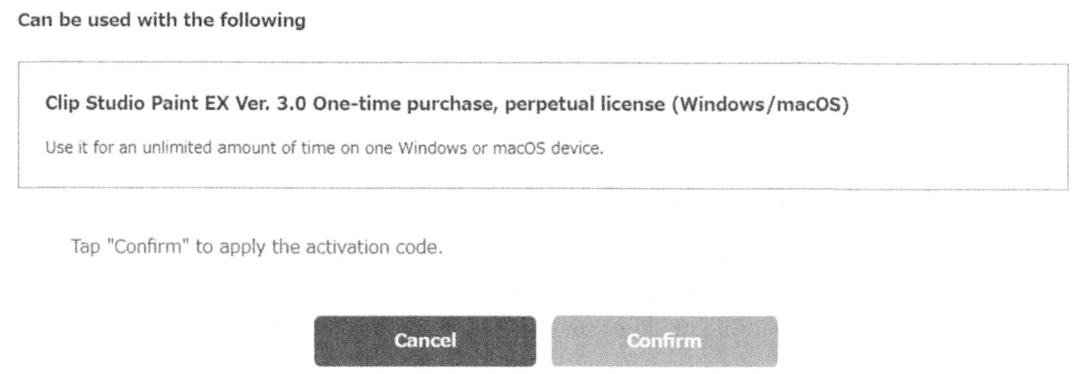

Figure 2.4: Screenshot of the confirmation page

The following screen will appear, and the activation code verification will be completed.

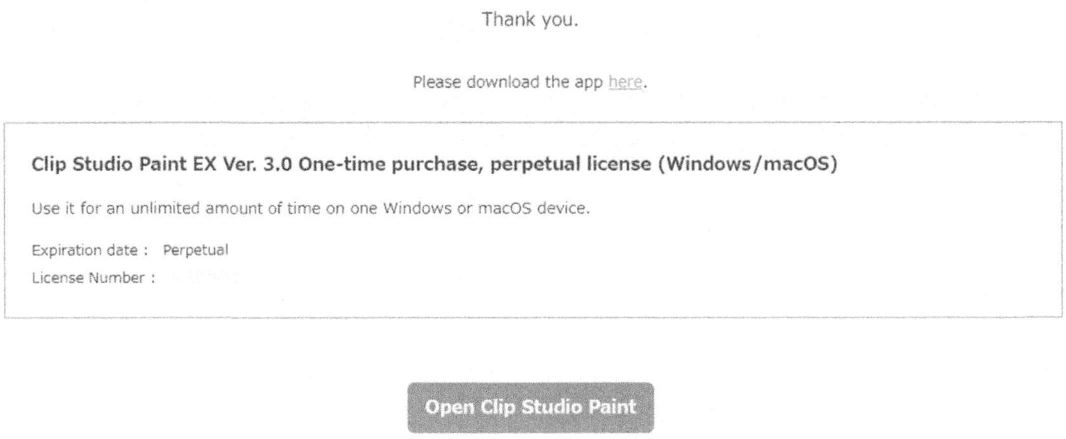

Thank you.

Please download the app here.

Clip Studio Paint EX Ver. 3.0 One-time purchase, perpetual license (Windows/macOS)

Use it for an unlimited amount of time on one Windows or macOS device.

Expiration date : Perpetual
License Number :

Open Clip Studio Paint

Figure 2.5: Screenshot of the completion of activation

Click the link on here in **Please download the app here,** as pointed out by the arrow in the following screenshot:

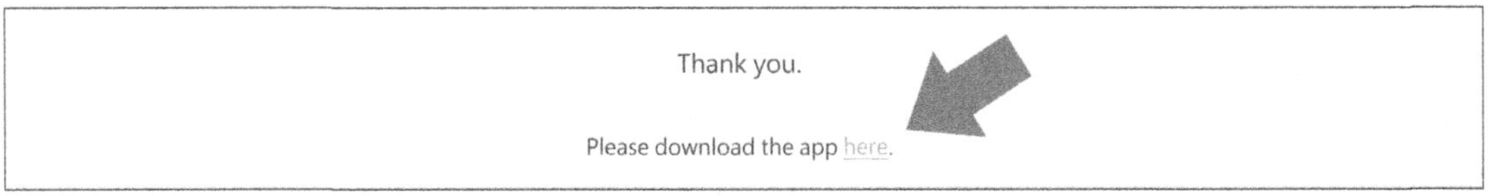

Thank you.

Please download the app here.

Figure 2.6 – Screenshot of the link

It will take you to the download page. The installer for your operating system will be automatically downloaded. If you exited and reopened the page in *step 5*, click the operating system of your computer and download the installer for Clip Studio Paint Ver. 3.0.0.

Great! Now that you have your Clip Studio installer on your device, let's install the application!

Installing on a Windows computer

Complete the following steps to install Clip Studio Paint on your Windows computer:

1. Locate the install file named CSP_XXw_setup.exe that has been saved to your computer, and double-click it to launch the setup program.
2. The welcome screen will be displayed. Click on **Next** to continue.
3. Read the license agreement. Click on the circle next to **I accept the terms of the license agreement** to accept the terms. Click **Next** to continue.

4. The **Choose Destination Location** window will be displayed. The setup will default to a folder in `Program Files` for installation. If you wish to change the location of this folder, click on the button labeled **Change** to the right of the currently selected folder name, and choose the location of the desired folder. Once the desired folder is selected, click **Next**.

5. On the next screen, choose the desired language for installation. Note that when using a purchased version, the language that correlates with the serial number must be used. If using the trial version, select the language you wish to install. Then, click **Next**.

6. Click **Install** to complete the installation.

7. When the installation completion screen appears, click on the **Finish** button to exit the setup.

Installing on a Mac computer

Complete the following steps to install Clip Studio Paint on your Mac computer:

1. Locate the file named `CSP_XXm_app.pkg` that has been saved to your computer, and double-click it to launch the **Installation** window.

2. Once the setup program launches, click on **Continue**.

3. Read the license agreement, and then click on **Continue**.

4. To continue, you must click on **Agree** on the next screen to accept the terms of the license agreement.

5. On the **Installation Type** screen, click **Install** to continue.

6. Select the desired language for installation. Note that when using a purchased version, the language that correlates with the serial number must be used. If you're using the trial version, select the language you wish to install. Then, click **OK**.

7. Once the installation completes, you will see a screen stating that the installation was successful. Click on **Close** to exit the setup program.

Important note

If you see a warning message when you try opening the file, you need to go to **System Preferences**, then **Security & Privacy**, and click the key icon to be able to make changes. In the **General** section, check **App Store and identified developers** and try opening the file again.

Figure 2.7: Screenshot of the Clip Studio icon

8. Double-click the Clip Studio application icon, which looks like the image on the right:

Once Clip Studio is open, click **Draw** on the upper-left of the screen, as pointed out by an arrow in the following screenshot:

Figure 2.8: Screenshot of the Draw icon

9. Select **I already have a license / I have signed up for a free offer** from the **Getting Started with CLIP STUDIO PAINT** dialog. When the login screen appears, enter your email address and password to log in.

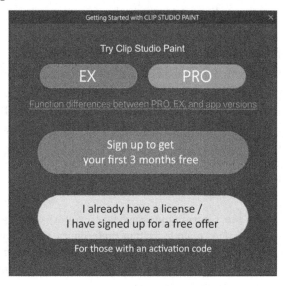

Figure 2.9: Screenshot of the Getting Started with CLIP STUDIO PAINT dialog

10. The license will be automatically authenticated and Clip Studio Paint will start up. If a license list opens, select the one for Ver. 3.0 and click **Activate**.

It is very important to keep this code in a safe place where you can locate it! Your Clip Studio Paint activation code allows you to register the software on up to four computers, so long as the following conditions are met.

You must also have your serial number if you purchase a new PC and need to install Clip Studio Paint on it again. Save the email from your registration in a safe folder in your email client. I also keep important serial numbers in a text file in a cloud backup, such as Dropbox or Google Drive, in case something happens to my emails. You may also want to make another backup of your serial number on a removable drive, such as a USB drive, to be extra certain that it is safe and can be recovered if there is an emergency.

Important note

If you see a warning message when you try opening the file, you need to go to **System Preferences**, then **Security & Privacy**, and click the key icon to be able to make changes. In the **General** section, check **App Store and identified developers** and try opening the file again.

Starting the program for the first time

Now that we have the program installed, we're ready to launch it for the first time. On the initial launch, you will have the opportunity to download additional materials, such as new brushes, patterns, and 3D models. Enter and verify your serial number, or register to use the trial version. This is the last step before we can open the Clip Studio Paint program and begin exploring the interface, so let's get started.

Changing a license

There are a few cases where the license may need to be changed:

- When changing from the trial version to the purchased version
- Upgrading the software from the Pro version to the EX version

To change a license, follow these steps:

1. Launch the Clip Studio Paint software.
2. From the **Help** menu, select the **Register/Change License...** option (or the Clip Studio Paint menu in macOS).
3. Enter your registered email address and password, and then click **Log in.**
4. Click **Enter** to enter the new serial number or activation code and click **Activate.**
5. Follow the instructions on the screen to complete the license registration and click **Launch.**

Downloading additional materials

The additional materials you can download inclue many extra tools, patterns, or models that go beyond basic tools. If they were not downloaded during the initial registration of the program, they can be downloaded later by using the following steps:

1. Launch the Clip Studio application by double-clicking the icon.
2. Once Clip Studio is open, click on the settings menu (the gear icon) in the top-right-hand corner.
3. Click **Download additional materials now** from the menu.
4. When the download confirmation message is displayed, click **Yes** to begin the download. Depending on the size of the materials, this download may take several minutes.

Once we install the program, we need to have a tool to draw on the program! Let's start finding out what we use to create art in Clip Studio Paint.

About graphics tablets

When working with art software such as Clip Studio Paint, having a graphics tablet makes life a lot easier. So, what is a graphics tablet, and where can you obtain one?

What is a graphics tablet?

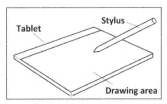

A graphics tablet is a computer peripheral that comes with a stylus. It allows you to hold a stylus and draw the way that you would with a pencil or pen on paper. The following diagram on the right illustrates a basic tablet and stylus:

Figure 2.10: A graphics tablet

There are many different types and brands of graphics tablets, all ranging in price from under $100 to over $2,500, so it is easy to find a tablet that is within your budget. I cannot express enough how much easier working in Clip Studio Paint is when you have a tablet!

There are many different factors to consider when shopping for a graphics tablet. Let's break some of those options down so that you can make a good choice when purchasing your tablet.

What type of tablet should I buy?

There are two primary types of tablets: traditional tablets and monitor tablets. Traditional tablets are slates that plug into or connect wirelessly to your computer. You then use the stylus to draw on the tablet while looking at the separate monitor, just like using a mouse on a computer.

A monitor tablet is a tablet with a monitor screen built into it. You then use the stylus directly on the screen so that you can see your hand and what you're drawing at the same time. This method feels more like using traditional paper and pencil and requires less of an adjustment period for new tablet users, as there is less of a disconnect between what your hand does and what your eyes see. A traditional tablet is fantastic for painting, but for detailed drawings that require accuracy, such as inking, a monitor tablet plays a great role.

However, this comes at a price. Monitor tablets are becoming more affordable every year, but they are still much more expensive than traditional tablets. If you are purchasing a tablet for a young artist or are someone just getting into digital art, I always recommend getting a traditional tablet. They are far more affordable and usually easy to find second-hand, but still in good working order. For more established artists who do a lot of art and know for certain that they like working digitally, investing in a larger tablet or a tablet monitor will usually speed up your workflow and make life easier, so it makes sense to invest in a higher-end tablet.

How large of a tablet should I buy?

Tablets come in all sizes, from no bigger than a traditional mouse pad to the size of a tabletop. The size of the tablet that you buy is very much dependent on how you draw. Sit down and draw on a piece of regular paper, and try to pay attention to how large or small you draw. You'll need to figure that out before you can decide on the size of the tablet you want to buy!

Another thing to consider when looking at different sizes of tablets is the space you have to store them. If you are using a tablet with your laptop and will be traveling with it often, or if you have only a small amount of space on your desk, you will want to purchase a smaller tablet that is more easily transported. However, if you have a larger area or will only be using the tablet at a desk, a larger tablet could be the right fit for you. I find that people who draw small can be comfortable with a small tablet size. Personally, I draw rather large and tend to take up the whole sheet of paper when I draw, so I like a larger tablet when I work because it gives me more room to work with.

What tablet brand should I buy?

There is a wide selection of tablets available, all with their own pros and cons. Some of the most well-known of these tablet brands are Wacom, XPPen, and Huion. Each brand has a wide range of different-sized and priced tablets, most of which you can find on their websites or by searching for them on sites such as Amazon.

I often get asked what brand of tablet I would recommend, and for me, there is one clear winner: Wacom. From my personal experience, Wacom tablets are of the highest quality and last the longest.

It's always good to know which models are great for your budget. The following is a list of Wacom, Huion, and XPPen recommendation models, organized by price range:

- **50–199 USD range:** Wacom Intuos Medium, HUION HS610, and XPPen Artist 12 Pro 11.6"
- **200–300 USD:** Wacom Intuos 5 Touch Medium, HUION Kamvas Pro 16, and XP Pen Artist 15.6
- **+400 USD:** Wacom Cintiq 13 HD, HUION Kamvas Pro 16 2.5k, and XP Pen Artist 22R Pro

You can often find them used on eBay and Amazon as well, so with a bit of searching, you should be able to find a tablet for any budget.

Important note

The Clip Studio Paint iPad version is as good as the computer version. But please remember that purchasing Clip Studio Paint on a computer doesn't mean you can use the iPad, iPhone, Galaxy, and Android versions for free. You need to pay the monthly fee for these versions, regardless of whether you already have Clip Studio Paint on your computer. To learn more about the Clip Studio Paint price range, go to ClipStudio.net/en.

Now that we have Clip Studio Paint installed and chosen our graphics tablet, it's time to start getting to know this amazing art software.

Taking a look at the default interface

Once you launch Clip Studio Paint, you will be greeted by the default interface. New users often get to the default interface and panic. It can be a bit overwhelming at first, but I promise it's not so scary! With a little bit of exploration, we can break down the default interface and understand what each section is. In the next section, we'll even learn how to customize the interface to suit our own needs. But for now, let's take a look at the default user interface.

The following screenshot shows what you may see when starting up your program for the first time:

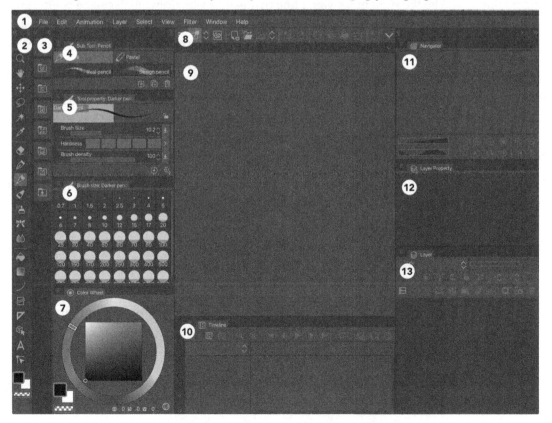

Figure 2.11: Screenshot of the default interface

The numbers in the preceding screenshot correlate to the following.

1. The **menu bar** is where you will find many of your options, such as creating and saving files, program preferences, viewing preferences, and more.

Figure 2.12: Screenshot of the menu bar

2. The **tool palette** holds all of the various tools that we'll use to create our comics and illustrations. At the top of the **tool palette** are tools such as **Zoom, Move, Move layer, Selection, Auto select,** and **Eyedropper.** In the middle are the drawing tools, such as **Eraser, Pen, Pencil, Brush, Airbrush, Decoration**, and **Blend.** In the bottom third of the tool palette are tools such as **Fill, Gradient, Figure, Frame border, Ruler, Operation, Text,** and **Correct line.** The final part of the tool palette displays our current foreground and background color selections, as well as a transparent color selection. We'll discuss all of these tools as we continue through this book, so don't worry if you don't know what all of them do just yet.

Figure 2.13: Screenshot of the tool palette

Figure 2.14: Screenshot of the Quick Access and Material palettes

3. The **Quick Access** and **Material palettes,** shown on the left, have a lot going on, but they are an extremely useful part of the Clip Studio Paint software. The Quick Access palette gives us access to more frequently used actions, much like the command bar. The Quick Access palette can also be customized, but unlike the command bar, it has two sets inside of it. This allows more flexibility, as Set 1 could be used for functions such as save and undo, while Set 2 could be set up with the most widely used tools or other commands to make tasks like coloring easier. We'll explore the Quick Access palette in more depth in *Chapter 5, Pages and Panels to Shape Manga.* This part of the software also contains the **Material** palette, shown right. Materials can be everything from comic frame templates, word balloons, and photographs to special brush designs and 3D models. There's a huge variety of items contained in the Material palette. We'll learn more about 3D models in *Chapter 14, Using 3D Figures and Objects,* and more about the Material palette in *Chapter 9, Inking Special Effects and the Material Palette.*

4. The **Sub Tool** palette contains options for each of the tools in the **tool palette**, and it changes depending on which tool we currently have selected. At the top of this palette are the different categories of tools in the Pencil category. In the central area of the palette are the different types of pencil tools. The tools displayed in your Sub Tools may be different than what is shown in the following screenshot on the right:

5. **The Tool property** palette displays options for the currently selected tool , as you can see in the screenshot on the right. Each tool can be customized to meet our individual needs, which we will discuss in more detail later in this chapter.

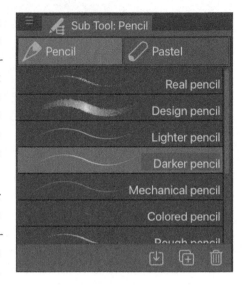

Figure 2.15: Screenshot of the Sub Tool palette

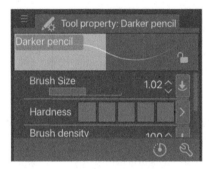

Figure 2.16: Screenshot of the Tool property palette

7. The **Color palette** offers us several options to choose and mix colors, all of which we'll explore later on in *Chapter 15, Color Palettes*.

Figure 2.18: Screenshot of the Color Palette

6. The **Brush size** palette allows us to quickly change the size of our brush by selecting one of the preset brush sizes from the icons shown in the palette:

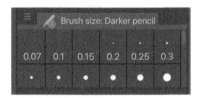

Figure 2.17: Screenshot of the Brush size palette

8. **The command bar** is a powerhouse in Clip Studio Paint, even though it doesn't look like much. This little piece of the interface gives us quick access to frequently used functions, such as creating a new file, saving, undoing, and even exporting files. The best thing is that it's completely customizable, too!

We'll learn how to customize the command bar in *Chapter 3*, *Pages and Panels to Shape Manga*.

Figure 2.19: Screenshot of the command bar

9. When there is a drawing or file currently open in Clip Studio Paint, it will be displayed in the Canvas display in the center of the program.

10. The **Timeline** palette is for displaying an animation timeline. We will learn more about creating animations in *Chapter 18*, *Exploring Clip Studio Assets and Animation*.

Figure 2.20: Screenshot of the Timeline palette

The **Sub View** palette shows the currently active file, along with a red rectangle that outlines the currently viewed section of the canvas. This is useful when working zoomed in on a page.

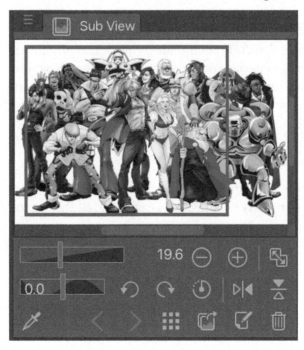

Figure 2.21: Screenshot of the Sub View palette

11. Beneath the **Navigator** palette is the 12, the **Layer Property** palette, which gives us the options available for the currently active layer. We'll discuss layers and layer properties in more detail in *Chapter 3, Pencilling: Layer and Layer Property Palettes*.

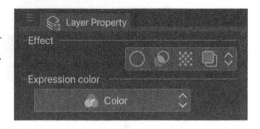

Figure 2.22: Screenshot of the Layer Property palette

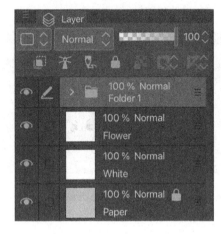

Figure 2.23: Screenshot of the Layer palette

12. The final part of our interface is the **Layer** palette, which shows all the layers in our currently active file:

Now that we have a better grasp of the default parts of the interface, we can learn how to move elements of the program around and customize it to suit our needs. Read on to learn more!

Moving, collapsing, and closing palettes

One of my favorite things about Clip Studio Paint is how customizable it is. We can customize not only our tools but also the interface of the program to make it look however we want it to look. This means that we can set up the program palettes and toolbars to give us the most efficient workflow, making our process as streamlined as possible. The process of moving, closing, and rearranging palettes is very easy, so let's get right to it.

Moving a palette

Let's start off by moving a palette to a new location in the Clip Studio Paint interface. I'll be working with the **Tool property** palette in this example, but this can be done with any palette you choose. Follow these steps to move a palette:

1. Locate the palette to be moved.

2. Put the mouse cursor over the name on the tab of the palette. The tab will be highlighted in blue when the mouse cursor is in the correct position.

3. Hold down the left mouse button to grab the palette, and then move the mouse to drag the palette out of its position. The palette's new location will be shown in red, as shown in the screenshot on the right:

Figure 2.24 :Screenshot of the palette location

Drag the palette to the new desired location. A red line will appear when the palette is in line to be dropped in a new place in the interface, as shown by the red line below the **Layer Property** palette in the following screenshot:

When the palette is in the desired new location, release the left mouse button to finish moving the palette. In the following screenshot, the **Tool property** palette is now below the **Layer Property** palette:

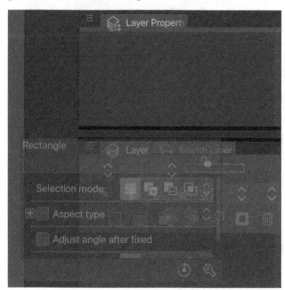

Figure 2.25: Screenshot of the palette location 2

Figure 2.26: Screenshot of the palette location 3

A palette can also be popped out of the interface, by dragging the palette out to the canvas display window and releasing it when it is surrounded by a red rectangle. This will place the palette out on its own and not as part of the side-bars of the interface, as shown in the screenshot on the right:

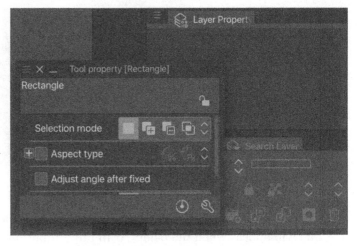

Figure 2.27: Screenshot of the palette location 4

Closing a palette

There are two ways to close a palette that isn't needed. Follow these simple steps to close a palette:

1. Follow the preceding instructions to move a palette, and make sure to *pop out* the palette, as shown in *step 6*.
2. Click on the X button in the upper-right-hand corner of the palette to close it.
3. To retrieve a palette once it's been closed, simply go to **Window** in the **File** menu. Click on the name of the palette to show it again. Alternatively, the **Window** menu can also be used to close palettes by clicking on the names with check-marks next to them.

Collapsing and expanding palettes

Clip Studio Paint can also temporarily hide entire banks of palettes and then retrieve them when needed. In the screenshot on the right, the **Quick Access** and **Material** palettes are collapsed so that we can only see the category icons:

Figure 2.28: Screenshot of the Quick Access and Material palettes

Let's learn how to expand and collapse these palettes by following these steps:

1. To fully expand the palette, click on the single right-facing arrow at the top of the palette window. The palette will expand, as shown in the screenshot on the right:

   To collapse the palette back down to icons only, click on the single left-facing arrow at the top of the palette.

2. To fully collapse the palette, click on the double left-facing arrows at the top of the palette.

Figure 2.29: Screenshot of an expanded palette

Tip

Remember that palettes on the right-hand side of the screen will have arrows facing the opposite direction, but they still perform the same function! They just collapse the palettes to the right instead of to the left. Collapsing palettes is a great way to give yourself more drawing space when on a small monitor, so be sure to use this if the interface feels cramped and you want to temporarily move things out of the way while creating your art!

The tool palette and command bar

Now that we've explored how to move palettes around, let's discuss the tool palette and command bar in more detail. Both of these parts of the Clip Studio Paint interface are very important, and you'll use them often, so let's get to know them before we start drawing.

The tool palette

The tool palette is found in the default interface down the left-hand side of the program. This is shown in the following screenshot:

The tool palette gives us access to the various drawing and editing tools in Clip Studio Paint. The tools are separated into categories, designated by the horizontal lines going across the tool palette, and are divided into thirds.

In the top third of the tool palette are the selection and editing tools. From top to bottom, they are listed in the following order with the corresponding shortcut keys in brackets:

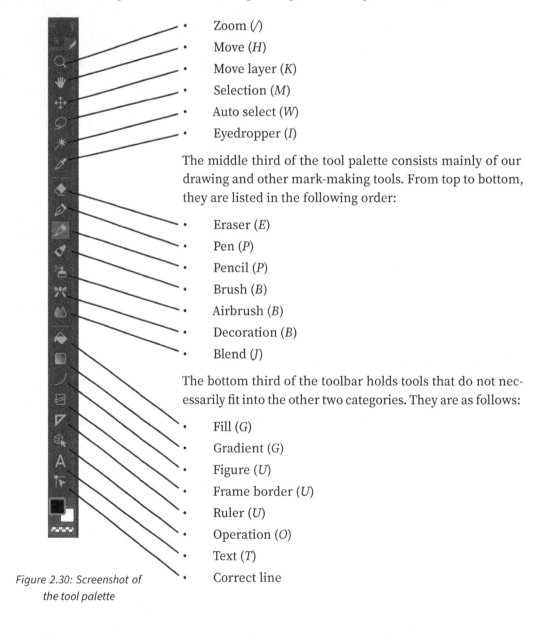

- Zoom (/)
- Move (H)
- Move layer (K)
- Selection (M)
- Auto select (W)
- Eyedropper (I)

The middle third of the tool palette consists mainly of our drawing and other mark-making tools. From top to bottom, they are listed in the following order:

- Eraser (E)
- Pen (P)
- Pencil (P)
- Brush (B)
- Airbrush (B)
- Decoration (B)
- Blend (J)

The bottom third of the toolbar holds tools that do not necessarily fit into the other two categories. They are as follows:

- Fill (G)
- Gradient (G)
- Figure (U)
- Frame border (U)
- Ruler (U)
- Operation (O)
- Text (T)
- Correct line

Figure 2.30: Screenshot of the tool palette

The very bottom of the tool palette shows the current foreground and background colors, as well as a transparent *color* that can be selected to allow mark-making tools to act like erasers. More information on this is in *Chapter 6, Erasers, Selections, and the Sub View Palette*.

It is best to think of the tool palette as a collection of categories of tools. Clicking on one of the icons in the tool palette will change the options available in the **Sub Tool** palette. The desired tool is then selected from the **Sub Tool** palette. You can think of the tool palette as drawers holding supplies in each one. For instance, if we click on the pencil in the tool palette, it is like opening a drawer where all of our pencils are stored. Then, we can select the specific pencil we want out of that category of pencils. It is always good to have the tool palette and **Sub Tool** palette open near each other to make tool selection quick and easy.

Customizing the tool palette

Just like all the other parts of the Clip Studio Paint interface, the tool palette can be customized to suit our needs. Let's take a look at the different options we have to customize the toolbar.

Reordering tools

Just like the palettes of the interface, the tools in the toolbar can be moved around to suit our individual needs. For the following instructions, let's move the Pencil tool up above the Zoom tool so that it is the first tool in the tool palette. Accomplish this by following these steps:

1. Click on the icon of the tool in the tool palette to be moved and hold down the left mouse button.
2. While holding down the button, drag the tool icon to the new location. A red line will show the current position.
3. Once the red line is in the new, desired place, release the mouse button.
4. To put the tool icon back in its previous place, repeat the preceding steps to move it again.

Renaming tools

Any of the tools in the tool palette can be renamed. To do this, complete the following steps:

1. Locate the icon of the tool to be renamed in the palette.
2. Right-click with the mouse on the icon to bring up the menu shown in the screenshot on the right:

Figure 2.31: Screenshot of renaming tools 1

3. Select **Tool settings...** from the menu. The following dialog box will appear:

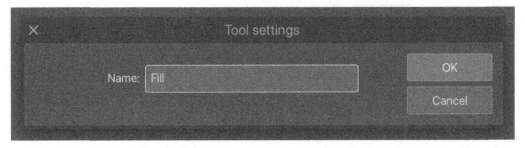

Figure 2.32: Screenshot of renaming tools 2

4. In the text entry field, type in a new name for the tool.
5. To accept the name change, click **OK**. If you change your mind and don't wish to rename the tool, click **Cancel**.

Deleting tools

Sometimes, you just don't use a certain category of tools, and you don't want them cluttering up your space. With Clip Studio Paint, we can get rid of some of the visual clutter and delete tools that we don't use from the tool palette. Use the following steps to delete a tool and all of its sub tools:

1. Locate the icon of the tool to be deleted in the tool palette.
2. Right-click on the icon to bring up the menu shown in *step 2* of the *Renaming tools* section.
3. Select **Delete tool...** from the menu. The following message will appear:

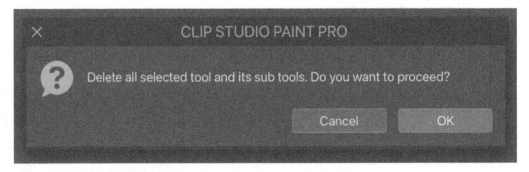

Figure 2.33: Screenshot of deleting tools

To proceed to delete the tool and all of its sub tools, click **OK**. If we've changed our mind and want to leave the tool icon in the tool palette, we can simply click **Cancel**.

Tip

If you accidentally delete an important default tool from the tool palette and need to get it back, all of the default sub tools are available from the tool palette menu. Click the top-left icon of the palette and select **Add from default...** from the drop-down menu. Select the tool you want to add to the tool palette from the list and select **OK**. Ta da! The deleted tool is now back on the tool palette!

Now that we know all about customizing the tool palette, let's take a minute to talk about the command bar.

The primary command bar

The primary or permanent command bar is located between the **File** menu and the canvas display area. It is shown in the following screenshot:

The default options on the command bar in the preceding screenshot are as follows, from left to right:

- **Clear:** Deletes the current content (of a layer or a selection).
- **Clear Outside Selection:** Deletes any content outside of the currently active selection.
- **Fill:** Fills in the current area with a foreground color.
- **Scale up/Scale down/Rotate:** Resizes or rotates the current layer or selection content.

- **New File:** Creates a new file.
- **Open File:** Opens an existing file.
- **Save File:** Saves the current file.

- **Deselect:** Clears the active selection.
- **Invert selected area:** Reverses the selected area.
- **Show border of selected area:** Turns the visibility of the selected area off and on.

Figure 2.34: Screenshot of the command bar

- **Undo:** Reverses the last action.
- **Redo:** Redoes an undone action.

- **Snap to ruler:** Toggles snapping when there is an active ruler.
- **Snap to special ruler:** Toggles snapping on a special ruler.
- **Snap to grid:** Toggles snapping on an active grid.
- **Clip Studio Support:** This is a direct link to the Clip Studio website for help or downloads.

We will discuss customizing the command bar in *Chapter 5, Pages and Panels to Shape Manga*.

Summary

In this chapter, you learned how to obtain Clip Studio Paint and install it. You are now familiar with the default interface, can move, close, and temporarily collapse menus and palettes, and know how to reorder tools in the tool palette. We also took a closer look at the command bar in the main menu and the selection launcher.

In the next chapter, we are going to take a look at the program's preferences before we get into our actual drawings. They are very helpful for creating a comfortable art studio for you to work in, by decluttering and placing frequently used tools closer to you. Let's build a unique environment for your creation! Read on to learn more.

Join us on Discord!

Read this book alongside other users. Ask questions, provide solutions to other readers, and much more.

Scan the QR code or visit the link to join the community.

https://packt.link/clipstudiopaint

3

Penciling: Layer and Layer Property Palettes

Most people have probably heard the word **penciling** before. Penciling is a stage of the manga or comic creation process in which an artist sketches out a layout of the page with their pencil before they move on to the "inking" stage. In Clip Studio Paint, we have a great function for it! One of the best features of working in a digital art program is the ability to work in **layers**. We can use layers to edit and separate finished pencil artwork from ink artwork, and you will find tons more benefits as we read through this chapter!

Layers are like stacks of transparencies used for projection: every transparency carries a bit of text or an element of the image, so that we can separate the pencil sketch layer from the inked art layer, and when all the transparencies are stacked on top of each other, they form the complete image. You can make each layer visible or invisible with only one click, and manipulation of one layer doesn't affect the other layer's art. Most digital art software allows the creation of layers, and Clip Studio Paint is no exception. This chapter is all about the layers!

The topics discussed in this chapter will include the following:

* Penciling
* The Layer palette
* Properties of layers
* Different types of layers
* Layer groups and layer colors
* Layer effects

Let's jump right in!

Technical requirements

To get started, you need Clip Studio Paint installed on your device and a new blank canvas ready. Any size is fine, but I recommend creating a 300 DPI square canvas to go through the content in this chapter. You can create it by clicking **File**, selecting **New file...**, selecting the **illustration** icon, and then clicking **OK**.

What is penciling?

Penciling is one of the manga creation stages in which you draw a pencil sketch referring to a manga script before the inking stage. In the manga process, there's often a first-draft pencil sketch and a second-draft pencil sketch. The first one is called **Ne-mu**, pronounced like "Name," which is a very rough pencil drawing, with panels and speech bubbles to create an overall page draft.

We do this to get a good visual plan of the page, and it's important to show it to an editor, a designer, and/or a scriptwriter if you're working with a publisher. After getting approval, we move on to a second pencil sketch, which is more detailed and easier to work on with inking pens. In the image on the right, we can see the whole process of the manga page creation, including the Ne-mu on the very left top and the second penciling sketch next to it:

Figure 3.1: A sample image of a manga page creation process

Chibi

When we draw Ne-mu with Pencil tools, what we care about is the layout, so only basic figures are fine at this stage as long as it's clear which character the figure is. I often write an initial of the character's name on the face of the figure. We can see how figure drawings are composed in the following sketches:

7Heads

8Heads

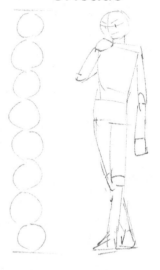

The penciling sketch is a good place to start. Keep working on the rough figure until the proportions look right. The heads rule shown here is a good start! You may need to spend some time getting the head, arms, and legs the right sizes. It may be frustrating at first, but once you're happy with the overall shape, you won't have to worry about it again as you go into more detail with clothes, expressions, and so on. Of course, the more you practice proportions, the more intuitively they'll come to you.

Sometimes, we realize we want to change the character's pose after drawing the figure, but still want to refer to the original pose without erasing it. Layers come in handy in this case. Simply create a new layer, use a different colored pencil tool, and start drawing alternative poses on the new layer.

Figure 3.2: A penciling image of various proportions

We can also use layers when we have different elements on one panel overlapping each other. Each element is drawn on a different layer, so we can move one element around at a time without affecting other drawings.

We can see these two cases in the following image:

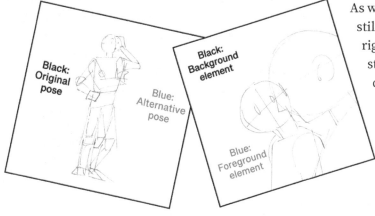

Figure 3.3: Sample images of multi-layer penciling

As we can see, your first sketch can still be useful even if isn't quite right. It's important when you are starting out to not be too critical or erase too much! It would have been more difficult to draw the blue alternative pose shown here if we didn't have the black original pose as a reference. Penciling is a good time to make mistakes, so long as you iron them out before inking.

That's right, we benefit a lot from using layers on digital drawings. Let's have a closer look at what they are.

What is a layer?

A layer, in a piece of digital art, is a magical thing that can make our workflow smoother and easier, and it can also save a lot of headaches in the future when we go from pencils to inks to colors too. Okay, so maybe it's not *actually* magic, but it's pretty darn close!

Layers are like stacks of transparencies used for projection: every transparency carries a bit of text or an element of the image, so that we can separate the pencil sketch layer from the inked art layer, and when all the transparencies are stacked on top of each other, they form the complete image. You can make each layer visible or invisible with only one click, and manipulation of one layer doesn't affect art on another layer.

But what are layers and how do they work? Let's look at the following example images. Now that the sketch has been done, the art can be completed by inking and coloring on it. The colored drawing in this screenshot is made from five layers on top of it:

Figure 3.4: A sample colored drawing

What exactly are those layers? In the following screenshot, we can see exactly what they are:

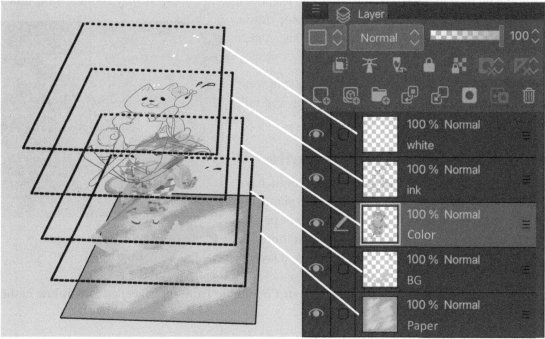

Figure 3.5: Layer diagram of a colored piece of art

Here, we can see the transparencies that we mentioned earlier. Every transparency has its own bit of text or part of the image, and when they are stacked on top of each other, they form the complete image. The pink background is a paper layer. On top of that, there is a layer with some gray, which is the carpet the character is standing on. Then, there is a layer with most of the colors of the drawing. Above that is the actual line art (ink) for the character. Finally, on top is a layer with white dots for the shining effect.

It's entirely possible to create digital art without using layers, but layers can make your digital art life easier. Here's a list of things you can do with layers:

- Manipulate, add extra, or organize pencil sketches
- Change and edit inks even after coloring started
- Add special effects to certain parts of an image
- Easily correct color using adjustment layers, blending modes, and layer masks
- Revert your image to inks only if a mistake is made in coloring
- Change the color of the line art without affecting the other parts of an image
- Separate out individual characters or elements for reuse in other images
- Organize image elements

There are many more benefits to using layers. Of course, there are also some downsides. Depending on how many layers you choose to use, the number of layers may begin to slow down computers with less RAM and disk space. Keep this in mind, especially when working on larger images with a high DPI.

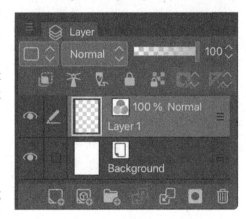

Now that we know what layers are and why we'd want to use them, let's explore the **Layer** palette and talk about different types of layers.

Introducing the Layer palette

Just like most options in Clip Studio Paint, layers have a palette that acts as a *command center* for managing and creating layers. When we look at the **Layer** palette in the following screenshot, we can see that there are many icons and options that apply to different layers:

Figure 3.6: A screenshot of the Layer palette

If you cannot locate the **Layer** palette in your Clip Studio Paint interface, go to **Window** in the **File** menu and click on **Layer** to display it.

There are two drop-down menus and a slider on the top row. The first drop-down menu on the left is used to decide the palette color, changing the color of the icons next to the layer name in the **Layer** palette. It is used to organize layers easily by grouping them by color. For instance, when making an image with many characters, each layer related to one character can be assigned a layer color for easy identification.

The second drop-down menu on the left is **Blending Mode**, which applies different color effects to the drawings beneath the layer. A full explanation of **Blending Mode** can be found in *Chapter 16, Using Clip Studio Paint to Color Your Manga*.

To the right of the **Blending Mode** drop-down menu is a slider. This controls the opacity of the layer. Opacity refers to the amount of transparency that the objects on the layer have. If the slider is set to **100**, then the layer contents are at full opacity. If it is set to zero, then the layer contents will be completely transparent and therefore invisible. I normally set the sketch layer opacity to 30% when I start inking on the layer above it so that we can see the inked line clearly!

Below **Blending Mode** and the opacity slider is a group of icons. The following is a list of them from left to right and a description of what each one does:

Figure 3.7: A screenshot of the icons

- **Clip to layer below:** This hides some parts of the image in the current layer using the layer below. Content in the current layer will only be shown in areas where there is also content in the layer below. This is a very useful function for coloring when you need to color in a limited area. For example, we can use this for skin color, clothing patterns, and shading. In the following screenshot, the cheek color layer is clipped by the below skin color layer, so that the cheek color doesn't exceed the outside of the face:

Figure 3.8: A screenshot of the Clip to layer below function

- **Set as reference layer:** Some tools, such as the **Fill** tool, can be set to reference their parameters with another layer. This icon turns the currently selected layer into a reference layer for these tools. Using this setting stops the color overflowing the borders drawn on the reference layer. We can also link it to the **Anti-overflow** setting on brush tools, which you can find in the *Anti-overflow* section in Chapter 4, *Introducing Clip Studio Paint Brushes*.

- **Set as draft layer:** This option turns the layer into a draft layer. Exporting and printing images can be set to ignore a draft layer, even if that layer is visible in the file.

- **Lock layer:** This sets the layer so that it cannot be drawn on or changed at all until it is unlocked.

- **Lock transparent pixels:** This sets the layer so that transparent pixels cannot be drawn on. Only pixels that are currently drawn on will be able to be changed.

- **Enable mask:** This enables or disables the layer mask, which can hide some parts of an image. This is a great function to add patterns to clothing! You can learn more about layer masks in *Chapter 12, Making Layer Masks and Screentones*.

- Once you click the **Apply mask to layer** icon, mark any areas that you don't want to edit and pick the deselect option. With those areas masked, you can edit your art without affecting those areas.

  As an example, the following image shows masks applied on clothing pattern layers. The black areas in the thumbnails are the parts that are masked with the deselect option:

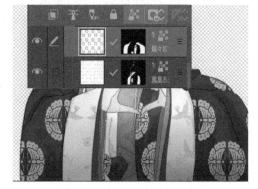

Figure 3.9: A screenshot of the Layer mask function

- **Set showing area of ruler:** This controls what layers or layer folders the ruler is visible on, such as only being visible when in the layer that contains the ruler or being able to see the ruler from any layer of the drawing.

The following screenshot is of another set of icons called the command bar. This set of icons allows us to execute many common layer operations directly from the **Layer** palette. It looks as follows:

Let's explore these icons in the command bar, once again going from left to right:

- **New raster layer:** This creates a new layer for raster art. It's good for any organic feel drawings, such as pencil sketches, inking figures, and coloring.

- **New layer folder:** This creates a new folder that layers can be placed into for organization.

- **Create layer mask:** This creates a mask on the currently selected layer. It's a brilliant function when you want to add effects and patterns to the limited area, as we briefly saw earlier.

- **Apply mask to layer:** This makes the layer mask permanent in the layer.

Figure 3.10: A screenshot of the layer command bar

- **Create vector layer:** This creates a new layer for vector art. It's good for precise geometric shapes or super smooth lines. It's not pixelated even when blown up to print bigger scale.

- **Delete layer:** This deletes the currently selected layer and all its contents.

- **Transfer to layer below:** This option transfers the contents of the currently selected layer to the layer below it in the stack, while leaving the empty layer behind.

- **Combine to layer below:** This option merges the currently selected layer with the layer below it while getting rid of the empty layer.

Below or above the command bar, depending on the device you use, is a list of the current layers of your image.

As you can see in the following screenshot, each one has a symbol that looks like an eye that indicates whether the layer is visible. You can check on your inking process by clicking this eye icon to hide the sketching layer. Similarly, you can check on any art underneath by making the above layers invisible.

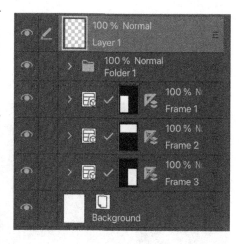

To the right of the eye icon of the currently active layer, there is an icon that looks like a pen. This indicates that this layer is the one that's currently being worked on. Above the layer name, the current blending mode says **Normal** in the image, and you can find more about the layer blending mode in the *Exploring layer blending modes* section in *Chapter 16, Using Clip Studio Paint to Color Your Manga*. It also tells us the opacity, which is at **100%**. These details are displayed so that specific layers can be found easily:

Figure 3.11: A screenshot of the layer list

Now that we've learned all about the **Layer** palette, let's look at its companion: the **Layer Property** palette.

The Layer Property palette

The **Layer Property** palette is shown above the **Layer** palette in the default interface layout. If you cannot find the **Layer Property** palette, it can be restored by going to the **File** menu and clicking on **Window | Layer Property**.

The **Layer Property** palette has fantastic functions to add on top of the ones of the Layer palette. It is shown in the following screenshot:

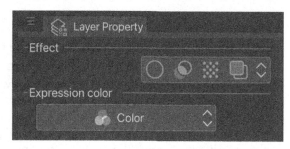

Figure 3.12: A screenshot of the Layer Property palette

Though it's a little palette, it can do big things. Let's explore each of its options now.

Border effect

The **Border effect** icon, which is the first icon on the left of the top row, can be used to get two different looks on a layer. The most common way to use it is to add a stroke to the outside of the content of a layer.

To do this, click on the left-most icon of the **Border effect** options to activate the **Edge** option. The following is a screenshot of **Border effect** in action on a layer of text:

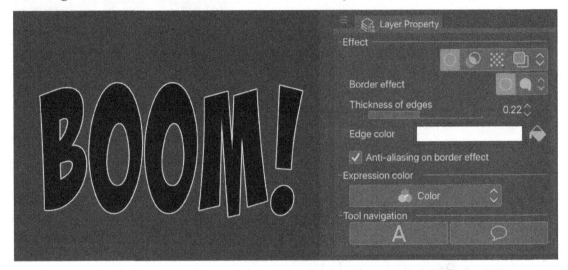

Figure 3.13: A screenshot of a text sample and the Layer Property palette

By adjusting the **Thickness of edges** setting, the thickness of the border can be made thicker or thinner by adjusting the slider or using the up and down arrows to the right of the slider. **Edge color** can be set by clicking on the rectangle showing the current color and choosing a new color using the color picker window.

Border effect also has another setting, though, and that is the **Watercolor edge** effect. This effect looks very different from other edge effects and has a lot more options, and it can be used to give a piece of art a slick look that is reminiscent of traditional watercolor.

To access the **Watercolor edge** effect, click on the icon next to the **Edge** option under the **Border effect** heading of the **Layer Property** palette.

In the following screenshot, the **Watercolor edge** effect has been applied to the brushstroke on the right:

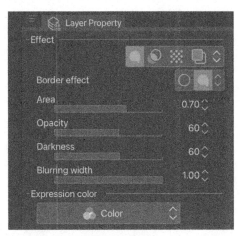

Figure 3.14: A screenshot of an image sample with the Watercolor edge effect applied

Notice how the stroke on the right has a dark edge around the outside, which is just how watercolor paint would react if it was layered over dry paint. The look of this effect can be changed by moving the **Area**, **Opacity**, **Darkness**, and **Blurring width** sliders. There is no *ideal* setting for this option, but moving the sliders around will update the layer in real time, so it's very easy – and fun – to play with.

When we apply this as a layer property, we're affecting the whole layer. If you want to add a watercolor edge effect only to a specific brush, see the *Watercolor edge* section in *Chapter 4, Introducing Clip Studio Paint Brushes*.

Now that we know about the **Border effect** option, let's explore another: the **Extract line** effect.

Extract line

The **Extract line** icon is another icon under the **Effect** options in the **Layer Property** palette. This option is only available in the EX version and is especially useful for incorporating 3D objects into your art. This is usually used as a stencil, on top of which you can draw the object.

In the following screenshot, I have taken a photo of some scenery and used the **Extract line** effect on it. It's always better to use a photo that is properly focused, and taken in enough light with high contrast. The settings used are shown in the **Layer Property** palette in the following screenshot:

Figure 3.15: A screenshot of a line extraction image

Using this option turns the photo into a line drawing. By adjusting the options in the **Layer Property** palette, we get a real-time preview of the line drawing. Using this layer effect does not change the source photo permanently, as the effect can be turned off at any time if we change our mind, so feel free to play around with the sliders!

> **Important note**
>
>
>
> Only use photographs in your art that you have taken yourself or that you have permission to use. Remember, just because you found a photo through a Google search doesn't mean that you have the right to use it! Be sure that the owner of the photo is okay with it being used, even if you're not going to be selling the piece of art that you're making.

This option also has another effect, called **Convert to lines and tones.** This is mostly used by comic artists on 3D objects or background photographs, but we can also keep using it on our scenery photo. Once we have the settings shown in the preceding screenshot just how we want them, we can click on the **Convert layer to lines and tones** button at the bottom of the **Line Extraction** settings. The following dialog will appear:

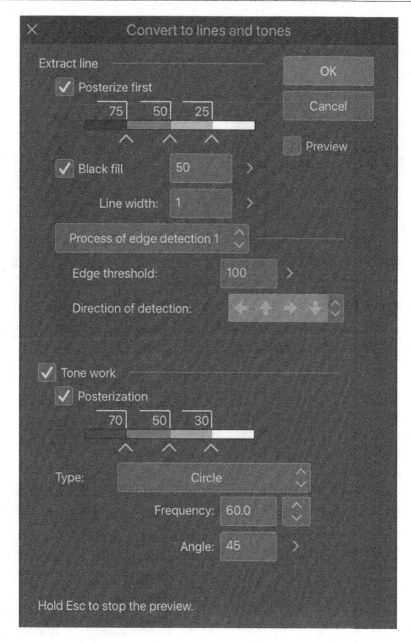

Figure 3.16: A screenshot of the line and tone conversion of layer settings

Settings can be modified in this window again before continuing. To see the changes being made, make sure to check the **Preview** checkbox below the **Cancel** button. Note that the preview may be slow on computer systems with a low amount of RAM or hard disk space.

When we click on **OK**, we will get something like this:

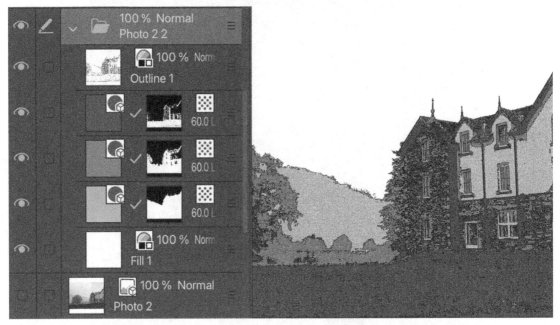

Figure 3.17: A screenshot of a photo with the Layer palette

Clip Studio Paint automatically creates an outline layer and several layers of tones, depending on the settings we specified in the previous window. Looking in the **Layer** palette, we can also see our original image safely saved on a layer below the tones and the outline layer. This means we don't have to worry about making changes to a photo and then not being able to undo them. If we don't like the final result of the conversion, the action can be undone, or the layers deleted, and we can try again to get a different result. The ideal result would blend nicely with your other drawings on the image, as we can see in the following sample:

Figure 3.18: A sample image with a photo background

Remember that, to keep your style consistent, it's best to draw over the automatically created background.

Tone

The next icon in our **Layer Property** effect options is the **Tone** effect. Just as the name implies, this takes our layer and turns it into screentones, depending on the contents of the layer.

What is a screentone? If you read Japanese manga, you've probably seen screentones but never knew what they were called! A **screentone** is a pattern of dots, lines, or hatches used to apply shading or texture to any area. In traditional pen-and-paper drawing, these tones were applied using a sticker-like sheet of pre printed patterns that would be applied over the top of the drawing. Some companies even started printing background images, such as photos of city skylines or forests, to make the comic creation process faster and easier. This is now easy to create using digital tones. Using digital tones means we don't have to replenish our screentone supplies, because we never run out, and we can make custom tones. We can find more about using screentones in the *Adding screentones* section in Chapter 12, *Making Masks and Screentones*.

In the following screenshot, the **Tone** layer effect has been applied on a layer containing a shade of a drawing:

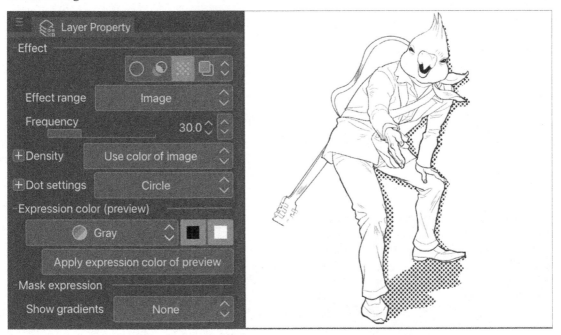

Figure 3.19: A screenshot of a piece of art with a Layer Property palette

We also have several options for this effect, such as setting **Frequency**, which will make the screentone dots more or less numerous. Note that the higher the number set with this slider, the smaller the dots will become. **Density** can be set in accordance with the color or brightness of the image. Changing this setting to increase the brightness will make lighter parts of the image more transparent. **Dot settings** can be used to change the shape of the dots that make up the screentone pattern. There are many options, from the standard circle to stars, flowers, hearts, and more!

Now, let's talk about the last effect option.

Layer color

The **Layer color** effect is simple and is the one that you will use most for day-to-day artwork. Here's an example of the Layer color effect on a pencil sketch in the following screenshot:

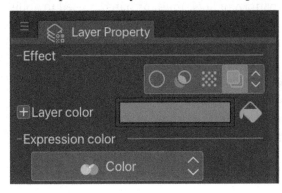

The **Layer color** option takes the contents of the selected layer and tints them based on the color set by the user in the **Layer color** selection box. By default, this is set to a light blue color that is reminiscent of non-photographic blue pencil art from traditional comics. This is a non-destructive way to tint our layer, as we can simply click on the **Layer color** icon again to change the layer back to its original colors.

Figure 3.20: A screenshot of a pencil sketch with a Layer color effect

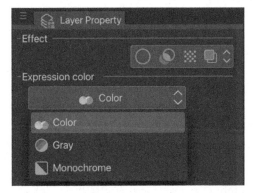

Figure 3.21: A screenshot of the Expression color options

The most common way to use this option is to make your finished pencil sketch layer blue before inking.

Expression color

The final part of the **Layer Property** palette is the **Expression color** drop-down menu. This menu is shown in the following screenshot:

With this menu, we can set the color mode of each layer in our document. For instance, for crisp line art, we could set our ink layer to be only black and white pixels by selecting the **Monochrome** option. Layers for pencil sketches can be set to **Gray**, and only layers that contain color content can be set to **Color**. This control over the individual layers' color modes can help to reduce file sizes in large files with lots of layers, so keep that in mind when you're working!

Now that we know what the icons and menus in the **Layer** and **Layer Property** palettes do, let's explore some things that you can do with layers.

Organizing layers

Layers are a powerful digital art software tool, but only if you know how to use them effectively. Many artists switching from doing their pieces on paper have a difficult time figuring out how to work in layers. In this section, we are going to create a few new layers and keep them organized by renaming them and changing their color in the **Layer** palette.

Follow these steps in order to create a new file with layers set up to take a drawing from a rough draft to ink:

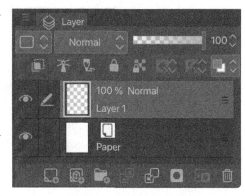

1. Create a new file. Use the **A4 Color** template under the **Show all comic settings** icon for more information on creating new files and using templates. If you are using Clip Studio Paint EX, don't turn on the **Multiple Page** option for this file. We just want one page to work on for this exercise.

2. Once we have hit **OK** and our file is created, we should have a **Layer** palette that looks as on the right:

Figure 3.22: A screenshot of the Layer palette with a new layer

3. Double-click on the words **Layer 1** in the **Layer** palette to rename the layer. When the text entry box appears, name the layer **Roughs**. Hit the *Enter* key on your keyboard to confirm the new layer name. Now, our **Layer** palette looks like on the right:

Figure 3.23: A screenshot of a layer with a new name

4. Use the **Change Palette Color** drop-down menu to change the **Roughs** layer to blue. This is to allow us to quickly identify the **Roughs** layer in the stack of layers. Now, our **Layer** palette looks like this:

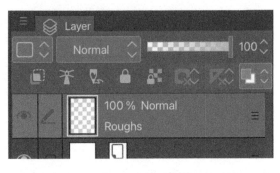

Figure 3.24: A screenshot of the Layer palette

5. Create a new layer by either clicking on the **New Raster Layer** icon above and left of the layer or at the bottom of the **Layer** palette, depending on your interface or device. You can also go to **Layer | New Raster Layer** in the **File** menu at the top of the screen. Raster layers suit organic drawings, whereas Vector layers suit geometric shapes with super smooth lines, and avoid pixelation when blown up to a bigger size. Using the process outlined in *Steps 3* and *4*, name this new layer **Finished pencils** and set the color to green. Now, our **Layer** palette should look as it does in the following screenshot:

Figure 3.25: A screenshot of three layers

6. Using the preceding steps, create another layer with the name **Inks** and set **Palette Color** to **Red**.

7. Now, we are going to create a **Layer Folder** to hold our **Roughs** and **Finished pencils** layers. Create a **Layer Folder** by clicking on the **Finished pencils** layer in the stack to select it (the currently selected layer will display as blue in the **Layer** palette). Now, click on the **New Layer Folder** icon at the top of the palette (or at the bottom of the **Layer** palette, depending on your device). Also, you can use **Layer | New Layer Folder** in the **File** menu. Now, our **Layer** palette looks like this:

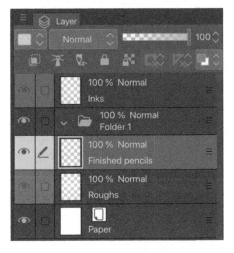

Figure 3.26: A screenshot of four layers and a folder

8. Double-click on the words **Folder 1** to bring up the text entry box to rename the folder. Change the name to **Pencils** and press the *Enter* key on the keyboard to finalize the name change.

9. Select the **Finished pencils** layer and hold down the *Shift* or *Ctrl* button on the keyboard as you click on the **Roughs** layer in order to select both pencil layers at the same time. Both layers will turn blue when they are selected together. Now, use the mouse to drag the layers into the **Pencils** folder. You will know they are in the correct position when a red rectangle is shown around the folder while the mouse is over it, as in the following screenshot on the right.

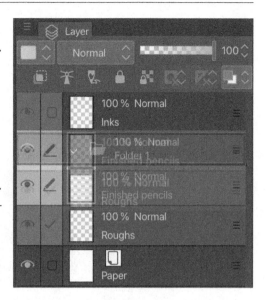

Figure 3.27: A screenshot of us adding layers to a folder

10. Release the mouse button to complete the move to the layer folder.

11. Save your file. We will be drawing on these layers in the next chapter.

We now have a stack of layers (and a layer folder) that looks like this:

Tidying up layers into folders brings you another benefit aside from the organization clarity – you can move, edit, change opacity, and add layer blending mode effects on all layers in the folder at once!

Of course, this is just one of the many ways to use and organize layers. As you continue to work in digital layers, you will find your own style of using them. Some artists use many, many layers in a completed work, while some may only use a few layers.

Personally, I try to keep my layers down to a minimum, but larger color pieces with lots of characters can quickly see the stack get pretty high!

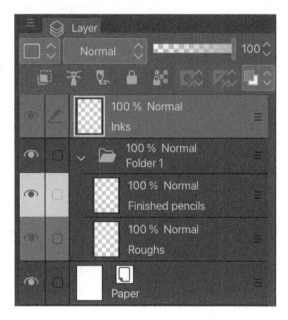

Figure 3.28: A screenshot of layers in a folder

Tip

Do you have lots of layers and are you having a hard time finding the one that you need to work on? Change **Thumbnail display settings** to display only the area in which some elements are drawn in the thumbnails in the **Layer** palette. **Thumbnail display settings** can be found by clicking three bars next to the **Layer** tab name. In the **Layer** drop-down menu, click **Thumbnail display settings**, and click **Show only layer area** as in the following image:

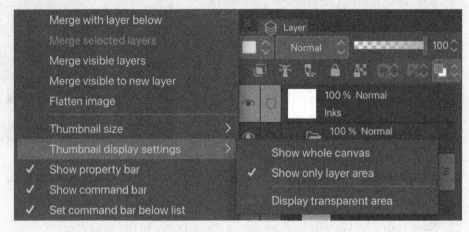

Figure 3.29: A screenshot of the Layer drop-down menu

Brilliant – your layer thumbnails are more comprehensive and it is easier to spot which element is on which layer!

Summary

In this chapter, we learned about the penciling sketch as part of the manga creation process. This is the best time to make mistakes, keep practicing, and eventually get the proportions right. It may be frustrating if you're new to drawing figures, as well as being new to drawing on a tablet, but it will get better as you go. In fact, this could be seen as the hardest part of a composition; if you've got a good pencil sketch, the rest of the details will fall into place naturally.

As a significant step in your journey into digital art, we learned what layers are and how to use them when creating your penciling sketch. We can use layers to add sketches in alternate poses or with additional foreground elements. Remember that, when you start inking your artwork on a new layer, you should reduce the pencil sketch layer's opacity so you can focus on the ink. It's also helpful to change the color of the penciling layer, to further distinguish it from the ink.

We also explored the benefits of layers when coloring digital art; they offer freedom for experimentation while protecting each element of your artwork, making your piece easy and safe to edit. With that in mind, we learned about the **Layer** palette and the various options and icons it has. We also learned about the **Layer Property** palette and the different effects it can have on our layers. In *Chapter 15* and *Chapter 16*, we will explore coloring in much more detail when we look at creating your color palette and exploring layer blending modes.

As you grow as an artist, your drawings will get increasingly complex. It's best, after all, to start with simple sketches and work your way upward. To handle the increasing number of layers, we learned how to make layer folders.

Now, it's time to get into the pen tools that you will use every day in Clip Studio Paint, whether for penciling or inking. In the next chapter, we will learn about Clip Studio Paint brushes.

Join us on Discord!

Read this book alongside other users. Ask questions, provide solutions to other readers, and much more.

Scan the QR code or visit the link to join the community.

`https://packt.link/clipstudiopaint`

4

Introducing Clip Studio Paint Brushes

In the analog world, drawings are made on paper or canvas with pencils, ink, paint, brushes, and many other tools. In the digital world, too, we have a myriad of tools—many that imitate real-world art supplies and techniques. In Clip Studio Paint, the bulk of these mark-making tools fall under the heading of brushes, which includes sub-categories such as pencils, pens, markers, pastels, oil paints, and more. We're going to get familiar with the toolbox of brushes with sample images so that when we start drawing, we will be familiar with the default tools and how we can change them to suit our individual style of working.

In this chapter, we will cover the following topics:

- Understanding the categories of Clip Studio Paint brushes and navigating them
- An introduction to the Clip Studio Paint brush engine
- Exploring the tool properties and settings
- Copying, saving, and restoring brushes

Let's jump right into learning about these versatile digital art tools!

Technical requirements

To get started, you need Clip Studio Paint already installed on your device, and then you need to open a new blank canvas. Any size is fine, but I recommend creating a 300 dpi square canvas to go through the content in this chapter.

Navigating the brushes

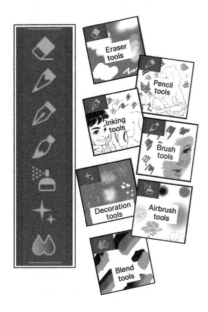

In the world of analog art, a brush is a very specific tool. In Clip Studio Paint, however, the word *brush* can refer to several different tools. Usually, we use the term *brush* to refer to a digital tool that is used with a stylus or mouse to draw lines, as opposed to other tools that fill colors or select or perform the other operations that can be performed in digital art.

Most of the tools that we will refer to as brushes can be found in one section of the toolbar in the user interface. These tool icons are labeled as **Eraser**, **Pencil**, **Pen** (aka **Inking** tools), **Brush**, **Airbrush**, **Decoration**, and **Blend**. The icons for these tool categories are shown in the creenshot on the left:

Figure 4.1: Toolbar and art samples

Clicking on one of these icons in the toolbar results in a change in the **Sub Tool** palette.

In this chapter, we'll be closely looking at the most important paintbrush tools – in this case, Pen tools. When we click on the *Pen* icon in the toolbar, we can see the categories of pencils in the **Sub Tool** palette, as shown on the left of the following screenshot with inking and shading examples:

Figure 4.2: The Sub Tool palette

The buttons on the top of the **Sub Tool** palette show the different categories of tools available under the **Pen** heading.

The **Pen** categories include **G-Pen** and further down, **Real G-Pen**. These tools are a collection of settings that change how the stylus interacts with the canvas and the look of the digital marks that are made. For instance, the following screenshot shows art that has been drawn with the **G-pen tool** on the left and the **Real G-Pen** tool on the right:

Figure 4.3: Sample pen drawings

See the difference in the look of the lines? The **Real G-Pen** tool produces more precise thickness, depending on the pen pressure, and bolder lines with more variation, similar to what you would get using a traditional G-pen. Although both pens are pressure sensitive, the **Real G-Pen** tool creates more sensitive results and with more textures as you draw.

Take a moment now to look under each brush tool category and **Sub Tool** category, and check out the different tools. Open a blank canvas and use the tools that look the most interesting to you to make marks on the canvas and test them out. One of the best things about doing digital art is how forgiving it is. If you don't like a mark that you have made, it can always be erased or undone, so take this opportunity to play around and familiarize yourself with the tools

When you've done that, let's move on and become familiar with the brush engine, a powerful tool that allows you to customize your tools to suit your style!

Figure 4.4: Sample brush drawings

The brush engine

Clip Studio Paint makes it easy to create your own tools with its powerful—but simple-to-use—brush engine. There are lots of options in the brush engine, such as brush size, shape, and how it's corrected. But once you learn what each one does, it's easy to make the best tools for your own needs. Let's get started right away by looking at the brush options and learning what each one does.

Accessing the brush options

To access the options to create and change brushes, click on one of the brush tools. In this example, we'll be looking at **G-pen**, which is a sub tool under the **Pen** tool. Once you have chosen a brush tool as your currently active tool, locate the **Tool Property** palette. In the lower right-hand corner is an icon that looks like a wrench. Click on the wrench icon, which is displayed in the following screenshot, to open the **Sub Tool Detail** palette.

Figure 4.5: The Sub Tool Detail icon

The **Sub Tool Detail** palette is shown in the following screenshot:

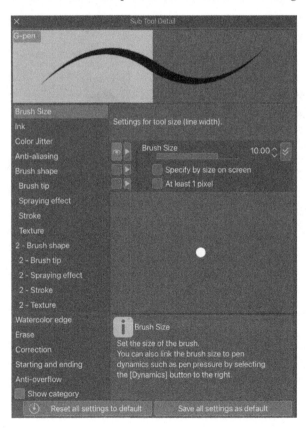

The categories of options are listed on the left-hand side column, and the actual options to edit are shown on the right-hand side.

We're going to discuss making a custom brush for special effects in *Chapter 9, Inking Special Effects*, so we're going to cover more of these brush options in that chapter. In this chapter, we're just going to get a feel for customizing the existing tools, so we'll be covering the options that are most useful to tweak the feel and look of existing brushes. Now, let's examine the options under the **Brush Size**, **Ink**, **Anti-aliasing**, **Correction**, and **Starting and ending** categories of options.

Brush Size

When we are drawing a rough sketch, we might want very thick pencil lines on a sketch layer, while we might want thinner lines to draw the detailed background sceneries or eyelashes. For these reasons, we can take control of the thickness of our mark-making tools. The **Brush Size** category has options related to the size of a brush or the line width.

Figure 4.6: The Sub Tool Detail palette

The size of the brush is set using the slider, by clicking on the current number to the right of the slider and using the number pad to enter the size manually, or by adjusting the brush size by using the up and down arrows to the right of the number display. The brush size can also be changed according to other factors, such as the pressure applied to the tablet stylus.

> **Tip**
>
> There are more options in the brush engine that can also be adjusted according to source settings. Look for the rectangular button to the right of those options to access the source settings menu for them.

 Directly under the **Brush Size** slider, there are two checkboxes. The first is **Specify by size on screen**. When this option is activated, the size of the brush will not change according to the amount of zoom. Therefore, a tool that is *4.00* in size when the document is at 100% zoom will be the same size when the document is scaled up or down, instead of becoming larger or smaller as the zoom changes. The other checkbox is **At least 1 pixel**. This option ensures that the mark being made is at least one pixel, even if the pen pressure becomes so light that the line should be interrupted.

Ink

The next category of options is the **Ink** category, which is related to the thickness and blending of the ink color. Here, you can find settings such as **Blending mode**. This settings are quite advanced, and you can find out more about coloring in *Chapter 16, Using Clip Studio Paint to Color Your Manga*.

Color Jitter

Under the **Ink** category, there is a **Color Jitter** category, which can make the brush color vary in terms of its stroke. If the brush tip color is fixed, the **Color Jitter** setting will not affect the brush color. The options are in the following screenshot on the right:

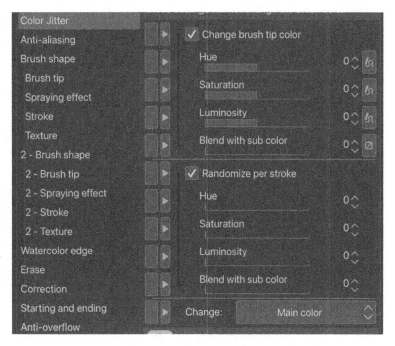

Figure 4.7: The Color Jitter category

Let's have a look at each setting to see how it affects brush color:

- **Change brush tip color** gives you control over the brush tip color dynamics settings, with four options when it's turned on.
- **Randomize per stroke,** when it's turned on, gives you control in terms of randomizing the color of each stroke as you draw.

Let's see the four options for each checkbox:

- The **Hue** slider controls the degree of variation of the color to add to your brush stroke.
- The **Saturation** slider controls the vividness of the color to add to your brush stroke. Higher values result in more vivid colors.
- The **Luminosity** slider controls the value of the color mixed in your brush stroke.
- The **Blend with sub color** slider allows us to draw using a combination of the main drawing color and the sub-drawing color. The larger the value, the stronger the sub-drawing color becomes in the drawing.

Let's have a look at some samples of the **Randomize per stroke** settings:

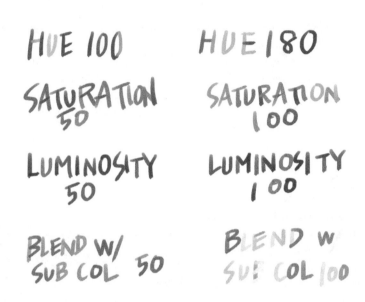

Figure 4.8: Sample strokes of the various Randomize per stroke settings

You can see that each stroke changes its ink color, depending on the settings. I've written the setting name for each stroke, so you can see the effect that they have. In these examples, copper is the main color and white is the sub-color. You can enjoy discovering things through serendipity with this random color effect on your ink.

At the far right of each slider on the **Color Jitter** settings, there are pen image icons. If you click one of them, a **Hue Dynamics** sub-menu will appear, as shown in the following screenshot:

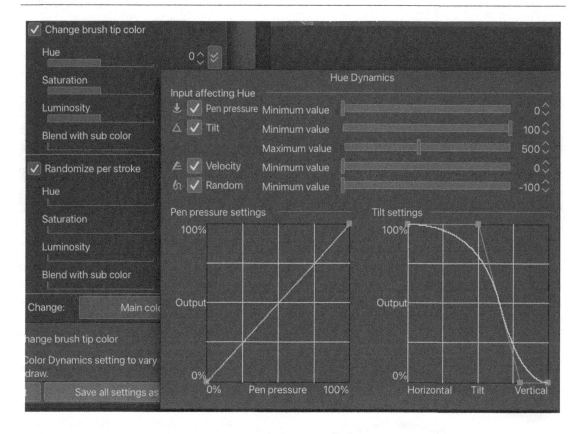

Figure 4.9: The Hue Dynamics palette

Each option controls how the input source affects the brush stroke color.

My favorite setting is to turn the **Pen pressure** input on, under the **Blend with sub color** slider, with a value of **50** for **Change brush tip color.** This way, I can enjoy having a sub-color appear naturally when I apply pressure to the brush, gradually increasing it while drawing. This gives you great control while merging two different colors. The following example shows a brush using my favorite settings, with red as the main color and white as the sub-color:

This category provides you with endless experiments in terms of brush stroke colors! Let's now move on to more interesting settings that maximize the benefit of using digital art tools.

Figure 4.10: Brush example

Anti-aliasing

The next category that we will look at in this chapter is the **Anti-aliasing** category, which controls the appearance of smoothness on the border of brush strokes. The options appear as follows:

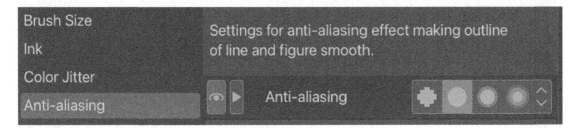

Figure 4.11: The Anti-aliasing category

Anti-aliasing is a fancy way to describe how jagged or smooth a digital line looks. Using the icons in the **Anti-aliasing** category, the smoothing of a line can be set to **None**, **Weak**, **Middle**, or **Strong**. The following are two examples of lines made with the **G-pen**. The top one has anti-aliasing set to **None**, while the bottom one is set to **Strong**:

Figure 4.12: The Anti-aliasing category

Notice how the top line has lots of sharp edges that make it look like it's pixelated. Anti-aliasing adds tones of gray to the edge of a line to smooth it out, avoiding this jagged look. The bottom line, with the option set to **Strong**, looks soft and almost blurry because of the amount of gray added around the edges. I generally select **Middle** or **Strong** unless I want to have a pixelated texture in my art.

Dual brush

Let's have a look at the Dual brush settings under the category 2 – **Brush shape**. You can combine two different brush shapes to express unique brush strokes. Start by clicking the **Dual brush** tick box, and then you will see all **Dual brush** options appear. The setting is the same as the normal brush settings; there are shape, tip, effect, stroke, and texture options. There are millions of possibilities for inventing your own combinations.

In the following image, you can see some sample drawings of a grass-shaped brush, created using some Dual brush effects:

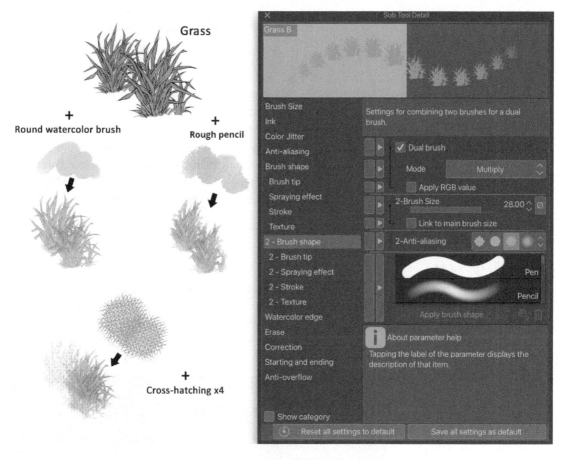

Figure 4.13: Sample Dual brush drawings

You can recreate the sample drawings by following these steps:

Download or create the Grass decoration brush, store it in Decoration brush Sub Palette, and select it. You can learn how to download brushes in *Chapter 18*, *Exploring the Clip Studio Assets and Animation*, or how to create it in *Chapter 9*, *Inking Special Effects and Material Palette*.

1. In the preceding image, underneath the **2-Anti-alising** setting, you can see the stroke samples of the second brushes. Select one of them and click **Apply brush shape**.
2. Try it out on the canvas.

By picking various-shaped secondary brushes and trying out the Dual brush settings, you might encounter fantastic unexpected results!

Watercolor edge

Now, let's jump into the Watercolor edge category!

Traditionally, watercolor is an art material that uses water to thin the color and creates special textures, such as smudge, blur, stain, a transparent background color, and darker edges around the stained areas, which all create a very tender and crafted artistic effect. Clip Studio Paint has a function to recreate the effects digitally, as you can see in the art on the left:

Figure 4.14: Sample Watercolor brush drawing

With these watercolor effects in mind, let's have a look at a list of **Sub Tool Detail** categories under the **Watercolor edge** settings. **Watercolor edge** creates an edge on brush strokes when it's active. Combine this with textures for a watercolor effect. This effect is not visible with dense color brushes. The following screenshot shows a watercolor edge brush stroke along with the **Watercolor edge** settings:

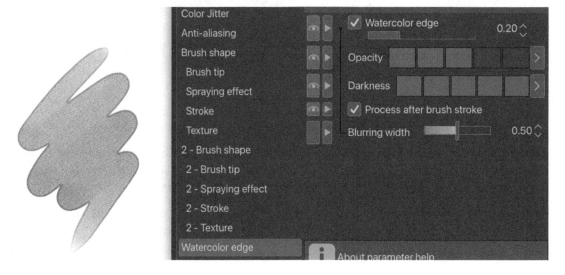

Figure 4.15: Watercolor edge category with an example stroke

When you click on any option, a description of it will appear on the palette. The most important one is **Watercolor edge**, which controls the strength of the edge appearance. By clicking the checkbox and changing its value, we will have a desirable edge appearance on the canvas!

Correction

Now, let's jump into the list of **Sub Tool Detail** categories under the **Correction** settings. **Correction** settings can assist us in making clean, sharp lines in our drawings, even if we have shaky hands or aren't used to doing digital art and inking yet. The trade-off for relying too heavily on some of these options, however, is that high settings on some of them can cause computer lag, depending on the specs of your system.

The following is a screenshot of the **Correction** settings:

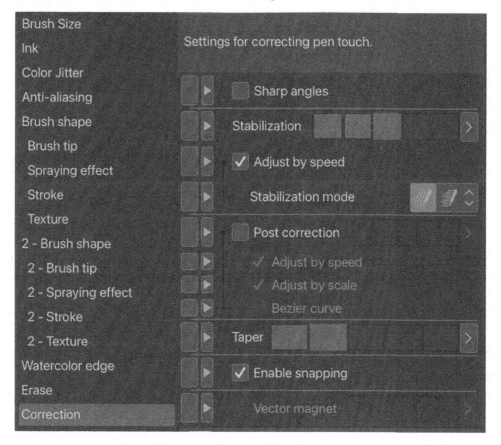

Figure 4.16: Correction category

Here are each of the **Correction** options explained:

- **Sharp angles** automatically turns corners in drawn lines into sharp points, even if they are slightly curved.
- **Stabilization** is used to smooth out your lines. The larger the value of the **Stabilization** setting, the smoother the line will be (even if the line you actually draw is shaky). The **Adjust by speed** checkbox will allow the stabilization level to adjust, depending on the moving speed of the brush. You can choose whether you want more stabilization when you move your brush more slowly or more quickly.

- **Post correction** will stabilize the line and smooth it out once the line has been drawn. There is a slight lag between the line being drawn and the smoothing process. **Adjust by speed** smooths the line more, depending on the speed at which the line is drawn. **Adjust by scale** controls the amount of smoothing of the line, based on the zoom of the canvas. **Bezier curve** converts the line to a quadratic Bezier curve once the correction is completed.

- **Taper** automatically tapers the end of lines, depending on the value set. The larger the value, the more tapered the end of the line will get after the brush mark is made.

- **Enable snapping** controls whether or not this tool will snap to an active ruler. We'll be learning all about rulers in *Chapter 13, All about Rulers*.

- **Vector magnet** is used on vector layers. It allows the new line to merge automatically with existing vector lines. More information about vectors will be presented in *Chapter 10, Exploring Vector Layers*.

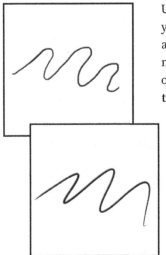

Using **Stabilization** and **Post Correction** can make a huge difference in your inking. It's great if you're just starting to work digitally or your hands aren't very steady. It's OK to have shaky lines for a sketching stage, but you need steady lines for inking, especially background buildings or metal objects. In the following screenshot, the line above is before **Post Correction**, and the line below is the same one after being corrected:

Notice how much smoother the line below is when compared to the one above, especially around the curves. However, sometimes, this computer correction can make lines look less organic, so depending on your personal art style, you may want to use it sparingly if you want to have an organic and crafty style of artwork. If your style blends well to super-smooth curves, such as when you're drawing loads of futuristic buildings and robots, then go crazy!

Figure 4.17: Line drawings

> **Tip**
>
> In the section that follows, *Playing with brush settings*, we're going to learn how to copy a tool and make changes to the copy. I like to ink my figures with a very organic-looking brush tool, but I also have a copy of that tool with the stabilization set high to ink robotic objects and inorganic backgrounds. Saving copies of your favorite tools can help save time, so give it a try!

The following image shows a sample artwork that uses the same G-pens, but one uses light stabilization to draw organic shapes, such as flowers and stones, and another uses heavy post-correction to draw the straight lines of bamboo and wooden objects:

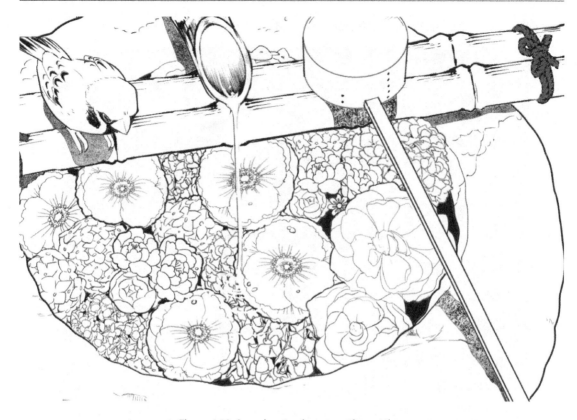

Figure 4.18: Sample art using correction settings

The **Correction** tool is like having an invisible assist as you draw!

Starting and ending

Let's now take a look at the **Starting and ending** category. These options alter how the beginning and end of a drawn line appear. If you are struggling to get a perfectly tapered line, these settings will help you to achieve the look you desire, as shown in the following samples:

The image on the left shows samples of pen strokes with and without the **Starting** and **Ending** options.

The strokes above are great for drawing 1980s-style simple drawing patterns or handwriting. The strokes below were made with **Starting and ending** turned on, with the **Brush size** using a **Starting** and **Ending** value of **800** each. Read on to how to adjust it!

Figure 4.19: Sample strokes with Starting and ending off and on

The following is a screenshot of the **Starting and ending** settings screen:

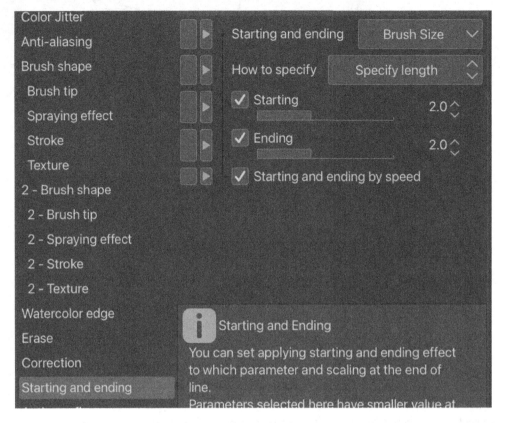

Figure 4.20: Starting and ending category

The very first option beneath this category is a drop-down menu with options to change the beginning and end of lines. Each of the items listed is a factor that the start and end of the line can be modified by. Checking the box next to the desired parameter activates it, and the slider to the right is then used to set the minimum value of that setting, but normally, we use the **Brush size** option only, with the value set to 1 in the drop-down menu.

The following options are also present in the **Starting and ending** settings:

- **How to specify** allows the **Starting and ending** settings to be set by **Length**, **Percentage**, or **Fade**. **Length** and **Percentage** will produce lines that go from the set minimum value to the full value and then back again, depending on the length of the drawn line. Selecting **Fade** will only change the ending of the line and not the beginning.

- The **Starting** checkbox and slider allow us to configure the length of the effect at the start of the line. The **Ending** checkbox and slider do the same thing, except at the end of the line!

- **Starting and ending by speed** will set the values of the starting and ending effect according to the speed at which the line is drawn.

The next brush option is the final one.

Anti-overflow

The last brush category is **Anti-overflow**. It comes in handy when we are adding color to images. We need to set a line art layer as a "reference layer" first to stop brushstrokes from going beyond the lines. You can do this by selecting the line art layer and clicking the **Set selected layer as a reference layer** icon, which looks like a lighthouse image on the layer palette.

The **Anti-overflow** settings appear as shown in the following screenshot:

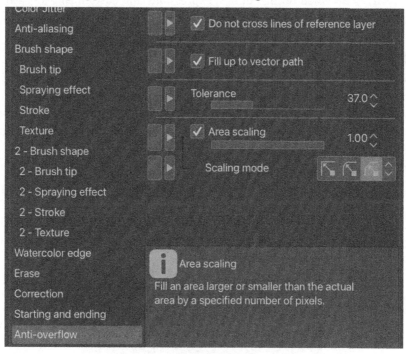

Figure 4.21: Anti-overflow settings

These are amazingly useful when you color your art. The following sample shows some artwork with **Do not cross lines of reference layer** off on the left top and on on the bottom. The detailed settings on the right side are 10% for **Tolerance**, **Area scaling** ticked with a 1.00 value, and **Rectangle Scaling mode**:

As you can see on the below of the image, the color doesn't overflow from the line art as you start adding the color. We don't need to tediously erase any overlapping color afterward!

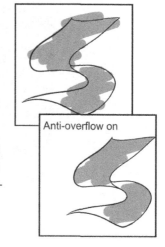

Figure 4.22: Sample art of Anti-overflow settings

Tip

Not sure what a particular brush setting does? Hover over it with the mouse or stylus, and the bottom of the **Sub Tool Detail** screen will show a description of the option.

There are many, many possibilities in terms of fiddling around with brush settings, and mastering these options really helps when trying out new expressions and customizing a brush for your own needs. Let's read on to try out different settings!

Playing with brush settings

Now, we have an idea of what these brush settings do. One of the best things about digital art is that almost nothing is permanent. If you make a mark with a pen, you can almost always undo it (or erase it). With Clip Studio Paint, if you make a change to a tool that you don't like, you can always revert the tool to its initial settings. That said, let's learn how to make a copy of an existing brush tool, make changes to the copy, and then make marks with the copy to see what some of the brush options do when utilized.

Follow these steps to create a copy of a brush tool and change the settings:

1.   Select the tool to be copied. For these instructions, we are going to use the **G-pen sub tool** tool.
2.   In the **Sub Tool** palette, as shown in the following screenshot, click on the icon that is pointed by arrow. This is the **Duplicate sub tool** icon:

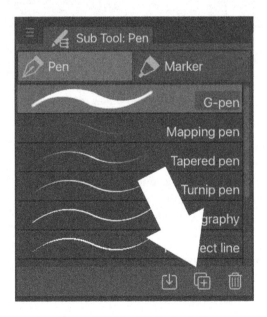

Figure 4.23: The Sub Tool palette

3. In the pop-up **Duplicate sub tool** window that appears, as shown in the following screenshot, enter a name for the new sub tool. I've left the name as **G-pen 2** for this example:

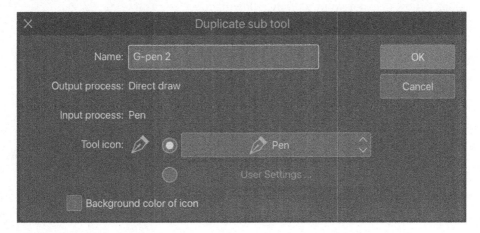

Figure 4.24: The Duplicate sub tool window

4. Make sure that a canvas is open in the canvas window so that the new tool can be tested as changes are made.

5. Open the **Sub Tool Detail** window. Make sure that you can see and draw on the canvas behind the **Sub Tool Detail** window. We are going to use this blank canvas to test our changes.

6. Continue changing the settings and testing the new brush on the canvas to see the effects.

7. Once you've finished changing the settings and seeing what they do in practice, you can either click on the **X** in the upper right-hand corner of the **Sub Tool Detail** window to close it and save the tool as it is, or you can reset the tool to its initial settings.

8. To reset the tool to its initial settings, press the **Reset all settings to default** button in the lower-left corner of the **Sub Tool Detail** window.

9. To save the settings as the new default (and overwrite the current default settings of the tool), press the button marked **Register all settings to initial settings** in the lower right-hand corner of the **Sub Tool Detail** window.

Now that we've copied a brush tool, made changes, and experimented with the settings, let's learn how to save a backup copy of our new brush tool and how to load a brush into the **Sub Tool** palette. Read on for more details.

Exporting and loading brushes

Whether you simply want to have a backup copy of all your custom tools if a catastrophe should happen, or you want to share your brushes with the world by giving them away or selling them, knowing how to export your tools is a great thing. It's an extremely simple process that can save you hard work in the future or provide an income stream if you're particularly good at making specialty brushes! But before we get into making specialty brushes in *Chapter 9, Inking Special Effects and Material Palette,* let's learn how to export and load brushes to make backup copies of our tools. You can export and import any type of sub tool in Clip Studio Paint, not just brushes!

Exporting a tool

Now, let's look at how to export your tool. By following these easy steps, you will save a backup copy of the tool you created originally on your device. You don't have to worry if you modify your tool; the original is always there, in a folder on your device!

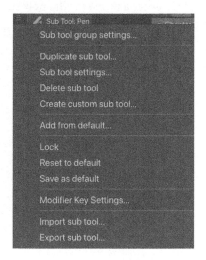

1. Select a sub tool to export. For this example, we will use the **G-pen 2** tool that we created in the previous section.

2. In the upper left-hand corner of the **Sub Tool** palette is an icon of three horizontal lines. This is the **Sub Tool** drop-down menu. Clicking on the menu will display it, as shown in the following screenshot:

3. Click on the **Export sub tool…** option in the menu.

4. In the next screen, navigate to a folder where you wish to save the sub tool. Then, enter the name of the tool. In the following screenshot, we leave the name as **G-pen 2**:

Figure 4.25: A part of the Sub Tool group menu

Figure 4.26: The Sub tool saving window

5. Click **Save** to complete the export.

Now, let's learn how to load a tool into Clip Studio Paint.

Importing a tool

Now that we've exported our custom tool, let's learn how to import a tool. You can find and download new tools from digital art supplier websites such as True Grid Texture Supply (https://www.truegrittexturesupply.com/). There are free and priced tools available for download. You can find more information by joining Clip Studio forums on SNS, or simply following digital art tip accounts.

Once you have some tools to import to your Clip Studio Paint tool palette, you can actually do so in two ways, and we'll cover both of them here!

The following are the steps to use the **Import sub tool...** option method of importing a tool:

1. Click on the **Pen** category in the toolbar and then the **Pen** category in the **Sub Tool** palette, where the tool is to be exported.

2. Click on the **Sub Tool** drop-down icon, which looks like three horizontal lines, in the upper left-hand corner of the **Sub Tool** palette. Then, click on the **Import sub tool...** option.

3. Navigate to the folder where the sub tool file is located. Click on the file of the sub tool, and then click on the **Open** button to complete the import.

The following is the click and drag method to import a tool, which can also be used to import multiple tools simultaneously:

1. Either in your operating system in Windows or **Finder** on Mac, open the folder containing the tools to be imported.

2. In Clip Studio Paint, choose the **Sub Tool** palette category that the tool or tools will be stored in.

3. Click and drag the window with the folder where the tool files are located so that Clip Studio Paint's **Sub Tool** palette can be seen at the same time as the folder. This is shown in the following screenshot:

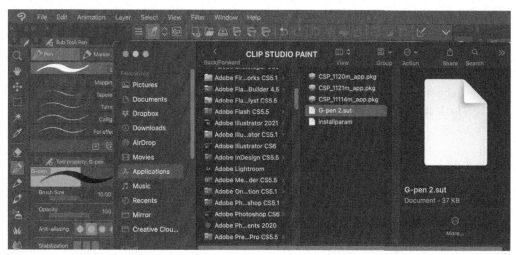

Figure 4.27: The Sub tool category and the Finder window

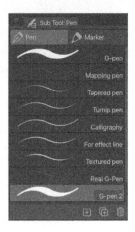

4.   Select the tool or tools to be imported. Click and drag the tool or tool files over the **Sub Tool** palette. The mouse cursor will turn into a + symbol. Release the mouse button to complete the import.

5.   The import of the tool or tools will then be completed. In the following screenshot, we can see that **G-pen 2** has been added to the **Pen** Sub Tool group:

Done! You have exported and imported sub tools. Isn't it great to know how to customize and move tool files? Now, you're able to create tools on your own and organize them! It's like having real brushes and tool cabinets to store them in at a traditional artist's studio!

Figure 4.28: The Sub Tool category

Important Note

From version 1.10.6 onward, Clip Studio Paint can import Photoshop brush files (.abr). You can import them by using the same method discussed in this section! The brush results may differ from their usage in Photoshop, but it's great to know that we can share brushes!

Summary

In this chapter, we learned how to navigate the brush categories and sub tools. We also learned how to customize our brushes using some of the options in Clip Studio Paint's brush engine. Then, we learned how to export our tools to make backups or share them with others, as well as two ways to import new tools into our software.

Now that we've learned about brushes, in the next chapter, we are going to take a look at the program's preferences. They are very helpful to create a comfortable art studio to work in, by decluttering and placing frequently used tools closer to you. Let's build a unique environment for your creation! We will also look at page and panel creations. Read on to learn more.

Join us on Discord!

Read this book alongside other users. Ask questions, provide solutions to other readers, and much more.

Scan the QR code or visit the link to join the community.

`https://packt.link/clipstudiopaint`

5

Pages and Panels to Shape Manga

Now that we've gotten Clip Studio Paint installed and have gone over the basics of layers and brushes, in this chapter, we'll take a closer look at our workspace. There are plenty of settings when preparing a new file that we should look at now that we've started creating artwork.

Importantly, we'll build on what we know about layers by setting up comic panels on new pages. This process is just like setting up a studio table to work on, choosing what paper to use, and knowing the correct tools to use to create panels.

In this chapter, we will cover the following topics:

- Making and saving workspaces
- Creating a custom-sized page and saving a preset
- Adding templates to a new file
- Making comic panels
- Creating new files and templates
- Using template panels and creating and editing them

Let's dive right in!

Making and saving workspaces

One of the best features of Clip Studio Paint is the ability to create and save different workspaces for different tasks. A workspace is a collection of palettes and their position on the interface. Clip Studio Paint comes with a few workspace options already in the program, but we can also create our own workspaces.

Saving a workspace

Follow these steps to create and save a workspace:

1. Use the directions in *Chapter 2, Installing Clip Studio Paint Pro and Interface Basics*, to move, collapse, and close palettes to set up a workspace. In the following screenshot, the palettes have all been moved to the left-hand side of the interface to make it easier to select items with your left hand, supposing you're a right-handed user drawing with your right hand:

Figure 5.1: A screenshot of a workspace

2. To save the current workspace, click on **Window** in the **File** menu, then go down to **Workspace** and click on **Register Workspace**. A box as shown in *Figure 5.2* will appear.

Figure 5.2: Register Workspace box

3. Enter a name for the workspace in the text entry box. Then, click **OK** to save the workspace settings.

Your workspace is now saved!

Switching between workspaces

Now that we've saved one of our own workspaces, we can switch to that workspace again whenever we like. Follow these steps to load a previously saved workspace:

1. Click on **Window** in the **File** menu, then go to **Workspace** to see the following options:

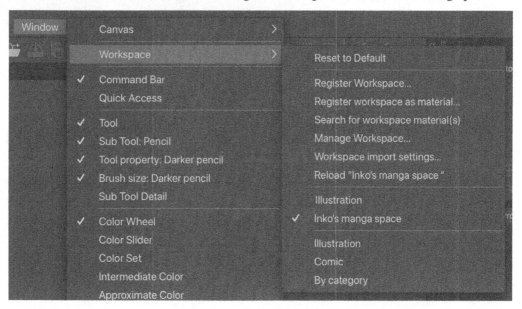

Figure 5.3: Workspace options

2. To switch back to the default workspace, click on the **Reset to Default** option.

3. To change to one of the workspaces included in Clip Studio, click on the **Illustration** or **Comic** option.

4. To load a custom workspace, locate it in the area above the **Illustration** and **Comic** workspace names and click on the name of the workspace to reload.

The new workspace will be loaded.

Managing and deleting workspaces

Sometimes, you may want to rename or delete workspaces that you've saved. We can do this easily just by following these steps:

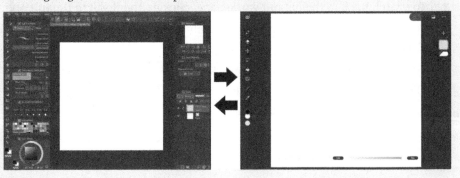

Figure 5.4: Manage Workspace box

1. In the **File** menu, click on **Window | Workspace | Manage Workspace…**. The menu in *Figure 5.4* will appear.

2. To delete a workspace, click on the name of the workspace on the left-hand side of the menu to highlight it in blue. Then, click on the button marked **Delete** on the right-hand side.

3. To rename a workspace, click on the workspace name to highlight it in blue. Then, click on the button on the right-hand side marked **Change name of settings**. Enter the new name for the workspace and click on **OK** to save the new name.

As you can see, it is easy to make new workspaces and change between them! Perhaps you want to make a workspace for drawing and inking, and another for coloring. The sky is the limit, so get creative with your workspaces and use them to maximize your workflow for efficiency.

Tip

If you're using a tablet or cellphone version of Clip Studio Paint, you might want a quick sketch with simple functions. In that case, you can switch between Studio Mode (the interface you are looking at now) and Simple Mode (limited tools and functions). The following diagram shows the comparison of the two different modes.

Figure 5.5: Studio Mode and Simple Mode interfaces

Tip

The step to switch is easy: just click the Clip Studio icon in the **File** menu, then select **Switch to Simple Mode** from the drop-down menu. When you want to go back to Studio Mode again, click the three-dots icon on the top right of the screen, then select **Switch to Studio Mode.**

In the next section, we'll start making new files and also learn about file templates.

New files and templates

Making a new file in most computer programs is pretty easy, and it is no different here. In Clip Studio Paint, you can simply start the program, click **Draw**, and then from **Project** select **Illustration,** then press **OK**. Now you have a blank canvas in front of you!

If you want to dive deeper into comic creation, there are some terminologies and options that need to be explained so that you can create files that will have the right specifications for your projects. For anyone planning to print manga later, they can be very important. In this section, we will discuss the relevant terms when creating a new file and learn how to create or load templates into new pages. Let's get started!

The New file window – explained

When first creating a new file in Clip Studio Paint, the number of options can look daunting. Not to worry though – in this section, we will learn about the most important options. That said, we can also explore each option in the new window and explain what each one means, so please feel free to choose whether you skip the parts that are not flagged as important.

The following screenshot shows the new file dialog box. Note that if you are using Clip Studio Paint Pro, you will not have the **Multiple pages** or **Cover page** settings that are available in Clip Studio Paint EX:

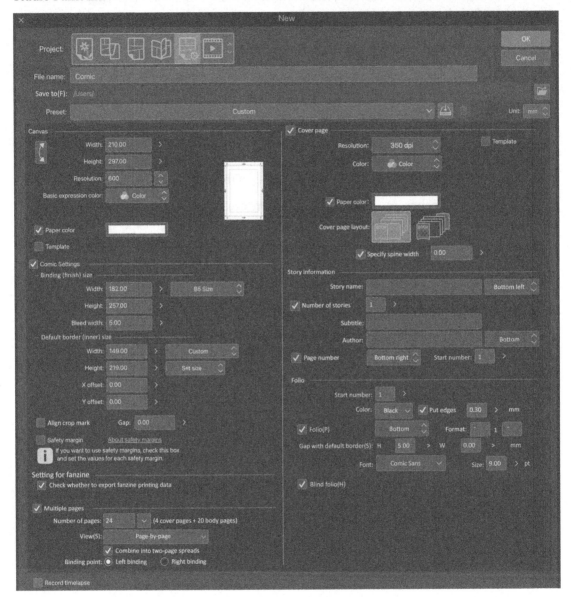

Figure 5.6: New file window

Wow, that's a lot of options! It can look scary at first, but let's break it down piece by piece and talk about each option individually so that we know what they all do. The most important are flagged as *important*, if you just want to know the crucial options:

- **Important: Project** is the area where we can select a category from preset document options.

The categories are **Illustration, Webtoon, Comic, Printing of fanzine, Show all comic settings,** and **Animation.** Clicking on one of these categories changes the available settings as well as the presets, depending on which **Project** category is selected. For instance, selecting the **Illustration** category hides any settings related to making a comic.

We will look closely at the **Webtoon** category in *Chapter 19, Exporting, Printing, and Uploading Your Manga.*

- **Important: File name** is a textbox where the name of the file can be added. This field must be filled in when making multiple-page files.

- **Important: Save to** is the folder where a multiple-page file is saved to. To change the destination folder, click on the **Browse** button to the right of the current file path.

- **Preset** is a drop-down menu of preset page sizes and settings that correspond to the current selection made in the **Use of work** section. This is also where any user-made page presets will appear. We'll learn more about saving our page settings in an upcoming section.

- **Important: Unit** is where we can set the unit of measurement for the page. In the preceding screenshot, it is set to **mm**. It can be set to **cm, in, px,** or **pt** via the drop-down menu.

In the **Canvas** section, we have several options. **Width** and **Height** are the measurements of the new canvas that will be produced, in whatever unit of measurement is set in the **Unit** drop-down menu. These can be adjusted either via the arrows to the right of the textbox, or we can click inside the box and simply type in a new measurement. To switch the measurements for the height and width, click on the curved double-headed arrow button to the left of the **Width** and **Height** boxes.

- **Important: Resolution** is where you can set the resolution in dpi for the new document. For print projects, this should be at least 300 dpi.

> **Tip**
>
> Create all of your projects in at least 300 dpi (or larger, if your computer can handle it!) so that you never have to redo something if you decide after making it that you want to print it. Images with low resolution will look pixelated and blurry when printed.

- **Basic expression color** is where you can set the default expression color of the image. **Basic expression color** can be changed via individual layers in the image later, no matter what the expression color is set to during this step. However, if you are creating a pure black and white or grayscale image, it can save time (and file space!).

- **Paper color** is where you can set a default paper color. Activating the checkbox here will create a **Paper** layer in the file with the indicated paper color as a fill. This paper color can be edited later. If the paper color is not active, then the new file will be transparent.

- **Template** is the checkbox where we can load a template into the new file. We'll discuss templates more in the next section.
- The **Comic Settings** section activates the **Binding (finish) size** and border size options. Let's discuss the **Binding (finish) size** and border size options in more detail:
- **Binding (finish) size** is the dimensions of the finished page after printing. In printing, we have a bleed area that is cut off the edges of paper after documents are printed. This is how a full bleed (an image going off the edge of the paper) is achieved:
    - The **Width** and **Height** settings in the Canvas area should be the paper size, including any bleed area.
    - The **Binding (finish) size Width** and **Height** should be the finished dimensions of the page after trimming has occurred. For instance, if we had a 6 x 9-inch finished page with a .25-inch bleed margin, then we would need to add .25 inches to all four sides of the paper.
    - This would make our canvas **Width** and **Height** 6.5 x 9.5 inches, but our **Binding (finish) size** would be 6 x 9 inches.
    - Preset finish sizes can be selected from the drop-down menu or entered manually via the text entry boxes.
- **Default border (inner) size** is the size of the margin on the finished page. This is sometimes called the safe area. We want to keep any important elements of the art in a comic or other printed design away from the very edges of the page, especially when doing a bleed. This is because the very edges of the paper are cut down to the finished size, and sometimes those cuts aren't precise. Having text or other important elements too close to the edge can result in those things getting cut off! As with the binding size, the border size can be selected from the drop-down menu or entered manually in the textboxes.
- **X offset and Y offset** are used to offset the border to the left, right, up, or down. This feature is very handy if you need to move the margins to the left or right to compensate for the binding of a book, or if you want to move the inner border up slightly to allow for page numbers or notes at the bottom of the page.
- **Align crop mark** is used to align crop marks on two-page spreads. When you turn it on, the crop marks are combined by aligning the positions of the cropped border. The position of the cropped border on the left and right pages can be adjusted by typing numbers in the **Gap** section. When it's off, crop marks are created at the position where the paper edges of the left and right pages match.
- **Safety margin** is a border for manuscripts printed in multiple formats, showing the areas that will be printed in all formats. When it's on, the safety margin border will be shown in green on a canvas.
- **Setting for fanzine** is used to export work with data capable of being used by a fanzine printer. This option is used mainly for Japanese doujinshi.

- **Multiple pages** is an option that's only available in Clip Studio Paint EX. Checking this box allows you to make a file with multiple page files nested in it. This option is invaluable for anyone making longer-chapter comics. By using a multiple-page file, you can look at all the pages in the file at once, check the flow of the work, and rearrange, delete, or add pages.

- The **Number of pages** box controls how many pages should be created in the new file and can be set either using the downward pointing arrow to the right of the text entry box or by typing in a number manually:

    - You can select how you want to view the pages, with either **Page-by-page** (like bound books) or **Webtoon** (vertical scrolling).

    - The setting and **Story** window will change depending on the view you selected.

    - The **Combine into two-page spreads** checkbox will turn facing pages into a two-page spread automatically.

    - **Binding point** controls which side of the book the binding will be on. For instance, English books are bound with the spine on the left-hand side while Japanese books have the spine on the right.

When creating a multiple-page file, the **Cover page** option can be used. When active, this creates a front and back cover for the file. Note that these covers are included in the page count. Therefore, a 24-page file will yield 20 inner pages, a front outside cover, a front inside cover, a back inside cover, and a back outside cover. Just like when setting up the rest of the canvas, **Resolution**, **Color**, **Paper color**, and **Template** can also be set for the cover.

There are also two options for **Cover page layout.** The first icon is to make the cover a two-page spread so that the back and front of the cover are one continuous page and can both be designed and drawn on at the same time. When this option is selected, the **Specify spine width** option can be used to set the width of the spine of the finished book so that the appropriate width spine can be added to the cover. The icon on the right under **Cover page layout** separates the cover pages into individual pages.

- The **Story information** section of the **New** file window is optional but can be very helpful, especially if working with a team or when sending files out to a printer. **Story name** allows you to enter the name of your story. The drop-down menu to the right of the text entry box controls where the story name will appear on the new page. By activating the **Number of stories** checkbox, the number of the current story can be entered.

The **Subtitle** textbox can be used to add any additional title information. The **Author** box can be used to add the name of the author of the comic story, and the drop-down menu to the right can be used to determine where on the page to display the author's name. By activating the **Page number** checkbox, a page number will be displayed automatically in the bleed area of the pages. The drop-down menu to the right of the **Page number** checkbox can be used to control where to display this number. The **Start number** box is used to indicate what number should be the first in the number series.

- The **Folio** section of the **New File** window is where folio information can be added to new pages. Folio is another name for page numbering. The **Folio** option will leave visible page numbers on the new pages, inside of the bleed area. **Start number** allows us to set the number to begin the page numbering with. The color of the page number can be set with the **Color** drop-down menu. To add a stroke to the outside of the page numbers, activate the **Put edges** checkbox and then indicate the desired thickness of the outline in the text entry box to the right. The **Folio** checkbox is used to activate the **Folio** options and indicate that folio information should be included in the new file.

The drop-down menu to the right of the checkbox allows you to customize where the page number shows up on the page. The **Format** text entry boxes are used to format any text around the page number (for instance, Page 1 of 35 could be entered in the text entry boxes). **Gap with default border** is used to set the gap between the folio information and the default border of the page. The larger the number in the gap options, the larger the space between the folio information and the default borderline. The **Font** drop-down menu allows us to set the desired font to use for the folio information, and the **Size** option next to it sets the size of the folio text. *Figure 5.7* is a screenshot of the **Folio** section.

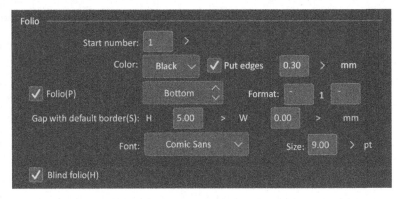

Figure 5.7: Folio section of the New file window

There is a **Blind folio** checkbox underneath. **Blind folio** puts a page number on the inside edge of the page, where the spine would be when the pages are bound into a book. These folio numbers are not visible when the book is bound.

Finally, if you wish to record a timelapse of your manga creation, click the **Record timelapse** checkbox at the very bottom of the window underneath the **Multiple pages** section, as shown in *Figure 5.8*. It will allow you to record and share the timelapse.

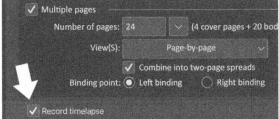

Figure 5.8: Timelapse section of the New file window

Now that we know what all of these terms and options are, we can make a new page! In the next section, we are going to create a custom page, sized to the standard American comic book size paper with the recommended margins. We will save this page as a preset and then create a new file with a template added to it as well. Let's get started!

Creating a basic square canvas

Let's start out by creating a basic illustration canvas, before we learn how to create custom pages for manga. It is pretty easy by following these steps:

1. Go to **File** | **New** or press *Ctrl + N* to open the **New** dialog box.
2. In the **Project** section, click on the **Illustration** icon on the far left.
3. Set **Unit** as **px**, **Width** and **Height** as 1000, and **Resolution** as 300.
4. Set **Basic expression color** as **Color**, then press **OK**.

Now you have a nice square canvas in front of you to draw anything!

Once you're ready to try controlling the specifications, we can move on to more precise file settings.

Creating a custom-sized page and saving a preset

While it provides Japanese and European comic sizes, Clip Studio Paint doesn't come with the sizes that are common to American comic books. We are going to create a standard American comic book size page and save it as a preset for use later. Follow these steps to complete this activity:

1. Go to **File** | **New** or press *Ctrl + N* to open the **New** dialog box.
2. In the **Project** section, click on the **Show all comic settings** icon.
3. Change the **Unit** drop-down menu to the right of the **Preset** dropdown to **in** (inches).
4. In the **Width** entry box, enter 7.00.
5. In the **Height** entry box, enter 10.50.
6. Set **Resolution** to 300 dpi (or more, depending on your computer hardware).
7. Set **Basic expression color**. I usually leave this as **Color**, but if the majority of your work is in black and white or grayscale, you may wish to choose a different mode. Individual layers can be adjusted later in the file, so even if we choose grayscale mode in this step, we will still be able to color our work later if we decide to.
8. Set **Paper Color** by clicking on the checkbox if it's not checked already, then click on the color selector box to choose the paper color. For this example, we will be leaving the paper color white.
9. Click the checkbox next to **Comic settings** to activate it if it is not already active. In **Binding (finish) size**, enter 6.75 for **Width** and 10.25 for **Height**.
10. Enter a **Bleed width** of 0.10.

11. Under **Default border (inner) size**, enter 6.25 for **Width.** Enter 9.75 for **Height.** Leave **X offset** and **Y offset** both at 0.00. Your settings should look like what's shown in the following screenshot:

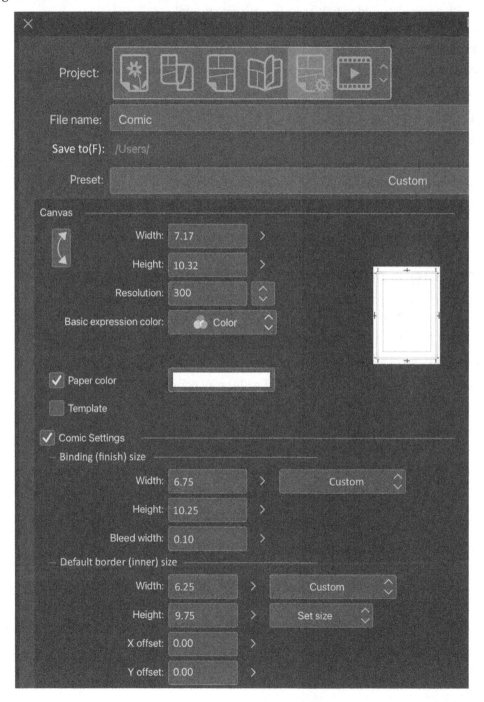

Figure 5.9: New comic settings window

12. Now, we are going to save this set of page settings as a preset so that we can use it again at a later time. To do this, all you have to do is click on the **Save** icon located to the right of the **Preset** drop-down menu. This will bring up the **Add to presets** window, which is shown in *Figure 5.10*.

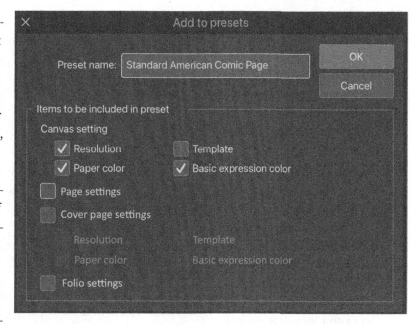

Figure 5.10: Add to presets window

13. Enter a name for the new preset in the **Preset name** box. Use the checkboxes to indicate which settings should be saved. When finished, click on **OK** to save the preset.

The new preset will be in the **Preset** drop-down menu and ready to use for future projects! In the next section, we will learn about adding templates to our files.

Adding templates to a new file

Templates can save a lot of time. For instance, if you are making a series of comics that all have the same four-panel layout, then by using Clip Studio Paint EX, you can make a multiple-page file and load the four panels into every page of the file upon creation, saving valuable time! No matter whether you're using the Pro or the EX version, though, using templates can save a lot of tedious work. So, let's learn how to load a page template into a new file by following these simple steps:

1. Open the **New** dialog box by going to **File | New** (or press *Ctrl + N*).

2. If you saved the preset page from the previous exercise, now is a great time to try it out by selecting it from the **Preset** drop-down menu.

3. Under the **Canvas** section, click the checkbox next to the word **Template**. This will bring up the **Template** dialog box.

4. Scroll down through the template selections to find the desired template. For this example, we will be using the **4 frames 2 strips with titles** template. Click on the template to select it.

5. Click on **OK** in the **Template** window. Now, the chosen template will be shown next to the **Template** checkbox. To change to a different template, click on the button with the name of the current template on it to bring the **Template** dialog box up again.

6. For EX users, check the box next to the **Multiple pages** option. In the drop-down menu, select 8 as the number of pages. Add a title in the **File name** textbox at the top of the window, and choose a folder to save the new file in.

7. Your screen should now look something like *Figure 5.11*. Click on **OK** to create the new file.

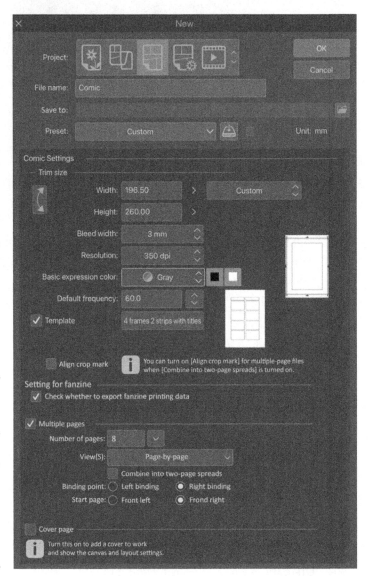

Figure 5.11: New comic page window

Tip

Creating a file with multiple pages can take a few seconds to a few minutes, depending on the number of pages and the speed of your computer system.

Be patient!

The following screenshot shows our eight-page file with the framing template we chose on each page:

Figure 5.12: Multiple-page window

Wow, now you have comic pages in front of you to work on! And you know how to use panel templates. Shall we proceed to the next stage – making your own comic panels?

Making comic panels

It's always faster to use already prepared templates for manga panels, but if you need to create your own, there is a variety of tools and options for frame border layers. These frame borders make comic panels – the individual boxes that each piece of sequential art in a story is drawn inside of.

These frame border layers can be created easily, edited in just a few clicks, and even set to mask out any content outside of the panel – which makes for a much easier drawing experience. If you want to know more about layers, check out *Chapter 3, Penciling: Layer and Layer Property Palettes*.

For now, let's start making some comic panels!

What are frame border layers?

First of all, frame border layers are what Clip Studio Paint calls the specific type of layers that it makes comic panels from. Panels in comics are like shots in a movie or TV show. They contain the action and can also give a sense of the amount of time that's passed or how much weight the action carries. Panels can also bring lots of drama and excitement to a page and can lead the reader's eye around the composition, telling them what is important and what they should be looking at.

Panel layouts can be straightforward or much more detailed. Let's take a look at a few comic panel examples, along with the way that their frame border layers are laid out in the **Layer** palette.

The following image is the first example of three panels on one page:

Figure 5.13: Manga page and the Layer palette 1

In a quiet, conversational-based storytelling layout, time passes at a consistent tempo. So, we use roughly the same-sized frames to indicate a stable passing of time. In the example shown here, there are two people talking. A girl is sitting; we can see her full body on the first panel, then the close-up of her face on the second panel (it is Japanese style, so it reads from right to left), and a boy is slowly leaving the place.

In the **Layer** palette at the bottom right of the screenshot, you will see the various frames of the comic. Each panel is created in its own frame or frame border folder, and you can tell which panel it is by looking at the black and white mask of each of the layers. (For more information on layer masks, see *Chapter 12, Making Layer Masks and Screentones*.) The following screenshot shows another example of comic paneling:

Figure 5.14: Manga page and the Layer palette 2

In the preceding example, the characters are involved in more actions than in the previous image! The bottom two frames depict the disappearing body of a boy, showing the two characters at the same angle. These two frames stay within the inner border of the page, but the top panel has been extended out beyond the margins to create a dynamic action scene of the characters.

This is called a **bleed,** as we discussed earlier in the *The New file window – explained* section. It refers to any art that goes off the edge of the page. When printed, the paper will be trimmed down to the final finished size so that there is no white margin around the edge of the paper. This trimming of the paper after printing occurs in traditional book publishing, which is why we must always keep the interior margins of the page (**Default Bordersize** in the **New** file options in Clip Studio Paint – see *Chapter 2, Installing Clip Studio Paint Pro and Interface Basics,* for more information on creating a new file) in mind. Artwork, text, and anything else that is too close to the edge of the page are at risk of being cut off in the trimming process, so it is a good idea to keep anything important, such as dialog and speech balloons, inside the inner margins at all times.

Here is a third example of a comic panel layout, along with its corresponding **Layer** palette from Clip Studio Paint:

Figure 5.15: Manga page and the Layer palette 3

It is a page showing the girl's confession of her indulgence in blind love, symbolized by the puppy in the middle of the page. The panels are round shapes that soften the impression of the page as it's told in a dreamy state of mind. Believe it or not, this set of panels was just as easy to create as the other panel examples; it just required a little bit of pre-planning to keep everything together!

Of course, these three examples do not cover the entire spectrum of comic book paneling. Just like shooting a movie, there are countless ways to tell a story. Page compositions depend on the style of the artist and the type of story they are telling to inform the style of paneling.

So, now that we've talked about panels and what they are, let's get into the tools we use to make them.

Creating, editing, and using template panels

In order to create frame border panels, you will need an open page. I recommend using one of the templates under the comic category to test out the panel creation tools, but use any size canvas that you feel comfortable with! I recommend the comic templates because they already have the inner border size set, so it's easy to see where you should keep the panels to avoid them getting cut off.

Before we get into actually creating some panels, let's take a look at the subtools used to make them and some of the options for those subtools. The **Frame Border** subtools can be found under the **Figure** category of tools in the toolbar. These subtools are shown in *Figure 5.16*.

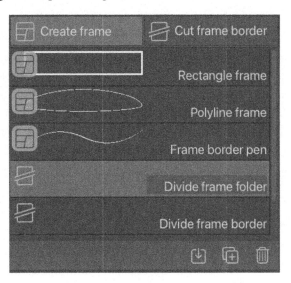

Figure 5.16: Create frame subtools

In this section, we are going to concentrate on the **Rectangle frame**, **Polyline frame**, and **Frame border pen** tools. We will discuss the other two types of subtools in the *Dividing and editing panels* section coming up later in this chapter.

Figure 5.17 shows the **Tool property** options for the **Rectangle frame** subtool. The list that follows provides details about each of these options:

- **Draw border:** This checkbox controls whether a line is drawn around the outside of the created frame or not. When unchecked, Clip Studio Paint will create a panel with no outline.

- **How to add:** The options under this drop-down menu are **Create a new folder** and **Add to selected folder.** Depending on the setting selected, new panels will either be made in a folder of their own or will be created all in the same folder. We will discuss this more in the next section of this chapter.

- **Raster layer:** When checked, this option will automatically create a new raster layer underneath the new panel folder.

- **Fill inside the frame:** Automatically creates a background fill layer in the new frame.

- **Aspect type:** When checked, this option controls the aspect ratio of the created panel with either a set ratio or a set length. For example, to create frames that are all exactly the same size, that size can be specified by setting **Width** and **Height** under the **Set Length** option.

- **Brush Size:** Controls the thickness of the created border outline.

- **Anti-aliasing:** Sets the anti-aliasing of the border outline.

- **Brush shape:** Controls the brush used to draw the outside border. For example, a border of dashed lines or hearts can be set using this drop-down menu.

Figure 5.17: Rectangle frame subtool

Now that we know a little about the panel options, let's create some panels using the first three subtools in the **Frame border** category.

Using the Rectangle frame tool

Follow these steps to create a comic panel using the **Rectangle frame** tool:

1. Select the **Rectangle frame** tool from the **Frame border** category.

2. Edit the tool properties to your desired settings.

3. Decide where you want your panel to be located on your open page.

4. Click and hold down the mouse button or stylus where you want the panel to begin.

5. Drag to create the panel and release when the panel is the desired shape and size.

6. Repeat to create additional panels.

The **Rectangle frame** tool can be used to create circle- and polygon-shaped panels, as well as squares and rectangles. Simply click on the icon at the bottom of the **Tool property** palette to bring up the screen shown in *Figure 5.18*.

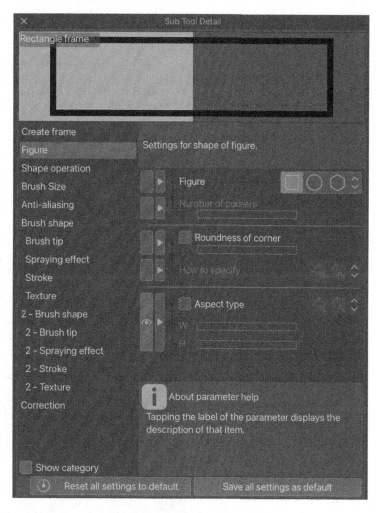

Figure 5.18: Sub Tool Detail pane

Under the **Figure** options, you will find icons to change the shape to a circle or a polygon, as shown in the preceding screenshot.

Tip

Want to see options from the **Sub Tool Detail** screen in the **Tool property** palette for easier access? Click on the box to the left of the option name to turn on the eye icon. Any options with the eye icon next to them will be available in the **Tool property** palette.

Using the Polyline frame tool

The **Polyline frame** tool allows us to create more complicated and irregularly shaped frames.

Select the **Polyline frame** tool and look at the **Tool property** palette. If the **Curve** options are not visible, they can be accessed through the **Sub Tool Detail** palette, as shown in *Figure 5.19*.

The very first icon will produce straight lines between the points of your frame, and the second option is the **Spline** setting, which will create curves between each point of the frame. To use either of these options, simply click on the point in the canvas where you want the frame to start. Then, click again where the second point should be. Continue clicking on each corner of the frame until you reach the starting point and double-click to finish the frame.

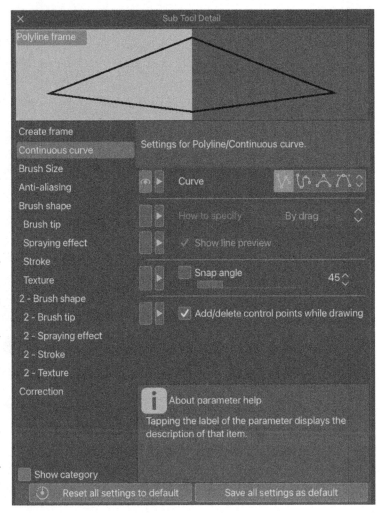

Figure 5.19: Sub Tool Detail pane

Frames made using the **Straight line** option are shown in *Figure 5.20*.

The sample image on the right is a scene where a samurai is captured, looking through a decorative hole in a castle wall. Using a specifically shaped panel depicts a feeling you are secretly looking through a scene through a hole in a wall, a keyhole, or some other crack. It can take a little time to effectively use the **Polyline frame** tool if you are using it for the first time. But don't worry, just try it step by step, and soon you will have perfect control of the tool!

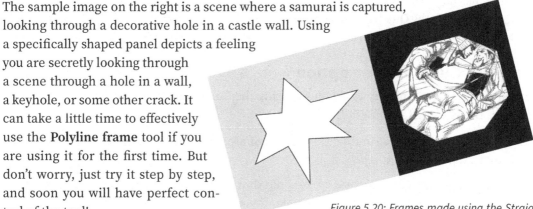

Figure 5.20: Frames made using the Straight line option

Using the Quadratic Bezier option

Using the **Quadratic Bezier** option for a panel takes a little getting used to and usually requires some refinement after the initial points are laid out. Follow these steps to create a curved panel with Quadratic Bezier:

1. Select **Polyline frame** and then the Quadratic Bezier option from the **Tool property** palette.

2. Click on the canvas once, at the point where you'd like the frame to start.

3. Click on the point where you would like the frame to start curving. This will create a small square handle at the clicked point.

4. Move the cursor to another point on the canvas. The line of the frame will bend according to where the second click was placed and where the cursor is now.

5. Continue clicking to add boxes and curves to the frame until it is the desired length. Double-click to end the frame when the starting point is reached.

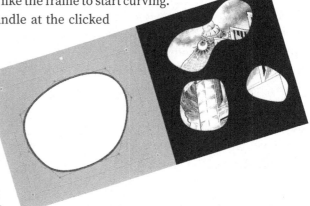

Figure 5.21: Frames made using the Quadratic Bezier line option

6. To adjust the frame, select the **Operation** category of tools and then the **Object** tool in its category. Click on the frame outline to select it and reveal the handle controls. In *Figure 5.21*, on the left image, the control handles are on the straight lines and the frame has the curved lines.

The right side of the preceding screenshot is a sample panel depicting a character's patchy memory, where the character only remembers parts of what they saw. This has been done by creating abstract shapes with the **Quadratic Bezier** option. This tool has its own way of handling the shape. You can try moving each point to see how the tool modifies the shape!

Using the Cubic Bezier option

Another option for making curved frames is using the Cubic Bezier setting. Follow these steps to create a frame using Cubic Bezier:

1. Select the **Cubic Bezier** setting from the **Tool property** palette of the **Polyline frame** tool.
2. Click on the first point of the frame.
3. When clicking to add the first curve, hold down the mouse button and drag it in the direction your line is going. (For example, if you are starting on the left-hand side of the canvas and heading toward the right, drag the mouse to the right while holding down the button. Going in the direction of the line will prevent the control handles from reversing and making "snarls" in the line.) The line between the two clicked points will curve.
4. Click on a third point and drag with the mouse while holding down the button to continue making the curve.
5. To end the frame creation process, click on the starting point to enclose the frame.
6. To edit the Cubic Bezier frame, select the **Operation** category of tools and select the **Object** tool. Click on the frame to reveal the control handles. The control handles are shown by the red lines on the left image in the following screenshot:

Cubic Bezier has a unique function with the red handles: they make it possible to create the exact smooth shape you need! In the image on the right, the scene captures a memory inside a man's silhouette. This is an example of how a panel can depict a past scene (in the character's memory) within a modern-day image (the silhouette of the man in a hat).

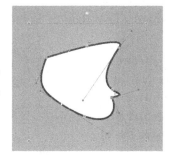

Figure 5.22: Frames made using the Cubic Bezier line option

Using the Frame border pen

The **Frame border pen** is a versatile tool that allows you to freehand any shape into a frame border. It's so easy to use!

Follow these steps to create a frame with the Frame border pen:

1. Select the **Frame border pen** subtool from the **Frame border** category.
2. Using the mouse or tablet stylus, draw the desired shape for the panel outline.

3. When the entire shape is enclosed, release the pressure on the mouse button or stylus tip to complete the frame creation process.

4. As shown in the following screenshot, more complex frame shapes can be made with the Frame border pen tool than with the other frame creation tools.

The Frame border pen is for more complicated shapes and is easy for just drawing freehand! It will give you more freedom with panel shapes. On the right hand side of the preceding screenshot, you can see a frame border of eerie blood streams created by the Frame border pen.

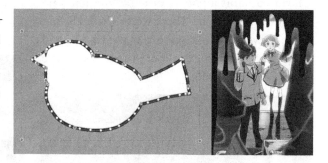

Figure 5.23: Frames made using the Frame border pen option

One layer and many panels, or one layer for each panel?

You may be wondering: why use the **Frame Border** tools to create panels when we can use the various shape tools to simply draw a border and create our art inside of it?

Frame Border panels come with a feature that makes them a lot more convenient than just using the **Direct Draw** tools to make a square and drawing your comic art inside of it. As you may have noticed from the screenshots, the outsides of the comic borders are shaded in purple. This is because the frame borders are made with a layer mask automatically on the outside of them. Because of this layer mask, we can create artwork that goes outside of the panel but that is automatically cleaned up. For instance, let's look at the images in *Figure 5.24*.

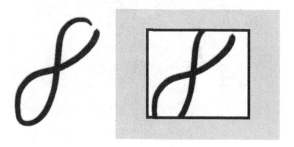

Figure 5.24: Drawing and the same image with a panel

The line on the left was drawn quite big, and in the right image, only the parts of the line inside the frame border panel are visible. Because of this layer mask, we don't need to spend time tediously making sure that our art doesn't go outside of the panels.

However, we can create our panels either all on their own layer or with every panel on the same layer. In *Figure 5.25*, one panel has been created on its own layer and two more panels have been created on the same layer.

You can see the outlines of each layer by looking at the black and white layer mask icons to the left of the layer names. The **Frame 1** layer contains one panel at the top, while the **Frame 2** layer contains a panel at the bottom left, and also the bottom right. These were created by toggling between the two options in the **How to add** drop-down menu in the Tool Properties for the **Rectangle frame** tool.

As shown on the left-hand side of *Figure 5.26*, the **Frame 1** layer allows us to see only what is inside the attached layer mask. The other two panels are shaded out and the contents of those frames will not be visible, and not affected when you draw.

Figure 5.26: Page with different layers selected

If we create all our panels on separate layers, then each will be independent of the others. However, with panels created on the same layer, artwork can be shown in multiple panels continuously, so you don't need to switch layers every time you are inking a different panel. Fewer steps, less hassle!

Figure 5.25: A layer with Frame Border panels

Ultimately, the decision of whether to put all your frames on their own layers or all on one layer is yours to make. Putting each on its own layer means more layers to manage and more clicking around to complete your comic page. But putting them all on one layer means managing more of your creation process to ensure that artwork is only in the frame it's supposed to be in.

Personally, I work more comfortably using only one or two panel layers, just because there are fewer layers to toggle around, and it can make the work simple. But of course, the right choice for you will depend on your working style and preferences. This is especially true when you're working on commissions and need to do a quick amendment of the panel order; it saves a lot of time having each panel in a separate layer so you can move the panel layer folders instead of re-drawing the contents!

You now know why we need frame border panels, and how to create them in various ways. If the panel shape you have created is not entirely as you desired, don't panic; you can always edit it! Read on to find out how.

Dividing and editing panels

A big advantage to working in the digital realm is the ability to make edits on the fly. Yes, our frame border panels can be edited even after we've created them. Resizing, rotating, and even completely changing the position of our frames is possible, as is adding a new one or deleting one entirely. In this section, we will learn how to modify the frames we've created.

If you haven't created panels already, follow the instructions in the *Making comic panels* section of this chapter and put some panels on a page!

To resize a comic panel, you'll need to first select the **Object** tool from the **Operation** category of tools. Then click on the outside edge of the comic panel to select it. When selected, a red line will show along the outline of the panel, as well as some light-blue handles and small yellow arrows. Around the outside edge of the panel, a rectangle with a light-blue handle at each corner and a handle at the center top will also show.

To resize the panel manually, click on one of the light-blue handles and drag. Once the desired size is reached, let go of the mouse button.

The small yellow arrows can also be used to resize a panel quickly. Clicking on one of the yellow arrows will automatically either take that edge of the panel out to the same size as a nearby panel (if there are any nearby panels) or take that side of the panel to the edge of the page. In *Figure 5.27*, the yellow arrow on the left-hand side of the panel was used to quickly make the panel bleed off the edge of the page.

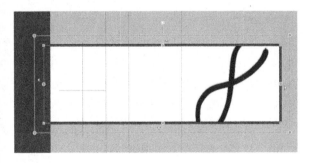

Figure 5.27: Panel resizing

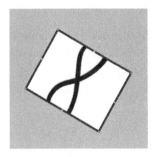

Rotating a panel is just as simple as resizing one! To rotate a panel, simply move the mouse over the light-blue handle sticking up outside of the bounding box at the top of the panel. The cursor will change to a curved double-headed arrow once it is in the correct position for rotating. Click and drag to rotate the panel to the desired position. In *Figure 5.28*, the handle was used to rotate the panel clockwise.

Figure 5.28: Panel rotating

To move the selected panel, put the **Object** tool over the red outline around the edge of the panel. Click and drag to move the panel to the new location. Release the button once the new position is reached to stop moving the panel. *Figure 5.29* shows that the panel edges have been moved down and to the right from their starting position.

So now you know you can move/edit panels around even after you have already drawn artwork. Phew, what a relief!

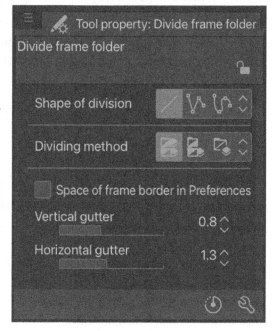

Figure 5.29: Panel expanding

Dividing existing frames

Remember how I said earlier that we would cover the **Divide frame folder** and **Divide frame border** tools later? Now is the time!

With these tools, it is easy to cut a whole framed page into pieces, rather than creating each frame using frame drawing tools. The **Divide frame folder** and **Divide frame border** tools can take one frame and turn it into two. But, just as their names suggest, they each perform that division a little differently.

Earlier, we discussed how we can either make our frames all on one layer or each on their own layer. These two dividing tools divide the existing frames into either separate layers or frames all on one layer. Let's look at each tool and how to use it.

Figure 5.30 shows the **Tool property** palette for the **Divide frame folder** tool. In the following list, you will find a description of each of these settings:

Figure 5.30: Tool property palette of the Divide frame folder tool

- **Shape of division:** Controls how the panel is divided. The options are **Divide by straight line**, **Divide by polyline**, and **Divide by spline.** Using the straight-line option will produce a panel division that is one straight line. Polyline division allows us to create a panel division using a segmented line. The spline division option allows us to create a curved panel division.
- **Dividing method:** Controls how the panel division operation is carried out. The options are **Divide frame folder and duplicate inside layer**, **Divide frame folder and create empty layer**, and **Divide not folder but frame border.** The first two options will create a new panel folder after the division is completed, but the first option will duplicate the layer inside the existing panel, while the second will create an empty layer inside the folder.

The third option turns the **Divide frame folder** tool into the **Divide frame border** tool by splitting the frame but keeping both new frames on the same layer.

- **Space of frame border in Preferences:** Uses the value set in the program preferences to set the gutter space between panels.

- **Vertical gutter:** When the option to use program preferences isn't in use, this sets the width of the vertical gap between panels.

- **Horizontal gutter:** When the preceding option is not checked, this sets the height of the horizontal gap between panels.

Using the **Divide frame folder** tool is easy. Simply select the tool and click on or near the edge of the panel to divide. While holding down the mouse button or stylus, drag to where you want to divide the panel. A set of lines will show a preview of the panel division so you can see exactly what your new panels will look like. Once the preview lines are in the correct spot, release the mouse button to complete the division.

In *Figure 5.31*, our panel has been divided into two panels, each in its own folder. This comes in handy when you want to apply different effects to a scene divided into two frames. For example, you might want to divide a scene to show a fall into a character's monologue, or into the past. The left-hand side panel in *Figure 5.31* is selected for editing. The **Divide by straight line** option in **Shape of division** was used to split the the frames.

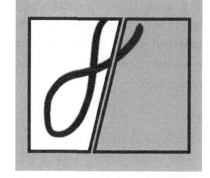

Figure 5.31: Panel divided into two

Figure 5.32 shows the **Tool property** palette for the **Divide frame border** tool. Refer to the preceding list for a breakdown of each of these options. This tool divides an existing frame but keeps each new frame on the same layer, making connected panels. In *Figure 5.33*, the panel has been split using the **Divide by spline** setting, in order to make a curved division.

Now we know how to create, edit, and divide panels. We can also use panel templates to help save time with page creation. Keep reading to find out how!

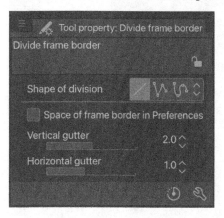

Figure 5.32: Tool property for the Divide frame border tool

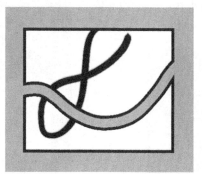

Figure 5.33: Curved division

Using framing template materials

The **Material** palette has tons of useful resources that can save lots of time when working on your creative projects. Included in the **Material** palette are a large number of framing templates that can be used to easily and quickly set up a comic page.

You will find out more about the **Material** palette in *Chapter 09, Inking Special Effects and the Material Palette.*

The comic panel templates can be found in the **Material** palette, under the **Manga material** folder, and in the **Framing template** sub-folder. This folder is shown in *Figure 5.34*.

The icons on the right-hand side of the **Material** palette show a preview of the layout of the comic panels. To add one of these to your page, locate the desired framing template and click to select it. The selection will be highlighted in blue. To add the material to your page, click on the **Paste selected material to canvas** icon at the bottom of the **Material** palette, which looks like the following screenshot:

Figure 5.35: Paste selected material to canvas icon

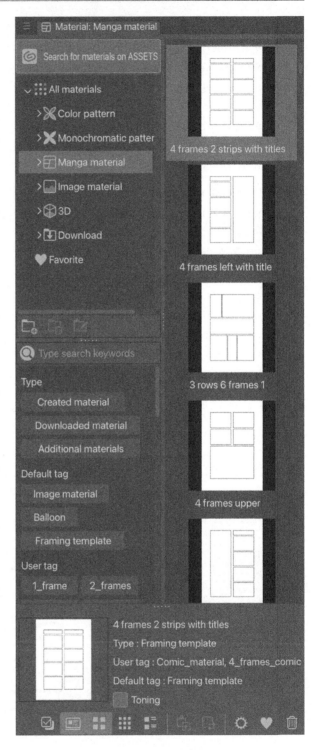

Figure 5.34: Material palette

The left-hand side of the following screenshot shows the **4 frames 2 strips with titles** framing template added to canvas, and the right-hand side shows that each panel in the template is in its own empty folder in the **Layer** palette. By using the framing templates, we can also concentrate more on the art of drawing our comics!

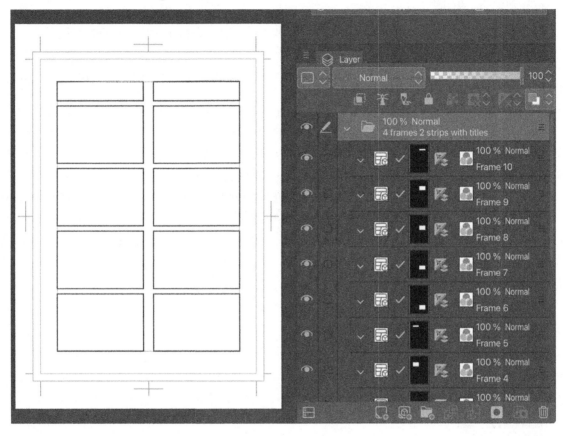

Figure 5.36: A screenshot of a pasted template and its layers

Tip

Want to save some time by using a framing template but each of your comic pages has a different panel layout? Create a framing template with one large panel around the inner border of the page and apply it to the story file. Then, use the **Divide Frame Folder** or **Divide Frame Border** tool to slice one large panel into smaller panels!

Summary

In this chapter, we covered all manner of ground regarding manga creations! First, we learned how to set up workspaces, then about creating new files and templates, and finally, all about frame border panels!

You may come back to this chapter for more adjustment of your workspace as you find easier workspace layouts, and to try out new file settings or panel layouts for more complex storytelling.

For file configurations, I personally recommend you stick to the new file template settings we used in the example in the *Adding templates to a new file* section, unless you are required to create your manga in specific settings. In that way, you don't need to worry about what settings you should configure each time you create a new file; it's great to jump into creation quickly! Just ensure to keep the file resolution around 300 dpi.

Now you have a great manga workspace to draw your stories onto and panel variations, shall we move on to exploring erasers? In the next chapter, we will learn about erasers, selection tools, Sub view palette, and how we can use them. Let's read on!

Join us on Discord!

Read this book alongside other users. Ask questions, provide solutions to other readers, and much more.

Scan the QR code or visit the link to join the community.

`https://packt.link/clipstudiopaint`

Erasers, Selections, and the Sub View Palette

Whether you draw with pencils on paper and then ink digitally or draw digitally from start to finish, a certain amount of refinement is needed in most art processes. We will use a variety of tools in this chapter to refine our images, from erasers to selection tools that allow us to scale and rotate sections of our image. We will also learn about a great feature of Clip Studio Paint, the **Sub View** palette, which allows us to store and use reference images easily.

In this chapter, we will cover the following topics:

- Erasers and using transparent color as an eraser
- Lassos and other selection tools
- Loading reference images to the Sub View palette
- Using Layer Color to prepare a sketch

Let's get started with refining our pencil work!

Technical requirements

To get started, you need Clip Studio Paint installed on your device and a new canvas opened with any dark color. Any size is fine, but I recommend creating a 300 dpi square canvas to go through the content in this chapter.

Eraser tools and transparent color

No matter whether we are penciling, inking, or coloring, mishaps do happen. Especially when we are creating very neat and slick styles of art, eraser tools and transparent color become our guardians. They are not only for erasing unnecessary marks; we can also use them tactically, such as for brightness, light reflections, cut-out frames, disappearing objects, and rainy scenes. Read on to find out more.

There is a selection of dedicated eraser tools in Clip Studio Paint that is accessed by clicking on the **Eraser** icon in the toolbar and then choosing an option from the **Sub Tool** palette. Each of these **Eraser** sub tools has a different use. But, by using the transparent color selection in the Color Picker option in the toolbar, we can also transform any mark-making tool into an eraser. We will touch on transparent colors in more detail in the *Using transparent color* section later. Before we get into transparent colors, though, let's talk about some of the eraser tools in Clip Studio Paint and what they do.

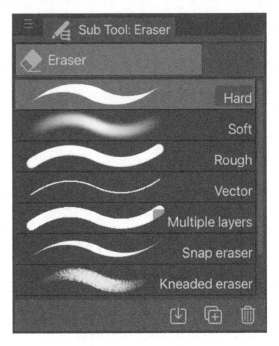

Figure 6.1: The Eraser sub tool menu

The eraser tools

Once you start drawing, you need an eraser to correct a mistake or give a half-erased texture to your image, which is the same in digital drawing. There are various useful erasers in Clip Studio Paint. The screenshot on the right shows the Eraser sub tools in Clip Studio Paint.

Each of these tools has a different look and use. Let's briefly explore each one now.

> **Tip**
>
> If you are using a graphics tablet that has an eraser end to the stylus, like some models of **Wacom** tablets have, then the currently selected **Eraser** sub tool will be the one used when the **Eraser** button on the stylus is activated.

Hard eraser

The Hard eraser is a pressure-sensitive eraser tool with a hard edge. Since it is pressure-sensitive, when a graphics tablet is being used, it is a very versatile tool because simply varying how hard you are pressing with the stylus changes how small or large the area being erased becomes. So, this eraser tool is just like a pressure-sensitive pen: you can use it to control the line width, as if you're drawing with a pen tool!

The screenshot on the right shows some examples of the Hard eraser tool in action.

Adding light expression

Sharpen siluettes

Figure 6.2: Hard eraser usage

You can see this eraser has a very clear edge; it comes in handy when you want to erase sections with defined edges. I can say that this is the most basic eraser!

Tip

I strongly recommend using the **Undo** button when you don't feel right about the line you have just drawn, rather than using the Hard eraser tool to refine it, because the Hard eraser tool is best for chiseling the edge of lines, not refining them. I normally rest my left hand on top of *Cmd + Z*, then repeat: draw, undo, draw, undo... until I create the desired line. I find I always get the best result and can work faster this way. You can also map this shortcut to a button on your tablet, so it is easily on hand.

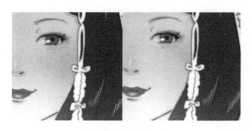

Figure 6.3: Soft eraser

Soft eraser

The Soft eraser is also a pressure-sensitive tool. It has a soft, blurry edge to it, and the best usage is to reduce color in a very soft way, as shown on the right of the screenshot on the left.

This eraser is great for using in effects, such as fading one color to another or making a subtle gradient. It can be used for general erasing as well.

Rough eraser

The Rough eraser tool is a non-pressure-sensitive tool with a hard edge. Because it is not pressure-sensitive by default, the size of the tool will remain consistent, despite any variations in the pressure on the stylus.

The screenshot on the right shows an example of the Rough eraser in use.

Since it is not pressure-sensitive, it's better to use it for rough sketches rather than detailed drawings.

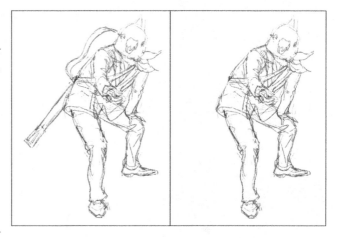

Figure 6.4: Rough eraser

Vector eraser

The Vector eraser can be used on raster layers, but it is most useful on vector layers because on vector layers, you can erase a whole line or a shape with one stroke of the Vector eraser! We will be discussing vector layers in detail in *Chapter 10, Exploring Vector Layers*.

Multiple Layers eraser

Got a speck or splotch on your image that shouldn't be there, but you can't find the layer it's on? The Multiple Layers eraser can take care of it quickly. Just make sure you're not erasing part of the image that you want to keep in the process of using it, though!

The Multiple Layers eraser tool erases content from multiple layers at a time. It will delete the content of the area where it is used from every layer in the stack. The following screenshot shows an image composed of multiple layers. The background color layer is locked, as you see a lock icon next to it:

Figure 6.5: Multiple layers

There are three splotches in the preceding image, which are circled, waiting to be erased but... we don't know which layer they are on! Instead of going through each layer to make it invisible to check which one they are on, let's use the **Multiple Layers** eraser tool. Since it affects all layers, we can clean these marks up no matter which layer they are on. One warning, though; don't forget to lock the background color layer if you don't want the background color to be erased, so that the layer is unaffected.

Snap eraser

If you need to erase only a part that is aligned to the ruler, this is the tool for you.

This eraser snaps to the ruler shape, so other parts of the image will not be affected. You can see this in the following screenshot on the right:

Figure 6.6: Snap eraser

The Snap eraser tool erases following the ruler line, to express the lighting on the building. We discuss **rulers** further in *Chapter 13, All about Rulers*.

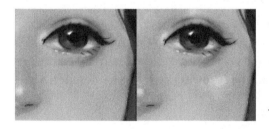

Figure 6.7: Kneaded eraser texture work

Kneaded eraser

For artists who want more of an analog look to their drawings, the Kneaded eraser (or as some artists might refer to it, a *putty rubber eraser*) does a good job. It offers very delicate erasing work on the drawing, such as a skin texture, as seen in the screenshot on the left.

Now that we've talked about our dedicated eraser tools, let's talk about using the transparent option in the color picker to turn any tool into an eraser.

Using transparent color

At the bottom of the toolbar in the Clip Studio interface are two squares that show the currently selected foreground and background colors. Below these is also a rectangle filled with a checkerboard pattern. This is shown in the screenshot on the right, underneath the foreground and background color selections:

Figure 6.8: Toolbar color swatch

The checkerboard pattern is how transparency is shown in digital art programs. Having this transparent swatch means that we can quickly turn any tool into an eraser just by changing our color selection to transparent.

This option is used to make special effects with textured erasers. The screenshot on the right shows the **G-Pen** tool and **Soft** decoration tool being used as an eraser with the transparent option to express the rain and atmosphere on the left, and the **Pampas grass** decoration tool is used as an eraser on the right:

Figure 6.9: Erasing by using the various drawing tools

Of course, these are just a few examples of the effects that can be achieved by using transparency as a painting color.

Surprisingly, there are more ways of erasing and editing your art! Let's move on to the various selection tools that can be utilized in Clip Studio Paint.

Lassos and other selection tools

One of the most useful features of creating art in a digital space is the ability to move, scale, rotate, flip, and otherwise transform all or parts of the drawing to obtain exactly the right look. In this section, we will use selection tools to clean up and correct a sketch with several errors in it. You can follow along with a sketch of your own or use the following sketch as a reference. These tools can be used with any sketches on your canvas.

The following is the sketch that we will be looking at in this section:

Figure 6.10: A sketch with the Clip Studio Paint interface

There are several issues with this drawing, and we will use the selection and transformation tools to correct them. The character's left hand is a little too big, the bunch of hair on top of the head needs to be a different shape, and the headdress ribbon needs to be shaped better. Let's use the selection area and other selection tools to fix these problems.

The Rectangle and Ellipse selection area tools

The **Rectangle** and **Ellipse** tools both work in the same way; the only difference is the shape of the selection they produce. We can use these tools when our selection doesn't need to be precise. For the sketch we are going to be correcting, we will use the Rectangle tool to correct the size of the character's left hand in our drawing.

> **Tip**
>
> I recommend that any overlapping objects, such as an arm in front of the body, or characters standing in front of others, should be in different layers to make manipulation easier.

Even though we are going to use the Rectangle tool, the Ellipse tool operates in exactly the same way.

Let's use the Rectangle tool and the **Selection Launcher** options to resize a portion of our drawing by following the steps here:

1. Identify the area of the drawing that needs refining. In the case of our sketch, we will be resizing the character's hand to correct the proportions.

2. Select the **Selection area** icon from the toolbar. Then, select the **Rectangle** tool from the **Sub Tool** palette.

3. Using the mouse or stylus, hold down and drag the **Selection area** tool around the section of the drawing to be selected. When the appropriate area is outlined, release the mouse or stylus button to complete the selection. The following screenshot shows an example of a rectangle selection:

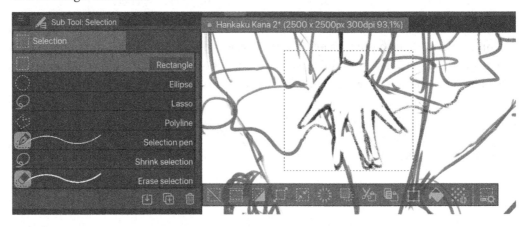

Figure 6.11: A rectangle selection

4. Select the **Scale/Rotate** icon, which is the fourth from the right on the **Selection** command bar. Use the square handles at the corners of the selection to resize the section of the drawing by dragging them in or out.

5. If an undesired change is made, click on the **Cancel** icon beneath the selected area.

6. Try keeping the wrist of the hand aligned with the arm. Once the area matches the newly desired size, click on the **OK** button beneath the selection, as in the following screenshot, or press *Enter* on the keyboard to commit the changes:

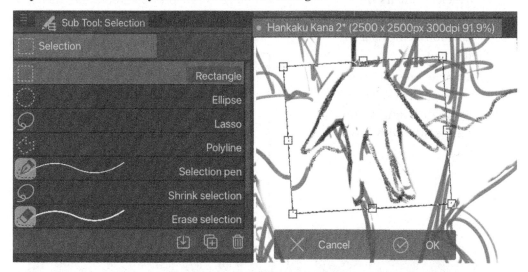

Figure 6.12: Resized hand image

Note that if you try to select a different tool or perform another operation while the selection is still in transform mode, a message will appear asking whether you would like to commit the changes.

7. Use the **Eraser** and **Brush** tools to correct any areas in the sketch that do not align, such as wrists and ankles.

Selecting with rectangles and circles is all well and good, but what about when we have an area that is a much more complicated shape than that? Let's learn how to use the other tools from the **Selection** command bar.

The Selection Launcher

Let's look at the launcher that appears just underneath the selection you made. You can usually get by using only your favorite functions in the launcher, but it's always good to know other important functions too. The selection launcher contains useful tools, as the following screenshot shows.

From left to right, the options in the selection launcher and their functions are as follows:

- **Deselect:** Clears the active selection; the same function as the *Cmd + D* shortcut.

- **Crop:** Resizes the image to the current selection. Good for changing the canvas size with just a click!

- **Shrink selected area:** Makes the selection smaller for smooth **Fill** tool coloring.

- **Delete:** Deletes the contents of the selection without tedious erasing with eraser tools. The same as pressing *Command + X* shortcut.

- **Delete outside selection:** Deletes the contents that are outside of the selection for easier clean-up of the outside area!

- **Cut and paste:** Cuts the selected content out and pastes it to a new layer. It comes in handy when you accidentally draw on the wrong layer!

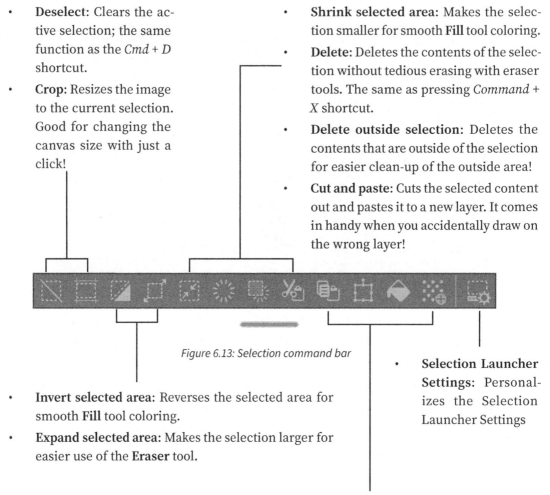

Figure 6.13: Selection command bar

- **Invert selected area:** Reverses the selected area for smooth **Fill** tool coloring.

- **Expand selected area:** Makes the selection larger for easier use of the **Eraser** tool.

- **Selection Launcher Settings:** Personalizes the Selection Launcher Settings

- **Copy and paste:** Makes a copy of the current content of the selection and pastes it to a new layer. One of the most useful functions when you reproduce the same element on a new layer!

- **Scale/Rotate:** Scales or rotates the contents of the selection using displayed handles to edit the contents. Another very popular function.

- **Fill:** Fills the selection with the currently active color for smooth coloring.

- **New Tone:** Fills the area with a screen tone based on set parameters for efficient shading.

If you hover a cursor on the horizontal bar under the command bar, the cursor turns into a hand. If you click and hold, you can move the command bar anywhere on the canvas!

The Lasso and Polyline selection area tools

For more complicated selections, the **Lasso** and **Polyline** tools are good tools to know about. They work in basically the same way. The Lasso tool is being used in the next set of instructions, but the Polyline tool will also be covered.

The Lasso tool allows curved and rounded selection areas, while the Polyline tool can make complex shapes, but each segment of the selection area must be a straight line.

Follow these steps to select and horizontally flip a selected area of the drawing:

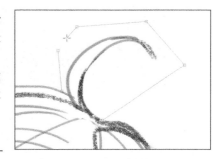

1. Identify the area of the drawing to be selected and choose the appropriate tool from the **Selection area** category of sub tools. To use the Lasso tool, hold down the mouse or stylus button and drag to trace around the area, releasing the button once you're back to the starting point. An example of the Lasso tool is shown on the right.

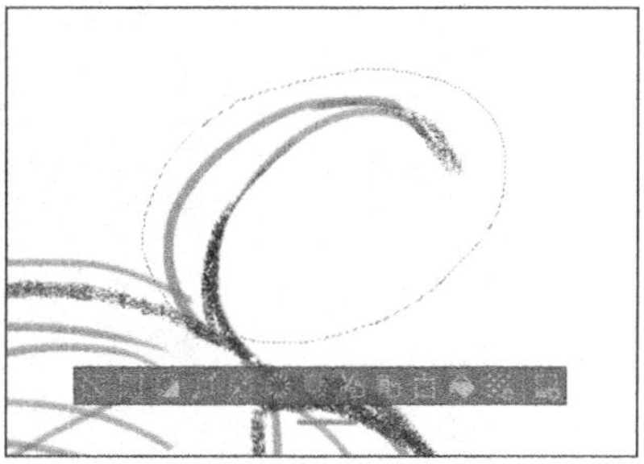

Figure 6.14: Lasso selection area

2. To use the Polyline tool, click with the mouse or stylus and move to another area. Click again to set another point of the selection area border. Continue this process until you come around to the beginning point to complete the selection area, or double-click to draw a straight line from the current point to the starting point. The screenshot on the left shows the process of selecting a section using Polyline just before clicking the starting point.

Figure 6.15: Polyline selection area

3. To begin the transformation process, click on the **Scale/Rotate** icon, which is fourth from the right in the Selection Launcher.

4. In order to flip the selection area horizontally, we need to look at the **Tool property** palette. The **Tool property** palette is shown in the following screenshot:

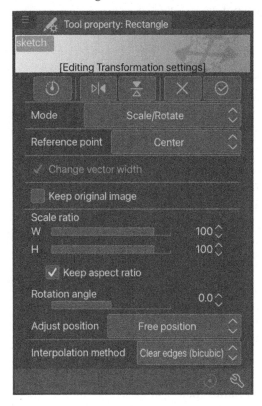

Figure 6.16: The Rectangle tool's Tool property palette

5. In the set of rectangular icons at the top of the **Transformation settings**, click on the **Flip vertical at center of rotation** icon, which is the second from the left, to mirror the currently selected area vertically.

6. Adjust the selection area to the correct position, then click on the **OK** icon beneath the selection or press *Enter* on the keyboard.

7. The flipped and adjusted section of the drawing is shown here:

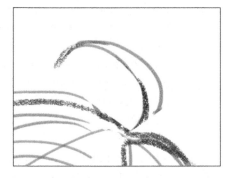

Figure 6.17: The flipped part

Yes, the bunch of hair is now a mirror image! Use the **Pencil** and **Eraser** tools to clean anything that might have been jutting out or missing after flipping the image.

You have seen several different ways to erase part of your art. Isn't it great to know more about editing your art using rich functions for selection tools?

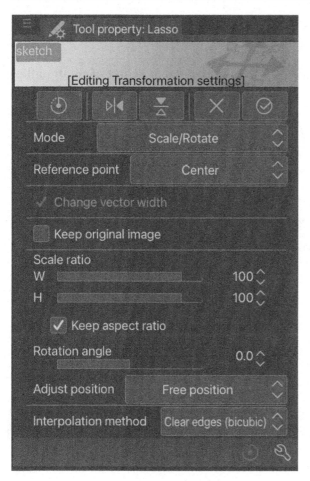

Figure 6.18: Lasso tool properties

Using the Tool property palette to scale or rotate a selection

As mentioned previously, the **Tool property** palette for the Selection area tools changes its contents when the **Scale/Rotate** function is activated with a selection. The **Tool property** palette becomes a transformation command center, and it's really important to know what it's capable of! Let's take a closer look at this palette before we move on.

The **Transformation settings** area in the **Tool property** palette is shown on the left.

These settings are accessible when either a selection area or the contents of an entire layer are being scaled or rotated. To transform the contents of an entire layer, simply select the layer from the **Layer** palette, then click on the **Scale/Rotate** icon in the main menu at the top of the interface window, between the **File** menu and the **Canvas Display** area. A bounding box will appear around the contents of the layer.

The **Transformation settings** area has five icons at the top of the palette, as you can see in the following image.

From left to right, the following list describes the function of each of these icons:

- **Reset current transformation** will undo all changes made to the current area being transformed and revert it to the initial settings.

- **Flip horizontal at center of rotation** flips the area being transformed in the horizontal direction based on the center of rotation.

- **Flip vertical at center of rotation** flips the area being transformed in the vertical direction based on the center of rotation.

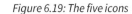

Figure 6.19: The five icons

- **Cancel current transformation:** Cancels the present or newly made transformation.

- **Confirm current transformation:** Commits the transformation change. This icon does the same as pressing the **OK** icon below the bounding box or pressing the *Enter* key on the keyboard.

Below these icons are other transformation options, described here:

- **Mode types:** You can pick a mode type that decides how you transform the image from the drop-down menu: **Sacle/Rotate**, **Scale**, **Rotate**, **Free Transformation**, **Distort**, **Skew**, and **Perspective**.

- **Reference Point:** Allows the rotation point to be set in the current bounding box. The default setting is the center of the area being transformed, but other options can be chosen from the drop-down menu.

- **Change vector width:** This is only used when transforming vector images. We will discuss vectors in more detail in *Chapter 10, Exploring Vector Layers*.

- **Keep original image:** This will retain the original image when the transformation takes place. For instance, with this box checked, if we move a selection to the left, then Clip Studio Paint will copy the area being transformed and create two instances of it. It's so useful when you want to duplicate the element without growing the number of layers or layer folders! In the the screenshot on the right, the duplicated scene has been moved and re-touched to the next panel while this box is checked, resulting in a time-passing scene being created:

Figure 6.20: Panels using duplicated image

- **Scale ratio:** Controls the ratio of both the width and height of the area being transformed. Using the sliders, the selection can be transformed precisely on either axis. Activating the **Keep aspect ratio** checkbox below the sliders will ensure that the original proportions of the transformed area are preserved so that the image doesn't become skewed in either direction.

- **Rotation angle:** This is a slider that controls the rotation of the area being transformed. This slider can be used to rotate a selected area precisely. Alternatively, moving the mouse cursor to a corner of the bounding box and slightly to the outside of it will produce a curved double-headed arrow that can be used to free-rotate the selection.

- **Adjust position:** This is a drop-down menu that controls the position of the transformed area. Setting this to **Free position** allows us to move, rotate, and scale the transformed area however we wish. Another setting is **Canvas**, which automatically resizes the selection area to the size of the canvas and sets it in the center.

- **Interpolation method:** This contains the options for how Clip Studio Paint blends colors of adjacent pixels during scaling up and down. The **Smooth edges (bilinear)** setting blends colors of adjacent pixels and smooths them, but this may lead to a blurry outline, depending on the content being transformed. **Hard edges (nearest neighbor)** maintains a sharp color separation by not blending based on adjacent pixels; however, this may lead to unwanted rough edges. **Clear edges (bicubic)** blends and smooths the color separations for a smooth transition, and when the image is rotated, the outline is processed so that it is more emphasized than the **Smooth** option. White noise may occur around the outline, however. **High accuracy (average colors)** calculates the average color of each pixel contained in an image after transformation. The image becomes clear when it's enlarged, and softer when it's shrunk. A thin line will not be interrupted when it's shrunk. However, the edges of the shrunk image can be blurred, and you may need to go back and forward with other options to get your desired result on an image that contains a lot of thin lines.

| Smooth edges (bilinear) | Hard edges (nearest neighbor) | Clear edges (bicubic) | High accuracy (average colors) |

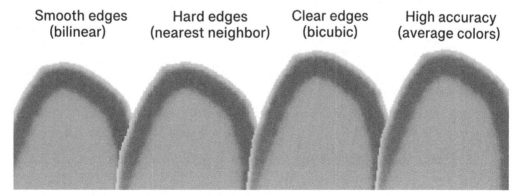

Figure 6.21: Various interpolation methods

The most commonly used methods are the **Smooth edges** option for black and white images and **High accuracy** for color images.

Now, let's learn about some more organic selection tools.

Selection pen

The **Selection** pen is another sub tool of the Selection area tool category. To use the **Selection** pen, select it from the **Sub Tool** palette. Then use the mouse or stylus to draw out a selection. The green area in the screenshot on the right is our area of selection:

Figure 6.22: Area selected with the Selection pen

Figure 6.23: Area selected with the Selection pen

Any area highlighted by the Selection pen (which defaults to a bright green highlight color) will be included in the selection. The screenshot on the left shows the selection that is made from the highlighted area:

The Selection pen makes highly precise selections easier. If you need to make a smaller selection, simply make the Selection pen brush size smaller. To select large areas, make the brush size larger.

>
>
> **Tip**
>
> To add more areas to a selection, hold down the *Shift* button on the keyboard while moving the mouse or stylus. To remove areas from a selection, hold down the *Alt* key. A + or - symbol will appear next to the selection tool cursor to indicate whether areas are being added or taken away.

Shrink selection

The **Shrink selection** tool allows us to quickly and easily isolate elements of a drawing without the tedium of having to be overly precise. Follow these steps to use the Shrink selection tool:

1. Select the **Shrink selection** sub tool from the **Selection area** category of tools.

2. Use the mouse or stylus to drag around the elements to be selected. As shown in the following screenshot, this selection does not need to be precise:

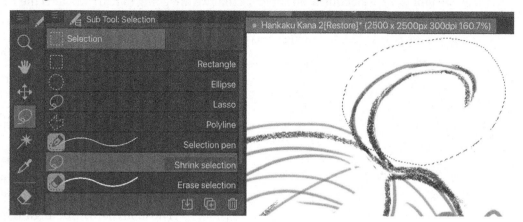

Figure 6.24: Shrink selection area

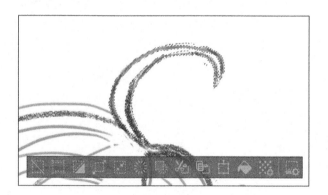

Figure 6.25: Shrink selection area and command bar

3. Once the mouse button or stylus is released, Clip Studio Paint will automatically shrink the selection down to the outside of the elements that were in the selection area. The selection made is shown in the screenshot on the left.

Tip

Note that some refinement may be needed, as is the case in the selection made in the preceding screenshot. The lighter color lines were not included in the final selection. The Shrink selection tool makes its best selections on areas with sharp, clearly defined lines, such as ones created with the Pen tools.

Erase selection

The final sub tool in the **selection area** category that we are going to learn about is the **Erase selection** tool. Note that this is used to adjust the selection area by using eraser tools, not to erase that part of your artwork. The following steps outline how to use this tool:

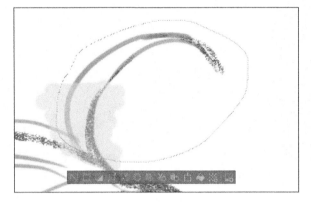

Figure 6.26: Erase selection tool

1. Make a selection with one of the other selection tools.
2. Select the **Erase selection** sub tool from the **Sub Tool** palette.
3. Use the **Erase selection** tool to *draw* over the areas that are currently selected and that should be deselected. Those areas will be highlighted in green as they are drawn on, as shown in the screenshot on the left:

4. Release the mouse button or stylus when all areas to be cleared have been highlighted.
5. Clip Studio Paint automatically deselects areas based on the highlighted area, as shown in the screenshot on the right, where now only the left area is selected.

Now that we've learned all about the selection tools, let's learn about a palette that is a big help in organizing your reference images. Read on to learn about the **Sub View** palette.

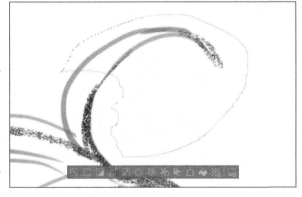

Figure 6.27: The selected area after using the Erase selection tool

The Sub View palette

The **Sub View** palette can seem like an enigma to some, but I find it to be one of the handiest palettes in the entire Clip Studio Paint interface. Let's delve into this simple yet powerful little palette.

When you first start using Clip Studio Paint, the **Sub View** palette looks as shown in the screenshot on the right.

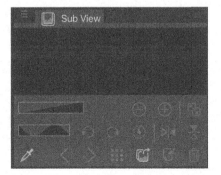

Figure 6.28: Sub View palette

It doesn't seem to have any purpose when you first look at it! So, what is it for?

The **Sub View** palette allows us to load images into it and view, zoom, rotate, flip, and select colors from those images. If you are a comic book artist, this palette can be used to hold character designs, concept art, background design sketches, color swatches, and any other images you may need access to on a regular basis while making comics. For illustrators, this can be used to hold reference images or other inspiration. It's a little reference library that remembers the images loaded into it so that you don't have to go through the process of opening them in new windows every time you open Clip Studio Paint.

Let's learn how to use the **Sub View** palette now.

Loading images into the Sub View palette

Follow these steps to load images into the **Sub View** palette and navigate through the images in the library:

1. In the **Sub View** palette, click on the **Import** icon (it looks like a folder – or a picture, depending on your device – with an arrow pointing to the right). This will open your file browser.

2. In the file browser, navigate to the image to be imported. Click on the file to select it. Click **Open** to complete the import.

3. To add several images at once, hold down the *Shift* or *Ctrl* key on the keyboard and select the files, then click **Open** to import all the selected files at once.

4. Once images are loaded into the **Sub View** palette, we can see them in this palette and flip through them. The screenshot on the right shows the **Sub View** palette with some of my character designs.

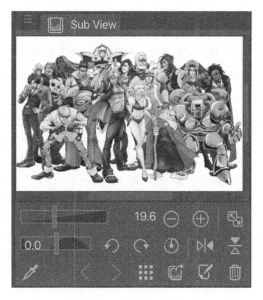

Figure 6.29: Sub View palette with an image

5. To see the other images loaded into the **Sub View** palette, locate the left and right arrows next to the **Eyedropper** icon. Clicking on either of these arrows will navigate to the previous or next image in the **Sub View** palette.

   Note that these arrows will only be active if more than one image is imported into the **Sub View** palette.

Alternatively, you can also pick an image that you want to display from an image list view by clicking the 9 square grid icon, which is the fourth from the right, as shown in the screenshot on the right.

6. You can also open the image as a new canvas by clicking the second from bottom icon, which looks like a paper and a pencil. To delete an image from the **Sub View** palette, click on the **Clear** icon in the bottom-right corner of the palette. This icon looks like a trash can. This will only clear the image from the **Sub View** palette and will not delete it from your computer.

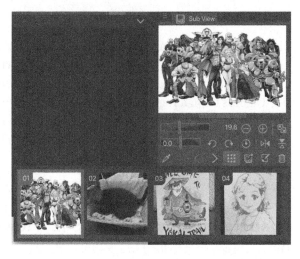

Figure 6.30: Image list view

Zooming, rotating, and picking a color from the Sub View images

In addition to being able to build a reference library in the **Sub View** palette, we can also zoom, rotate, flip, and select colors from those images.

To zoom into an image loaded into **Sub View**, use the slider located directly below the image view area of the palette. Alternatively, the - and + magnifying glass icons located to the right of

the slider can also be used to zoom in and out little by little. The **Fit to Navigator** icon ensures that the image resizes to fit the **Sub View** window as the palette is resized. When an image is zoomed in and the eyedropper is not active, placing the cursor over the image will change it to the **Move** tool and allow you to drag the image around to view specific areas.

To rotate an image in **Sub View**, the slider below the zoom slider can be used. Drag the rectangle in the center of the slider to the left or right to rotate the image. The **Rotate left** and **Rotate right** arrows can also be used to rotate the image incrementally and precisely in either direction. The screenshot on the right shows a rotated **Sub View** image.

Figure 6.31: Rotated Sub View image

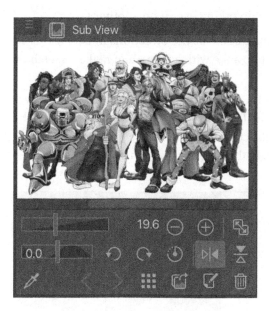

Figure 6.32: Flipped Sub View image

To reset the image to its original rotation, click on the **Reset Rotate** icon to the right of the rotate arrows.

To the right of the rotation settings are two icons. They are **Flip Horizontal** and **Flip Vertical**, and they flip the current **Sub View** image on either axis. The screenshot on the left is our **Sub View** image example, flipped vertically:

As mentioned previously, color selection is also possible from **Sub View** images. To switch from the default hand tool used to interact with the loaded image to the color picker, click on the eyedropper icon located at the bottom right. The eyedropper will now be active over the **Sub View** image. Clicking with the eyedropper will select the color from the image and make it the active foreground or background color, depending on which is selected in the toolbar.

In the next section, we will learn how to prepare a sketch for digital inking using the **Layer Color** setting that was briefly mentioned in the previous chapter. Read on to learn more.

Using Layer Color to prepare a sketch for inks

We're going to wrap up this chapter by learning about one way that Clip Studio Paint solves a common digital art problem. Those of you reading this book who have done digital art in the past might be familiar with the following scenario.

You finalize your sketch and create a layer for your final inks. You ink for a bit and then realize that something in the sketch needs to be changed. You switch back to the sketch layer and make the correction, then continue inking. It isn't until you finish inking that you realize you never switched back to your ink layer, and now you have your inks on the same layer as the pencil sketch and must start over.

This is an extremely frustrating and common problem when working with digital layers. Thankfully, the makers of Clip Studio Paint have given us a feature that makes this a thing of the past. Sure, you could prevent this by locking the sketch layer so that no changes can be made to it at all, but then if a change needs to be made, you have to spend the time unlocking it before you can correct an error or adjust a detail. This seems minor, but locking and unlocking a layer takes precious time, and I am all about streamlining the workflow as much as possible!

Follow these steps to turn a sketch layer blue and begin inking over it on another layer:

1. Open a file with a sketch layer. If you don't have one, use the directions in *Chapter 3, Penciling: Layer and Layer Property Palettes*, to set up a file with layers, then make a sketch on the sketch layer.

2. Once we have our finished sketch layer and made sure it is the active layer in the **Layer** palette, we click on the **Layer Color** icon in the **Layer Property** palette. This will turn the entire contents of the selected layer into a blue color that is reminiscent of the non-photo blue used in traditional pencil and paper art. In the following screenshot, the pencil layer has been turned blue:

Figure 6.33: Sketch turned blue

3. To change the color of the layer, click on the blue rectangle that will now appear in the **Layer Property** palette. This will bring up the color picker. You can select any color from the color picker to use as the layer color.

4. In the screenshot on the right, we can see that our colored layer is easy to discern in the list of layers because of the icon that shows above the layer's name. Look for this icon if you have lots of layers and need to find the one that has been colored:

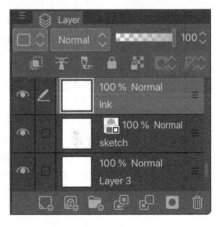

Figure 6.34: Layer palette

5. With the **Layer Color** option active, any new marks made on this layer will show up in the layer color. In the following screenshot, an inking pen tool has been used to make a mark on the sketch layer. Since the marks are blue, we know that we are still on the pencil layer and not on the ink layer:

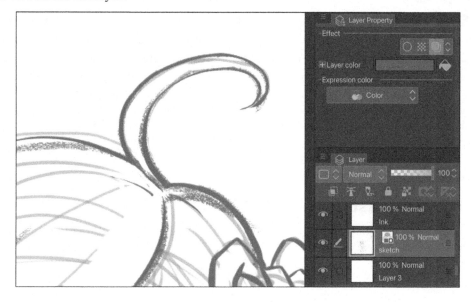

Figure 6.35: Inking on the sketch layer

6. Select the **Inks** layer in the **Layer** palette, above the **Finished pencils** layer, and begin inking. The ink lines will now have the currently selected color in the toolbar instead of using the layer color. In the following screenshot, the ink line is black because we are on the correct layer:

Figure 6.36: Inking on the Ink layer

This is such a simple solution to a common digital art problem, and a useful feature that I hope you'll incorporate into your own workflow!

Summary

In this chapter, we talked about eraser tools and using transparent color to turn any brush tool into an eraser. We talked about the different selection tools and how to make adjustments to a piece of art with them by using the **Selection** command bar. We also discussed the **Sub View** palette and how to use it to store various reference images. Finally, we learned about how the **Layer Color** feature can completely eliminate a common digital art problem.

In the next chapter, we are going to learn all about the ruler tools that make Clip Studio Paint a truly powerful piece of art software. Keep reading to learn more.

Join us on Discord!

Read this book alongside other users. Ask questions, provide solutions to other readers, and much more.

Scan the QR code or visit the link to join the community.

`https://packt.link/clipstudiopaint`

7

Using Text and Balloon Tools

One of the brilliant things about manga and comic creations is you can make your characters have dialog! Lettering for this media can be a complex and nuanced topic that could fill an entire book of its own. The rules and conventions for lettering a comic are varied, and lettering in and of itself is a skill that takes lots of time and practice to master. Back in the days before computers, a comic would have a dedicated letterer who would draw all the dialog boxes, balloons, and words by hand using various tools. Thankfully, we can use Clip Studio Paint and the fonts installed on our computer to handle lettering, rather than having to draw every letter on our own!

In this chapter, we will take this basic theory of speech in comics and learn how to apply it using the Text and Balloon tools in Clip Studio Paint. Since Clip Studio is made for comic book artists, it naturally has tools to make the creation of speech balloons easy, as well as tools to create different balloon tails, and more.

The following topics will be covered in this chapter:

- The basic theory of speech bubbles
- Text tool basics
- Advanced text settings
- Creating custom text tools
- Making and editing speech balloons
- Connecting speech balloons
- Using speech balloon materials

Let's get started!

Technical requirements

To get started, you need Clip Studio Paint already installed on your device and a new canvas open, and preferably, one character should already be drawn on it. Any size is fine, but I recommend creating a 300 dpi square canvas to go through the content in this chapter.

The basic theory of speech bubbles

Before we learn how to create speech bubbles, let's think a little about where to place them.

It is important to consider speech bubbles and text boxes as part of a manga panel and its composition on a page. Even as early as the sketching stage, we need to think of these elements as part of the composition along with the characters and environment.

This means that, first of all, the text (and the panels they are a part of) must be in an order that's easy to follow. This may seem obvious, but it makes a big difference to how people read your comic. Who is replying to who? Are the characters speaking before, during, or after the action shown in the artwork? Is it clear, from one panel to another, how much time has passed? Reading is, after all, a linear experience, and it's important that we handle the flow of information to the reader effectively.

Perhaps more important, though, is to consider the impact of text boxes and balloons on a composition as a whole. The text must be placed *around* the center of the piece, rather than in the middle of it.

With these two aspects in mind – the sequence of the dialog and its incorporation into the composition – we should look at some examples. The following samples show text in a Western comic on the left and Japanese manga on the right:

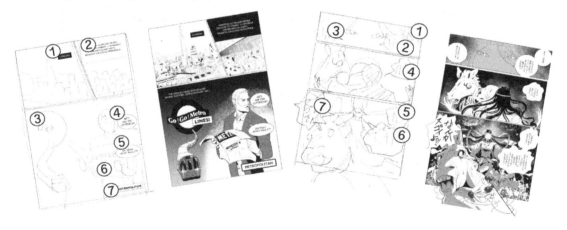

Figure 7.1: A sketch and a manga page with text

You can see from these examples that the placement of text boxes is influenced by the direction of reading – from left to right in the Western comic and from right to left in the Japanese manga. In both cases, the boxes generally flow from top to bottom and are near the character who is speaking. In neither case, however, do they overlap with important parts of the art piece.

Generally, text boxes are for announcements and speech balloons are for character dialog. For example, you may have seen text boxes used to announce details like the passage of time from one panel to another. As we can see in the left example, announcements about the passage of time are typically placed in the corners of the composition.

Speech balloons can be created using different shapes, depending on the tones and pacing of the dialog. In the previous examples, the character's pondering in the Western comic is shown with round bubbles with small tails. In comparison, the action-packed manga uses zig-zagging shapes and larger text.

Now, let's start learning how to create these balloons.

The basics of the Text tool

In this section, we're going to learn the basics of how to use the Text tools and their basic settings, before building on our knowledge in the sections that follow. Let's add some text to a drawing using the following steps:

1. Open a blank canvas or a drawing to add some text to.
2. Choose the **Text** category of the tools from the toolbar.
3. Make sure that the **Text** subcategory is chosen in the **Sub Tool** palette.
4. Select the **Text** tool.
5. In the **Tool property** palette, select the desired font from the drop-down menu. This menu will populate with fonts that have been installed on your computer system.
6. Select the size of the font by using the slider or the up and down arrows.
7. The alignment of the text (left, center, or right) can be set in the Justify section of the **Tool property** palette.
8. Set **Text Direction** to either Horizontal or Vertical.
9. Set **Text Color** using the options shown. **Text Color** can either be the currently selected main color, the currently selected sub color, or a user color.
10. Click on the canvas where you'd like to place the text, and type out your desired dialog or words.

Figure 7.2 shows a panel from my manga with the dialog text added.

The text in the screenshot on the left is center justified and set at a size of 9.0 points. Depending on the font you use, as well as your style of writing and art, a larger or smaller size may be more appropriate for you. However, keep readability in mind, as you don't want to make your words so small that they are illegible! If you are posting your comic to the internet and also printing it, make sure to check that your text is legible in both formats. Sometimes, text that is legible in print can become illegible on the internet.

Figure 7.2: A comic panel with text

Tip

Once your text is typed out, you can resize it on the fly by using the control boxes around the text. In the preceding screenshot, they are the circular and rectangular handles around the outside of the box surrounding the text. Clicking and dragging on one of these boxes will make the text inside larger or smaller.

Those are the basic controls to make words in Clip Studio Paint. In the next section, we will take a deeper look at the text settings to make finer adjustments to things such as line and character spacing.

Exploring advanced text settings

In some cases, you may need to adjust parts of the font that you use. Whether that is the spacing between individual characters or the spacing between lines of text, Clip Studio Paint gives you options to fine-tune your fonts to perfection. Whether letters look too condensed together or the lines seem too close, you just need to use the following settings to deal with them. Any settings I think important are marked as **Important**, which are **Font**, **Font size**, **Alignment**, and **Text color**. Let's look at these settings now. To access the settings, open the **Sub Tool Detail** palette from the **Tool property** palette in the user interface.

Editing properties settings

The left-hand side of the **Sub Tool Detail** palette contains categories of options. Each added category contains options for whether the changes in the **Tool Property** palette apply to new or selected text. Figure 7.3 shows this category of **Editing properties** options.

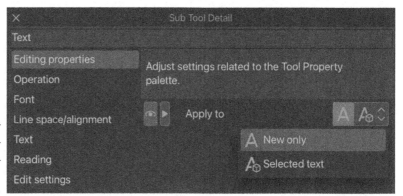

Figure 7.3: Editing properties options in the Text tool's Sub Tool Detail palette

Sometimes, you may want to change a font or the size of letters of only the new text without altering the existing text in the same sentence. The **Editing properties** option deals with this issue! When you select **New Only**, changes in the **Tool Property** will not affect any selected text. It is useful when you want to emphasize only some parts of the text in the same speech balloon/text box. When set to **Selected text**, the properties will apply to new and selected text. Normally, I set it as **Selected text**.

Operation settings

The second category is **Operation** settings. This is also a very useful new function. These settings let you decide how to operate previously typed-in text. Figure 7.4 shows the **Operation** settings options.

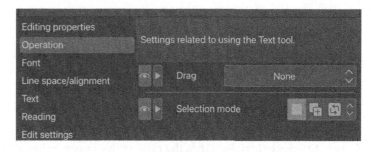

Figure 7.4: Operation options in the Text tool's Sub Tool Detail palette

The first **Operation** option is **Drag**, which allows you to decide whether you want to create a text box.

If you select **Create text box** from the drop-down menu, a text box with word wrapping is created. Word wrapping is a great new function to align text inside a created frame! When the option is set to **Select text**, any text in the area will be selected to drag around on the canvas. When set to **None**, either of the above options are applied. I normally set this as **None**.

Font settings

This category contains options for the font and size of characters, word and character spacing, and the style of the font.

Figure 7.5 shows this category of font options and the following list describes each of those options:

Figure 7.5: Operation options in the Text tool's Sub Tool Detail palette

- **Font (important):** This drop-down menu lists the currently selected font. This list is populated with fonts that have been installed on your computer's operating system.
- **Mixing font:** This option is used mainly when mixing Japanese and Chinese characters with English characters, so we will not use it in this book.
- **Size** (important): Sets the size of the font.
- **Horizontal ratio:** This option sets the horizontal spread of the letters, making them wider or thinner.

- **Vertical ratio:** Use this option to control the vertical ratio of the font, making the letters taller or shorter.

- **Kerning:** sets the spacing between kerning pairs. When you select **Manual** from the drop-down menu, you can adjust the spacing of chosen kerning pairs by setting a number. Selecting **Matrix** will automatically adjust the spacing of specific kerning pairs based on the font information. If there is no information in the font, the characters will be spaced as standard.

- **Character spacing:** Adjusts the spacing between the letters of the font.

- **Condense text:** Specifies the ratio of the gap on either side of each character.

- **Style:** This option allows you to set the font to the bold, italic, underline, or strikethrough font styles.

- **Outline:** Turns the font into an outline-only font, where the letters are not filled in with a solid color.

- **Ligatures:** Turns ligatures on or off. It's a niche feature. The only likely use that you'll encounter is needing to turn ligatures off because small letters stick together and are illegible when printed.

Line space/alignment settings

The fourth category of options in the **Sub Tool Detail** palette is **Line space/alignment**, which gives you control over editing lines. This category of options is shown in Figure 7.6.

These settings are described in the following bulleted list:

- **Alignment (important):** Set the alignment of the lines of text to **Left**, **Center**, or **Right**.

- **Wrap text at frame:** By ticking this box, text will wrap within the frame. When

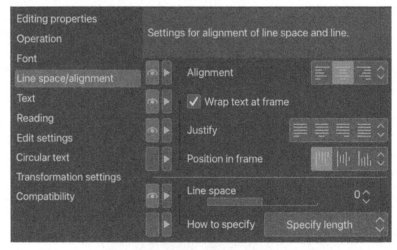

Figure 7.6: Line spacing options in the Text tool's Sub Tool Detail palette

it's off, the size of the frame will adjust to fit the text.

- **Justify:** Aligns text so that it aligns with both sides of the text box. This setting is only available when **Wrap text at frame** is turned on.

- **Position in frame:** Sets where the text is placed inside the frame. This setting is only available when **Wrap text at frame** is turned on.

- **Line space:** Adjusts line space by length when selecting **Length** in **How to specify**, but by percentage when selecting **Percentage** in **How to specify**.

- **How to specify:** This drop-down menu controls how to specify the **Line space** option. It can be set to either **Specify length** or **By percentage**.

Now, you know how to edit lines. Next, we are going to explore more detailed settings of text appearances.

Text settings

In this section, we will look at the **Text** category, which grants us control over even more detailed settings, such as text directions and background colors. Figure 7.7 shows the **Text** category of the **Sub Tool Detail** palette.

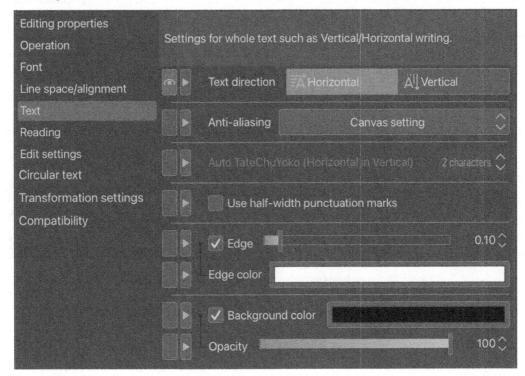

Figure 7.7: Text options in the Text tool's Sub Tool Detail palette

Each of the **Text** settings is described in the following list:

- **Text direction:** Sets the text direction to either **Horizontal** or **Vertical**.

- **Anti-aliasing:** Sets the anti-aliasing used for text. The options are **Canvas setting**, **On**, and **Off**.

- **Auto TateChuYoko (Horizontal in Vertical):** Sets how many consecutive half-width characters to show automatically in **TateChuYoko** (Horizontal in Vertical). It only applies to the Japanese language, so we can skip this.

- **Use half-width punctuation marks:** Having this checkbox selected uses punctuation marks that are half the width of the normal size, which is only effective in languages that use two-byte characters, such as Japanese.
- **Edge:** Adds an outline around the selected text. The thickness of the outline can be controlled using the slider that is activated after the checkbox is clicked.
- **Edge color:** Allows the user to select the color of the edge outline. Click on the rectangle to the right of the option name to select the color.
- **Background color:** Sets a background color around the text.
- **Opacity:** Controls the opacity of the background color.

In the next section, we will look at **Edit settings**, skipping the **Reading** settings, as they are specifically made for Japanese comics. **Edit settings** lets you decide the text color and which layer to add text to.

Edit settings

In this section, we will look at the text color settings and which layer to add text to. Figure 7.8 shows the **Edit settings** category of the **Text** options:

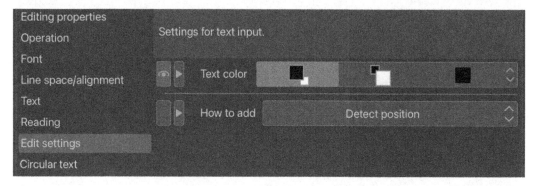

Figure 7.8: Edit settings options in the Text tool's Sub Tool Detail palette

The following explains these options:

- **Text color** (important): Controls the text color by setting it to either the main color, sub color, or user color. The user color can be selected by clicking on the user color icon and then selecting the color with the color picker.
- **How to add:** This drop-down menu controls how Clip Studio Paint inserts text, such as always creating a new layer, adding to selected text, or detecting a position.

Now, we know what **Edit settings** are. Did you know you can transform the text you have just typed in? Read on to find out.

Circular text

If you want to create a fun design with circular text that goes around a round shape, this is a function for it! By clicking the **Circular text** box, the settings will become available, as shown in the Figure 7.9.

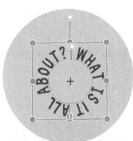

- **Radius:** You can adjust the radius of the circle where the text will be placed.

  - **Direction:** When set to **Clockwise** from the drop-down menu, the characters will be arranged in a clockwise direction. When set to **Counter-clockwise**, the characters are arranged so that the text reads counter-clockwise.

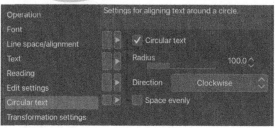

- **Space evenly:** When this is turned on, characters or words will be spaced evenly between the start and end points. You can adjust the start and end points with handles on the canvas, as shown in the preceding screenshot.

Figure 7.9: Sample text and the Circular text options in the Text tool's Sub Tool Detail palette

Transformation settings

If you want to resize, rotate, and skew text, these settings come in handy. Figure 7.10 shows the transformation square with a handle, and the **Transformation settings** category of the **Sub Tool Detail** palette.

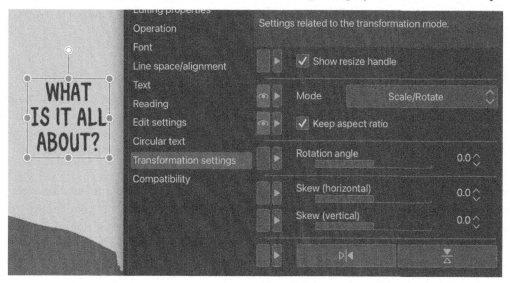

Figure 7.10: Transformation settings options in the Text tool's Sub Tool Detail palette

The following list explains the **Transformation settings** options:

- **Show resize handle:** At the top part of the resize box, you can see the handle with a small ball at the end of a bar. By turning it on, you can resize text with the handle.

- **Mode:** This drop-down menu controls how you want to transform text, such as **Scale/Rotate**, **Scale**, **Rotate**, **Skew**, and **Scale/Rotate/Skew**.

- **Keep aspect ratio:** When this is turned on, it maintains the aspect ratio while transforming the text.

- **Rotation angle:** Adjusts the rotation angle around the horizontal axis.

- **Skew (horizontal):** Adjusts the horizontal skew of the text.

- **Skew (vertical):** Adjusts the vertical skew of the text.

- **Flip:** The left-hand side button flips the text horizontally, and the right-hand side button flips the text vertically.

Now, you can gain control of the transformation of text. Next, there is one last setting you might want to know about.

Compatibility

In some cases, fonts have slight differences in appearance, depending on the version of Clip Studio Paint you are using. For example, when you're adding new text to a manga you created in version 1.13, the same fonts might have new designs in version 3.0.

If you want to keep all text in your manga consistent, the safest option is to use the same font in the same version. You can select the version you are using from the drop-down menu. The only other option would be to edit the settings manually, although this would be a losing battle.

Now that we're familiar with all the different options available to edit and fine-tune our text, let's create a custom text tool preset to save these settings for a specific comic project.

Tip

Do you find yourself opening the **Sub Tool Detail** window often to get to a setting? The **Sub Tool Detail** settings for any tool can be added to the **Tool property** palette in the interface by clicking on the rectangle to the left of the setting name. Settings with an eye icon next to them will appear in the **Tool property** palette, making them easily accessible!

Wow, that was quite a lot to take in – the many, many text settings, such as alignment, line space, and text color! But they allow you the freedom to control how your text appears in your comic; you can also change them depending on the scenes, tones, and mood of your comics. How about having a fixed setting that is made by you, which you can use throughout your comic without resetting it each time? Let's make that possible by reading the next section.

Creating custom text tools

For some projects, you may need to use the same set of text settings many times. Making a comic is just one example of when you may want to customize a text tool that saves your font, font size, justification, and other settings so that you don't have to set them over and over again!

Creating a custom text tool is easy. Follow these steps to make a saved text tool:

1. Select the **Text** sub tool.

2. At the bottom right of the **Sub Tool** palette, click on the **Create copy of currently selected sub tool** icon.

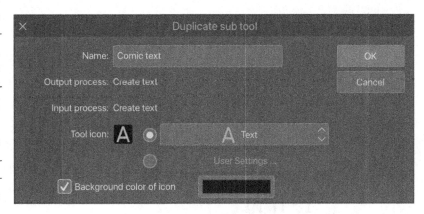

3. The **Duplicate sub tool** window will appear, as shown in Figure 7.11.

Figure 7.11: Duplicate sub tool

4. Enter a name for your new text tool in the **Name** text entry box.

5. Select a tool icon, if desired.

6. Click on the **Background color of icon** checkbox and select a color to display around the icon when this sub tool is selected.

7. Click on **OK** to create the new sub tool.

8. Using the text settings and advanced settings, make changes to the new text tool to set the font, font size, and any other options to make the text look as desired.

Now, whenever you need to create text with these settings, you can select your custom text tool preset and immediately start typing!

Making and editing speech balloons

Since Clip Studio Paint is made primarily for creating comics, there are tools included to create speech balloons easily in the program. With just a few clicks, we can make speech balloons and tails that can be edited like vector objects.

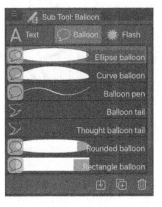

Follow these steps to create a speech balloon and a tail:

1. Add some text to your canvas using the directions that we gave in the first section of this chapter.

2. The **Balloon** tools are in the same category of tools as the **Text** tool. They are shown in Figure 7.12.

Figure 7.12: Balloon sub tool

3. Select the desired **Balloon** tool. For this set of instructions, we will use the **Ellipse balloon** tool.

4. With the text layer selected, click on the **Ellipse balloon** tool, and drag it to make a balloon surrounding the text. Don't worry about making it perfect—we will adjust the position in the next step.

5. With the **Operation | Object** tool, click on the previously created balloon. Clicking directly on the balloon with this tool will reveal the individual control points and allow them to be manipulated like the vector points. If you want to know more, go to *Chapter 10, Vector Layers and the Material Palette*. Use the handles around the outside of the bounding box to resize the balloon as needed, as shown in Figure 7.13.

Figure 7.13: Ellipse balloon example

6. To reposition the text inside of the balloon, use the **Object** tool to click on the text to reveal the text bounding box. Clicking and dragging on the text within the box will reposition the text, and the outside handles can be used to resize the text.

7. To create the balloon tail, select the **Balloon tail** sub tool from the **Text** category.

8. In the **Tool property** palette, select the desired option from the **How to bend** drop-down menu. In this example, we will use the **Spline** option.

9. Click inside the speech balloon to start the tail. When using the **Spline** option, click for a second time on the point where the balloon tail should curve. Continue clicking to place curve points until the desired length of the tail has been reached, and then double-click to end the tail. You can see the perfect tail in Figure 7.14.

Figure 7.14: Balloon with a tail

The Object tool can be used to edit the look of the balloon tail as well as the balloon. The preceding instructions show us how to make a simple balloon and tail. Let's take a few minutes now to look at the **Tool property** options for the **Ellipse balloon** tool before we discuss the other balloon tools.

The Ellipse balloon tool

Figure 7.15 shows the **Tool property** palette for the **Ellipse balloon** tool, which is the most generic and easy balloon to create. In Clip Studio Paint, you can decide how speech balloons appear, such as their color, shape, and which layer to add them to. Let's look at how to adjust the balloon's appearance to your desired one.

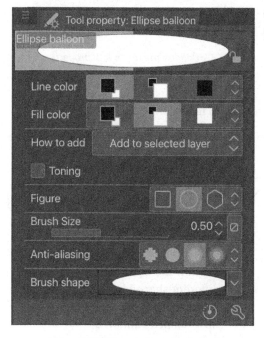

Figure 7.15: Ellipse balloon tool's Tool property palette

The following list describes each of the options shown in the **Tool property** window:

- **Line color:** The color of the outline around the edge of the balloon. Usually, we set it to use the main color, which is black.

- **Fill color:** Sets the color of the inside of the speech balloon. Usually, we set it to use the sub color, which is white.

- **How to add:** Controls how the balloon will be added to the image. The options are **Create new layer** and **Add to selected layer**. I normally select **Add to selected layer** to keep the amount of layers down.

- **Toning:** Creates the balloon by using a dot tone effect.

- **Figure:** Sets the shape of the balloon. A rectangle, ellipse, or polygon can be created. The most common use is ellipse.

- **Brush size:** Controls the thickness of the outline. Thinner looks smart, while thicker makes it easier for the reader to identify areas to read texts. So again, you have to think about the composition as a whole.

- **Anti-aliasing:** Sets the anti-aliasing level for the outline of the created balloon. Select **Weak** for normal usage.

- **Brush shape:** This dropdown allows a variety of effects to be applied to the outline of the balloon. In addition to the most common setting of **Pen**, more settings are available, such as **Pencil**, **Airbrush**, and **Spray**, and watercolor designs such as **Waved**, **Rough Edged**, **Bumpy**, **Dashed Line**, **Dotted**, **Heart**, **Star**, **Laced Ribbon**, and **Melody** can be applied to the outline.

Isn't it easy and simple enough to create your own preferred balloon? We will look at how to edit balloon tails, which is even simpler to do, in the following section!

The Balloon tail tool

In a comic, especially when there are multiple characters in the same panel, we need to indicate which dialog comes from which character to avoid confusion. So it is necessary to have an accurate balloon tail for each dialog. Let's look into what the balloon tail options are.

Figure 7.16 shows the options for the **Balloon tail** tool.

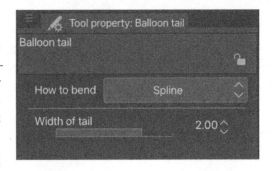

Figure 7.16: Balloon tail tool's Tool property palette

The following list describes each of the options for the **Balloon tail** tool:

- **How to bend**: Sets the type of tail to be created. These are **Straight line**, **Polyline**, and **Spline**.

Figure 7.17: Various Balloon tail tools

- **Width of tail**: Controls the width of the tail at the starting point. The width was set to 142.0 in the preceding screenshot.

Great, now you know how to set the balloon tail options! Let's move on to different-shaped balloons, which come in handy when you need more than ellipse-shaped balloons.

The Curve balloon tool

The **Curve balloon** tool is another way to create speech balloons, allowing for greater flexibility in shaping balloons. Figure 7.18 shows the options for this tool.

Many of these options are the same as the **Ellipse balloon** tool. The following list explains the options that are unique to this tool:

- **Curve**: Controls how to make the curves of the balloon. For a detailed description of each of the **Curve** options, see the *Curve ruler* section in *Chapter 13*, *All About Rulers*.
- **Sharp angles**: Changes corners from smooth curves to hard corners.

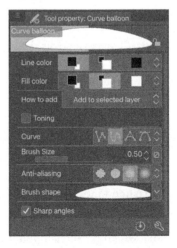

Figure 7.18: Curve balloon tool's Tool property palette

So a balloon doesn't have to be round all the time! Let's look at even more different shapes of balloons in the next section.

The Balloon pen tool

Most of the time, the Clip Studio Paint tools to make ellipses, tails, and curves are sufficient to tell your story. If you use them right, they are customizable and easily legible.

However, sometimes you may want to create your own balloons. If you have a very ornate style of comic, then you will most likely want to create your own balloons and even start learning calligraphy. Alternatively, maybe you just want to draw your own balloon because you want to convey a tone, such as an angry or panicked character.

The **Balloon pen** tool allows us to create speech balloons by drawing them freehand. Figure 7.19 shows the **Tool property** options for this tool.

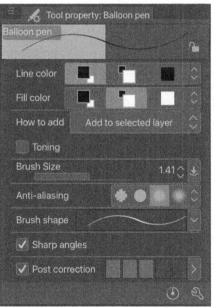

Figure 7.19: Balloon pen tool's Tool property palette

By now, we have seen most of these settings already. In fact, there is only one new option to keep in mind:

- **Post correction**: When this option is checked, the program will smooth out lines after they are drawn. The amount of correction is based on the value selected in the bar to the right of the option name. I normally put this setting at a minimum value, as the reason I use the **Balloon pen** tool is to create hand-drawn lines, such as a shaky-lined balloon for a scared character's dialog.

That just leaves us with one more question: *what shape should I draw?* This is really a wonderful question, as it's something you'll always be learning. I'd suggest that you look through some of your favorite comics for inspiration, as well as the speech balloon materials available in Clip Studio Paint. If you need to, you can put these materials (or even images found online) onto a canvas and trace them for practice.

You now have mastery over speech balloons; using the options we have learned about, you can add balloons, change their shape and color, edit their tails, and even draw freehand-shaped balloons!

How about having more than one dialog in one panel? You can also connect them if they come from the same character! Isn't that fun?

We will discuss how to do this in the next section!

Implementing connected speech balloons

In this section, we are going to learn how to implement connected speech balloons. Connected speech balloons are used when you have dialog in multiple speech balloons that are connected together with balloon tails, as shown in Figure 7.20.

Figure 7.20: Screenshot of connected balloons

This style of speech balloon is easy to do in Clip Studio Paint, but it does require a bit of forethought. Setting up connected speech balloons actually occurs during the text tool phase of making speech balloons. Follow these steps to create connected speech balloons:

1. Type in the text for the first speech balloon by using the **Text** tool. Click on the checked-circle icon below the text entry to commit the text. This icon is shown in Figure 7.21.

Figure 7.21: Text typing command bar

2. With the **Text** tool selected, move the cursor close to the box surrounding the first text you entered. A + icon will appear next to the cursor when you are in the correct spot to make a connecting text box. Click and enter the text for the second balloon.

3. Click on the checked-circle icon once the second area of text is entered. A box will appear around any text areas that are connected, as shown in Figure 7.22.

Figure 7.22: Two different texts on the same layer

4. Create a balloon around each section of text, using the instructions in the *Making and editing speech balloons* section of this chapter.

5. Select the **Balloon tail** tool and drag a tail from the first balloon to the second, as shown in Figure 7.23.

Figure 7.23: A tail connecting speech balloons

6. Once the tail is created, it will automatically connect the two balloons, as shown in Figure 7.24.

Wow, the two dialogs are connected! Comic readers would perfectly understand that both balloons come from the same character!

Now, you know how to handle multiple balloons in one panel, so you won't panic when there are multiple dialogs. You can just type the next dialog by clicking the + icon under the first dialog, create balloons, and then connect them with tails.

In the next section, we are going to learn how to use ready-made special balloons. You might find one that is really suitable for your comic or manga creation.

Figure 7.24: Connected speech balloons

Using speech balloon materials

In addition to having the speech balloon sub tools at your disposal, Clip Studio Paint also has a library of speech balloon materials for special dialog, emotional moments, and almost anything else you can imagine.

We will cover materials in more depth in *Chapter 10, Vector Layers and the Material Palette*, but let's take a look at the specific speech balloons in the **Material** palette now.

This section of the **Material** palette is shown in Figure 7.25.

Balloon materials are located in the **Manga material** category of the library. There are three subcategories of balloons, as detailed in the following list:

- **Dialog: Dialog** balloons include balloons for shouting, mumbling, announcements, whispering, thought clouds, and more.

- **Feeling: Feeling** balloons are more specialized, with color borders of flowers, stars, and more.

- **Narration:** The **Narration** category contains various rectangle balloons, perfect for narration in comics.

Note that some of these materials may need to be downloaded from the Clip Studio Assets before use. For more information, please refer to *Chapter 18, Exploring the Clip Studio Assets and Animation*.

To use a speech balloon material, select the material to highlight it, and then click on the **Paste selected material to canvas** icon at the bottom of the **Material** palette.

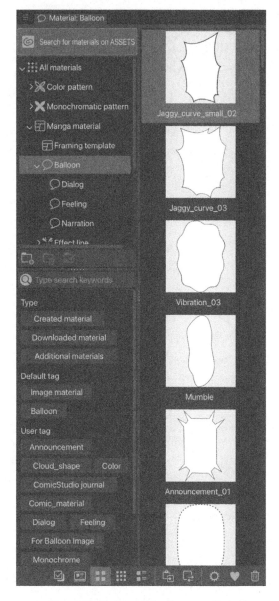

Figure 7.25: Speech balloon materials

The icon is shown in Figure 7.26.

Speech balloon materials will not automatically attach themselves to text that is present in an image, so the material may need to be repositioned and resized to fit the text.

Figure 7.26: Paste selected material to canvas icon

Summary

In this chapter, we learned about how to use the **Text** tool and the settings to edit and fine-tune text. We learned how to create a custom text tool to save text settings for our comic projects. Then, we learned how to create speech balloons with tails, how to connect speech balloons, and about the speech balloon materials.

These skills are great to have, not only for lettering and drawing speech balloons faster and more accurately but also so you can give dialog your own unique look. Text in comics and manga is indeed part of your creation and is as important as your art in telling a story.

As you read more manga and comics, you'll notice how the fonts and their placement perfectly complement the scenes, pacing, and story themes. It's good to know what is appropriate for your manga – if you are after overall artistic consistency, you should consider creating your own fonts. It's a skillset of its own, but you will start seeing meaningful differences without being an expert in calligraphy and letter design! Having said that, we need to remember that the most important thing is readability; choose legible design over an artistic look to be able to tell your story, always.

In the next chapter, we will learn about some techniques to ink artwork while also looking at the many available inking tools.

Join us on Discord!

Read this book alongside other users. Ask questions, provide solutions to other readers, and much more.

Scan the QR code or visit the link to join the community.

`https://packt.link/clipstudiopaint`

8

Getting Started with Inking Tools

Back in the early days of comics, pencil lines were too light to be picked up by the cameras used to replicate comic art. So, artists used a brush or pen and black ink to redraw over the pencil lines and make them dark enough for the cameras to pick up. Inking has become an art in and of itself. Clip Studio Paint has some of the best inking tools in the digital art world, packaged with it when you purchase the software. There are also a multitude of third-party tools available either for free or to purchase that provide specialty inking functionalities that give different looks and feels to inked lines.

We are going to start with a step-by-step inking process in the first section, so don't worry if you don't know much about digital inking! You will also see many of the inking tools Clip Studio Paint offers, then we will find out how to customize them in a later section of this chapter. Finally, we will end the chapter by finding out how to use inking tools on vector layers!

In this chapter, we are going to talk about the following topics:

- Principles of inking
- Inking tools
- Customizing pressure sensitivity settings
- Inking on vector layers
- Tips for inking comic panels

Let's get started!

Principles of inking

Inking in the world of non-digital tools is the process of using pens or brushes and black India ink to finalize pencil lines and make them ready for toning or coloring. The printing presses back in the early days of comics weren't capable of printing grayscale, so dark black ink lines were needed to reproduce the comic art.

In the digital world, we aren't restricted to simply black ink for our lines, and we have a multitude of tools we can use to make our finalized lines. There is an art to good inking that we should discuss briefly.

Inking is the art of taking a rough pencil sketch and providing finalized edges, volume, and a sense of light and shadow. To see this process in action, let's take a look at an inking from a sketch to final shades and examine how the inked lines accentuate the mood of the piece.

Creating a great pencil sketch

Before you start inking, you need to create the pencil sketch, which we learned about in *Chapter 3, Penciling: Layer and Later Property Palettes*. In that chapter, we touched on how to use the pencil sketch to establish characters' proportions. Before we start inking, let's touch on that method again while introducing some more complexity – this time looking at **perspective**.

When you compose a visual, you should think about how perspective performs wonders when you want to create dynamism in a still image. Once you're comfortable with proportions, delving into perspective is the natural next skill to learn to create great pencil sketches.

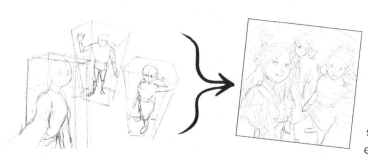

Perspective is something quite simple in theory, yet needs practice to utilize in art. We know that objects closer to you look bigger than objects far away. In the image to the left, we can see I drew my 7-heads proportion characters in one frame with perspective on the right, which created a more dramatic look than just lining them up without overlapping or perspective.

Figure 8.1: Image of a composition in pencil sketch

In the preceding sketch, the lady in front is taking a group selfie, which means she is the closest object to the camera, such that her right arm looks big, hiding her body. Then the character on the right is the next closest object, drawn slightly smaller. Finally, the character at the rear, standing far from the camera, has his body hidden by the other two characters.

If you drew all three characters in separate layers, it would be easier to move them individually to edit the composition. For example, you could select each individual character and move them around the composition, resizing them as you go. You can edit or re-sketch till you feel it looks right.

Once you have the basic form established in the first few sketches, you'll want to think about adding detail. It's best to do this iteratively, adding new layers and progressively delving into more complexity.

Depending on what style of manga you want to create, learning how to draw details could be a long and rewarding journey for you. Really, it is a never-ending experience. That said, one basic aspect to get right is creating expressions. Along with perspective, training yourself to draw expressions will produce much livelier artwork!

Take a look at the character below, expressing a gallery of emotions:

As you can see, a lot of a person's expression comes from their mouth and their eyes. If you're new to drawing expressions, this is worth thinking about and practicing – how does a character frown with their eyes? How do they

Figure 8.2: Screenshot of various facial expressions

smile with their eyes? Try drafting different expressions on top of each other using different layers. Notice how much difference the position of their eyebrows makes. Additionally, you'll want to think about blushes, wincing marks around the eyes, and other details.

As with all drawing skills, the best way to learn is by studying how others do it, and then practicing it yourself. You can also use Clip Studio Paint materials or images downloaded online and try tracing their expressions.

As you may have noticed, *Figure 8.2* is not a messy sketch, but an inked composition. Now that you have used pencil sketches to work on your art to the point that you're happy with it, it's time to ink your art in the same way, cleaning it up and making a few extra artistic decisions along the way.

Beginning inking

Once you think your sketch is ready to be redrawn in ink, turn the finalized pencil sketch blue using the **Layer Color** settings on the **Layer Property** palette, and decrease the **Opacity** setting of the sketch layer to 30% to see the new inking lines more easily.

Don't worry, your sketch should be quite rough at this stage, with multiple attempts at each line and a few guiding lines from organizing the perspective, the facial details, and so on. That is why we'll be going over it now with finalized lines in ink.

When you ink the image, the most orthodox way to do this is using **G-pen**, which is popular due to it having a higher touch and tilt sensitivity setting for outlines of characters, and the **mapping** pen, which is great for drawing very fine lines over content, as well as detailing.

Higher touch and tilt sensitivity means the line width changes from fine to bold depending on how much pressure or tilt you put on your pen. This can be seen in the following screenshot of the **pen pressure** setting and a corresponding line sample.

To change the **Pen pressure** and **Tilt** inputs, you can find the options by clicking the button to the right of the **Brush Size** setting:

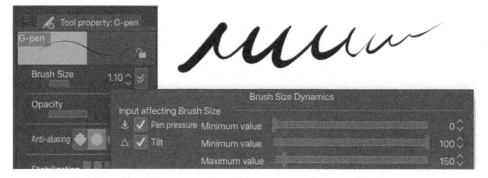

Figure 8.3: Screenshot of high Pen pressure setting and line

The following screenshot shows an inactive pressure and tilt sensitivity setting, which means the pen's width doesn't change no matter how much pressure you put on it or how much you tilt your pen:

Figure 8.4: Screenshot of low Pen pressure setting and line

We will explore more of the pen settings in the *Customizing pressure sensitivity settings* section later in this chapter.

Drawing with great control of line width gives the image a crafted and soft look, especially when you draw things such as human skin, hair, and fluffy dress garments—these would be perfect to create with a higher touch- and tilt-sensitive G-pen!

A mapping pen has less touch and tilt sensitivity, but I assure you that using it with the tiny brush setting and going around the details of hair, eyes, and clothing will give you a perfect and accurate look for the contents of your drawing. Let's have another look at the inking tool that was used in *Figure 8.2:*

Figure 8.5: Screenshot of various facial expressions

Using these pens helps you depict the delicate details of facial expressions!

The following screenshot shows the first stage of inking using a **G-pen** and **mapping** pen:

There are two things you might notice:

- The first thing is the line thickness; the outlines of characters are drawn with thicker **G-pen** lines to make the characters stand out from the background, and details are added with thinner mapping pen lines. If all the lines were of the same thickness, readers of the manga would have trouble finding where to focus. For an extreme perspective scene, you can use very thick lines for the closest object!

- The second thing is that there is already shade in this line drawing. Take a look under the characters' faces, and under the flower crown, noticing how the black section that is filled with ink depicts shade. This is a trick to create a three-dimensional effect on a simple black-and-white line drawing.

Figure 8.6: Screenshot of the first inking stage

We can add more shade and dark color expressions in the next stage, as in the following screenshot:

Boom! The character on the right has dark hair, the middle character has dark but shiny hair, and the left character has light-colored hair. You can express dark hair by adding some lines to create a closed section with any pen tool, filling the sections with the **Fill** tool on the layer below, and leaving a small section untouched for a shiny hair effect.

Not just hair; if you look at their eyes, the eye color is also depicted in a different shade. The character on the left has a lighter eye color, so the eyes are not filled with black ink like the others.

Figure 8.7: Second inking stage

What happens if we have a background too? See the following screenshot:

The trees, leaves, and floor tiles are added to the drawing! The background image was drawn in thinner lines with a mapping pen compared to the character outlines, because the nature in the background is further away from the camera and less important in this image. Additionally, you can change the color of the background layer to light gray. This helps create more contrast with the objects in the foreground.

But wait a minute... this image is visually too busy! You will need space between characters or objects and the background.

First, we will add a new layer between the layer that contains the characters and the layer with a background. Then, we use white to draw space around the character figures with brush tools.

Figure 8.8: Screenshot of the background inking stage

In this way, you can emphasize the focus of the image, as seen in the following screenshot:

Figure 8.9: Screenshot of the background with the extra inking stage

This is just a tiny change, but it makes a big difference in guiding readers' eyes to the desired objects in the drawing. One last thing to add is a puddle of black shade underneath the characters to make them really stand out, as in the following screenshot:

Figure 8.10: Screenshot of the last inking stage

By adding the darker shade underneath, we can see the characters clearly now.

Of course, there are lots of ways to do inking. Many inkers use the color black to fill certain spots to indicate deep shadows. Feathering, hatching, and cross-hatching can be used to add shading, detail, and texture. The following image is the same inked art but using hatching to shade:

Figure 8.11: Screenshot of shading with hatching

There are even styles of art that use ink with no line weight, a style called *ligne claire*, or clear line. Inking is as individual as each artist's style and if you're new to it, it may take a while to develop your own style. The key is to keep practicing!

Now that we know some of the principles of inking, how to change the layer color of the pencil layer, how to use thin and thick lines, how to add shade, and finally how to draw a background, let's explore some of the inking tools in Clip Studio Paint in the next section.

Exploring inking tools

Clip Studio Paint has a variety of tools for inking, and thanks to the customizable brush engine, we can also modify tools to better suit our needs. For the experienced inker, there are tools that mimic traditional inking tools, such as the G-pen, turnip pen, calligraphy pen, and textured pen. There are also a variety of marker tools that can be used for inking as well.

Alternative inking tools

There are some manga artists that decide to use the **Pencil** tool for final inking while others just use it for drafts. One of the reasons for using **Pencil** as a final inking tool is the "handmade" feeling it gives. Not only is it light and easy to draw with, but it also gives a warm, hand-drawn impression, just like looking at an artist's sketchbook. The screenshot on the right shows a panel drawn with the **Pencil** tool.

There are differences here from a pen drawing, such as that the lines are not very smooth and clear, the shading is not a flat black patch, and we can still see pencil marks.

Figure 8.12: Screenshot of a pencil drawing

With the **Pencil** tool, we can also create other art elements such as speech bubbles and sound effects in harmony with our art. Slice-of-life or fantasy story manga often use pencils or pastels for final ink drawings for a warm and cozy feeling.

Let's have a look at another alternative of using a brush instead of ink in the screenshot on the left.

In this screenshot, we see a brush drawing and other brush mark samples. What's great about using a brush is we can instantly change the visual to something dramatic and easily create black to gray tones. The shadow of the character at the bottom of the image shows textured gradation. The lines are not as smooth as those made with **Pen** tools, but **Brush** tools give us the space to have fun using smudges, smears, or blur effects. We often find manga artists using **Brush** for horror, suspense, and traditional oriental-style manga.

Figure 8.13: Screenshot of a brush drawing

> **Tip**
>
> Once you pick an inking tool, make sure to stick to that tool throughout the whole manga, except where you want to add a different impression to particular parts of the story, such as episodes from someone's past or a dream sequence. For instance, if you started using the **G-pen** in 12 pt, keep using it until the end. Otherwise, the visuals of the manga will not hold consistency, and readers will not be able to concentrate on the story anymore.

The **G-pen** default tool is pretty good as a substitute for a real brush and ink experience because of its pressure sensitivity settings, as I mentioned in the previous section.

I get a lot of people asking what inking tools I use. Personally, I use several inking tools from third-party designers that I love! You can download ready-made pens created by other Clip Studio Paint artists, some of which are priced. You can check out *Chapter 18, Exploring the Clip Studio Assets and Animation*, to get to know more about these ready-made materials and how to download them.

But if you don't want to pay for a tool, you can always make one that suits your needs and style! The "right-feeling" tool will vary for every artist because every artist is different and wants a different look from their tools. We will explore this more in the *Customizing pressure sensitivity settings* section later.

> **Tip**
>
> Having trouble getting smooth-looking inks? Ink while zoomed in! I find that zooming in to 250% on an image of 300 dpi or larger and then inking works best for me. The lines look a little shaky when I'm zoomed in, but upon zooming back out, the lines look smooth and crisp!

Let's briefly discuss each of the categories of tools that we can use to ink in Clip Studio Paint.

Marker tools

From Micron pens to the basic Sharpie, most artists have used marker tools on paper to ink their work at some point in their lives. In Clip Studio Paint, marker tools are characterized as having a set line width, meaning that they don't get thicker or thinner no matter how light or hard we press with the stylus, as you can see in the comparison of pens and markers in the screenshot on the right.

Figure 8.14: Screenshot of pen and marker samples

Even though the markers give us a line with no variation in width, they are still valuable in some inking situations. For instance, backgrounds with patterns of mascots and objects, machines, and other inorganic objects look great when inked with a line that has less variation:

Figure 8.15: Screenshot marker samples

Despite not getting thicker and thinner as we press, we can always change the size of the marker tip to get some variation in our lines by making them thicker or thinner manually, instead of with pressure.

The marker tools can be found under the **Pen** category as a tab of sub tools under that category. Here is a screenshot of the **Marker** tools in the **Sub Tool** palette:

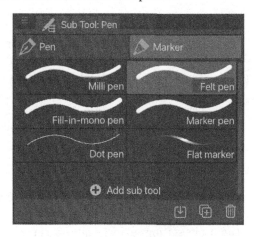

Figure 8.16: Screenshot of the Marker Sub Tool palette

Let's have a look at some more inking tools.

Pen tools

Pen tools are the primary tools for inking, both in the digital and the analogue art worlds. With a bit of practice, we can ink anything with pen tools. Pen tools in Clip Studio Paint have pressure sensitivity, allowing us to make thick and thin lines depending on how hard we press with the stylus.

Tip

Having issues with your tools in Clip Studio Paint? Go to the website of your tablet brand and make sure that you have the most up-to-date drivers for your model of tablet installed. Some of the most common software issues are just problems with outdated drivers. Make sure to have a backup of the previous drivers too, just in case there's a bug in the newest drivers!

For the traditional artist switching to digital who inks with brush or nib pens, the pen tools in Clip Studio Paint are going to give you the most familiar feel when inking, especially if you have a tablet stylus with a changeable nib. Wacom brand tablets usually have different tips that can be put on the stylus to give a different feel against the tablet, whether it be extra friction to make the experience more like working on paper or a spring-loaded nib that gives the squishy feel of a brush or nib. So, if you have one of these tablets with a nib that can be changed, be sure to experiment with it! Also, you'll want to make sure you have a few extra nibs on hand, because nibs can and will wear out over time and need to be replaced. You don't want to have a stubby nib and no fresh one when there's a deadline coming up!

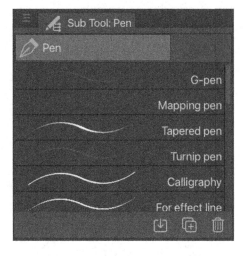

Figure 8.17: Screenshot of the Pen Sub Tool palette

The following screenshot shows the **Pen** tool category in the **Sub Tool** palette:

Tip

If you find your hand sticking to your tablet (or smudging your tablet, for those with screens or working on tablet PCs), you'll want to get a smudge guard! These gloves go on your dominant hand and are fingerless except for the pinkie and ring fingers, which have fabric to keep your skin from touching the tablet. You can make one yourself by getting a cheap pair of gloves and cutting off the thumb, pointer, and middle fingers, or you can buy one. A popular brand is www.smudgeguard.com.

We have been looking into pen tools and marker tools and the differences between them in this section.

We can customize our inking tools in many ways, but one of the easiest ways to start making tools on our own is to change the pressure sensitivity settings. In the next section, we will duplicate an existing tool and adjust its settings to make our own custom inking tool.

Customizing pressure sensitivity settings

All artists have their own preference on how to tilt a pen and how much pressure they put on paper. We can control this by using traditional pens on paper, but we need to configure our digital tools to make them understand what our preferences are.

We're going to create a sensitive pen that will give us thin lines, but also get thick rather quickly. Follow these steps to complete this exercise:

1. Select the **G-pen** tool from the **Pen Sub Tool** palette.

2. Click on the **Create copy of currently selected sub tool** icon at the bottom right of the **Sub Tool** palette to make a copy of the **G-pen** tool.

3. Name the new tool with a name of your choice. In the screenshot on the right, we are naming the tool Responsive Pen:

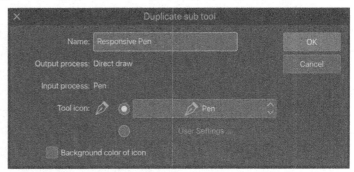

Figure 8.18: Screenshot of the pen Duplicate sub tool window

4. Click on **OK** to complete making the tool copy.

5. In the **Tool Property** palette, click on the wrench icon to open the **Sub Tool Detail** window.

6. Change **Brush Size** to 8.0.

7. Click on the button to the far right of the **Brush Size** option to open the **Brush Size Dynamics** options.

8. Ensure that the checkbox next to **Pen pressure** is checked. The **Brush Size Dynamics** window should look as in the screenshot on the right.

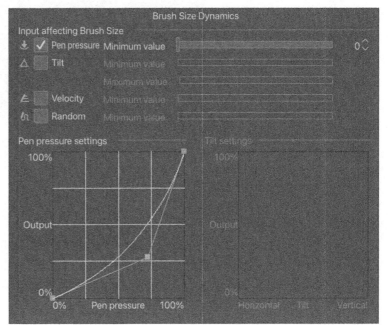

Figure 8.19: Screenshot of the Brush Size Dynamics window

9. The **Minimum value** slider controls how small our pen can get. It is set to 0, indicating that if we use light pressure, we can create a break in the line. You can change this slider to a different minimum value if you want to make a tool that always gives lines of at least some thickness.

10. The curve graph at the bottom marked **Pen pressure settings** controls how quickly the pen goes from 0% to 100% as we increase the pressure on the stylus. We are going to change this from the gentle curve it currently is into an S-curve. To do that, click on the curved line to add a second control point. Then, adjust the purple handles in order to make a shape like the one in the following screenshot:

11. Test out the pen on a new canvas. Press lightly and then press harder as you make strokes. Experiment with making lines slowly and quickly. Adjust the curve settings as needed until you like the feel of the new pen tool.

12. If your tablet supports **Tilt** settings, you can also experiment with these settings by enabling the checkbox next to the **Tilt** option in the **Brush Size Dynamics** window and adjusting them in the same way as we did for the pen pressure.

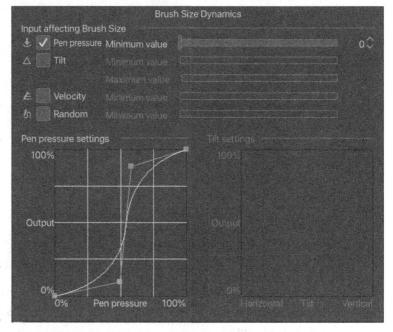

Figure 8.20: Screenshot of the Brush Size Dynamics window with an S-curve setting

13. The more control points you add to the curve, the more erratic the pen will behave. Experiment with the settings until you get the results you like!

14. Once you have finished adjusting the settings, close the **Sub Tool Detail** palette. You are now ready to use your new pen on your drawings!

Doesn't it feel like your pen understands how you behave when you draw? Great, you can now change pressure settings anytime using the steps we learned in this section whenever you want more suitable drawing tools.

In the next section, we are going to discuss how to ink on vector layers. Yes, it's different from inking on raster layers as we have been learning, but believe me, it's equally useful. Let's find out more!

Inking on vector layers

For a beginner inker, inking on a vector layer is very forgiving because of the editable nature of vector lines. (For more information on vector lines, see *Chapter 10, Exploring Vector Layers.*) If you are just starting out with inking, or if you want to be able to draw an inked line once and then tweak it until it's perfect, inking on a vector layer is going to be perfect for your needs! However, beginner inkers, remember that in the digital realm, even ink can be erased, and the **Undo** button will forgive most sins. So long as you remember to begin inking on a layer separate from your sketch, you will be able to erase and tweak your lines regardless of whether you go with raster or vector inks.

For an example of how we can tweak ink lines on vector layers, let's take a look at the screenshot on the right, showing lines we made with the **Pen** tool and that hasn't had any vector adjustments made yet.

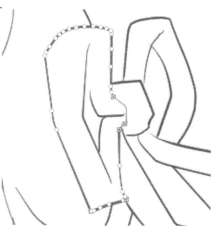

Figure 8.21: Screenshot of a vector free-hand drawing

Note that some of the lines are shaky and lack the smoothness of a confident inking hand seen in the previous example. After we use the **Control point** tool and the **Simplify vector line** tool on the lines, we end up with the smoother and more elegant lines, shown in the following screenshot:

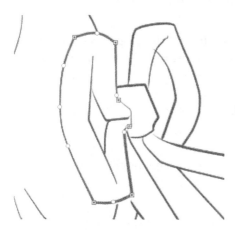

Figure 8.22: Screenshot of the corrected vector free-hand drawing

Whether you ink on raster or vector layers is, of course, up to you and your preferences. The more you practice with inking, the better you will become! In the next section, we will look at some tips on how to ink comic panels effectively.

Tips for inking comic panels

Now that we have some foundational knowledge of inking and inking tools in Clip Studio Paint, let's talk about inking a comic page. These are general tips, of course, because we could write an entire book just about inking comics (and entire books have, in fact, been written about this!). But for those just starting out, here are some general tips that make the inking process a little easier:

- Start with the panels that you're most excited about inking. In traditional inking, we would start from the opposite corner of our dominant hand and ink diagonally across the page and down to avoid smearing drying ink, but with digital inks, we don't have to worry about that. Start with whatever panels you wish to ink first and move around the page as you like.

- Remember to turn on the **Layer Color** option on any pencil layers before beginning to ink. This ensures that we can easily see where we've inked already and any lines we may have missed and keeps us from inking on the wrong layer and having to start all over again.

- Ink on separate layers for characters and backgrounds, or the foreground and background. I like to separate my characters from the backgrounds and then apply layer masks as needed. This not only allows me to adjust the position of characters or background elements more easily, but also ensures that backgrounds can be reused in other panels if needed.

- Use the eraser tools or the transparent color to correct your mistakes. Remember that digital ink isn't permanent! We can adjust it, delete the ink layer, and start over, or add textures using erasers or tools set to the **transparency** option.

If you really want to improve your inking, there are hundreds of resources on the internet where artists post their penciled work for others to ink and/or color. Make sure that you have the permission of the original artist to use this work, and that you give credit and a link to the artist's website if you post your inked version somewhere! Practice is the best way to improve and to find your own style.

Now you know the basic inking methods that Clip Studio Paint offers. You also understand in real terms what digital inking is all about.

Summary

In this chapter, we covered the reasons for inking and some basic principles for making clear and dynamic inked lines. We explored the **Marker** and pen tools, two of our workhorses for making inks in Clip Studio Paint, and learned how to adjust the pressure settings in the **Pen** tools to customize our tools. We talked about inking on vector layers and the benefits of doing so. Now you can take control of inking tools!

Let's take another step in becoming a Clip Studio Paint master. In the next chapter, we will discuss how to ink some special effects. We will also make a brush with custom brush tips to produce a special effect, and discuss more of the special tools, such as creating textured ink brushes, which will expand your digital drawing utilities.

Join us on Discord!

Read this book alongside other users. Ask questions, provide solutions to other readers, and much more.

Scan the QR code or visit the link to join the community.

`https://packt.link/clipstudiopaint`

Material Palette and Inking Special Effects

Sometimes, inking requires us to answer a set of questions relating to how to render something. How can we make a textured, grungy look? How can we use the digital space to make repetitive inking tasks easier and more efficient? Becoming familiar with the other drawing tools and how to customize them is the best way to save time when drawing. When you have a core understanding of how to create and customize tools, you can make special ones that solve problems and speed up your workflow.

Digital art materials are a contentious topic, as over-relying on them is sometimes seen as cheating. The important thing to remember is that the materials used for custom brushes still need to be drawn; you still need to know how to draw the materials, it just saves the repetition of drawing hundreds of leaves or blades of grass. Making custom tools that can create a grungy effect, make lightning, or even create a crowd scene for us is no more cheating than using a ruler or a compass on a piece of paper.

In this chapter, we will learn how to use the Material palette and build a foundation that will allow you to create your own custom tools. Each exercise is designed to build on the skills learned in the previous one to take you through the different options in the brush engine. The following topics will be covered in this chapter:

- Exploring the **Material palette**
- Creating a textured inking brush
- Making a broken glass shard brush
- Creating a foliage brush
- Texturing with a cross-hatching brush

Let's get going right away!

Technical requirements

To get started, you need Clip Studio Paint installed on your device, and a new canvas should be open without any background color. Any size is fine, but I recommend creating a 300 dpi square canvas to go through the content of this chapter.

Exploring the Material palette

Did you know you can save your art to the **Material** palette for later use in brushes, patterns, designs, backgrounds, and more? It certainly is one of the most useful techniques to have in digital drawing!

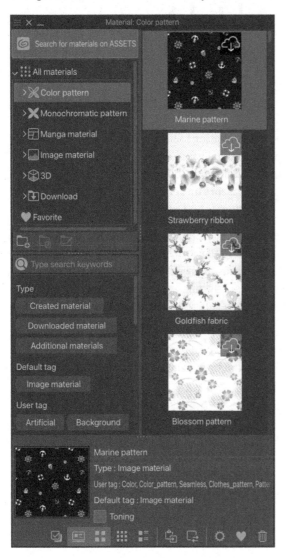

Figure 9.1: The Material palette

In this section, we are going to take a design and save it to the **Material** palette so that it can be used as a design on a character's shirt. First, though, let's take a look at the **Material** palette categories, which are shown in *Figure 9.1*.

- **Color pattern** contains patterns and background assets that are in color. Most of these assets are seamless tiles, but not all of them. They are separated into subcategories according to type.

- **Monochromatic pattern** is for black and white patterns, backgrounds, and textures. Included in this category are many different types of screentone patterns for manga creation.

- **Manga material** contains assets such as framing templates for comic page creation, speech balloons, sound effects, and effect lines.

- **Image material** contains illustrations and photo assets, as well as brush tip material assets.

- **3D** contains all 3D assets. For more information on 3D materials, see *Chapter 14, Using 3D Figures and Objects*.

- **Download** contains any assets downloaded from the Clip Studio Paint app. For more information on downloading new materials, see *Chapter 18, Exploring the Clip Studio Assets and Animation*.

- **Favorite** contains any materials you add to the Favorite category by pressing the heart-shaped icon at the bottom of the palette when a particular material is selected. It's a good idea to favorite any frequently used materials.

Now that we know about the different types of assets in the **Material** palette, we should learn how to save our own artwork to the palette as well. Let's see how to do that in the next section.

Saving artwork to the Material palette

There are many reasons why we might want to save a piece of art to the **Material** palette. Perhaps it's the title logo for your comic series and you want to be able to easily add it to your covers. Maybe it's a watermark that you intend to put over any image that you post online to deter art theft. Maybe it's a special speech balloon you designed for the villain of your manga, or it's a special repeating plaid pattern for your protagonist's outfit. You can also lay out complex tattoos and save them to the **Material** palette so that you can use them again instead of drawing them over and over every time you draw the character. Alternatively, you can create a T-shirt design for a character and simply paste it in and edit it slightly to fit the angle your character is standing at instead of redrawing the design each time!

The possibilities with materials are limited only by your own imagination, and the preceding points are just a few ideas of ways to use them.

Let's use the artwork shown below as an example. We'll learn how to save your art assets to the Material palette and then apply them to your drawings:

I have left the design with a transparent background because it will be used for a character's clothing in another creation so that, later, I will be able to change the color of the clothing by isolating the design itself from the selection.

The following steps will walk you through the process of saving an image to the **Material** palette:

1. If your image is made of multiple layers, either flatten the image or go to the **[Layer] menu | Merge visible to new layer** to create a new layer with a copy of the layers on it. Only the contents of the currently active layer will be saved to the **Material** palette, so make sure that all of the parts of the image that are going to be saved are on the same layer and that this layer is selected before continuing.

Figure 9.2: Example material design

2. In the **File** menu, click on **Edit**, select **Register Material**, and click on **Image....**

3. The **Material property** window will appear, as shown in the following screenshot:

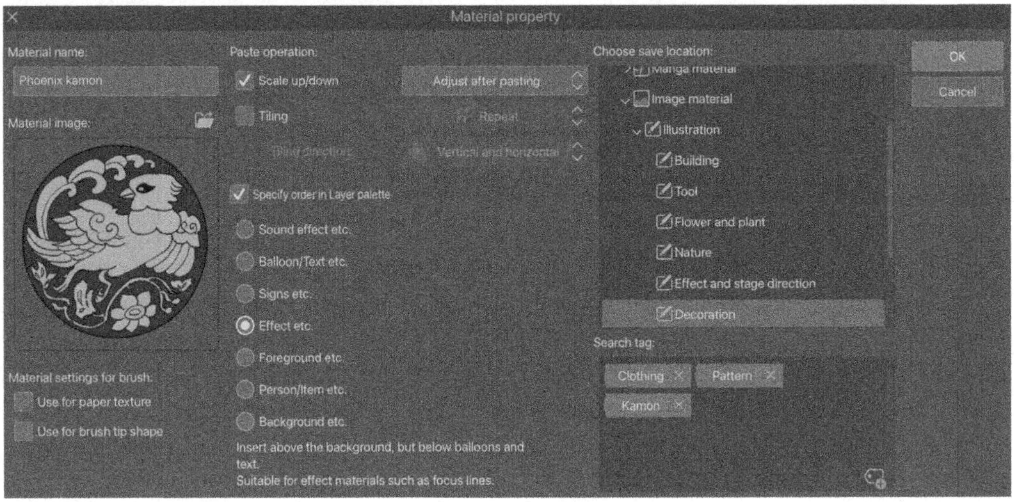

Figure 9.3: The Material property window

4. Enter a name in the **Material name** text entry box.

5. The **Material image** box will show a preview of the image that is being saved. If this image isn't correct, click on the **Cancel** button and follow the instructions in *step 1* to ensure that your image is all on one layer.

6. Under **Paste operation**, make sure that the **Scale up/down** option is checked, and that **Adjust after pasting** is selected in the drop-down menu. This will allow us to resize the material after adding it to the canvas.

7. The **Specify order in Layer palette** setting allows us to choose where in the stack of layers the material will be added. For instance, if we were adding a background image, we could select the **Background etc.** option so that the image will always be pasted beneath the other layers in the stack. Since we are creating a clothing design for this example, we will select **Effect etc.** so that the design will appear over the top of the characters.

8. Choose the desired category to save the **Material** under in the **Choose save location** window. In this example, we are using the **Image Material | Illustration | Decoration** folder to save this design.

9. Click on the icon in the lower-right corner of the **Search tag** window to add tags to the material. I always recommend using a unique tag on any materials you create and save so that you can find all of your assets quickly. I used the tag **clothing**, but you can come up with your own name, or maybe even the name of your comic project if that is what you want!

10. Click on **OK** to save the design to the palette.

Once our image is saved, we can view it in the **Material** palette. In the following screenshot, the **Phoenix kamon** design (which I saved by following the preceding instructions) is shown under **All materials** at the top of the list, since it has just been added:

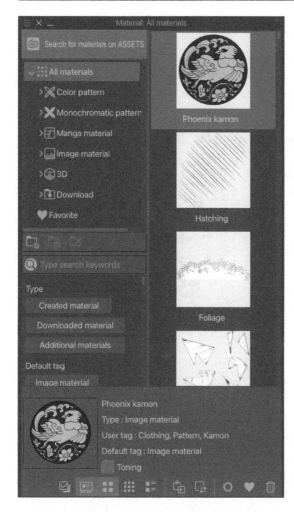

Figure 9.4: The Material palette

By selecting the material and clicking on the **Paste selected material to canvas** icon at the bottom of the **Material** palette, the material will be added to the currently active canvas. The **Paste selected material to canvas** icon looks as shown in the following screenshot:

Figure 9.5: The Paste selected material to canvas icon

In the following screenshot, the design has been added to the character's clothing, so now you don't need to redraw the image over and over again in every scene where the same character appears in your manga! Just to note, to make the design fit the clothing, we can click **Edit** in the **File** menu, select **Transform | Mesh transform...**, and then move control handles to shape the design.

Figure 9.6: Artwork with the pasted material

I'm sure you have a variety of designs you would like to use in your manga, and now you know how to store and use them without going through the hassle of creating them again and again!

Tip

This tip will save you a lot of time! Create a panel layer folder that contains a page full of panels before being divided into shapes, layers with speech balloon samples for each of the fonts used in your manga, a sketch layer, and an ink layer. Then, click the folder and drag it into the **Material** palette where your desired category is already open.

This can be used for the following pages as you continue to draw the manga series, and you don't have to recreate the set all over again. On each new manga page, just click on the **Paste selected material to canvas** icon! Now all you need to do is to edit the elements without creating them from scratch.

Creating a textured inking brush

In this section, we will use the materials we have explored to create a textured inking brush that will help us depict a certain grungy look. This exercise will get us familiar with creating and saving a custom brush tip and adjusting some of the brush tip settings in the **Sub Tool Detail** palette. Complete the following steps to make this textured inking brush:

1. On a new canvas, create a new raster layer. Make sure that **Expression color** in the **Layer Property** palette is set to **Gray**.

2. Select the **Airbrush** tool and the **Droplet** sub-tool. On the gray layer, make a circular shape with the **Droplet** tool, using pure black as the active color. Don't make this too precise; we want some variation to it. Your shape should look something like in *Figure 9.7*.

3. Turn off all layers apart from the one with the shape we created in the previous step. This includes any paper layers! We only want to see our new brush tip shape before completing the next step.

4. In the **File** menu, click on **Edit | Register Material | Image....** This path is shown in the following screenshot:

Figure 9.7: The Droplet tool's mark

Figure 9.8: The Register Material menu

5. This will bring up the **Material property** window. Enter a **Material name** value that is descriptive and unique. **Material image** shows us a preview of the shape we are saving. Check this to ensure that there is nothing else showing that we don't want to have in our brush shape.

6. Click on the checkbox next to **Use for brush tip shape**. Then, select the **Brush** sub-folder under the **Image material** folder in the **Choose save location** window to store the material.

7. Finally, enter a few tags by clicking on the + icon at the bottom of the **Search tag** window. This will allow us to search for our material easily when we go to make our tool. Your **Material property** window should look like the following screenshot:

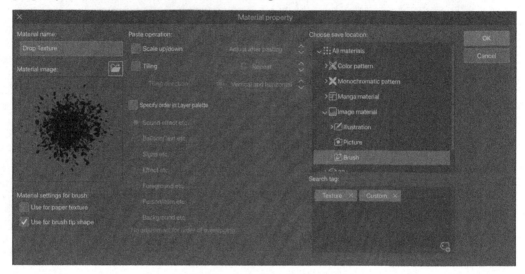

Figure 9.9: The Material property window

8. Click **OK** in the **Material property** window once all the parameters are set. This saves our new material.

9. Using the instructions from *Chapter 8, Getting Started with Inking Tools,* create a copy of the G-pen tool. Name this new tool Drop Texture.

10. Use the wrench icon at the bottom of the **Tool Property** palette to open the **Sub Tool Detail** palette.

11. Click on the **Brush Tip** category on the left side of the **Sub Tool Detail** palette.

12. Next to **Tip Shape**, click on the button marked **Material**. The box beneath **Tip Shape** will now say **Click here to add tip shape**. Click in this box to bring up the **Select brush tip shape** window.

13. In the **Select brush tip shape** window, locate the brush tip we made at the beginning of this exercise. Click on it to select it, as shown in the following figure:

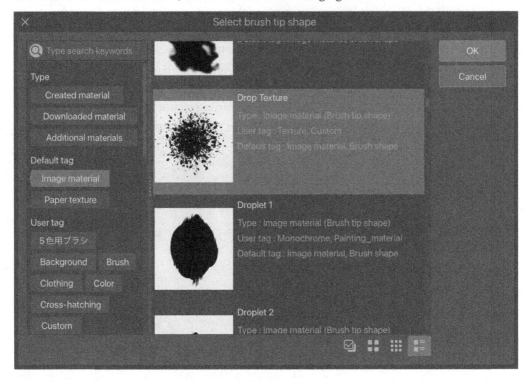

Figure 9.10: The Select brush tip shape window

14. Click **OK** to confirm the tip shape. This will take us back to the **Sub Tool Detail** palette.

15. While still in the **Brush tip** options, click on the button to the far right of the **Thickness** option. Check the **Random** box to turn on this parameter, as shown in the following screenshot:

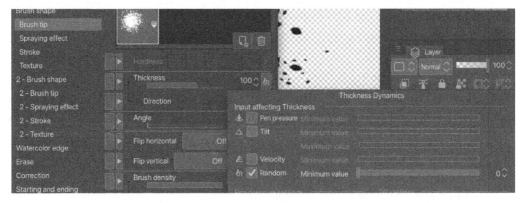

Figure 9.11: The Thickness Dynamics window

16. Repeat *step 15* for the **Angle** option as well, as shown in the following screenshot:

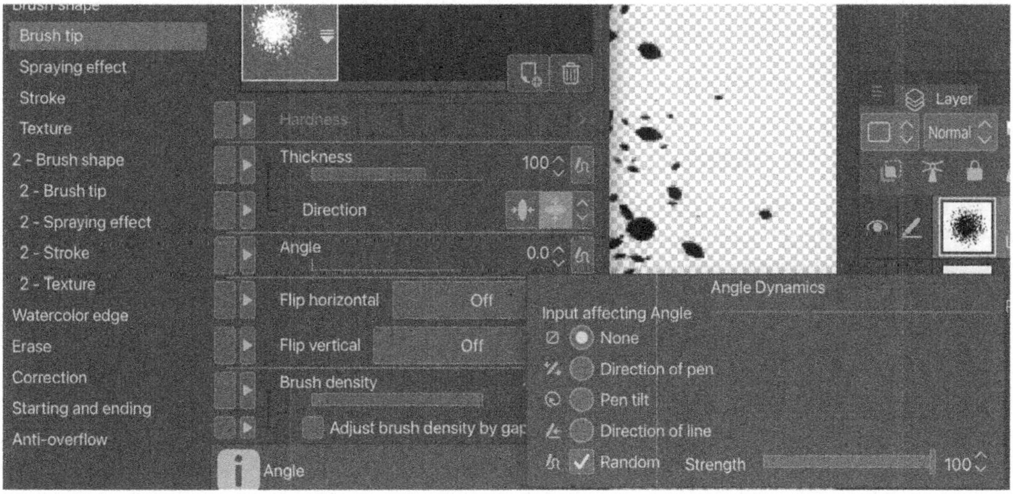

Figure 9.12: The Angle Dynamics window

17. Test your new textured inking brush!

This textured inking brush will give you results like what you see in the artwork below, on the left.

Note that the other lines are slightly out of focus to emphasize the mood. I duplicate the line art layer, check the new layer is selected, then click **Filter** from the file menu, select **Blur | Gaussian blur...**, set **6.00** for **Strength**, then click **OK**. Now the line art looks nicely blurred.

You can also create your own interesting pattern by creating a brush from a simple shape drawing, as seen in the following sample image:

Figure 9.13: A sample image with the new texture brush

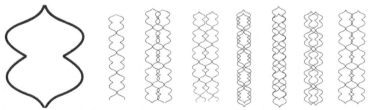

On the far left of the Figure 9.14 is the brush tip shape, and on the right are a few ribbon images showing different ways of overlapping the brush strokes.

Figure 9.14: Using patterns as textured brushes

This works well for creating interesting patterns!

For brush settings, turn the **Ribbon** function on in the **Stroke** category, turn **Post correction** on, and make the value maximum in the **Correction** category. We will learn more about the Ribbon function in a later section: *Creating a foliage brush*.

Wow, you have made a special brush tip of your own!

Do you want to learn more about these special brushes? Read on to learn about a different brush.

In the next section, we will create a brush that will help us create a more complex effect.

Making a broken glass shard brush

By utilizing the features of Clip Studio Paint, we can save time with a brush that will make applying an otherwise tedious-to-achieve special effect a simple affair. We will create a brush that will make shards of broken glass rain down on our images. Follow these steps to create this brush:

1. Open a blank canvas, preferably at least 300 dpi. You do not need to use the **Paper** option in this canvas; in fact, we want a transparent background.

2. Using your preferred drawing tools on an empty layer, draw the outline of several jagged, broken glass shapes. Use black or dark gray for the outlines.

3. Create a new layer beneath the outline layer. In this layer, fill the glass shapes with solid white.

4. Lower the opacity of the white layer to 50% by using the slider at the top right of the **Layer** palette.

5. Merge the outline layer with the 50% transparent white layer by clicking on **Layer** in the **File** menu and clicking on **Merge visible layers**. (Note that this will combine any layers that are currently visible, so make sure that your only visible layers are the glass shard outlines and the 50% white fill.) You should have a transparent background and your canvas should now look something like the following screenshot:

Figure 9.15: Broken glass drawing

6. In the **File** menu, click on **Edit | Register Material | Image....** This path is shown in the following screenshot:

Figure 9.16: The Register Material menu

7. This will bring up the **Material property** window. Enter a **Material name** value that is descriptive and unique. **Material image** shows us a preview of the shape we are saving.

8. Check this to ensure that there is nothing else showing that we don't want to have in our brush shape.

9. Click on the checkbox next to **Use for brush tip shape**. Then, select the **Brush** sub-folder under the **Image material** folder in the **Choose save location** window to store the material.

10. Finally, enter a few tags by clicking on the + icon at the bottom of the **Search tag** window. This will allow us to search for our material easily when we go to make our tool. The settings will look as follows:

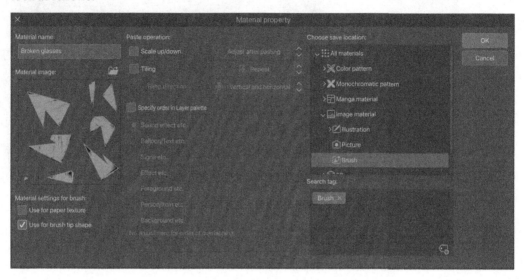

Figure 9.17: The Material property window

11. Click **OK** in the **Material property** window once all the parameters are set. This saves our new material.

12. Duplicate the G-pen as we did in previous sections. Name the new sub-tool Broken glass. Click **OK**.

13. In the **Tool Property** palette, click on the wrench icon in the lower-right corner to open the **Sub Tool Detail** screen.

14. Change **Brush Size** to **60.0**. Open **Brush Size Dynamics** to set **Minimum value** to **15** and edit the curve to look like the one in the following screenshot:

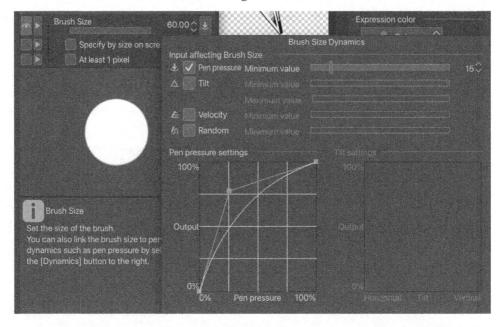

Figure 9.18: The Brush Size Dynamics window

15. Click **Anti-aliasing** and select **Medium**, then click on **Brush tip** in the **Sub Tool Detail** palette.

16. Click on the **Material** button under the **Tip Shape** option. The box beneath **Tip Shape** will now say **Click here and add tip shape.**

17. Click in this box to bring up the **Select brush tip shape** window, then locate the glass shard shapes we made at the beginning of this exercise. Highlight them as shown in the following screenshot, and click **OK**:

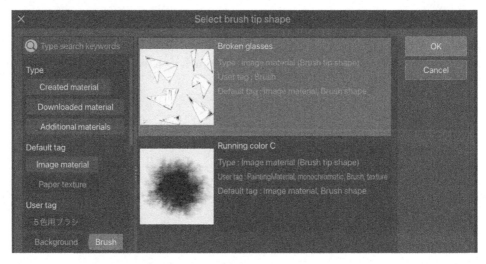

Figure 9.19: Select brush tip shape window

18. In the **Brush tip** settings, click on the icon to the right of the **Thickness** option. Check the box next to the **Random** option and set the minimum value to **65**, as shown in the following screenshot:

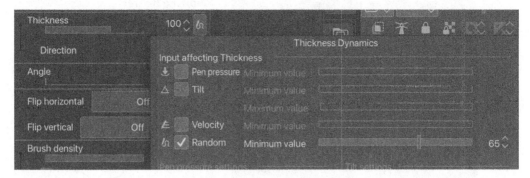

Figure 9.20: Thickness Dynamics window

19. Click on the icon to the right of the **Angle** option and select the **Direction of line** option. Check the box next to the **Random** option and set **Strength** for the effect to **100**, as in the following screenshot:

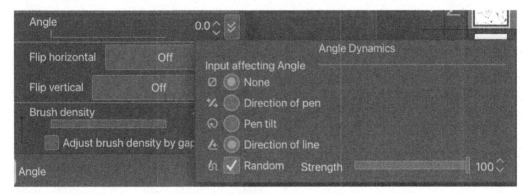

Figure 9.21: Angle Dynamics window

20. In the **Sub Tool Detail** window, click on the **Stroke** category.

21. Set the **Gap** option to **Fixed** by clicking on the first icon (the one with one full circle in the center of it).

22. Use the slider under the **Gap** option to set the value to **150.0**.

23. Set **Repeat method | Random**, as in the following screenshot:

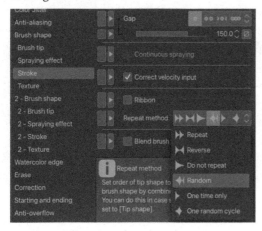

Figure 9.22: Repeat method drop-down menu

By changing the **Thickness, Angle,** and **Repeat method** options to **Random**, we get a random rotation and direction of the glass shard shapes as we use the brush. By changing the **Gap** option, we make the brush tip shapes show up far apart from each other, instead of in a continuous stroke like with other drawing tools.

24. Test your new brush!

The brush will give us the effect shown in the following figure:

Figure 9.23: Sample image using the Broken glasses brush

You can also use perspective transformation to change glass sizes at once. You can try this by selecting **Edit** from the **File** menu, then selecting **Transform | Perspective....** Now you can move the control handle around to change perspective, as in the following screenshot.

Figure 9.24: Perspective transformation

Next, we will create a brush that helps us draw different aspects of nature. With a customized foliage brush, you can draw a tree and its leaves super easily! Let's have you make your own by following the steps in the next section.

Creating a foliage brush

I don't think I need to keep it a secret that the foliage brush is one of my favorite specialty brushes ever created. This brush makes drawing detailed trees and bushes easier, and it introduces us to the **Ribbon** options in the brush details.

In the following set of steps, we will create a leafy material and then make it into a brush that rolls out like a spool of ribbon:

1. Open a new blank canvas with at least 300 dpi resolution.

2. Using an inking pen, draw a row of leaves similar to the top of a tree or bush.

3. Fill the leaves with white. Use the following screenshot as a guide to create your leaves and the white fill. You need a transparent background as we had in the previous sections of this chapter.

4. From the **File** menu, click **Layer | Merge visible layers**. The image is now similar to the following screenshot:

5. In the **File** menu, click on **Edit | Register Material | Image...** This will bring up the **Material property** window. Enter a **Material name** value that is descriptive and unique. **Material image** shows us a preview of the shape we are saving. Check this to ensure that there is nothing else showing that we don't want to have in our brush shape.

Figure 9.25: Drawing leaves

6. Click on the checkbox next to **Use for brush tip shape**. Then, select the **Brush** sub-folder under the **Image material** folder in the **Choose save location** window to store the material.

7. Finally, enter a few tags by clicking on the + icon at the bottom of the **Search tag** window. This will allow us to search for our material easily when we go to make our tool. Your **Material property** window should look similar to the following screenshot:

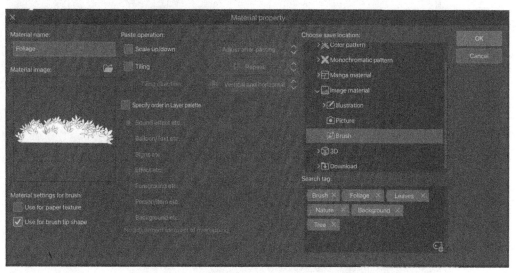

Figure 9.26: Material property window

8. Click **OK** in the **Material property** window once all the parameters are set. This saves our new material.

9. Make a copy of the G-pen and name this new tool `Foliage brush`.

10. In the **Tool Property** palette, click on the wrench icon in the bottom-right corner to open the **Sub Tool Detail** palette.

11. Set the **Ink** category accordingly:

    a. Ensure that **Opacity** is set to **100**

    b. Set **Blending mode** to **Normal**

    c. **Anti-aliasing**: set to **None**

    For the **Brush tip** category:

    a. Click on the **Material** button under the **Tip Shape** option; the box beneath **Tip Shape** will now say **Click here to add tip shape**.

    b. Click on that box to bring up the **Select brush tip shape** window.

    c. Locate your leafy shape and click on it to select it. Click **OK** to load this material into the brush.

    d. Set **Thickness** to **100**.

12. In some cases, the leaf material is loading vertically instead of horizontally, as in the following screenshot, which is not what we want:

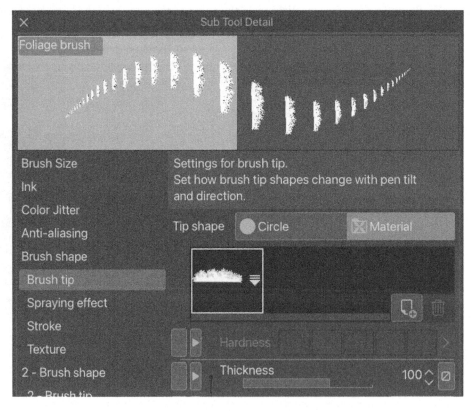

Figure 9.27: Brush tip menu with vertical leaf material

13. No worries; to change the orientation of the material shape, change the value of **Angle** from **0.0** to **100**. This should rotate the material to be horizontal, as shown in the following screenshot:

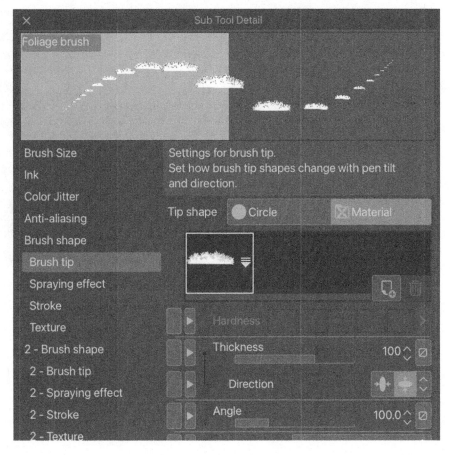

Figure 9.28: Brush tip menu with horizontal leaf material

14. Click on the icon to the right of the **Angle** settings to open the **Angle Dynamics** window. Make sure the box next to the **Random** option is deselected, as shown in the following screenshot:

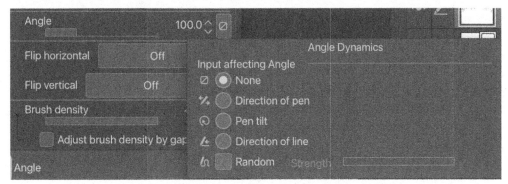

Figure 9.29: Angle Dynamics window

15. Click on **Stroke** on the left-hand side of the **Sub Tool Detail** screen. Click on the checkbox next to the **Ribbon** option to activate it. Now the brush looks like the following screenshot:

16. Test out your new brush.

This brush works best when it's used in layers. To understand what I mean, let's look at the process of creating a tree using this tool.

After sketching the trunk of the tree and the general shape of the leaves at the top, use the brush to go around the outline of the top. Work in a clockwise direction to ensure that the bottom leaves are in the correct orientation. Look at the following screenshot and note the direction of the arrows. This is the direction we are working in:

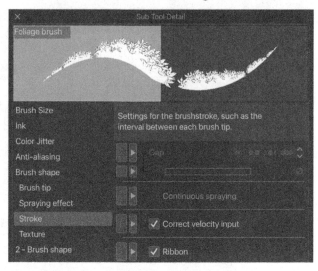

Figure 9.30: Stroke menu

Not bad, but it could look better! By continuing to work in the same clockwise direction, but slightly inside of the already-existing leaves, we can make more layers of foliage that will grow outward from the tree branches, as shown in the following screenshot:

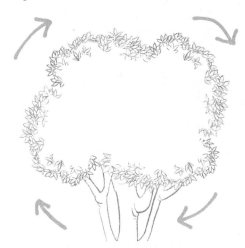

Figure 9.31: Foliage brush's brush-strokes

Figure 9.32: Foliage brush's brush-strokes with layers

By using the **Ribbon** setting, we get a brush that repeats in a pattern, unrolling like a pattern printed on tape. This is also what allows us to get the pattern to go upside down to make the bottom leaves without having to create a second brush with the brush tip material upside down. Layering the leaves gives us a detailed finished product!

By using the **Ribbon** option and playing with the **Repeat** method, we can make brushes that simulate patterned fabric trim, lace, ruffles, knit patterns, and even shoelaces!

Overly relying on material brushes can cause your art to look generic, especially when multiple compositions use the same brushes. To get a more organic look, you should start hand drawing the elements of your artwork instead.

Alternatively, try making new materials by hand so that you have a bigger variety to choose from. You can also go over the results of the material brush with hand-drawn details.

In short, material brushes are convenient tools to create foundations, which you finalize in your art yourself.

In *Chapter 18*, *Exploring the Clip Studio Assets and Animation*, we will learn how to access the Clip Studio Paint Assets download library, where you can get more ideas for custom tools to make or download tools made by other users.

Next, we will look at one of the most useful brushes – the cross-hatching brush. Read on to find out how to create one in the next section!

Texturing with a cross-hatching brush

Hatching is a shading technique achieved using groups of parallel lines. Cross-hatching is a group of parallel lines that cross another group in another direction, adding texture and the appearance of darker shading. Hatching and cross-hatching can add a lovely look of depth and texture to monochromatic illustrations. By making a hatching brush, we can achieve this look without the tedium of having to make all the lines by hand. When creating your new canvas to draw your brush tip, make sure that **Basic expression color** is set to **Gray** instead of **Color**. The following screenshot shows the drop-down menu in the new file creation window where this change can be made:

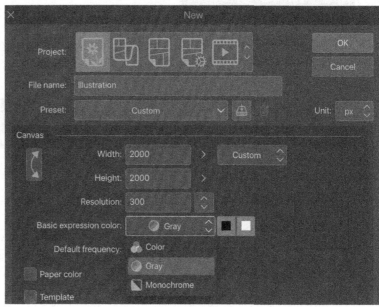

Figure 9.33: Screenshot of the Basic expression color options

The following steps will walk you through the brush creation process:

1. Select the **Ruler** tool category and then the **Create ruler** sub-tool category.

2. Select **Special ruler** from the **Sub Tool** palette.

3. In the **Tool property** palette, choose **Parallel line** from the **Special ruler** drop-down menu, as shown in the following screenshot:

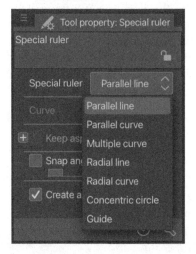

Figure 9.34: The Special ruler drop-down menu

4. Click inside the canvas and hold down the mouse button or stylus. While still holding, drag the cursor across the canvas at an angle. Release the mouse button to set the ruler. The canvas should now look like this:

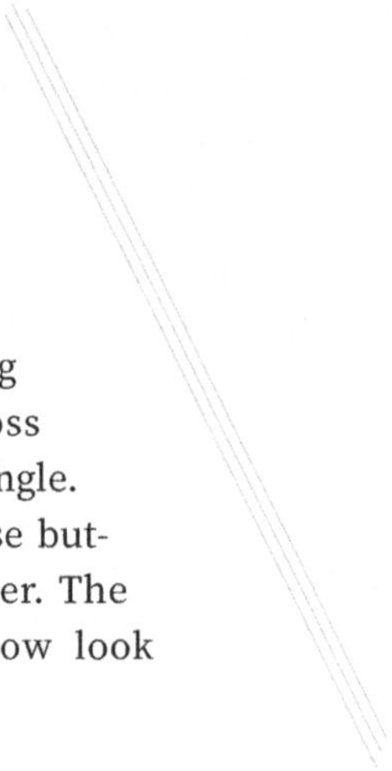

Figure 9.35: Parallel lines being set diagonally

5. Select your preferred pen tool from the **Pen** subtools.

6. Ensure that the **Snap to Special Ruler** option in the main command bar above the canvas is active. This will make the pen follow the parallel line ruler. Refer to the following screenshot for the location of this icon:

Figure 9.36: The Snap to Special Ruler option

7. Using your preferred pen tool, draw a group of parallel lines, as shown in the following figure:

Figure 9.37: Lines drawn by snapping to the ruler

8. Turn off or delete any **Paper** color layers or any fill layers behind the parallel line layer, leaving only the group of lines and a transparent background.

9. Before we can set the new brush tip material, we must clear the parallel line ruler. To do this, select the **Object** sub-tool from the **Operation** category of tools. Click on the ruler to select it. Then, click on **Edit | Delete** from the **File** menu. (You can also right-click and select **Clear** from the pop-up menu.)

10. In the **File** menu, click on **Edit | Register Material | Image....**

11. This will bring up the **Material property** window. Enter a **Material name** value that is descriptive and unique. **Material image** shows us a preview of the shape we are saving. Check this to ensure that there is nothing else showing that we don't want to have in our brush shape.

12. Click on the checkbox next to **Use for brush tip shape**. Then, select the **Brush** sub-folder under the **Image material** folder in the **Choose save location** window to store the material.

13. Finally, enter a few tags by clicking on the + icon at the bottom of the **Search tag** window. This will allow us to search for our material easily when we go to make our tool. Your **Material property** window should look similar to the following screenshot:

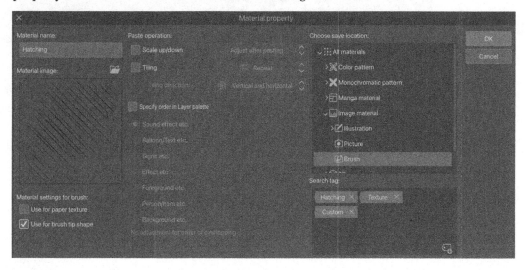

Figure 9.38: Material property window

14. Click **OK** to register the material.

15. Copy the G-pen, as we have in the other sections of this chapter. Name this new tool `Cross-hatching`.

16. In the **Tool property** palette, click on the wrench icon in the bottom-right corner to open the **Sub Tool Detail** palette.

    a. Click on the **Brush tip** option.

    b. Click on the **Material** button under the **Tip Shape** option. The box beneath **Tip Shape** will now say **Click here to add tip shape**. Click on this box to bring up the **Select brush tip shape** window.

    c. Search for and select the brush tip shape created earlier in this section.

    d. Click on the icon to the right of the **Angle** settings to open the **Angle Dynamics** window.

e. Click on the circle button next to **Direction of line** to activate this option, as shown in the following screenshot:

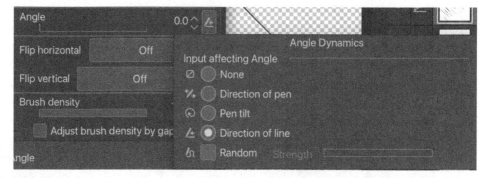

Figure 9.39: Angle Dynamics window

This option will set the direction of the brush tip material, depending on the direction we move the stylus in to make our line, allowing us to overlap the hatching to get cross-hatching lines.

17. Under the **Stroke** category of options, set **Gap** to **Fixed**.

18. Test your new tool!

Because we created the brush material in a **Gray** color mode canvas, it means that we can set the color of the brush as needed. This can be seen in the preceding figure with the white highlight cross-hatching on the left side of the face, the hair, the shoulder, and the tip of the newspaper.

You can now apply textured shade and light to your artwork!

Summary

This chapter has given us knowledge about the **Material** palette and a foundation for making our own custom tools, and with this knowledge, you should be able to make pretty much any special brush that you can dream up! We learned how to make and save our own custom materials that can be used as brush tips. We created a grittily textured inking brush and learned how to set the **Sub Tool Detail** settings to get the look we wanted. We made a glass shard brush that utilized **Opacity** and a **Random** direction to give us the appearance of hundreds of hand-inked glass shards in an illustration. Then, we used the **Ribbon** options to create a foliage brush. Finally, we used the parallel line ruler to create a brush tip material and used the **Direction of line** brush option to create a layered cross-hatching brush.

Figure 9.40: Cross-hatching brush effect in use

In the next chapter, we are going to move on to how to use vector layers. We will have a closer look at how vector layers are different from raster layers, which have a few different capabilities that might be useful for you.

Join us on Discord!

Read this book alongside other users. Ask questions, provide solutions to other readers, and much more.

Scan the QR code or visit the link to join the community.

https://packt.link/clipstudiopaint

10

Exploring Vector Layers

One of the benefits of using Clip Studio Paint is that it can produce both raster and vector images. In fact, rasters and vectors can be used on different layers of the same canvas by simply creating the corresponding layer type. Creating vectors in Clip Studio Paint, however, is different in many ways compared to other vector programs.

Vector images are different from raster images. Raster images are made up of small squares of color, called pixels. Raster images are used in many situations, but they do have some disadvantages – primarily that since they are composed of pixels, they lose quality when made larger. Vector images are made of points that are connected together in the program and can be edited on the fly and resized at will without any loss in quality.

In this chapter, we will learn both how to create vectors in Clip Studio Paint and how to save artwork to the **Material** palette for use again later. The following topics will be covered:

- Creating a vector layer
- Drawing on vector layers
- Editing vectors

By the end of this chapter, you will know how to deal with vector line drawing and will have gained knowledge of using materials.

Let's get started with vectors!

Technical requirements

To get started, you need Clip Studio Paint already installed on your device, and a new canvas opened with a white-colored paper layer. Any size is fine, but I recommend creating a 300-dpi square canvas with which to work through the content in this chapter.

Vectors in Clip Studio Paint

In this section, we will start by learning about vectors, so don't worry if you are new to the term. We will start with what they're all about, and then you will try creating some vector art with our step-by-step tutorials.

Vector images are made from points, lines, and curves that are based on mathematical expressions. Because these images are defined by mathematical expressions instead of pixels, they can be scaled up or down infinitely without losing quality or becoming pixelated.

Vectors are most often used for logos, but they can be useful to create comics as well as illustrations. The lines can be adjusted without being redrawn, so if you have trouble confidently making lines for inking, then working with vectors may be a solution for you.

Some graphics software will only work with either vector or raster information. Clip Studio Paint can do both, even within the same image file. We can have one layer of the image filled with vector information while all the others are filled with raster information if that's the way we want to do our work!

NOTE

It's worth noting here that if you are already familiar with working with vectors in another program, you may need to adjust to the way that Clip Studio Paint handles vector graphics. Also, Clip Studio Paint's vectors are not exportable from the program as vectors, and vector graphics from other programs cannot be imported as vectors into Clip Studio Paint.

Let's get into creating your vector art!

Creating a vector layer

To start working with vectors, we need to create a vector layer. There are two ways to do this: through the **File** menu or through the **Layer** palette. We will look at these methods in the following sections.

Creating a vector layer via the File menu

Follow these steps to create a vector layer using the **File** menu:

1. In the **File** menu, click on **File**, then go to **New Layer**, and finally click on **Vector Layer**.
2. Enter a name for the layer in the **New vector layer** dialog box that appears.
3. Choose an **Expression Color** (**Black** and **White**, **Gray**, or **Color**) from the drop-down menu in the **New vector layer** dialog box.
4. Click on **OK** to create the new layer.

We will see how to create a vector layer from the **Layer** palette in the next section.

Creating a vector layer via the Layer palette

Follow these steps to create a vector layer using the **Layer** palette:

1. Locate the **Layer** palette in the user interface.
2. Click on the **New vector layer** icon in the **Layer** palette. The icon is pointed out with an arrow in the screenshot on the right:
3. The new layer will be created and will show up in the layer stack in the palette.

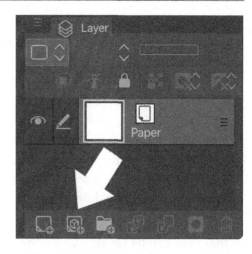

Figure 10.1: Screenshot of the Layer palette

Anything drawn on a vector layer will be a vector image, meaning that it is not made up of pixels, but of control points. Now we know two methods for creating a vector layer. They can be created either from the **File** menu or from the **Layer** palette. The second method is definitely easier since it's just a click on an icon!

In the next section, we will learn how to draw on a vector layer with our favorite tools.

Drawing on vector layers

Once you have created a vector layer, you can use any tool that you'd like to draw on it, including pencils, pens, or the direct drawing tools (line, curve, ellipse, and so on).

Some editing may be needed to create a smooth line, and we prefer a line with the fewest control points possible to make it easier to edit the line.

Let's look at two similar vector lines, as shown in the screenshot on the right:

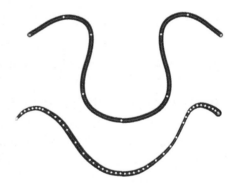

Figure 10.2: Two vector lines

The line at the top was created using the **Continuous Curve** tool. The line at the bottom was created using the **Pen** tool. The small circles shown along each line are the control points that are used for editing vector lines. On the line that was created with the **Continuous Curve** tool, nine control points are shown at each point where the curve changes direction.

The line created by drawing a curve with the **Pen** tool has many more control points because Clip Studio Paint automatically places them wherever the program thinks they may be needed. This makes editing the vector lines more difficult without some extra work beforehand.

Thankfully, Clip Studio Paint provides us with tools to make the cleanup process easier, which is exactly what we'll explore in the next section.

Editing vectors

In this section, we are going to look at different ways to edit vector lines. First of all, we will get to know editing tools, then we will try out some tools on the vector lines that we created in the previous section. Finally, we will learn how to change line widths.

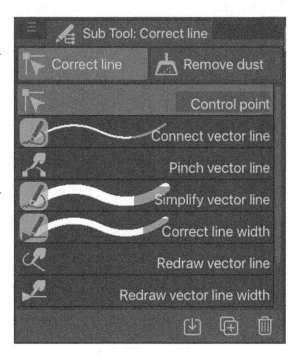

One of the advantages of using vector graphics is that lines can be tweaked and edited endlessly until they are perfect, unlike working with raster layers, where a line must be erased and redrawn until it's just right. Vector lines can be manipulated and reshaped using their control points.

Clip Studio Paint has tools that allow for the easy cleanup and editing of vector lines. These tools can be found in the **Correct line** group of tools, as shown in the screenshot on the right:

Figure 10.3: Screenshot of the Correct line sub-tool options

Let's take a closer look at some of these **Correct line** tools, what they do, and how we can use them.

Using the Pinch vector line tool

I think it's best to talk about this tool first, because using **Pinch vector line** is an easy way to make a small change to the line position. Click on this tool, then click on the line you want to move and drag it around to the desired place. As you can see, the **Pinch vector line** icon shows a circle pinching a line. It's that easy – if you only need to make a small tweak, this is the tool you need!

For example, in the screenshot on the right, I wanted to add more curve to the guitar outline behind the character. So, I used the **Pinch vector line** tool to edit the line retroactively:

Figure 10.4: Screenshot of the Pinch vector line sample

Let's have a look at its settings.

The settings of the **Pinch vector line** tool options are described as follows (and are shown in the screenshot on the right):

- **Fix end:** This sets which ends of the pinched line to edit. If you select the **Fix one end** option, as highlighted in the screenshot, you can move one end of the line but not the other.

- **Pinch level:** This option adjusts how much the line bends when editing with this tool. Bigger values pinch the whole line while smaller values pinch a smaller part of the line.

- **Effect range:** This adjusts the extent of the line affected when you drag along the line. The larger the value, the more the part of the line is moved at once.

- **Add control point:** When activated, this automatically adds control points as you bend a line so that the parts without control points are not dragged along as you edit. When it's not activated, a whole line will be dragged as it is, so the drawing shape might be distorted.

- **Connect lines:** When activated, if you pinch one line and move it to touch the end of another line, these lines will be connected. You won't be able to activate this if you select the **Fix both ends** option in the **Fix end** setting.

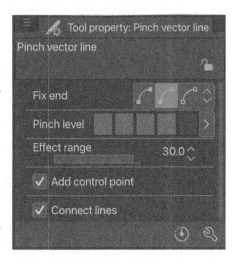

Figure 10.5: Screenshot of the Pinch vector line sub-tool settings

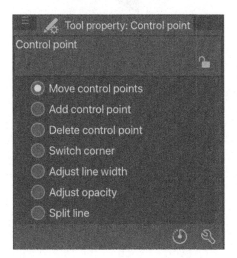

Figure 10.6: Screenshot of the Control point sub-tool property palette

Now you know how to control the **Pinch vector line** tool, so you can adjust your vector lines as you please using this tool! We will now look at some different ways of editing vectors in the next section.

Using the Control point tool

The **Control point** sub-tool can be used to perform various actions on the control points along a vector line. These functions can be accessed via the **sub-tool property** palette when the **Control point** sub-tool is selected. The screenshot on the left shows the **sub-tool property** palette:

The different modes of the **Control point** tool are described as follows:

- **Move control points:** Allows the control point to be moved by clicking and dragging.
- **Add control point:** Adds a control point by clicking on the vector line at the point where the additional control point should be placed.
- **Delete control point:** Deletes control points with a click.
- **Switch corner:** Switches the corner of the control point. Control points can be hard corners or curves, and using this tool will change a hard corner on a vector line into a curve, and vice versa.

- **Adjust line width:** Easily manipulate the width of the vector line by clicking and dragging to the right or left on a control point. Dragging in either direction will either make the line thinner or thicker at that control point. *Figure 10.7* shows sample lines of the same line width after dragging the stylus from left to right, and right to left, respectively:

Figure 10.7: Screenshots of Adjust line width in action

- **Adjust opacity:** This is similar to the **Correct line width** option and allows us to change the opacity of the line at the control point by clicking and dragging. It works great when you don't want a solid thick line edge. *Figure 10.8* are before and after using **Adjust opacity:**

Figure 10.8: Screenshots of before and after using Adjust opacity

- **Split line:** Separates the vector line at the point where the tool is clicked.

By switching back and forth between these options, you get a great level of control for manipulating your vector lines! But aren't there too many control points? We will see how to simplify this in the following section.

Using the Simplify vector line tool

This is the tool that I use the most when creating vector graphics in Clip Studio Paint. I love the look of hand-inked lines for most of my art, especially lines that go from thin to thick and back again, like they were made using a traditional brush pen. However, as seen in the *Drawing on vector layers* section of this chapter, using the drawing tools on a vector layer produces a line with an abundance of control points, making editing the line difficult.

The **Simplify vector line** tool can be used to reduce the number of control points in a hand-drawn line to only the points needed. The line in the screenshot on the right has had the **Simplify vector line** tool used on the left-hand side, while the right still has the control points that were created automatically:

Figure 10.9: Screenshot of a half-simplified line

Notice how close together the control points are on the right side of the curve compared to the control points on the left. This is because Clip Studio Paint puts too many control points along vector lines when they are drawn with a pen or a brush tool.

Using the **Simplify vector line** tool is easy. Simply select the tool, set the brush size, and then click and drag it over the areas of the vector line that need to be simplified. A green highlight shows where you've already used the tool during that stroke. When the mouse button is released, the program will simplify the line automatically.

Note that after using this tool, some control points may need slight tweaking for accuracy. Now your vector line looks simplified and more manageable. Let's move on to learn how to change the line width.

Using the Correct line width tool

The **Correct line width** sub-tool under the **Correct line** group allows for a vector's line width to be changed in an instant. This is only one of the tools that allow us to change the width of a line. Let's take a look at the **Correct line width** sub-tool properties, which are shown in the screenshot on the right:

Figure 10.10: Screenshot of Correct line width sub-tool property

The white circle to the left of the option name indicates which operation is currently active:

- **Thicken:** This will make the vector line thicker, depending on what value the slider is currently on and where the tool is used.
- **Narrow:** This does the opposite, making the vector line thinner. If you click the small + icon next to it, it tells you it should be at least 1 pixel to reduce the width.

- **Scale up width** and **Scale down width:** Make the line thicker and narrower by scaling it up or down, according to the value set under those options. This means if you input **2** in the **Scale up width** value, the part of the vector line where the tool is used will become two times thicker.

  The outline in the screenshot on the right has thickened using this tool. You can see how this is helpful for certain styles, or if you just want to add more emphasis to your character!

Figure 10.11: Screenshot of a
drawing with line width corrected

- **Fix width:** Sets any part of the line the tool is used on to the width indicated by the slider, no matter how thick or thin it is before being used.
- **Process whole line:** The checkbox will complete the indicated action on the entire vector line at once. This can be a great time-saver when wanting to make an entire line thicker or narrower, because one click anywhere along the line will change the whole line at once, instead of us needing to select the entire line with the tool!
- **Brush Size:** Its slider controls the size of the cursor of the **Correct line width** tool.

Using the Redraw vector line tool

The **Redraw vector line** sub-tool is pretty neat because it allows you to push and pull the vector line around as you like. Simply select the tool, click somewhere along a vector line, and drag it around to change the line. It's an easy way to adjust vector lines quickly and organically without having to completely redraw them! In an earlier section, we learned about the **Pinch vector line** tool, used to make simple adjustments to vector lines. The tools are quite similar realistically, but this one is generally more handy for complicated shape line adjustment.

Using the Redraw vector line width tool

The **Redraw vector line width** sub-tool is another method of adjusting the thickness or thinness of our vector lines after they've been created. Honestly, this is the tool I tend to use the most when needing to adjust vector line thickness, simply because it is much more visual than the **Correct line width** tool. The **Redraw vector line width** sub-tool uses the **Brush Size** setting to adjust the thickness of the line. The larger the brush size is set, the thicker the tool will make the parts of the line it is used on. When the brush is set to a size smaller than the current line, the tool will make the line narrower. In the screenshot on the right, this tool was used with varying size settings along the length of the line:

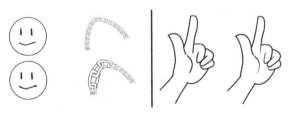

Figure 10.12: Screenshots of drawings edited
with the Redraw line width tool

Whatever size the brush was set to is the size that the line becomes after the tool is used. The Chain decoration pen line was created by making the brush size much, much larger than the current width. This was done by tracing just once on that section of the line.

That's how we can change the width of lines to suit our needs. We will look at how to make two separate vector lines connect in the following section, so let's read on.

Using the Connect vector line tool

If you see that there's a gap between two vector lines that you want to fill, this is the tool for you. You only need to stroke the tool over the line gap and it will be filled automatically! As with the other tools, there are several settings available for this tool, as you can see in the following screenshot:

Let's have a look at each of these settings in the sub-tool properties:

- **Simplify:** Reduces the number of control points in the area where you stroke to connect the lines. As you can see in the following screenshot, a smaller value makes the lines connect with a more complicated shape, and a larger value makes the connection with a simpler shape:

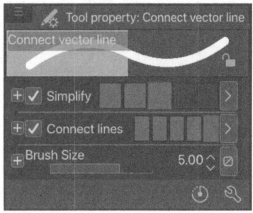

Figure 10.13: Screenshot of the Connect vector line sub-tool properties

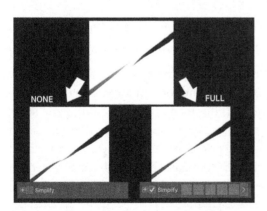

Figure 10.14: Screenshot of the Connect vector sub-tool's Simplify property

- **Connect lines:** This option, when activated, connects overlapping lines into a single one. The larger the value, the more lines can be connected. Be careful not to set this value too high, otherwise some unintended connections might happen.

- **Brush Size:** This sets the size of the brush.

Phew, seems like those were a lot of options to take in! But you can now move, add, erase, and simplify control points, and you can even change line width without having to redraw the line again and again. Because they're vectors, your lines also won't lose quality when you increase the size of the canvas. So, now you're familiar with the **Pinch vector line**, **Control point**, **Correct line width**, **Redraw vector line**, **Connect vector line**, and **Redraw vector line width** tools, and know how they work!

Did you make a mistake or just want to hide parts of a vector line? No problem, read on to find out how to erase a vector line.

Using the Vector eraser tool

Back in *Chapter 6, Erasers, Selections, and the Sub View Palette*, I mentioned that we would talk about the **Vector eraser** in a later chapter. Now, that time has arrived!

The **Vector eraser** can be used just like a regular eraser, but it also has some settings that turn it into an incredible time-saving device when working with vectors. Let's take a closer look at these settings now, as shown in the following screenshot:

Figure 10.15: Screenshot of the Vector eraser tool properties

Take special note of the **Vector eraser** section of the **Tool property** palette. This special setting is what makes the **Vector eraser** tool so special among the other eraser tools. In the screenshot on the left, we can see three icons, each accompanied by a black and blue + sign. These icons are **Erase touched areas**,

Figure 10.16: Screenshot of Erase touched areas icon

Erase up to intersection,

Figure 10.17: Screenshot of Erase up to intersection icon

and **Whole line.**

Figure 10.18: Screenshot of Erase Whole line icon

To illustrate what each of these settings does, a simple grid of straight lines on a vector layer will assist us.

The **Erase touched areas** option will erase only what is gone over with the tool, just like any of the other eraser tools will do normally. In the following screenshot, this setting was used, and then a stroke was taken down through the grid of lines with it. Only the sections of the lines that the tool passed through were erased:

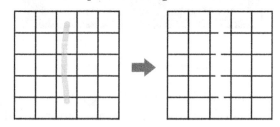

Figure 10.19: Erase touched areas action

Using the **Erase up to intersection** option allows us to clean up a grid of lines quickly and easily.

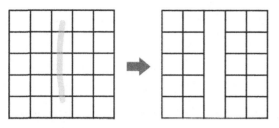

Figure 10.20: An action with Erase up to intersection

This setting will erase the vector line up to the point where it intersects with another vector line. In the screenshot on the left, it was used to make one stroke down through the third column of the grid. Note that, unlike the previous option, all of the horizontal lines from that section have disappeared, despite the fact that the tool only moved through the center of the lines in the column:

This setting can be used to quickly clean up the edges of the grid in the preceding screenshot. One swipe around the edges of the grid of squares and stray lines are erased entirely, up to where they intersect with other vector lines, as shown in the screenshot on the right:

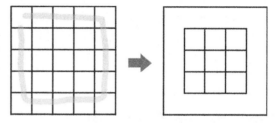

Figure 10.21: Another action with Erase up to intersection

Instead of tediously erasing the ends of the lines and trying desperately to get them perfect, the **Erase up to intersection** tool does it for you with one stroke. You can utilize it in your art, such as on strokes on fringes of hair and lines on face outlines, as in the sample art on the left:

Figure 10.22: Erase up to intersection used on art

The **Whole line** setting will erase the entirety of the vector line that is clicked on, no matter how small of a brush size the eraser tool is set to. In the screenshot on the right, this setting was used on two horizontal grid lines to make a set of rectangles instead of squares:

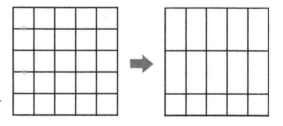

Figure 10.23: The Whole line action

Need to draw windows on the side of a building quickly? Create a vector layer. Draw a grid of vector lines in perspective with the building, then use the vector eraser to quickly clean up the edges of the grid and put spaces between the windows with the **Erase up to intersection** setting!

Aren't these options useful? They will save a lot of your precious time in making your drawings look neat.

Let's move on to how to save your precious art to use again later. It's like a drawer in an art studio, keeping art materials for later use again and again, whenever you need them!

Summary

In this chapter, we started off by getting familiar with vectors. We learned what a vector is and how vectors in Clip Studio Paint differ from vectors in other programs. We learned how to create a vector layer and how to draw on it with both the direct drawing tools and the brush tools. Finally, we learned about the different tools we can use to fine-tune our vector drawings.

You now know how to use raster and vector layers. Did you know that you can also create your own sound effects in Clip Studio Paint? In the next chapter, we'll learn about editing, modifying, coloring, and wrapping up text, while also getting creative by adding sound effects.

Join us on Discord!

Read this book alongside other users. Ask questions, provide solutions to other readers, and much more.

Scan the QR code or visit the link to join the community.

`https://packt.link/clipstudiopaint`

11

Creating Your Own Sound Effects

Making sound effects for manga is an art form in and of itself. It takes a lot of work and skill to turn sound into text! The letters that you choose to represent a sound are important, but so are the font, the colors, and even whether you choose to distort those letters for emphasis.

In this chapter, we will cover the following topics:

- Adding sound effects in speech balloons and how to group sound effect layers
- Using fonts for sound effects by adding color and lines to fonts
- Hand lettering and using the Mesh Transformation tool to warp text
- Making eye-grabbing titles

By the end of this chapter, you'll have learned how to user your skills in handling fonts, adding color, adding effects, distorting fonts into the shape you desire with the Mesh Transformation tool, and hand lettering to create the most dramatic sound effects and titles for your manga.

Let's dive right into these tools!

Technical requirements

To get started, you need Clip Studio Paint already installed on your device, and a new canvas opened with a white paper layer. Any size is fine, but I recommend creating a 300 dpi square canvas to go through the content in this chapter.

Adding sound effects in speech balloons

Sound effects are a part of art in manga. Manga readers encounter tons of them with and without noticing while reading through stories. It's not just about choosing the right word; there is creative space for sound effects, expressing the sharpness, loudness, and heaviness of sounds.

Most of the time, I add them in handwriting, because in that way the sound effects naturally blend into my art. If you look at the **India ink** subcategory in the **Brush** tools, there are good organic-feeling brushes, such as the **Bit husky** brush.

When you write a sound expressing solid objects being crushed, it would be better to turn **Stabilization** and **Post correction** on and set them to strong in the **Correction** setting to have good, clean straight lines.

It's good to remember that artistic writing still needs to be legible and placed close to the object that is making the sound. If you write sound effects on a separate layer, it will save a lot of time when you want to edit them later, such as changing the color or shape, picking a different sound effect, or even translating to another language! *Figure 11.1* shows a few examples of handwritten sound effects.

Figure 11.1: Various handwritten sound effects

Of course, this is not the only way to add them to your manga. You can also handle sound effects using speech balloons. You can apply this for popping, beeping, whispering, and shouting sounds. You can find out more about speech balloons in *Chapter 7, Using Text and Balloon Tools*.

Follow these steps to create a sound effect with a balloon:

1. Open a canvas and sketch your idea of a sound balloon with any drawing tool.
2. Click the **layer color** icon in the **Layer Property** palette to turn the sketch color to blue.
3. Create a new vector layer on top of the pencil drawing layer by clicking the **Create new vector layer** icon, select the **Felt pen** sub-tool from the **Marker** tool group, and trace your sound effect text in the vector layer as in *Figure 11.2*.
4. Since it's on a vector layer, you can correct the text to the exact shape you want by using **Correct line** tools. For more details on vector line editing, go to *Chapter 10, Exploring Vector Layers*. In *Figure 11.3*, the control points of the line stroke are visible for correcting.

Figure 11.2: Handwritten sound

5. Once you're satisfied with the shape of the sound text, select the **Ellipse balloon** sub-tool from the **Text** tool group, and then click on the canvas and drag to create a balloon that is big enough to cover all the text. Do not panic if the balloon hides the text – you can always move the balloon layer underneath the text layer after creating the balloon.

6. Select the **Balloon tail** sub-tool from the **Text** tool group, click on the canvas, and then drag your mouse or stylus to get the desired size for your balloon tail. You can always resize and adjust the position of the text, the balloon,

Figure 11.3: Control points on the vector image

and the balloon tail using the **Object** sub-tool from the **Operation** tool group. Try rotating the tail to aim it in a direction where the edge of the tail is pointing at the object that is the source of the sound. *Figure 11.4* shows a control handle and points for correction, which appear when you click on the canvas with the **Object** sub-tool.

This is a very easy and effective way to add sound effects. You can apply the method for various other sounds, too. But you might have noticed that you have too many layers for dialogs and sound effects in your **Layer** palette. You can organize them before losing the important sound effects layer in the chaos.

Grouping layers of sound effects and speech balloons

There are ways to organize your cluttered **Layer** palette. They are using a layer folder to group them, giving them a unique name, and adding color marks to a layer. You can always go

Figure 11.4: Control handle and points

back to *Chapter 3, Penciling: Layer and Layer Property Palettes*, for a reminder on layers and how to use the layer palette.

Follow these steps to declutter your sound effect and speech balloon layers:

1. While pressing the *Shift* key, click on multiple layers to select them. In this tutorial, select the layer that contains the writing and the layer that contains the speech balloon you just made in the previous section.

2. In the **File** menu, click **Layer | Create folder and insert layer**, as you can see in *Figure 11.5*.

Figure 11.5: Layer drop-down menu

3. Now, your selected layers are grouped in one folder in the **Layer** palette. Double-click on the folder name, which is currently displayed as **Folder 1**, then type a unique name for the folder. Press *Enter* to confirm the name.

4. With the folder you have just named still selected, click the square-shaped **layer color** icon in the **Layer** palette. The color variation drop-down menu will be displayed as in *Figure 11.6*.

5. Click on a color of your choice and the folder will automatically display a mark with the color on the **Layer** palette. You can repeat *Steps 1-5* every time you create sound effects. You can group layer folders in the same way as you have done with other layers. *Figure 11.7* shows a color-coordinated **Layer** palette.

Figure 11.6: Layer color drop-down menu

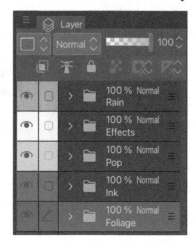

Figure 11.7: Colored layers in the Layer palette

Isn't your **Layer** palette much more organized and isn't it easy to find a particular layer at a glance? In this way, you can move layers that are combining similar sound effects together, but still be able to edit them separately.

You don't have to necessarily write the sound effect text yourself; there are huge amounts of ready-made fonts available. Read on to find out how to use them for sound effects.

Using fonts for sound effects

The easiest way to make sound effects is to use fonts, especially when you can't create sound effects exactly how you want yourself – especially when you can't create sound effects as professional looking as you want yourself. Don't worry, there are tons of great fonts available on the website, and some of them are free to use! Many specialty fonts exist that are perfect for creating the feeling of explosions, cracking, gunfire, and more. Let's see how to add fonts.

Important note

Some great resources for these types of fonts are www.blambot.com and www.1001freefonts.com, but be sure to check the terms of use for any free font that you download! Some free font creators do not allow their fonts to be used in commercial projects, so if you're making a comic to sell, you need to be certain you are not breaking any copyright laws!

After downloading a new font and installing it on your computer, you may need to shut down Clip Studio Paint and restart the program in order to get the font to appear in the font list in the **Text** tool. Once it appears in the font list, you can use the instructions in *Chapter 7, Using Text and Balloon Tools*, to lay out your basic text.

If you love collecting new fonts for every occasion that you can think of, the font list can get a little confusing and overwhelming. It can take a lot of time to find that specific font you downloaded last February for just this specific panel you knew was coming up in your script!

This is when it's hard to change how the font list is displayed in Clip Studio Paint. Click on the **Font** drop-down menu in the **Tool property** panel when the **Text** tool is active. An example of the font list is shown right, in *Figure 11.8*.

Figure 11.8: Font drop-down menu

At the bottom of the font list, on the left-hand side, there are three icons that control how the font list is displayed. The first-left icon is the **display font name icon**, shown below in *Figure 11.9*. It shows the font list in the default font of Clip Studio Paint's user interface.

The second icon is **display font name in specific font icon**, which is the option shown right, in *Figure 11.10*. Each font name is displayed in that particular font, making them easy to identify.

Figure 11.9: Display font name option

Figure 11.10: Display font name in specific font option

The third icon is **display text in specific font icon**, shown right, and it will use the currently selected text to display the font name. This is especially handy when doing sound effects because you can type out your letters and then see the way those letters will look in all the fonts that you have!

Figure 11.12 presents an explosion sound effect that has been typed in the Badaboom Pro BB font.

Figure 11.11: Display text in specific font option

This is a perfectly acceptable sound effect for an explosion, but what if we want to really make it pop and add some color? Read on to find out how!

Figure 11.12: Text in the Badaboom Pro BB font

Adding outlines, gradients, and patterns to text

Now that you know how to make your font appear in your font list, and you have text on your canvas, we can start manipulating text to make it more unique or more visually interesting.

Of course, you can select a color other than black or white for your text while entering it, but what if you want to apply a gradient, a texture, or create an outline for the text to make it pop off the page? In this section, we'll cover those exact topics! All of these are easy effects to accomplish with just a few button clicks and some tricks in the **Layer** and **Layer Property** palettes.

Adding an outline

This technique works for anything on a layer that you may want to add an outline to, not just text. Here, we'll use our **BOOM!** sound effect as an example. It's very easy to create an outline in Clip Studio Paint using the **Layer Property** palette.

Follow these easy steps to add an outline to the contents of a layer. In this case, we're using a text sound effect:

1.   Ensure that your text layer is the currently active layer by checking that it is selected in the **Layer** palette.

2. Locate the **Layer Property** palette. If you cannot locate it, ensure that there is a checkmark next to **Layer Property** in the **Window** menu.

3. In the **Layer Property** palette, locate the **Effect** section of the settings. Click on the **Border effect** icon to show the options that are shown in *Figure 11.13*.

4. Use the slider or the arrows next to the **Thickness of edges** option to set the width of the outline.

5. Click on the box next to **Edge color** to set the color for the outline from the color picker.

Figure 11.14 shows our sound effect from the previous section, with the font color set to white and with a black outline around it.

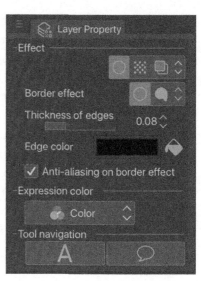

Figure 11.13: Layer Property palette

Figure 11.14: Text with an outline

Creating an outline with the **Border effect** options allows the outline to be edited later, so if you decide to make your outline a different color or to make the border thicker or thinner, simply select the layer again and change the settings in the **Layer Property** palette! There's no need to recreate your entire text layer from scratch!

Let's move on to using gradient color for your text.

Adding gradients to text with Lock Transparent Pixels

A great way to add a real punch to sound effects is to add a gradient. This can help your effect pop off the page when used correctly. Again, we can do this in just a few clicks! The following steps show you how to create a copy of a layer, rasterize it, and add a gradient:

1. Ensure that your text layer is active by locating it in the **Layer** palette and clicking on it to highlight it.

2. In the **File** menu, click on **Layer**, and then click on **Duplicate Layer** to create a copy of the text layer. Alternatively, you can also click on the layer in the **Layer** palette and drag it to the **new layer** icon to create a copy of the layer.

Figure 11.15: New layer icon

3. Click on the eye-shaped icon of the original layer to make it invisible on the canvas. Select the copied layer, then click on **Layer** in the **File** menu, and then click on **Rasterize** to convert the layer to raster.

4. In the **Layer** palette, click on the icon labeled **Lock Transparent Pixels**. This will allow us to apply our effects only to the filled pixels in the layer. The **Layer** palette with the **Lock Transparent Pixels** icon selected is shown in *Figure 11.16*.

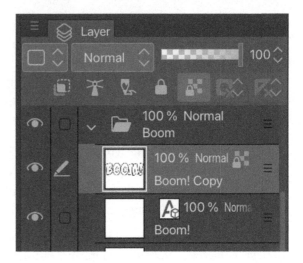

Figure 11.16: Lock Transparent Pixels icon selected

5. Select the **Gradient** category of tools in the toolbar and then select one of the **Gradient** sub-tools. Click on the canvas and drag it to apply the gradient to the text.

6. In the **Layer Property** palette, add the **Border effect** option to give an outline to your sound effect, if desired. In *Figure 11.17*, the Clip Studio Paint **Sunset Glow** preset gradient was used to give the sound effect a fiery look, and then a black outline was added to make the sound effect stand out:

Aside from using presets, you can also make gradients yourself by picking the appropriate colors, setting them as the foreground and background color, then selecting **Foreground to Background** in the **Gradient** sub-tool category.

Figure 11.17: Text with a gradient effect

Tip

When a text layer is rasterized, it becomes pixels that cannot be edited with the **Text** tools. If you need to rasterize text to apply an effect, it is recommended that you make a copy of the text layer and rasterize the copy so that you can go back to the original text if changes need to be made.

Great, now you have added a color, an outline, and even a gradient effect to your text! The text appears so dramatic. You can even go further by adding patterns. Read on to learn how.

Using clipping layers to add patterns to text

For extra-special sound effects, you may want to add a pattern to your text to add emphasis. This is where clipping layers come in handy. A clipping layer is a layer that clips to the layer below it, only showing the contents of the top layer in places where the bottom layer has pixels filled in.

Clipping layers are useful in all sorts of situations, but we'll create a striking sound effect in our example of how to use them.

Follow these steps to create a sound effect with a color pattern from the **Material** palette applied over it:

1. Ensure that your text layer is active by locating it in the **Layer** palette and clicking on it to highlight it.

2. In the **File** menu, click on **Layer**, and then click on **Duplicate Layer** to create a copy of the text layer. Alternatively, you can also click on the layer in the **Layer** palette and drag it to the **new layer** icon to create a copy of the layer.

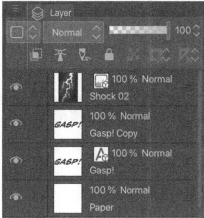

3. Click on the eye-shaped icon of the original layer to make it invisible on the canvas. Select the copied layer, then click on **Layer** in the **File** menu, and then click on **Rasterize** to convert the layer to raster.

4. Open the **Material** palette and select a pattern from the **Color Pattern** category to add to the text. For more information on using materials, see *Chapter 9, Material Palette and Inking Special Effects*.

5. The pattern of the material may be pasted in a layer below the rasterized text layer. Click and drag the layer in the **Layer** palette above the rasterized text layer. Your **Layer** palette should look something like what's shown in *Figure 11.18*.

Figure 11.18: Layer palette

6. In the **File** menu, click on **Layer**, then go to **Layer Settings**, and click on **Clip to Layer Below**. Alternatively, you can right-click on the pattern layer in the **Layer** palette and go to **Layer Settings**, then click on **Clip to Layer Below**, as shown in *Figure 11.19*.

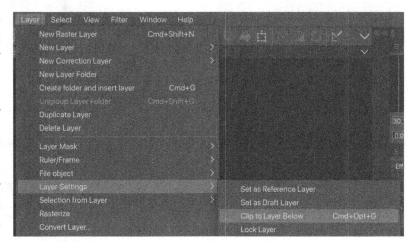

Figure 11.19: Layer drop-down menu

7. The pattern will now only be shown on the contents of the layer below it. The clipping layer is marked in the **Layer** palette by a red marker next to the layer thumbnail, which is next to the **Shock 02** layer, as shown in *Figure 11.20*.

8. To add an outline to the sound effect, follow the instructions in the *Adding an outline* section of this chapter, but apply it to the original text layer at the bottom of the stack. This will produce a sound effect along with the original text layer, as shown in *Figure 11.21*.

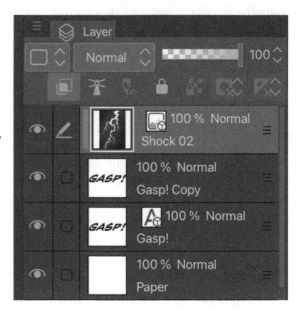

Figure 11.20: Layer palette with a layer mask on

Figure 11.21: Text with patterns

The text now has a strong impression of the lightning pattern. You can add any pattern you like with the same method. Next, we will create perspectives or flow on sound effects by using the **Mesh Transformation** tool.

Using the Mesh Transformation tool to warp text

Lots of sound effects in manga and comics follow curves or lines of action to emphasize the art on the page. In *Figure 11.22*, the sound effect for the explosion is angled and shaped to emphasize the action.

Though you can hand-draw sound effects like this if you want to (and hand-lettering is a great skill to have), you can also create curved and warped text using the **Mesh Transformation** tool just the same as we can use the tool on any hand-drawn text.

Figure 11.22: Transformed text

Follow these steps to create a warped sound effect:

1. Ensure that your text layer is active by locating it in the **Layer** palette and clicking on it to highlight it.

2. In the **File** menu, click on **Layer**, and then click on **Duplicate Layer** to create a copy of the text layer. Alternatively, you can also click on the layer in the **Layer** palette and drag it to the **new layer** icon to create a copy of the layer.

3. With the layer copy selected and the original text layer not visible, click on **Layer** in the **File** menu and then click on **Rasterize** to convert the layer to raster.

4. In the **File** menu, click on **Edit**, then go down to **Transform**, and click on **Mesh Transformation.**

   A grid of lines and points will appear over the layer contents.

5. In the **Tool property** palette, check the **Number of horizontal lattice points** and **Number of vertical lattice points** options. These both default to **4** points. For more fine control over the distortion of the text, make the number of lattice points higher. This must be done before you start moving any of the points around. The option to add more points will disappear after you start distorting the mesh! In *Figure 11.23*, the number of horizontal points has been increased to **6** to accommodate for the longer length of the sound effect.

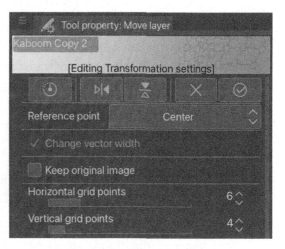

Figure 11.23: Part of the Mesh Transformation tool properties

6. Click on the points at the intersections of the grid and drag them to distort the sound effect. The areas around the moved point will shift and distort as the points are moved, as shown in *Figure 11.24*.

Figure 11.24: Mesh Transformation grid on text

Figure 11.25: Mesh Transformation grid on text 2

7. Continue moving the points around to reshape the contents of the mesh. In *Figure 11.25*, a curved effect has been created by staggering the control points.

8. Click on **OK** to commit the transformation. The final sound effect we've created in this example is shown in *Figure 11.26*.

Figure 11.26: Transformed text

Tip

Mesh transformation isn't just for sound effects! It can also be used on pattern materials to create more realistic clothing patterns. What will you use Mesh Transformation for?

It's even more useful to know a bit more about mesh transformation. Here, if you take a look at *Figure 11.27*, showing the rest of the **Mesh Transformation** tool property palette, you'll notice there are many ways to select grids to transform some areas together:

*   **Select grid points (tap)**: With this, you can choose the selection mode when tapping over grid points. The **New selection** mode selects points when tapped, the **Add to selection** mode adds points to the selection when tapped, the **Remove selection** mode deselects points when tapped, and the **Toggle selection** mode switches selection status.

*   **Select grid points (drag)**: This is only activated when **Select grid points** is on for **Drag mode**. This can choose the selection mode when dragging

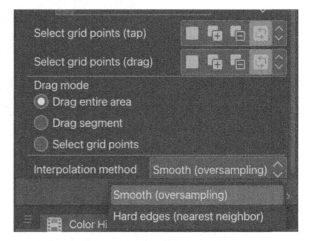

Figure 11.27: Mesh Transformation Tool property

over grid points. The **New selection** mode selects points when dragged over, the **Add to selection** mode adds points to the selection when dragged over, the **Remove selection** mode deselects points when dragged over, and the **Toggle selection** mode switches selection status.

*   **Drag mode**: With this, you can choose what happens when you drag over the area. **Drag entire area** moves the entire transformation area and **Drag segment** moves only the area within selected grid points, as in *Figure 11.28*.

Figure 11.28: Drag segment option sample

- **Select grid points** behaves as above regardless of what the **Select grid points (drag)** mode is. *Figure 11.29* shows four grid points are selected and highlighted with control handles and dragged along together.

Figure 11.29: Select grid points option sample

- **Interpolation method: Smooth (oversampling)** blends the colors of adjacent pixels and makes smooth edges. **Hard edges (nearest neighbor)** creates sharper lines without blending the colors of adjacent pixels. In *Figure 11.30*, the left *h* is transformed in the **Smooth (oversampling)** setting, and the right *h* is transformed in the **Hard edges (nearest neighbor)** setting.

Figure 11.30: Smooth and Hard edges setting samples

It was such a fun process transforming text with the *Mesh Transformation* tool! It gives text a unique charm and helps create drama on a manga page. Now, you know this function is not only for drawings but can be applied to text, too! Have a great, creative time when you add sound effects to your manga next time!

You can also be creative with manga title text with methods you learned in this chapter!

Making titles

We are going to look at some possibilities for creating title text by using methods we have just learned in this chapter. The title text is not only for telling us what the manga is called but also for showing the feeling and tone of the content, such as thriller, horror, romance, comedy, fashion, or tragedy. Let's have a look at the potential of title texts.

Figure 11.31 shows a title for a light-hearted manga story. I used a ready-made font and added a vector cloud drawing, then finally gave them the same color. The cloud shape is placed like a crown on top of the title, to emphasize the theme "sky." That's also the reason for the blue color.

Figure 11.31: Fluffy Sky title text

Figure 11.32: State of Emergency title text

Figure 11.32 shows the second example, which is a title for a science fiction, horror manga. I used a ready-made font and then fading, scratching, and dripping textures were added using ink tools. There is only a white color on a black background to emphasize the darkness of the story.

Figure 11.33 presents our third example of a thrilling adventure manga. The main content is strictly night scenes. With the color white, I created a handwritten title with the **Brush** tools, then added a spattering effect with star and crescent shapes on a navy-colored background, to depict a night scene. Finally, using the **Soft Airbrush** sub-tool, I sprayed the color gold around the center of the title on a new clipping layer. You can find more on clipping layers in *Chapter 12, Making Layer Masks and Screentones*.

Figure 11.33: Midnight title text

Figure 11.34 shows our final example, a title for a romantic comedy manga. A ready-made font is warped by the **Mesh Transformation** tool to create a slight perspective effect, which you can find in the preceding section of this chapter, *Using the Mesh Transformation tool to warp text*. Outlines are added with the layer property **effects** setting, then a rainbow color gradation is created by using the **Soft Airbrush** sub-tool on a new clipping layer. The vector pen and clapperboard drawings were created on a layer underneath the title. On the background, a downloaded flower and butterfly pattern was added by using the **Decoration** tool. Then, finally, it was partially colored with white by using the **Brush** tool on a new clipping layer with a layer mask setting.

You can find more on layer masks in *Chapter 12, Making Layer Masks and Screentones*.

Each of the title texts shows its own unique feeling and tone, depicting vaguely what the content is about.

You can be very creative with your own title text design with the methods we learned in this chapter!

Figure 11.34: The Writer & The Actor title text

Summary

In this concise chapter, we have explored ways to create sound effects. We have used specialized fonts to make sound effects and have learned how to make those fonts more punchy with outlines and gradient effects. We used clipping layers to add a pattern to a sound effect and learned about mesh transformation to distort and curve our sound effects. Finally, we looked at various title text artworks using some of the techniques we learned, such as downloading fonts, using the Mesh Transformation tool, and using clipping masks.

If you are wondering which sound effects to add to your manga, here is a useful resource: `https://www.writtensound.com/index.php`. It's fun to learn some more words you can use!

In the next chapter, we will explore the wonderful world of masks. Not masks for costumes, but layer masks! Read on to learn more about this feature of Clip Studio Paint.

Join us on Discord!

Read this book alongside other users. Ask questions, provide solutions to other readers, and much more.

Scan the QR code or visit the link to join the community.

`https://packt.link/clipstudiopaint`

12

Making Layer Masks and Screentones

In traditional painting, you might use masking tape to cover up the parts of the piece that you shouldn't touch, so that you can go crazy with your brush. There is a similar function in digital drawing, too! The layer mask is an extremely useful feature in digital art that has many applications. Thanks to the function, we can concentrate on drawing without caring too much about pen strokes going over boundaries.

We will also look at screentones; they are used less and less in modern printing but are still quite popular in black-and-white manga printing because they have their own beauty. You can use screentones together with a layer mask to create a nice shading effect for your manga art.

We are also going to learn about using screentones with clipping layers, which have a different masking effect from layer masks.

In this chapter, we will learn about the following topics:

- What is a layer mask?
- Using a layer mask
- Adding screentones
- Using a clipping layer

By the end of this chapter, you will know more about the benefits of digital drawing. You will be able to work on each part of a drawing tactically by using layer masks, screentones, and clipping layers.

Let's dive right in!

Technical requirements

To get started, you need Clip Studio Paint installed on your device and a new canvas open with a white paper layer and a layer with any art. Any size is fine, but I recommend creating a 300 dpi square canvas to go through the content in this chapter.

What is a layer mask?

A layer mask is a feature of digital art that allows parts of a layer to be hidden without being erased for good. This allows us to fine-tune a drawing or part of a drawing without losing what has already been done. Layer masks can be adjusted over and over, hiding parts of a drawing and then being removed again to bring those parts back.

A good way to think about a layer mask is as being like a Halloween mask. Putting a mask on your face conceals your real face. Take the mask off, and your face is visible again.

Unlike the case when using eraser tools, layer masks are not permanent and allow changes to be made without losing any data. We can see what a character looks like with a different hairstyle or temporarily hide parts of a background, for example. The best thing is that layer masks are easy to use and edit! In the next section, we will see how to use a layer mask.

Using a layer mask

In order to make a layer mask, you will need a canvas open with one layer and some sort of content on it. This could be a sketch, an ink drawing, a photo, or anything else you desire, so long as there is some sort of content to mask out so that we can see how the layer mask works.

Follow these steps to create a layer mask and hide and restore content:

1. Select the layer to add the mask to by clicking on it in the **Layer** palette.

2. Click on the **create layer mask** icon in the **Layer** palette. This icon is shown by the arrow in *Figure 12.1*.

Figure 12.1: Layer palette

A new thumbnail will appear to the right of the layer thumbnail in the **Layer** palette. This is the layer mask. When the layer mask is selected, a secondary outline will appear around the layer mask thumbnail. *Figure 12.2* shows a piece of art and a corresponding layer of the skirt color with a selected layer mask:

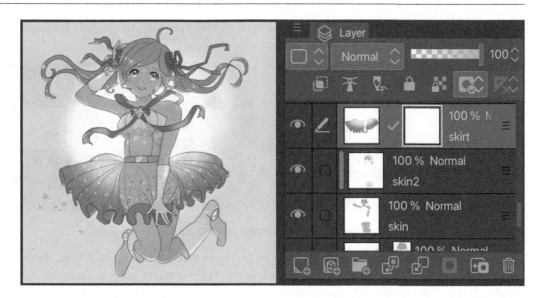

Figure 12.2: Image and the Layer palette with a layer mask

3. To hide the content on the layer, select the **Eraser** sub-tool. Erase the section of the layer that needs to be hidden. The masked area will show up in the layer thumbnail as blacked-out space. We can use this function to erase more skirt colors without losing them permanently. Because the masked area is still there, it can be unmasked at any time. We can use this great function to show elements on other layers better, but when we change the layout of the art, we can reveal the masked part again, so we don't need to redraw that part of the art all over again! *Figure 12.3* shows the black area where the skirt color layer has been masked.

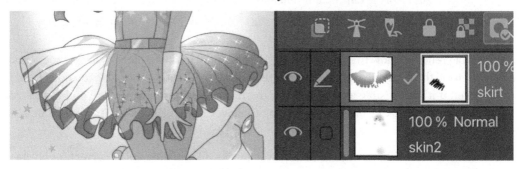

Figure 12.3: Image that is partially masked

4. To make masked content visible again, select any pen or brush tool. Draw over the masked area again with the tool to show the masked content.

Figure 12.4 shows that the middle of the masked area has been shown again because the area inside of the black mask is white again.

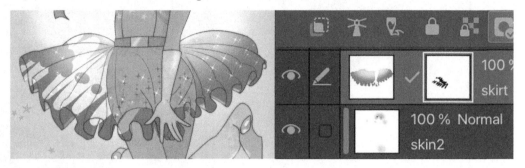

Figure 12.4: Image that is partially masked (continued)

If you are having trouble editing a layer mask or the layer that a mask is attached to, double-check the **Layer** palette to ensure that the layer mask or the layer is selected before moving on to other troubleshooting. Sometimes, the layer can be selected instead of the layer mask, or vice versa, which can have undesired results.

Tip

Want a part of your drawing to have a ghostly or faded look? Use the **Soft Eraser** or **Airbrush** tool with the translucent color on a layer mask to fade out the edges of the drawing. To select the translucent color, click the checkerboard pattern square underneath the two squares that show the currently selected foreground and background colors at the bottom of the Clip Studio Paint interface. By using the translucent color, you can turn any drawing tool into an eraser.

Isn't it a big relief to know that there is a way to hide some part of a piece of art without erasing it, in case you need the hidden part again later in the process of creating your art? You don't need to worry at all, even if it's not visible at the moment; the masked part is always there and can be recovered when you want it back by either deactivating the layer mask or deleting it. Something is only ever masked temporarily!

Figure 12.5 shows brilliant ways of using layer masks, like adding color correction layers, such as **Multiply** or **Overlay**, only on a character drawing, hiding parts of a hand fan/sword/gun/umbrella under a holding hand, and changing a hairstyle.

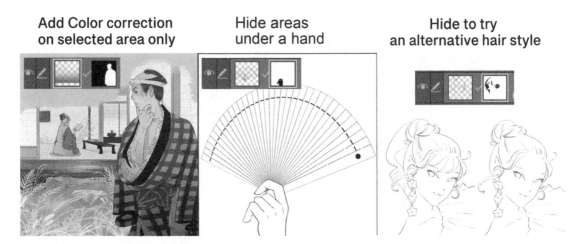

Figure 12.5: Three images that are partially masked

Let's look at a different way of hiding parts of an artwork!

Creating quick masks using selection tools

Layer masks can be created quickly by using the **selection** tools to select the areas of the drawing we want to hide and then adding the mask using active selection.

We covered a multitude of ways to make selections in *Chapter 6, Erasers, Selections, and the Sub View Palette*, so if you need a refresher on making selections, now is a great time to go back and review that chapter before continuing with using a selection to make a quick layer mask.

Once you've familiarized yourself with the **selection** tools, follow these steps to create a layer mask quickly:

1. First, make a selection using one of the **selection** tools. In *Figure 12.6*, the lasso marquee tool has been used to make a selection around the character's ribbon on the ribbon color layer.

Figure 12.6: Image with a selected area

2. In the **File** menu, click on **Layer**, then navigate to **Layer Mask** and click on **Mask Selection**. This path is shown in *Figure 12.7*.

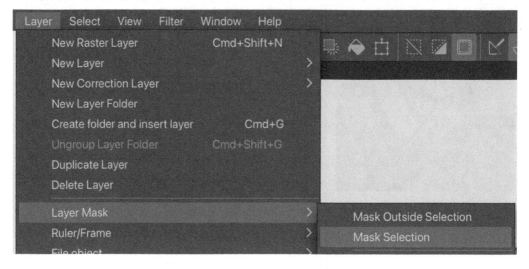

Figure 12.7: Layer drop-down menu

Using this method, the area inside the selection will be masked but everything outside of the selection will be visible. In *Figure 12.8*, the selected colored part on the ribbon is now hidden by the layer mask.

Figure 12.8: Image with a masked area

3. To mask everything outside of the selection, in the **File** menu, click on **Layer**, then navigate to **Layer Mask** and click on **Mask Outside Selection**. In *Figure 12.9*, all clothing color is gone except the end of the character's ribbon, because it was inside of the selection and so has not been masked.

Figure 12.9: Image with a masked area (continued)

Make any necessary edits to the mask, such as adding more masked parts using the erasing tool and an unmasked back with the pen or brush tool, as detailed in the *Using a layer mask* section of this chapter.

The Mask Outside Selection option works well when we want to hide the majority of the content but

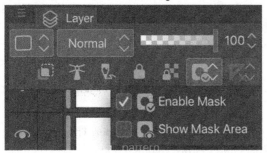

leave a tiny, complicated shape hidden, such as a clothing pattern on only a part of clothing –the very end of the skirt perhaps, or ribbons. Of course, we can add shade or lighting to a limited area in the same way.

Figure 12.10: Mask drop-down options

If you want to deactivate the mask temporarily, click on the **Mask** drop-down menu in the **Layer** palette and uncheck the box next to the **Enable Mask** option icon to deselect it, as you can see in *Figure 12.10*.

To delete the layer mask, go to the **File** menu and click **Layer | Layer Mask | Delete Mask**, as shown in *Figure 12.11*.

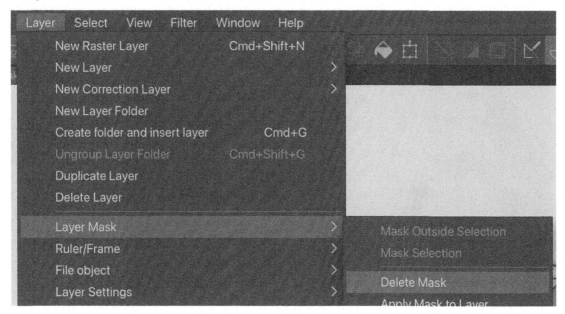

Figure 12.11: Layer drop-down menu

Tip

Want to mask everything outside of the selection quickly? Make your selection and then click on the **create layer mask** icon in the **Layer** palette. A mask will automatically be generated for the outside of the selection.

Using the selection tools allows us to make masks more quickly and easily. Rather than having to go over large areas with the eraser tools, instead, we can make a simple selection and create a layer mask for that selection with the click of a button. What a time-saver!

We have been looking at how to use layer masks using erasers and selection tools. Now, let's move on to find out about screentones and how we can use them with a layer mask!

Adding screentones

We're looking into how to use screentones with a layer mask to control shades of black and white for a manga.

In the old days, printers could only print black ink writing and drawings on paper. This meant that older printed illustrations didn't have gray tones. Artists had to draw detailed dots and line patterns using black ink in order to express gray tones for printing. But it's time consuming to do that! To make the process faster, people invented screentones.

Screentones, or halftones, are made of a pattern of dots that provide shading. Back in the days before digital art, these tones would be printed on a big sheet of sticky-backed plastic. Artists would apply this large, clear sticker over their art and then carefully use a sharp knife to cut out the areas that didn't need tone on them and peel away the excess. The downsides to this method were that you had to keep buying new screentone sheets and that, sometimes, a careless stroke would cut through your original artwork and ruin it!

But now, we can mimic these patterns of dots digitally. And, thanks to layer masks, we can simply mask out the areas that don't need to be shaded without doing any damage to the screentone pattern or our original sketch. This makes the screentone process easier and less stressful than it used to be!

Figure 12.12 is an example of using digital screentones. Note that the shadows are created using a pattern of circles that provide depth for the image.

Figure 12.12: Image with screentones

Follow these steps to add tone to a large area:

1. Open a new file. For this set of instructions, the size and resolution don't really matter.
2. Open the **Material** palette.
3. Open the folder under the **Monochromatic pattern** category in the **Material** palette by clicking on the arrow next to the folder name to view the contents beneath it.
4. Click on the arrow next to the **Basic** sub-folder to view the contents of that folder.
5. Click on the **Dot** sub-folder to view the materials located in this folder.
6. Select the desired screentone material to apply to the image. In this example, we are using the **50.0 LPI / 50% Circle Monochrome** material.

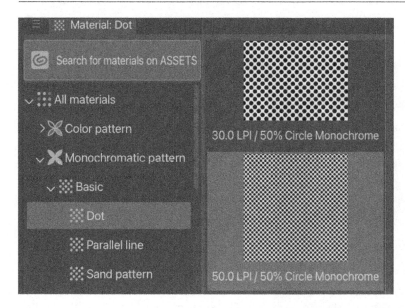

Figure 12.13: Material palette

7. Once you have selected the screentone material seen in the screenshot on the left, click on the **paste selected material to canvas** icon at the bottom of the **Material** palette, which looks like *Figure 12.14*.

Figure 12.14: Paste selected material to canvas icon

8. The tone material will be applied to the entire canvas, as shown in *Figure 12.15*.

Figure 12.15: Image with a screentone

9. The new **Material** layer will be made with an empty layer mask already attached to it. Use this layer mask to edit the screentone so that it only shows in the shadowed areas. *Figure 12.16* shows the drawing with screentone shadows.

Figure 12.16: Image with screentone shadows

You successfully added shades using **30.0 LPI / 50% Circle Monochrome** screentones! Brilliant! When dealing with a tiny area you need to add screentones to, there's a quick way to select and add screen tones, which we will cover in later sections.

But for now, are you wondering what the meaning of each screentone's name is? Let's find out more about that in the next section.

Lines and percentages in screentone names

Before we continue with our next method for adding tone to images, let's take a moment to understand the terminology used for the screentone names.

Figure 12.17 shows two of the tone materials in the palette.

Beneath each tone material is the name of the tone. We can break these names into four parts. Each of these parts of the name is detailed as follows:

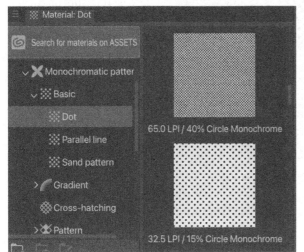

Figure 12.17: Types of screentones

1. **Screen frequency:** This is the number at the very beginning of each filename, appearing before *LPI* (line per inch). For example, in the first material in the figure on the left, the number for the screen frequency is **65.0**. This number refers to how many lines of the pattern are repeated in a set area. Much like DPI, the larger this number is, the smaller the overall shapes in the tone pattern will be. Compare the **65.0** thumbnail to the **32.5** one and note how much larger the circles are in the **32.5** example. The larger the number at the beginning of the material name, the smaller the dot pattern will be.

2. **Density:** This part of the name refers to the number with the percent sign shown in *Figure 12.17*. Density controls how dark the created shadow will appear to be. For example, a density of 10% would be a very light shadow, made of very small dots in the screentone pattern. However, a density of 95% would be made of very large black dots that might only have very small white gaps in the pattern because of the overlap. A density of 100% would be pure black. 50% density will provide a medium shadow in the completed artwork.

3. **Type:** This refers to the shape that the pattern is created from. Most commonly, screentones are made of solid circles. However, we can make tone patterns from many different shapes and symbols, as we will see in a later section. Each of the tones in the preceding figure uses the **Circle** type.

4. **Gradient style:** The tones in the preceding figure are of the **Monochrome** variety because they are located in the **Dot** screentone folder. This means that the tone has only one density and one screen frequency level throughout the entire tone. However, if we look in the **Gradient** folder instead of the **Dot** folder, we will find tones that have **Linear** and **Circular** gradients that fade from dark to light and back again in a pattern. These specialty tones can be used for effects or to get soft shading. In *Figure 12.18*, the gradient **60.0 LPI / 50% Circle Monochrome** was used to add the shading effect, and we can see the control handles, which means we can move and change the size of the circle.

Figure 12.18: Illustration with a Gradient screentone

Now that we know a bit more about the terminology of screentones, let's look at the fastest way to apply tones in Clip Studio Paint: the simple tone options.

Creating simple tones using selections

We can make a selection and then fill that selection with a customized tone, instead of using one that is already in the **Material** palette.

The following steps show how to add a screentone to a selection. You will need to have an open file ready to follow these steps:

1. Use the selection tool of your choice to make a selection.

2. Beneath the active selection in the command bar, click on the **new tone** icon. This is shown with an arrow pointing at it in *Figure 12.19*.

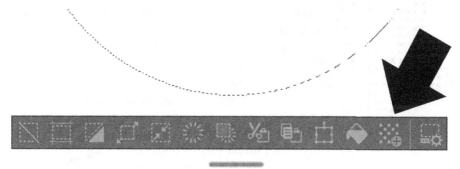

Figure 12.19: Command bar

3. Choose the desired settings from the **Simple tone settings** dialog box that will appear. Note that the **Frequency, Density,** and **Type** properties that we addressed earlier are also used in this dialog box's options. We can also adjust the angle of how the pattern is applied.

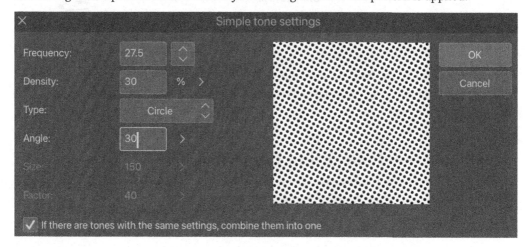

Figure 12.20: Simple tone settings dialog box

4. Click on **OK** to fill the selection with the new tone.

Tip

If you will be using the same simple tone settings in multiple selections, checking the **If there are tones with the same settings, combine them into one** option box will create all of those new tones on one layer. This can help save system resources and make layers easier to navigate.

I hope that you have started to understand more about how to handle screentones. Let's look at the variations for the shapes that create patterns of screentones!

Simple tone options

Let's talk for a moment about the different options available under the **Type** drop-down menu in the **Simple tone settings** dialog box. This allows us to choose shapes other than simple circles. These shapes include hearts, stars, asterisks, and flowers, among others. They can be used to create special effects in certain scenes, or just to provide a variety of tones. In *Figure 12.21*, the star shape has been made with the **Star** screentone.

The **Size** and **Factor** options in the **Simple tone settings** dialog box are only available when using the **Noise** option under the **Type** option. Using the **Noise** option makes the stars distort randomly; *Figure 12.22* is an example of the **Noise** screentone.

Figure 12.21: Star shape using the Star screentone

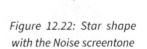

You can now select, paste, and edit screentones by using a selection tool, a layer mask, the **Material** palette, and the **Simple tone settings** dialog box!

Figure 12.22: Star shape with the Noise screentone

Creating screentones using Layer Property

There is also another incredibly easy way to add screentones to your art! With just one click on the **Layer Property** option, your drawing gets a screentone.

Follow these steps to learn how to do it:

1. Open a canvas that already contains some inking art. Create a new raster layer underneath, then use any drawing tool with any light-colored ink to fill in an area where you want to add a screentone.

2. Make sure the layer you have just drawn on is selected, then go to the **Layer Property** palette and click on the **Screentones** icon in the Effect options, which is pointed by an arrow in *Figure 12.23*.

Figure 12.23: Color-filled area and
the Effect options

3. Now, the colored area has become a screen-tone, as you can see in *Figure 12.24*.

Figure 12.24: Screentone settings
and the Layer Property options

4. But wait – the screentone now covers part of the character's jacket, which had a dark gray color but looks lighter now. That doesn't give the right shade for this character. You can fix this by clicking on the **Density** option on the **Layer Property** palette and selecting **Use brightness of image** from the **Density** drop-down menu, as shown in *Figure 12.25*.

Figure 12.25: Density drop-down
options

The jacket area is now shaded much better because the screentone's density has been adjusted for the brightness of the colors already on the canvas.

Alternatively, we can change the screentone layer's blending mode from **Normal** to **Multiply.** You can find out more about layer blending modes in the *Exploring layer blending modes* section in *Chapter 16, Using Clip Studio Paint to Color Your Manga*.

If you follow the same steps but fill an area with a dark color instead of a light one, the resultant screentone will be dense and dark, too!

When you use screentones incorrectly, your art can look bad, with the screentone shading for a character breaching the character's outline and intruding on the background. How can we fix this easily? Wouldn't it take too much time to adjust the screentones using eraser and pen tools here and there so that we don't go over the boundaries when we want screentones to stay inside the character's outline?

There is a good function to know for adding screentones to art right up to a boundary and no further. It is called the clipping layer function. It makes your shading very accurate! We'll look into this in the next section.

Using the clipping layer function

It's great to know that there is a clipping layer function for digital drawing when you are shading. A clipping layer is a layer that clips to the layer below it, only showing the contents of the top layer in places where the bottom layer has pixels filled in. It comes in handy when you want to add shading only inside a colored area.

I guarantee that you will find this feature very useful once you try it by following these steps:

1. Open your canvas and create a new raster layer with any inked art. Choose a light gray color from the **Color** palette and then use the **Fill** tool to fill with color any area that is enclosed by outlines.

2. Create a new raster layer *on top of the layer*, then use the **Soft Airbrush** tool with any dark color to paint an area where you want to add a screentone. Do not worry, as the color won't stay in the gray area; just add variations of thin and thick colors, something like *Figure 12.26*.

3. You can do this step from the **File** menu, too, but I'll show you the easiest way to create screentones from the **Layer** palette (in just one click). Make sure the layer with the airbrushed color is selected, go to the **Layer Property** palette, and click the **screentones** icon in the **Effect** options, shown with an arrow in *Figure 12.27*.

Figure 12.26: Airbrushed area

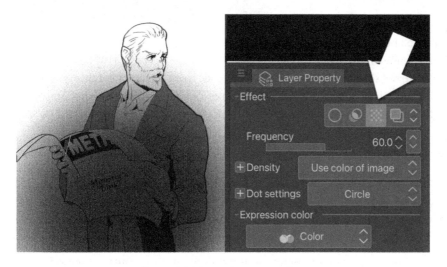

Figure 12.27: Layer Property options

4. As you can see in *Figure 12.27*, the airbrushed area has now turned into screentones. Click on the **clip to layer below** icon in the **Layer** palette, which is pointed to by a white arrow in *Figure 12.28*.

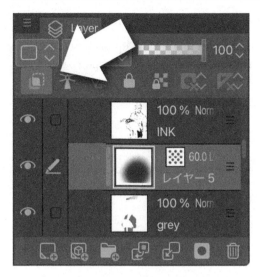

Figure 12.28: Clip to layer below icon

5. Once it's activated, the icon is highlighted in blue, and a pink line appears next to the clip layer thumbnail, as you can see in the figure on the left. The image now has screentones only on the gray area of the character's jacket, as shown in *Figure 12.29*.

Figure 12.29: Clipped screentones

Using clip layers, you can combine screentones and grayscale in some clever ways! You don't have to spend a lot of time using brush and eraser tools to make adjustments around the boundary edges to make sure your screentones neatly sit inside them.

In *Figure 12.30*, we have used screentones over flat gray fills to add more dimensions to the comic panel.

Figure 12.30: Image with grayscale and screentones

The clipping layer function is one of the huge advantages of digital drawing; you can use it with patterns, colors, shades, and screentones. Also, of course, you can use it in combination with a layer mask. You can activate it, deactivate it, and modify content anytime you want!

Summary

In this chapter, we learned what a layer mask is and how to create one. We also learned how to make a layer mask using selection tools to save time. We then learned about the benefits of using layer masks in comparison with eraser tools. We also used screentone materials and created simple tones by using selections and layer masks.

To finish off the chapter, we learned how to use a clipping layer to combine screentones with grayscale.

In the next chapter, we are going to learn all about the ruler tools that make Clip Studio Paint a truly powerful piece of art software. You won't worry about creating accurate angles and perspectives anymore. Keep reading to learn more!

Join us on Discord!

Read this book alongside other users. Ask questions, provide solutions to other readers, and much more.

Scan the QR code or visit the link to join the community.

`https://packt.link/clipstudiopaint`

13

All About Rulers

One of the handiest tools in an artist's toolbox is the humble ruler. Whether it's a regular straight ruler, a set square, or a set of French curves, rulers can really make a difference to your artwork.

Ruler tools in Clip Studio Paint work just like straight rulers or curved rulers in real life, except that they're digital—and they can be customized and made to produce certain special effects easily, such as all lines going to a specific focal point (or even curving to a specific focal point). If you draw or ink in the digital realm, you want to make sure you're familiar with these amazing tools.

We will cover the following key topics in this chapter:

- Introducing rulers and their types
- Using rulers in Clip Studio Paint
- Using the symmetry ruler
- Focus and parallel line rulers
- Understanding perspective rulers
- Making rulers inactive
- Drawing an ellipse in perspective
- Switching the active ruler
- Using grids and guides

We are going to take a deep dive into the special rulers in Clip Studio Paint in this chapter. We will briefly cover the basic rulers, and then we'll take a more in-depth look at the other ruler options and how they can be applied to drawing manga.

Now, let's get right into rulers!

Technical requirements

To get started, you need Clip Studio Paint already installed on your device, and a new canvas opened with a white-colored paper layer. Any size is fine, but I recommend creating a 300 dpi square canvas to work through the content in this chapter.

Introducing rulers and their types in Clip Studio Paint

When you draw a straight line digitally, you just need to pick the **Straight line** sub tool from the **Direct draw** tool group, and then click and drag. And it's done! It's quite a simple task. But when you want to create one with a textured brush, you need a ruler to guide you to create a straight line, no matter how steady your hand moves are. Alternatively, if you are going for a three-vanishing point perspective drawing, you need an accurate guide! Yes, there are good ruler tools for all these options.

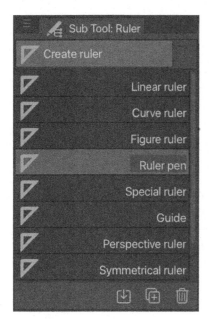

There are not only straight, **Linear** rulers but also **Curve** rulers, **Figure** rulers, **Ruler pen**, **Special** rulers, guides, **Perspective** rulers, and **Symmetrical** rulers available in Clip Studio Paint, which you can see in *Figure 13.1*. They will be introduced one by one with examples in this chapter. So if you get confused about which ruler is best for you, you can always come back to this chapter to check the descriptions with rich sample screenshots!

Using rulers

In this section, we are going to get to know the different ruler types, as well as how to snap to and manipulate rulers in Clip Studio Paint. Each ruler has its use, and they will surely help you to create accurate lines and shapes exactly how you need them to be!

Let's find out what rulers are available first and try using them. You will find the ruler sub tools under the **Ruler** section in the toolbar.

*Figure 13.1: Screen-
shot of the Ruler Sub
Tool palette*

The first four tools, **Linear ruler**, **Curve ruler**, **Figure ruler**, and **Ruler pen**, are the tools that we will briefly cover in this section. The tools listed below these four are a little more complex, and we'll delve into them in more detail as the chapter continues.

Ruler snapping options

Before we get into how to use each of the ruler tools, we need to learn about the snapping options. When a ruler doesn't work as expected, most of the time, it is because snapping is turned on or off. So when getting undesired results with the ruler tools, it is best to check these options first.

The three snapping options can be found in the command bar above the area where the currently active document is displayed. They are shown in Figure 13.2.

Figure 13.2: Screenshot of the ruler snapping options

From left to right, these options are **Snap to Ruler**, **Snap to Special Ruler**, and **Snap to Grid**. In the preceding screenshot, the **Snap to Ruler** option is the only one currently turned on and is marked by a light blue box. Now, let's look at what exactly they do:

- **Snap to Ruler** constricts the marks made by the current tools to any active basic ruler (linear ruler, figure ruler, ruler pen, and so on). If the active ruler is a special ruler, such as a perspective ruler, this option will not force the drawing tool to follow that ruler.

- **Snap to Special Ruler** forces tools to restrict their marks to any currently active special ruler, such as symmetry, focus line, and perspective rulers.

- **Snap to Grid** forces tools to stay within the confines of the grid when it is visible. There'll be more on the grid later in this chapter.

To turn a snap option on or off, simply click on it. Multiple snapping options can be active at one time. Remember that the snapping options will force your tools to constrain themselves to any currently active ruler that fits their criteria, so if you have a drawing tool that isn't drawing where you want it to and you have a ruler in your image, check the snapping option first to see whether that is the issue!

Now that we've discussed snapping, let's move on to the basic rulers and their functions.

— Linear ruler

The linear ruler works just the same as a regular old ruler that you might buy in any store. It is the simplest of rulers, used for making a single straight line.

To use the **linear ruler,** select the sub tool, click on your canvas, and drag. Release your mouse or stylus once you have reached the end of where you want the ruler to be. The ruler will be shown as a single-colored line, as shown in the following screenshot:

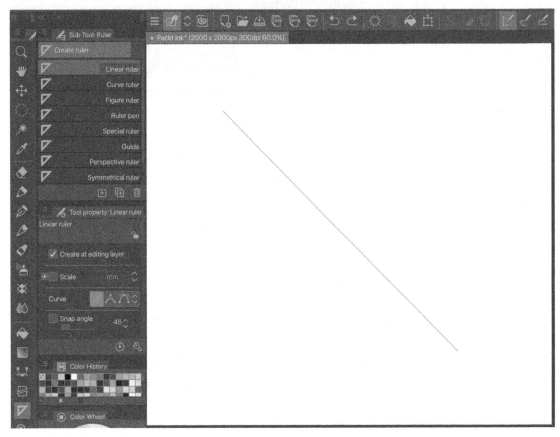

Figure 13.3: Screenshot of a linear ruler example

When the **Snap to Ruler** option is active, using a tool such as the G-pen will make a line along the ruler that we just made, as shown in the following screenshot:

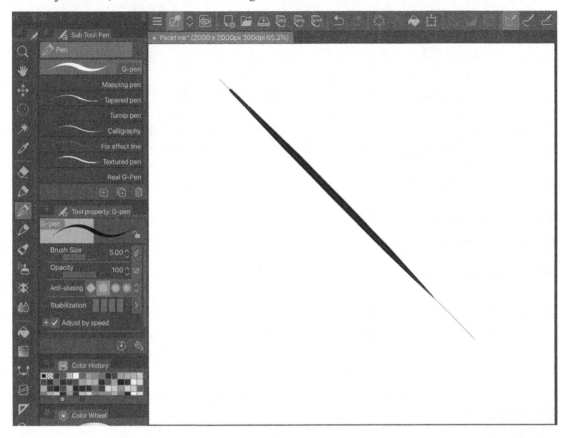

Figure 13.4: Screenshot of an inking on a linear ruler line

Tip

Need to adjust a ruler line that you already made? Use the **Operation | Object** sub tool and select the ruler, which is highlighted in Figure 13.5.

A bounding box will show up around the ruler, and a handle will appear at either end. By using this bounding box and the handles at either end, the angle and length of the ruler can be changed, the ruler can be resized, and it can even be rotated!

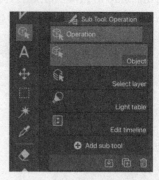

Figure 13.5: Screenshot of the Object sub tool

You can draw a smooth, straight line with your G-pen thanks to the Linear ruler's help. How about trying out a curved line? Read on to find out more.

⌒ Curve ruler

The curve ruler is a great help when we draw a mechanic object that has circles, such as a bicycle, car, motorcycle, and glasses. It supports us in drawing smooth lines, and it is good for editing a ruler shape whichever way you like. However, the curve ruler's name is a little bit misleading because it can be used to make polyline straight-line rulers as well as rulers with smooth curves, as shown in Figure 13.6.

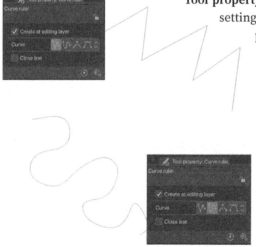

To use the curve ruler, select it from the **Ruler Sub Tool** palette. In the **Tool property** palette, you will see four options under the **Curve** setting. The very first icon is the **Straight** line, which will produce straight lines between the points of your ruler. The second option is the **Spline** setting, which will create curves between each point of the ruler. To use either of these options, simply click on the point on the canvas where you want the ruler to start. Then, click again where the second point should be. Continue clicking on each corner of the ruler until you reach the end of where you want the ruler to be. Double-click to end the ruler.

If you are making an enclosed shape, you can also go all the way around to the point where you started the ruler and click on the first point to end it, as shown in Figure 13.7.

Figure 13.6: Screenshot of curve ruler examples

The final two icons under the **Curve** setting in the **Tool property** palette are **Quadratic Bezier** and **Cubic Bezier**, which are simply two alternate ways to make and control the curve of the ruler. Let's learn how to create curves using each of these methods.

Using Quadratic Bezier

Using the Quadratic Bezier tool for a ruler takes a little getting used to and, usually, involves some refinement after the initial points are laid out. Follow these steps to create a curve ruler with Quadratic Bezier:

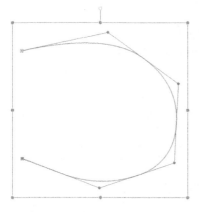

Figure 13.7: Screenshot of an enclosed shape

1. Select **Curve ruler** and then the **Quadratic Bezier** option from the **Tool property** palette.

2. Click on the canvas once, at the point where you'd like the ruler to start.

3. Click on the point where you would like the ruler to start curving. This will create a small square handle at the clicked point.

4. Move the cursor to another point on the canvas. The line of the ruler will bend according to where the second click was placed and where the cursor is now.

5. Continue clicking to add boxes and curves to the ruler until it is the desired length. Double-click to end the ruler.

6. To adjust the ruler, select the **Operation** tool | **Object** sub tool. Click on the ruler to select it and reveal the handle controls. In Figure 13.8, the control handles are on the straight lines and the actual ruler is the curved line.

To adjust the curve of the ruler, use the **Object** sub tool to click on one of the dot handles on the control line and drag it to a new position. The ruler in the preceding screenshot has been modified in Figure 13.9.

Let's look at a slightly different method of drawing a curve line, using Cubic Bezier.

Using Cubic Bezier

Another option to make curves is by using the **Cubic Bezier** setting. Follow these steps to create a ruler using Cubic Bezier:

1. Select the **Cubic Bezier** setting from the **Tool property** palette of the curve ruler.

Figure 13.8: Screenshot of a Quadratic Bezier example

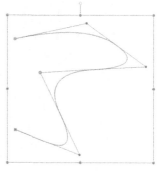

Figure 13.9: Screenshot of the Quadratic Bezier example adjusted

2. Click on the first point of the ruler.

3. When adding the first curve, draw in the direction your line goes. For example, if you start on the left side of the canvas and head toward the right, draw to the right. Going in the direction of the line will prevent the control handles from going in reverse and making "snarls" in the line. The line between the two clicked points will curve.

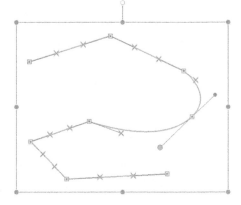

4. Click on a third point and draw to continue making the curve.

5. To end the ruler, double-click on another point. In this mode, the ruler will end at the point created before the double-click, so be sure the ruler is as long as necessary, click on the endpoint, and then double-click to finish the ruler.

6. To edit the Cubic Bezier ruler, select the **Operation** tool | **Object** sub tool. Click on the ruler to reveal the control handles. The control handles are shown by the red lines in Figure 13.10

Figure 13.10: Screenshot of a Cubic Bezier example

Using the **Object** tool, the handles along the red lines can be used to adjust the individual curves by clicking on the handles and dragging them. Clicking on the red squares that appear at the control points allows us to adjust their position. Dragging the red dot handles at either end of the red control line allows us to change the curve on either side of the control point.

Now that we know how to make curved lines using the Quadratic Bezier and Cubic Bezier options, we'll move on to ready-made figure rulers.

⬡ Figure ruler

The figure ruler allows us to create easy circle, rectangle, and polygon rulers with a few simple clicks. This is the best option to draw a perfect circle! Follow these steps to use the figure ruler:

1. Select the **Figure ruler** sub tool.

2. In the **Tool property** palette, select one of the shapes from the **Figure** tool.

3. Click on the canvas and hold down the mouse button or stylus. Drag to create the selected shape ruler on the canvas.

4. When using the polygon figure option, the number of vertices can be adjusted to create shapes such as triangles, pentagons, and hexagons. To edit the number of vertices, select the ruler, and then click on the **Show Sub Tool Detail Palette** icon at the lower right of the **Tool property** palette. Click on the **Figure** tool in the **Sub Tool Detail** palette. Beneath the **Figure** tool is the **Number of corners** option, which can be adjusted by using the slider or clicking on the number entry box and entering a number, using the keyboard. In Figure 13.11, the number of corners is 3, which will produce a triangle.

Beneath the Figure tool is the **Number of corners** option, which can be adjusted by using the slider or clicking on the number entry box and entering a number, using the keyboard. In the following screenshot, the number of corners is 3, which will produce a triangle:

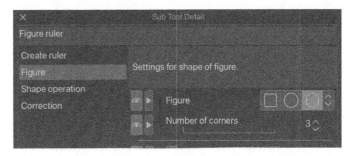

Figure 13.11: Screenshot of the Figure ruler Sub Tool Detail palette

After we draw the figure, we can always change its placement and size by selecting the **Operation | Object** tool and clicking the figure. Edit the figure using the control handles.

If we place a pen anywhere on the figure and start moving along the line, the figure will be drawn smoothly.

The final basic ruler that we will cover in this section is the versatile ruler pen. Read on to learn more about this tool.

⌒ Ruler pen

The ruler pen is a versatile tool that allows us to draw a ruler of any shape. It has **Stability** and **Post correction** settings, so we can create a smooth shape when we need to. We can find these settings in the **Tool property** palette or **Sub Tool Detail** palette.

In the following screenshot, I have created a free-hand drawing bird shape with the ruler pen:

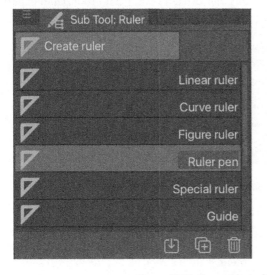

Figure 13.12: Screenshot of a Ruler pen example

Once we have finished drawing with the Ruler pen, any drawing tool can be used to trace the ruler!

Tip

Unsure about a layout you have just created? Try using the golden ratio, which is the so-called divine proportion, where you create a sense of beauty through the harmony and proportion of the 1:1.618 ratio.

In the following image, I have reworked the 1:1 composition on the left into the 1:1.618 composition on the right:

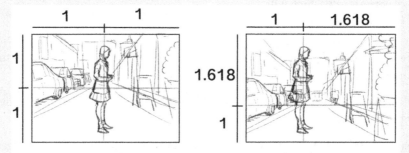

Figure 13.13: Screenshot of two different layouts

Notice how the horizon level and character placement are slightly different? We somehow feel more comfortable with this composition.

The aesthetics of the golden ratio can be applied to an animation storyboard, human face, book cover design, and more. You can add the **Golden ratio** scale to your **Linear, Curve**, and **Figure** rulers as well as **Ruler pen** by turning on **Scale**, and then selecting **Golden ratio** from the drop-down menu in the **Create ruler** category on the **Sub Tool Detail** palette:

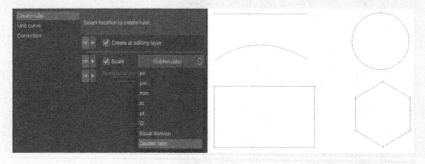

Figure 13.14: Screenshot of the Sub Tool Detail palette and various rulers with scale

Similarly, you should remember the **rule of thirds** when designing your composition. This is a guideline to place the subject in the left or right third of an image, leaving the other two thirds more open. If you look at the right-hand image of *Figure 13.13*, you can actually see this already, in the character placement. This is a good way of managing space when there are multiple elements in a composition, as well as making the composition more natural to look at.

We have covered how to snap to rulers and basic rulers, such as the ones to create lines, curves, and figures, and even covered how to create a hand-drawn ruler! Now, we will move on to specialty ruler tools in the following sections.

Using the symmetrical ruler

Have you ever wanted to create a design that was perfectly symmetrical on both sides, or make a beautiful digital mandala? If so, the symmetrical ruler is the answer to your prayers. As a bonus, it's really simple to use!

To begin using the symmetry ruler, select the **Ruler** tool from the toolbox and then select **Symmetrical ruler** from the **Sub Tool** palette. The **Tool property** palette is shown in Figure 13.15.

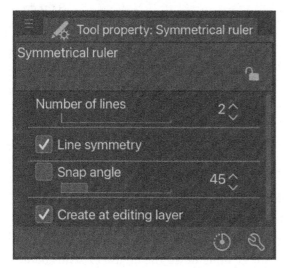

The most important option here in the **Tool property** palette is the **Number of lines** option. This controls how many sides of symmetry there will be in the completed ruler. Any number from 2 to 16 can be used in this option. Figure 13.16 shows an example of a ruler with **Number of lines** set to **2**.

Figure 13.15: Screenshot of the Symmetrical ruler tool property

Figure 13.16: Screenshot of a two-line symmetrical ruler drawing

The thin purple line in the center of the design is the ruler, and the design is mirrored on each side of the ruler's line.

This kind of symmetrical drawing is useful when designing manga characters where, on some elements, we want to add to both the right and left side of the body, as shown in Figure 13.17.

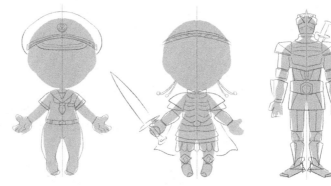

Figure 13.17: Two-line symmetrical ruler designs

Figure 13.18 shows a design drawn with **Number of lines** set to **8**.

The design now has eight symmetrical parts that radiate out from the center of the ruler. Figure 13.19 shows a design made with 16 lines, the maximum number a symmetrical ruler can have in Clip Studio Paint.

Figure 13.18: Screenshot of an eight-line symmetrical ruler drawing

Figure 13.19: Screenshot of a 16-line symmetrical ruler drawing

Creating a symmetrical ruler is easy and can be done by following these steps:

1. If desired, sketch a rough layout of your design before creating the ruler.
2. Select the **Symmetrical ruler** sub tool from the **Ruler** tool.
3. Set the desired number of lines in the **Tool property** palette.
4. Click and hold on the image canvas. While still holding down the mouse or stylus button, drag across the canvas to create a line. To constrain the ruler line to be perfectly straight or at a 45-degree angle, hold down the *Shift* key on the keyboard as you drag the mouse or stylus.
5. Release the mouse or stylus to finish creating the ruler.
6. Ensure that the **Snap to Special Ruler** icon in the top command bar is active in order to use the ruler.

Tip

Instead of holding down the *Shift* key to constrain the angle of the ruler, the **Snap angle** option can be used in the **Tool property** palette. Simply check the box next to the option and then set the desired angle using the slider or text entry.

Now that we know how to create and use a symmetrical ruler, let's learn about some more of the specialty rulers and how to use them.

Radial and parallel line rulers

Mostly, manga is in a black and white tone, so the lines must be bold and should clearly show actions, as well as the point on which the reader should focus their attention, hence the striking linework. One way that many manga artists do this is by using parallel lines to show motion, as well as radial lines to lead the reader's eyes to the point of interest in a frame or, in some cases, to express the impact of objects hitting each other. Clip Studio Paint comes with rulers ready to make parallel and radial lines, making the process of creating these effects much easier than with pen and paper.

Let's look at the following page from my manga adaptation of *A Midsummer Night's Dream*, showing some examples of how to use radial and parallel lines in a comic:

Figure 13.20: Screenshot of a manga comic with focus and parallel lines

In the left panel, parallel lines are used to show the motion of Bottom's head swung by Titania, who grips and shakes him. In the right panel, radial lines are used to draw the reader's eyes to the shocked face of Bottom.

Let's look at how to create and use the radial line ruler.

Radial line ruler

The radial line ruler allows us to set a central point and then draw lines that radiate out from that point. By using the snapping feature of Clip Studio Paint's rulers, making radial lines is much quicker and easier than making them in the traditional way with pen and paper. Simply set your central point and start drawing! Follow these steps to make a radial line ruler:

1. Select the **Ruler** tool from the toolbar, and then select the **Special ruler** sub tool.

2. In the **Tool property** palette, click on the drop-down menu to choose the **Radial line** option. The drop-down menu is shown in Figure 13.21.

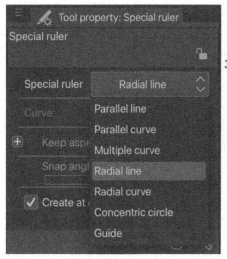

Figure 13.21: Screenshot of the Special ruler's Tool property palette

Click on the desired central point for the radial line. This is the point that all the lines drawn using the ruler will radiate out from.

3. Use your desired drawing tool to draw the radial lines. As you draw a line inward toward the center, you will see that the ruler assists you in maintaining a smooth straight trajectory at just the right angle with every stroke. In Figure 13.22, the focus lines have been drawn with the G-pen, and you can see the lines all stretching toward the center at the correct angle.

Figure 13.22: Screenshot of a radial line ruler drawing

Tip

There are also ready-made parallel and radial lines available under the **Figure** tool. They are **Stream line** and **Saturated line** in the **Figure Sub Tool** palette. You can use them in the same way as creating rulers, but lines will automatically be drawn for you—what a time saver!

A radial curve ruler can also be made. With a radial curve ruler, the lines still share the same central point, but they are curved instead of being straight. Follow these steps to create a radial curve ruler:

1. Select the **Radial curve** option from the drop-down menu in the **Tool property** palette.

2. Click where the central point of the radial curve ruler should be. Click again at the next point of the curve. Continue clicking until the desired curve is reached.

3. Double-click to end the curve.

4. Use a drawing tool of your choice to draw the focus curves. Figure 13.23 was done with the G-pen tool.

Note that the method to shape the curve is **Spline**. For a more in-depth explanation of these curve creation methods, refer to the *Curve ruler* section earlier in this chapter.

Now that you know how to create focus lines, let's study the other ruler we are covering in this section, the parallel line ruler.

Parallel line ruler

Follow these steps to create a parallel line ruler:

1. Select the **Ruler** tool from the toolbar.

2. Select the **Special ruler** sub tool.

3. From the drop-down menu in the **Tool property** palette, select the **Parallel line** option.

Figure 13.23: Screenshot of a radial curve line ruler drawing

4. Click on the canvas and drag to set the angle of the ruler. The ruler can be constrained to straight and 45-degree angles by holding down the *Shift* key on the keyboard.

5. Release the mouse button or stylus to finish creating the ruler.

6. Use the drawing tool of your choice to create parallel lines. Figure 13.24 shows an example of parallel lines drawn with a ruler.

As with the radial ruler we covered previously, parallel curves can also be made with a ruler. Follow these steps to create a parallel curve ruler:

1. Select **Parallel curve** from the drop-down menu in the **Tool property** palette.

2. Click on the canvas to begin the ruler. Click on the next point of the curve.

3. Select another point and click to continue the curve.

4. Continue clicking until the desired number and length of curves have been achieved. To end the ruler, double-click.

5. Use a drawing tool to draw your parallel curves. The lines in Figure 13.25 have been made with a G-pen tool.

Figure 13.24: Screenshot of a parallel line ruler drawing

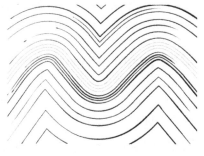

Figure 13.25: Screenshot of a parallel curve line ruler drawing

Note that the method to shape the curve is **Spline**. For a more in-depth explanation of these curve creation methods, see the *Curve ruler* section earlier in this chapter.

Tip

Do you need to change the angle or shape of your ruler once you've created it? Simply select the **Operation | Object** sub tool and click on the ruler to reveal the control handles. The **Object** tool can be used to move, rotate, and fine-tune your rulers.

Now that we've covered some of the advanced two-dimensional ruler tools, you can tell the differences between linear, curve, figure, ruler pen, symmetry, radial, and parallel rulers. Let's move on to perspective drawing, which is what you're probably most excited to learn about!

Understanding perspective rulers

In this section, we are going to look into what perspective rulers are, then understand one-point, two-point, and three-point rulers by creating them with step-by-step tutorials, and finally, learn how to use the Linear and Figure tools with perspective rulers.

Perspective rulers are a game-changer for any digital artist that draws backgrounds. Creating detailed cityscapes and backgrounds is easier than ever with the digital perspective ruler. However, having perspective rulers at your disposal will not suddenly make you an expert in perspective if you've never studied it before. Just like a real ruler in the physical world, perspective rulers are a tool that can make the drawing process easier.

Having access to a tool like perspective rulers does not replace knowledge of and practice with drawing in perspective. If you don't know the principles of drawing with depth, then these rulers can only aid you so much. You can find many good books explaining how to draw backgrounds in perspective.

Perspective rulers in Clip Studio Paint can be made as one-, two-, or three-vanishing point perspective rulers. You can also add other points as you get more comfortable with drawing in perspective, but for the purposes of this book, we'll focus on one, two, and three points of perspective.

Let's start with the easiest perspective ruler to grasp, the one-point perspective ruler. For each of the following ruler instructions, you will need a canvas to draw on and a rough sketch of the scene in perspective to draw. This is where that knowledge of perspective comes in! I recommend you properly place the perspective vanishing points when you create a rough sketch of the scene.

One-point perspective

As mentioned, we will start with a canvas with a rough sketch on it. For the one-point perspective, we are going to draw some buildings and a road going into the distance. For ideas, work from any references you have if you need to!

The following screenshot shows the sketch I will be basing my perspective ruler on. Having a rough sketch available makes it much easier to place the vanishing points and guidelines:

Figure 13.26: A rough sketch of a background

Now that the rough sketch is done, we can follow these steps to make the one-point perspective ruler:

1. In the **File** menu, click on **Layer**, go to **Ruler/Frame**, and then click on **Create Perspective Ruler.**

   A box will appear as shown in Figure 13.27.

2. Select **1-point perspective** from **Type.** Activating **Fisheye perspective** will distort the ruler into a Fisheye shape, but we won't use this function for now. Leaving the **Create new layer** box unchecked will create the ruler on the currently active layer. Since we want to create a layer to refine

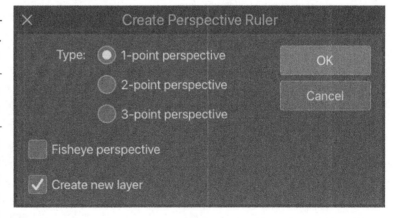

Figure 13.27: Screenshot of the Create Perspective Ruler window

our rough sketch above the rough sketch layer, we will leave the **Create new layer** box checked.

3. Click on **OK** to create the new ruler.

4. When the ruler is created on the canvas, the currently active tool will automatically switch to the **Object** sub tool. This will allow us to adjust our perspective ruler on the canvas.

Figure 13.28 is a screenshot of the perspective ruler without the rough sketch behind it, allowing it to be clearly seen. The line across the canvas from left to right is our horizon line. The two blue dots on either side of the line allow us to control the tilt of the horizon line. The circular point on the horizon line is the vanishing point for our perspective.

The two lines radiating out from the vanishing point are guidelines that will help us place our perspective ruler in the correct spot.

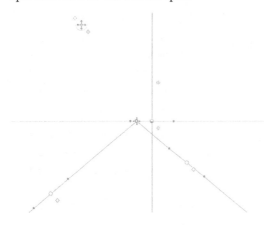

Figure 13.28: Screenshot of the one-point perspective ruler guidelines

Now that the perspective ruler is in position, we will ensure that the **Snap to Special Ruler** icon in the main command bar is active. We can now draw in our cleaned-up scene, and the drawing tools will snap to the lines of the ruler. Figure 13.30 shows the finished pencils for this perspective scene:

Figure 13.30: A sketch guided by the one-point perspective ruler

Using the **Object** sub tool, click on the vanishing point and drag it so that it is in the same place as the vanishing point on the rough sketch. Ensure that the horizon line of the perspective ruler also matches the horizon on the rough sketch. The handles of the guidelines can be used to check the perspective and ensure that the ruler is in the correct position. Figure 13.29 shows the perspective ruler in the correct position.

Figure 13.29: Screenshot of one-point perspective ruler guidelines on a sketch

Once the scene is sketched out, we can add another layer on top of the sketch layer to ink on and still be able to see and snap tools to our perspective ruler. In order to do this, look in the **Layer** palette. With the ruler layer selected, click on the **Set showing area of ruler** icon to open the dropdown, which you can see in the following screenshot as a triangular ruler shape, just above the drop-down menu:

Figure 13.31: Screenshot of the Set showing area of ruler menu option selected, with the dropdown displayed

Set the **Show in All Layers** option to see and use the perspective ruler no matter what layer is currently active.

The showing areas for the rulers are **Show in All Layers**, **Show in Same Folder**, **Show Only When Editing Target**, and **Link guide to ruler**. Descriptions for each of these options are as follows:

- When a ruler layer is set to **Show in All Layers**, the ruler will appear and be able to be snapped to any layer in the current canvas.
- When set to **Show in Same Folder**, the ruler will be shown only when it is on layers that are in the same layer folder as the ruler. (For instance, if our canvas includes a folder labeled **Sketches** that has a ruler in it, the ruler will only be visible and usable when on layers grouped in that same folder.)
- When set to **Show Only When Editing Target**, the ruler will only be shown when the ruler layer is the currently active layer.
- **Link guide to ruler** links the ruler and guide created on the same layer. When turned on, rulers and guides can be moved together with the **Move layer** tool.

Now, let's have a look at a perspective ruler with more vanishing points in the next section.

Two-point perspective

Creating a two-point perspective ruler can be achieved with the same method as shown in the *One-point perspective* section of this chapter. However, additional perspective vanishing points can also be added to an existing ruler. The following screenshot shows a sketch created with a two-point perspective ruler. Note that the two vanishing points are often far away from each other and out of the frame, as their being too close will distort the objects we draw:

Figure 13.32: Screenshot of the two-point perspective sample art

To create a basic two-point ruler, follow the instructions in the preceding section but select the **2 points perspective** option from the dialog box in *step 2*. To add a point to an existing ruler, follow these steps:

1. Click on the existing ruler with the **Object** sub tool to select it. If a ruler is currently selected, the control handles will be visible.

2. Select **Ruler** from the toolbar, and then click **Perspective ruler** from the **Ruler Sub Tool** palette. Confirm that **Add vanishing point** is selected from the **Process** drop-down menu in the **Tool property** palette, as shown in Figure 13.33.

3. On the canvas, click where you want to add a new vanishing point.

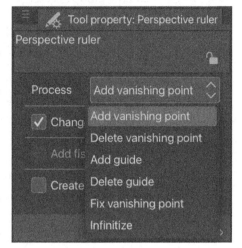

Figure 13.33: Screenshot of the Perspective ruler's Tool property palette

As you can see from the screenshot in *FIgure 13.33*, the perspective ruler **Tool property** palette has several options in the **Process** drop-down menu that can assist us with drawing perspective rulers. We have already covered the **Add vanishing point** option, and the following list describes the rest of the perspective ruler tools available in this palette:

- **Delete vanishing point** will delete the currently selected vanishing point.
- **Add guide** will create a new guide coming from the current vanishing point.
- **Delete guide** will delete the selected guide from the vanishing point.
- **Fix vanishing point** locks the selected vanishing point to its current position.
- **Infinitize** moves the vanishing point to infinity when selected.

Now, you can create multiple vanishing point perspective rulers. Let's look into how to create a three-point perspective drawing with a perspective ruler.

Three-point perspective

Once you have mastered one- and two-point perspectives, you can start creating some very cool scenes using three-point perspective. Scenes created in three-point perspective look flashy and cool and really add a feeling of three-dimensional space to your comic scenes. Figure 13.34 shows an example of a three-point perspective cityscape from my work.

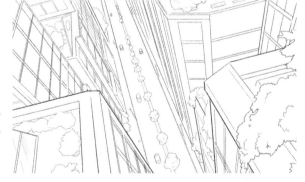

Figure 13.34: Background drawing by using a perspective ruler

By zooming out, we can see how the perspective ruler was set up to create this bird's-eye view of a city. As with two-point perspective, vanishing points shouldn't be too close, as they can distort the objects we draw, so it is worth remembering that they should be placed far apart. Figure 13.35 shows a zoomed-out view of the page with the perspective ruler showing. Note how far away the vanishing points are from the edges of the canvas.

Three-point perspective rulers can be created by using either method described in the one-point and two-point perspective sections of this chapter. However, they are trickier to work with, since there are so many points that the program tries to snap to. Sometimes, the program may pick up on the wrong guideline, and you may have to undo your line and try again.

Figure 13.35: Background drawing with vanishing points

Once you master three-point perspective rulers, they are an invaluable part of drawing really cool environments for your characters to inhabit, especially a scene where a camera looks up at a big building, or a bird's-eye view of a town, just like in the preceding sample art. It is like creating scenes with a drone camera, looking at the world freely from low on the ground or high in the air!

Before we move on from perspective rulers, did you know that you can draw perfect ellipses and other shapes with them? Let's learn more in the next section!

Using figure and line tools with perspective rulers

Did you know that you can use shape and line tools with perspective rulers? Follow these steps to use the **Direct Draw** sub tools with perspective rulers:

1. Using one of the methods listed previously in this chapter, create a perspective ruler on your canvas.

2. Select the **Figure** tool in the toolbar.

3. Select the **Direct draw** sub tool.

4. Select the **Rectangle** sub tool.

5. Ensure that the **Snap to Special Ruler** icon in the main command bar is active. Then, click and drag with the Rectangle tool to create a rectangle. The shape will conform to the perspective ruler automatically, so long as **Snap to Special Ruler** is active.

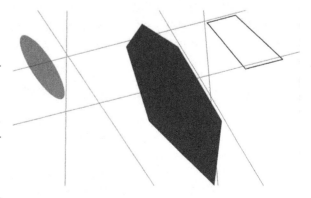

In Figure 13.36, we have drawn a circle, a rectangle, and a polygon in perspective using the **Snap to Special Ruler** option.

Figure 13.36: Figure tool drawings with a perspective ruler

By configuring the settings on shape tools, you can considerably speed up your object drawing.

There are ways to control multiple rulers to organize your canvas; let's find out how in the next section.

Making rulers inactive

In some instances, you may find it necessary to have multiple rulers in the same image. This can become confusing for the program, and for us as well! So in this section, we will examine the quick process of making rulers and vanishing points active or inactive. This will allow us to control how rulers work and what areas of a ruler are active at any time.

Turning rulers off and on with the control handle

Making a ruler active or inactive is simple but invaluable. Knowing how to manage multiple rulers can mean the difference between a smooth drawing experience and hours of frustration fighting with your tools! Follow these steps to make an active ruler inactive:

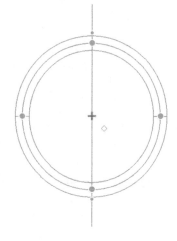

1. Create a ruler on a new canvas. In this example, we will look at a concentric circle ruler, but just about any ruler tool will do.

2. Click on the ruler with the **Object** sub tool if the ruler is not already selected. The currently selected ruler will show the control handles. In Figure 13.37, the control handles are the circular and diamond-shaped icons around the ruler that allow us to edit it and change its shape and rotation.

Locate the control handle shaped like a diamond. In the preceding screenshot, it is located just to the right of the center of the circle ruler. Click on the diamond-shaped control handle to make the ruler inactive. The ruler will change colors from purple to green, as shown in Figure 13.38.

Figure 13.37: Screenshot of the perspective ruler and figure ruler guidelines

To make the ruler active again, click on the circle with a slash icon. The ruler will change back to its active color and be able to be snapped to.

This method can also be applied to individual vanishing points along a perspective ruler. In Figure 13.39 showing the Fisheye perspective ruler, all upper vanishing points have been made inactive so that tools will only snap to the center vanishing point.

Figure 13.38: Screenshot with one of the rulers inactive

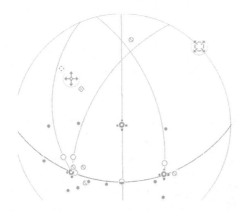

Figure 13.39: Screenshot of only one active ruler

Now that we've learned about all these specialty rulers, let's cover an often-overlooked tool that can save you from a headache and also save a lot of time if you know how to use it.

Using grids and guides

Many new users of Clip Studio Paint don't know that the software comes with a customizable grid that can be shown or hidden, or that you can create guides in the program as well. Grids and guidelines are handy for many tasks, of course, and provide a visual measurement that is easy to count and divide. Also, the grids and guidelines in Clip Studio Paint can be snapped to, making it very easy to get elements lined up precisely as they need to be.

In this section, we will learn how to show and hide the grid and how to make guidelines.

Showing and hiding the grid

To see the grid in action, let's look at the following screenshot:

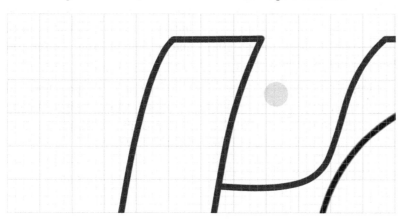

Looking closely, we can see that some of the lines are darker. These darker lines are our grid lines. Between each grid line are three grid-dividing lines that break each larger square of the grid up into four sections in each direction, giving a total of 16 squares between each line of the grid.

Figure 13.40: Screenshot of the canvas with a grid

Follow these steps to show the grid on your own work:

1. In the **File** menu, or on the top menu bar on a Mac, click on the **View** option.
2. Click on **Grid** to show the grid.
3. To hide a visible grid, click on **View**, and then click **Grid** again to uncheck the option.

The grid is also adjustable by changing its settings; read on to find out how!

Adjusting grid settings

There are grid settings that allow us to change grid divisions. These settings are accessible by clicking on **View** in the **File** menu and then clicking on **Grid/Ruler bar settings....** The grid/ruler settings menu is shown in the following screenshot:

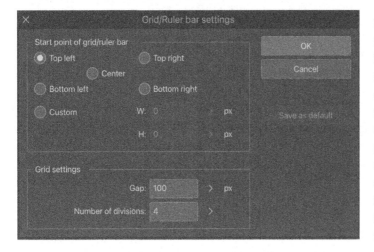

Figure 13.41: Screenshot of the grid ruler settings

Under **Start point of grid/ruler bar**, the point of origin of the grid can be set. By default, it is set to the top left, meaning that the grid will appear with its start point in the top-left corner of the canvas. The other options for the point of origin are **Top right**, **Center**, **Bottom left**, and **Bottom right**. There is also an option to set a **Custom** point of origin. Clicking the radio button next to the **Custom** option will activate the text entry box, and custom values for the number of offset pixels for both the width and height of the document can be set. For instance, if a value of **10** is entered in **W** and a value of **20** in the **H** setting, then the point of origin for the grid will be 10 pixels in from the left side and 20 pixels down.

Under **Grid settings**, the **Gap** and **Number of divisions** options can be set. **Gap** is the space between the grid lines, which is set to **100** pixels in the preceding screenshot. **Number of divisions** is the setting for how many times the larger grid lines should be divided. Setting this to a higher number will result in smaller squares occurring in the grid overall because of the additional divisions.

Let's look at another ruler that is easy enough to use for your creation.

Making guides

Guide rulers are simple to use, but their applications are endless. They can be used in combination with a grid to mark the margins of a document, to find the center of a canvas, or to align design elements such as different layers of text and illustrations.

Guides work like the line ruler sub tool, but they can only go straight horizontally or vertically on the canvas. Follow these steps to make guidelines on your canvas:

1. Click on the **Ruler** sub tool in the toolbar.
2. Click on the **Guide** sub tool.
3. Click on the canvas and drag either horizontally or vertically, depending on which direction you want your guide to go in.
4. When the mouse button or stylus is released, the guide will be made.

> **Tip**
>
> Guides automatically continue all the way across and beyond the constraints of the canvas, no matter the length of the line that was dragged to create them.

Grids and guides are really easy to use, so it's great to know that these rulers are available whenever you need them to draw straight lines!

Summary

Wow, that was a lot of information about rulers! I hope that you learned some great new tips and tricks that will help you with your digital art creation in the future.

In this chapter, we learned how to work with the basic rulers of Clip Studio Paint, as well as the radial, parallel, and symmetry rulers. We created one-point, two-point, and three-point perspective rulers and learned how to use the direct drawing tools with them. We learned how to make rulers active or inactive and how to use the snapping settings. Finally, we learned about grids and guides. In this chapter, you gained skills such as creating various rulers by yourself; manipulating and using perspective rulers, and using them with Figure tools; and using grids and guides, organized per your requirements. Background drawings won't scare you anymore now that you know about rulers.

In the next chapter, we're going to enter a new dimension: the third dimension! Keep reading to learn more about how to use 3D figures and objects in Clip Studio Paint.

Join us on Discord!

Read this book alongside other users. Ask questions, provide solutions to other readers, and much more.

Scan the QR code or visit the link to join the community.

`https://packt.link/clipstudiopaint`

14

Using 3D Figures and Objects

Clip Studio Paint is one of the leading pieces of software for creating top-notch manga and illustrations. But did you know that it can also import and display 3D assets? Many 3D assets come ready in the Material palette and can be applied to use 3D assets as poses or background references. In this chapter, we'll take a trip into the third dimension and learn about the following topics:

- Introducing the 3D Material palette
- Loading a 3D object onto the canvas
- Moving an object in 3D space
- Using preset poses on figure models
- Customizing character and figure models
- Saving 3D information to the Material palette
- Importing 3D models into Clip Studio Paint

We are going to look at 3D materials closely and learn how to apply them to your canvas and then customize them as per your needs. Finally, we will learn how to save and import them. By using 3D materials to study poses or to use them as a reference when you ink, you can have a deeper understanding of how to depict 3D objects in a 2D drawing!

Technical requirements

To get started, you need Clip Studio Paint already installed on your device, and a new canvas opened with a white-colored paper layer. Any size is fine, but I recommend creating a 300 dpi square canvas to go through the content in this chapter.

Introducing the 3D Material palette

First of all, we are going to look at the 3D assets in the Material palette. The Material palette is what we call the digital library of assets that are available through Clip Studio. Clip Studio comes with a huge library of brushes, images, screentones, 3D poses, objects, and more. More assets can be easily downloaded through Clip Studio Assets, which we will cover in *Chapter 18, Exploring Clip Studio Assets and Animations*. You can also save your own artwork to the Material palette, which is covered in *Chapter 9, Material Palette and Inking Special Effects*. For now, however, we will just concentrate on the 3D categories of the Material palette. In the 3D category, we have character heads, 3D figures, figures in poses, hands in poses, furniture, picture frames, accessories, and more! They are all great references or can be used to stencil to create our manga.

To access the Material palette, locate the appropriate palette location in your interface. If you cannot locate the Material palette, you can click on **Window** in the **File** menu and then navigate down to **Material**. From the menu under the **Material** option, click on **Material: 3D** to open the 3D Material palette, as shown in the following screenshot:

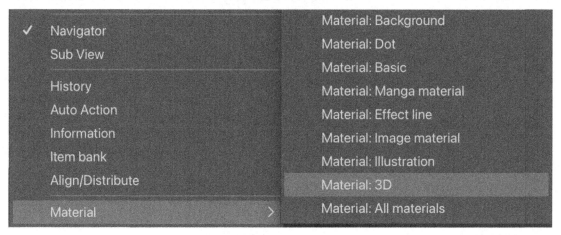

Figure 14.1: Material drop-down menu

Now, we can take a look at the **Material** palette to see the contents of the 3D category. The **Material** palette is shown in the following screenshot:

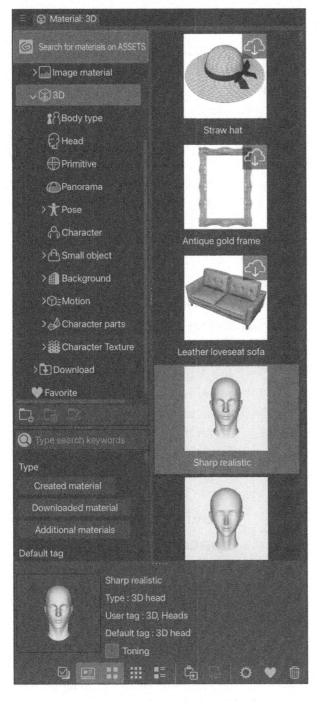

On the left-hand side of the Material palette is a list of the different categories of materials and their sub-categories. These categories organize our library of material assets and allow us to quickly find a specific material. The currently selected category will show up in the list with a blue highlight around its name. Any category name with an arrow symbol next to it means that that category can be expanded to show the sub-categories beneath it.

Sometimes, even sub-categories have more sub-categories, as can be seen next to the **Pose** sub-category in *Figure 14.2*.

The right-hand side of the Material window shows a list of the materials with images in the library. The currently selected material will have a blue highlight around it. Details about the current selection are shown in the bottom section of the Material palette.

Tip

If a material in the list has a cloud icon with a down-facing arrow in the top corner of the preview image, this means that the material must be downloaded from Clip Studio Assets before it becomes available for use. These assets are usually available at no cost to you, but they will increase the storage space Clip Studio needs on your hard drive!

Figure 14.2: 3D materials in the Material palette

Great, you found a variety of 3D assets in the **Material** palette! Let's move on to learn how to paste them onto your canvas.

Loading a 3D object onto the canvas

Now you know there are many 3D assets available in Clip Studio Paint, but you need to import them onto your canvas to work on! In this section, we will learn how to import those 3D assets from the Material palette to your canvas, so that you can start to move or manipulate them.

Follow these easy steps to add a 3D asset to a canvas:

1. Open a new canvas, if one is not already open. Material assets can only be added to a currently opened document.

2. In the 3D Material palette, click on the 3D asset to be added to the canvas. In this example, we are using the **3D drawing figure-Ver.2 (Male)** asset.

3. Once the material is selected, click on the **Paste selected material to canvas** icon at the bottom of the Material palette, which looks like the screenshot on the right:

Figure 14.3: Paste selected material to canvas icon

4. The asset will be pasted to the canvas. Note that, depending on your computer's specifications and the 3D asset, this may take a few minutes to complete.

The 3D figure we chose in the preceding steps is shown in the following screenshot:

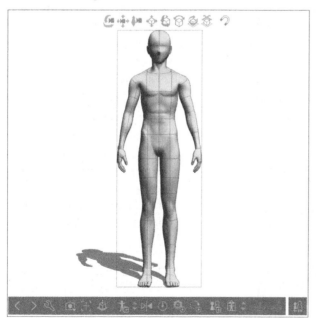

Figure 14.4: Pasted 3D material

As you can see, this is a decent 3D drawing doll that makes for a pretty good reference! But this pose is a little too static, and we need to move the limbs around to get some personality and life into this reference pose. Let's move this 3D figure and the camera around.

Moving objects in 3D space

Now that we've learned how to add a 3D object to our canvas, we can move and pose that object on our canvas. It requires time, practice, and patience to learn how to pose 3D characters in Clip Studio Paint, but once you know the basics of 3D space, you'll become an expert in no time!

The screenshots from *Figure 14.5* to *Figure 14.25* in the *Moving an object on the x, y, and z axes*, *Moving parts of a model*, *Moving the 3D camera*, *Using preset poses on figure models*, and *Customizing characters* sections show the **School girl B-Ver.** 3 3D character model. This model is available as a free download through the 3D character materials and Clip Studio Assets. For more information on how to download assets with Clip Studio Assets, see *Chapter 18, Exploring the Clip Studio Assets and Animation*.

The 3D object is now standing there, at its default angle. Let's learn how to move it around to fit your desired position in the next section!

Moving an object on the x, y, and z axes

To get your 3D asset into the correct position on the canvas for your scene, you may need to move or rotate it on the *x*, *y*, or *z* axis. This is true for 3D figures, objects, or any of the 3D backgrounds that can be used in Clip Studio Paint. Follow these instructions to learn how to move objects through 3D space:

1. Be sure that the **Operation | Object** tool is selected before continuing.

2. Click on the 3D object that you wish to manipulate if it is not already selected. A box will appear around the edge of the 3D object, and a command bar of icons will also appear both above and below the object. We will be using the top set of icons to move the object around in the space.

3. To move the entire object up, down, left, or right, hover the mouse cursor over the fourth icon at the top left of the box around the selected object. Click on the canvas, hold the left mouse button or stylus, and drag it to move the object in the desired direction. The screenshot on the right shows the location of the icon being used to move the object up, down, left, or right. It is highlighted in dark blue:

Figure 14.5: Pasted 3D material and icons

4. To rotate the object along the *x* axis (horizontal axis), and the *y* axis (vertical axis), hover the mouse cursor over the fifth icon from the left at the top of the box around the selected object.

5. Click and hold the left mouse button or stylus and drag. The object will rotate straight along the *x* or *y* axis, or diagonally to both axes, as shown in the following screenshot:

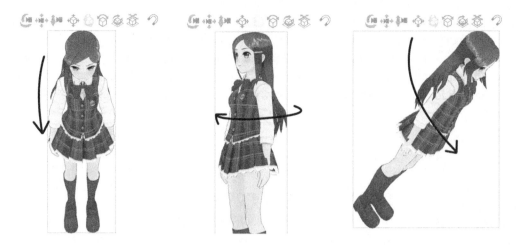

Figure 14.6: Rotated 3D material

To tilt the object clockwise and anti-clockwise, click the sixth icon from the left, click on the object, and drag it to the right or left, as shown in the following screenshot. Notice her hair dragged along with the motion and gravity in *Figure 14.7*.

6. To simply turn the object around, click the seventh icon from the left and click on the object, then drag it to the right or left, as shown in the following screenshot:

Figure 14.7: Tilted 3D material

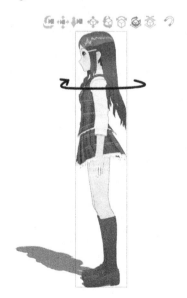

Figure 14.8: Turned 3D material

7. To move the object back and forth in a 3D space, click the third icon from the left at the top of the box around the selected object. Click and hold the left mouse button or stylus and drag up or down. The icon is shown in *Figure 14.9*, highlighted in dark blue, and the character has been moved back, away from the camera.

There is also an easy way to move the object around, which is using a manipulator sphere. It's always best when there is an alternative way to move an object because you can pick whichever you feel works best for you. Read on to learn what a manipulator sphere is and how it works!

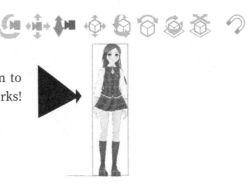

Figure 14.9: Backed-away 3D material

Moving an object using a manipulator sphere

A manipulator sphere is a group of circles that have three axes (x, y, and z), and with camera zoom directions, you can freely switch between these axes. You can apply all the editing we have done so far in the preceding sections by using a manipulator sphere, and you might find it easier. If you click on the object, the sphere appears as in the following screenshot:

Figure 14.10: 3D editing sphere

Once the manipulator sphere is visible, you can use it to adjust the object in the following ways:

1. Make sure to uncheck any icon at the top of the box. Click and hold anywhere on the canvas and drag your mouse or stylus along freely in whichever direction you want the object to turn.

2. If you want the object closer or farther away from the camera, click and hold the outermost spikey circle and drag along the inner (farther) or outer (closer) direction. All axes except the corresponding axis to the direction of movement will turn themselves off, as seen in the following screenshots – from left, vertical rotation, tilt, horizontal rotation, and camera distance:

Figure 14.11: Four directions of 3D editing

You can have fun watching the 3D character's hair and skirt being animated to show movement while dragging it around.

But isn't the character too static and lifeless? You can learn how to change her pose by reading on to the next section.

Moving parts of a model

Some models, such as figures and characters, as well as certain object models, can have individual parts of them moved. In this section, we will continue with the **School Girl B** model and move her arm, as an example of how to pose a character:

1. With the **Object** sub-tool, click on the model you'd like to pose. Once the model is selected, the movement controls will show. In the screenshot on the right, the blue circles are the movement handles for the major joints of the body.

2. Click on the movement control handle of the body part you want to move. While holding down the mouse button or stylus, drag the control handle to move that part of the model.

Figure 14.12: Movement handles

3. When a control handle is selected, a sphere made of red, green, and blue lines will also be visible. This control allows you finer access to the movement of a part of the model in the x, y, and z axes. Simply click and hold down the mouse button or stylus on the line of the sphere corresponding to the axis you wish to move the part of the model in and drag to complete the movement.

Using the motion control handles, a character can be posed quickly! The screenshot on the right was created in just a few moments by clicking and dragging the handles. The slight rotation of the right foot was achieved using the axis control lines.

With the new pose, the character looks lively and appears more natural!

Figure 14.13: Edited 3D object

Tip

You can attach one or more 3D objects to a main figure and move them along together. Paste one more 3D object on the same canvas, and in the **Tool property** palette, click on the wrench-shaped icon in the lower-right corner to open the **Sub Tool Detail** palette. Locate the object name you have just downloaded in the object list, then click and drag it to the other main object to make a hierarchy with sub-objects, as you can see in the screenshot on the right. Now you can move them together!

If you need to separate them later, simply click and drag the sub-object's name out of the hierarchy.

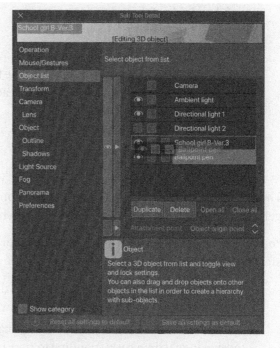

Figure 14.14: Object list category on the Sub Tool Detail palette

You can also edit the hand gesture. Read on to find out how.

Posing hands

Hands can be posed on a character either by clicking on each finger joint or by using the **Sub Tool Detail** menu to adjust the fingers. Let's take a quick look at the hand control in the **Sub Tool Detail** menu because it's a much faster way to pose hands than doing it by individual finger joints!

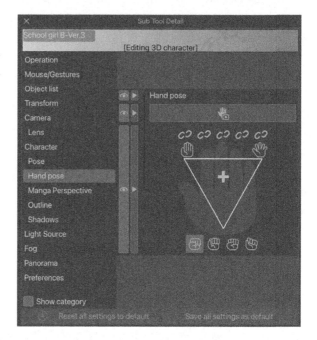

Follow these steps to change the hand pose:

1. Click on one of the hands of the character you wish to pose.

2. In the **Tool property** palette, click on the wrench-shaped icon in the lower-right corner to open the **Sub Tool Detail** palette.

3. Choose **Hand pose** in the **Character** category from the menu on the left-hand side of the **Sub Tool Detail** palette. The screen on the right will appear.

Figure 14.15: Hand pose settings on the Sub Tool Detail palette

4. By moving the crosshair icon inside of the triangle shape overlayed on the hand icon, the fingers of the model can be made to spread far apart or come in close together, and also to open or close into a fist.

5. Above the large icon of the hand in the screenshot in *Figure 14.15,* there are five icons that look like links in a chain. Clicking on one of these will lock the corresponding finger into the current position while allowing the other fingers to continue to be posed.

The best way to really understand these hand controls is to play around with them yourself and get a feel for them! So, give them a try and see whether you like them.

You can also take a picture of your hand and apply the hand pose to the 3D object. Follow these steps to use the Hand Scanner:

1. Click the icon of a camera on a hand in the **Hand pose** category in the **Sub Tool Detail** palette to open the **Hand Scanner** window.

2. Once the window opens, you will see the camera function is activated, and the 3D hand is posing in real time corresponding to your hand poses in the camera. You can see a sample in the following screenshot:

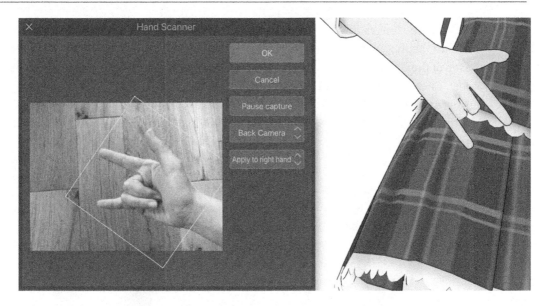

Figure 14.16: Hand Scanner window and the 3D figure

3. You can select **Back Camera**, **Back Camera (Mirror)**, **Front Camera**, and **Front Camera (Mirror)** to take the hand photo. Also, there is an option for which side of the hand of the 3D figure to apply the hand pose to. When you strike the ideal pose, click **Pause capture** to see how it applies to the figure.

4. You can repeat step 3 till you decide the ideal pose. When you make up your mind, click **OK** to finish posing the hand.

Wow, how easy and quick to create your ideal hand pose!

Not only can you move 3D objects in Clip Studio Paint but you can also move the 3D camera as well. Let's explore how to do this in the next section.

Moving the 3D camera

The 3D camera is another way of saying from what angle we are looking at the 3D object or scene. Instead of moving the 3D character or object, we can move the position from where we are looking at the model.

When moving the camera around the object, the object model will remain stationary. Follow these instructions to move the 3D camera:

1. To move the camera up, down, left, or right, click the second icon from the left at the top of the box around the selected object. Click and hold the left mouse button or stylus and drag. The selected icon is shown in dark blue in the screenshot on the right:

Figure 14.17: 3D camera icon

2. To rotate the camera around the object, click the first icon from the left at the top of the box around the selected object. Click and hold the left mouse button or stylus and drag. The icon and the camera rotation are shown in the following screenshot:

Click and hold the left mouse button or stylus and drag up or down. The following screenshot shows that the icon has been selected. Note that if you get the camera very close to the 3D character, the character will be displayed so big that it will eventually leave the canvas:

Figure 14.18: 3D camera icon 2

3. To move the camera back and forth in the 3D space, click the third icon from the left at the top of the box around the selected object.

Figure 14.19: 3D camera icon 3

Adding perspective

We can add extreme perspective to our 3D figure! Sometimes, we need to emphasize perspective to create dramatic scenes, such as a character punching toward a camera.

We can achieve this by changing the **Perspective** value of the camera. Let's try out the following steps to learn how:

1. With the **Object** sub-tool, click on the model, then create a pose that has the model's hand in front of its face.

2. Go to the **Sub Tool Detail** palette and increase the value of **Perspective** in the **Camera** category. You should get a result similar to the following screenshot:

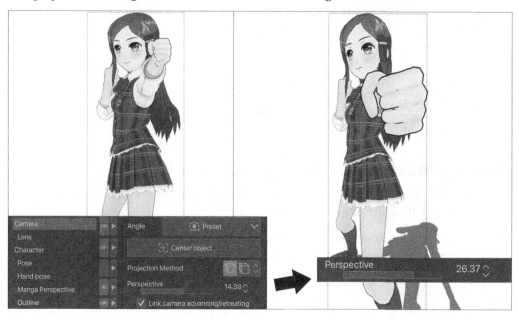

Figure 14.20: Perspective setting on the figure

3. Adjust the value to get the required amount of perspective. You can now apply it to your great punching scene, as in the screenshot on the right:

As well as a punching pose, we can also use this method to create a scene looking up at a physically huge character from the floor level. Have fun controlling the perspective of your 3D model.

Figure 14.21: Sample art referring to perspective figure

Tip

Rotate the camera when posing your character to check the position of the limbs for accuracy. See the *Moving parts of a model* section of this chapter for instructions on posing characters.

You can edit poses and camera angles using icons, the manipulator sphere, and the **Sub Tool Detail** palette. But isn't it handy to use the preset poses, skipping all the hassle? Let's see how to find and use them!

Using preset poses on figure models

There are many preset poses available for use in your creation. We will look into how to find and apply them to a 3D figure or character next.

The **3D** section of the Material palette includes many sub-categories. One of these categories is an entire library of premade poses that you can drag and drop onto a character model or one of the generic male or female figure models. Using these poses is a great way to get your character or figure reference into a pose quickly. You may need to make a tweak or two to get the pose absolutely perfect. But many of these poses work well on their own or are a fantastic starting point for creating your own poses. As a bonus, they're easy to use, too!

Follow these steps to find out how:

1. In the **3D** category of the **Material** palette, find the **Pose** category and expand it by clicking on the arrow to the left of the category. Then, click on the **Entire Body** sub-category.

2. Select a pose to add to the character. In this example, we are using a pose called **Rest chin in hand 01**.

3. Once the desired pose has been clicked, it will be highlighted in blue.

4. Click on the pose again and hold down the mouse button or stylus. Drag it over the top of the character or figure model while still holding down the button. The cursor will display a + symbol next to it when you're in the right spot.

5. Release the mouse button or stylus over the character. If you only have one 3D character on your canvas, just click on the clipboard-shaped **Paste selected material on canvas** icon at the bottom of the **Material** palette. The pose will change automatically to the selected preset pose, as shown in the screenshot on the right:

Figure 14.22: Figure with a preset pose

We can also edit preset poses we have just applied to make them look more interesting.

Did you know you can import poses from images, photos, and the Posemaniacs website? The Pose Scanner reads an image containing a figure and applies the pose to 3D figures or 3D characters. It can read various image formats, including BMP, JPEG, PNG, TIFF, and Targa. If you are using a tablet, you can take a photo with the camera and apply it to your 3D figures.

First of all, let's have a look at how to import a pose from an image or a photo:

1. In the **File** menu, click on **File | Import | Pose Scanner (image) (Technology preview)...** on Windows/macOS or **File | Import | Pose Scanner (image) (photo library)** on tablets, as shown in the following screenshot:

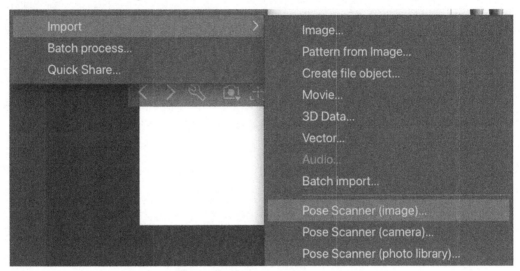

Figure 14.23: Pose Scanner options

2. It will bring up a dialog window in which you need to confirm whether you are happy to use an internet connection to use this feature. Check the small box if you don't want to see this dialog window again. If you're fine with it, click **OK** to bring up the **Open** window.

3. In the **Open** window, navigate to the location on your computer where the image or photo you want is saved. Click on the file and then click **Open**.

4. It may take a moment for the 3D data to apply. Once it does, you will be able to adjust and rotate the camera around it as normal.

It's amazingly easy to apply your desired pose if you already have a reference image on your computer!

Even if you don't have any pose reference images, don't worry. You can always take a picture of yourself posing and import it to your computer. And if you're using Clip Studio Paint on your tablet, it is much easier: just click on **File | Import | Pose Scanner (camera)...**, then take a picture of yourself or others posing. Click **Use Photo** to apply it to your 3D figure, or **Retake** to retake a photo.

You can also import useful poses from tons of lists on the Posemaniacs website when you need poses with an understanding of muscles. Follow these steps to find out how to do it:

1. In the **File** menu, click on **File | Import | 3D pose (Posemaniacs)**. Alternatively, you can access the Posemaniacs website by clicking on the up and down arrow triangles next to the clipboard with the human-shaped icon on the command bar beneath the 3D figure to display drop-down options, then click **3D pose (Posemaniacs)**, as shown in the screenshot on the right:

    Figure 14.24: Pose Scanner options on the command bar

2. After clicking "**yes**" on the confirmation dialog box, you will jump to the Posemaniacs website. You will see tons of pose samples there! When you decide on one, click the thumbnail of the pose, and then you will see the Clip Studio **Open** button beneath the image, as shown in the following screenshot:

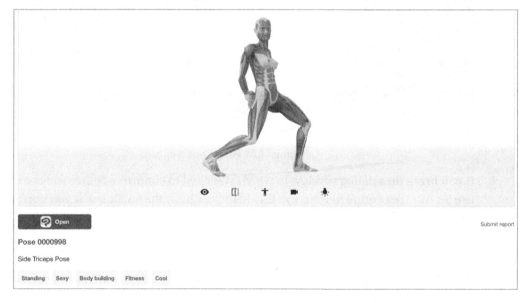

Figure 14.25: Pose view page on the Posemaniacs website

3. Clicking the **Open** button will bring up a dialog window to confirm connecting to Clip Studio Paint. Click the **Open** icon again to launch Clip Studio Paint.

4. It may take a moment for the 3D data to apply to the figure. Once it does, you will be able to adjust and rotate the camera around it as normal.

5. Apply the pose to your drawing by referring to it.

Importing poses from images, the camera, and Posemaniacs is a brilliant time-saver, especially when you need to have conventional poses such as aiming an arrow, a horse-riding posture, and sword-fighting kata.

Isn't it both easy and handy to use a preset pose and import the most suitable ones? You can also edit them after applying them to your canvas. Read on to learn how.

Figure 14.26: Pose model and art

Customizing character and figure models

Clip Studio Paint allows for the customization of both the character models and generic figure models that come with its 3D library. The character models can have their expressions, hairstyles, clothes, and accessories changed, while the generic figures can have their proportions altered. Let's find out how to alter the 3D model proportions, change and alter a head model.

Customizing figure models

The generic male and female drawing models don't have accessories and clothes to change. However, their head and body types can be altered to more accurately reflect the character you're drawing.

In this section, we will discover how to adjust the proportions of the body and head drawing figure. Follow these steps to learn how:

1. Follow the instructions in the previous *Introducing the 3D Material palette* section to load the male drawing figure model onto the canvas.

2. In the command bar, under the selected 3D figure, click on the icon on the far right, labeled **Adjust body shape and size of 3D drawing figure in detail**. This will open the **Sub Tool Detail** palette for the 3D model, as shown in the following screenshot:

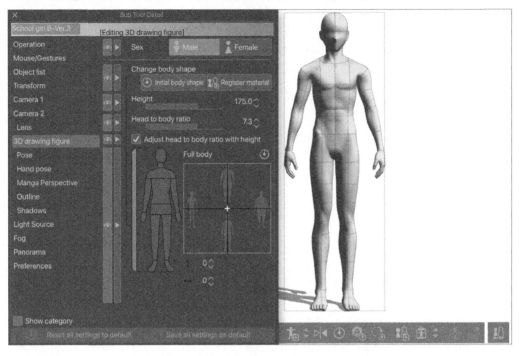

Figure 14.27: Change body shape Sub Tool Detail palette

3. In the following screenshot of the **Sub Tool Detail** palette, to the right of the image of the full body is a square menu that is divided into four smaller squares. By dragging the white + icon into the center of the four squares, we can change the proportions of the model by mixing attributes such as skinny, muscular, and fat. The **Height** and **Head to body ratio** sliders below this menu can also be used to adjust the model:

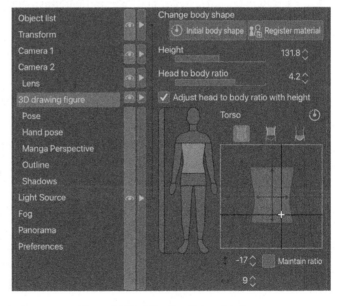

Figure 14.28: Adjusting the waist shape

4. To adjust the height and width of a specific part of the model, click on the corresponding section of the full-body figure in the **Sub Tool Detail** palette. In the preceding screenshot, the torso is the currently selected body part being adjusted.

5. Adjust any part of the model as needed to achieve the desired look for the drawing figure, checking how it changes on the canvas. Then, close the **Sub Tool Detail** window.

The screenshot on the right shows the figure model with proportions inspired by a *Chibi* anime character!

By using this option to adjust the body shape and size, you can have a variety of body shape references!

Figure 14.29: Adjusted body shapes

Now, let's have a look at how to customize a head model:

1. Follow the instructions in the previous *Introducing the 3D Material palette* section to load a 3D head model onto the canvas.

2. In the command bar, under the selected 3D figure, click on the wrench icon. This will open the **Sub Tool Detail** palette for the 3D model, as shown in the following screenshot:

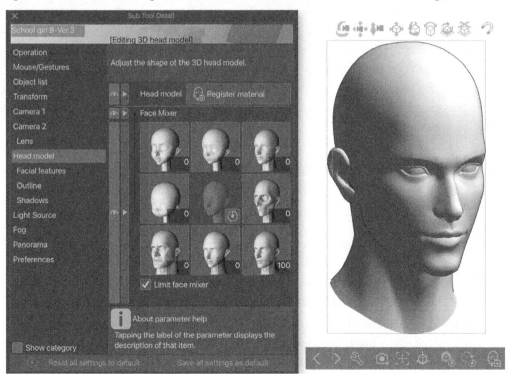

Figure 14.30: Editing 3D head model Sub Tool Detail palette

3. In the screenshot on the right of the **Head model** setting on the **Sub Tool Detail** palette, a variety of head models are displayed. You can mix the head model on the canvas with any of the models on this list using the slider. Simply click the head model you want to mix in the list and move the slider that appears next to the thumbnail image.

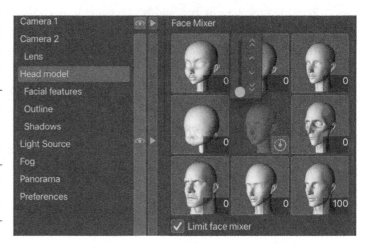

Figure 14.31: Head model setting

4. To customize facial features manually, select the **Facial features** setting in the **Head model** subcategory on the **Sub Tool Detail** palette. Click on the corresponding section of the face figure. In the screenshot on the right, **Eyes** is the currently selected face part being adjusted:

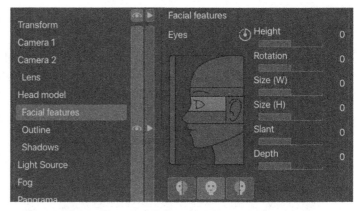

Figure 14.32: Facial features setting

5. Adjust any part of the model as needed to achieve the desired look for the drawing figure, checking how it changes on the canvas. Then, close the **Sub Tool Detail** window.

You have now grasped how to customize both the body and the head of your 3D drawing figure!

In the next section, we are going to save our customized model to our Material palette so that we can use it again later.

Saving 3D information to the Material palette

You put in a lot of effort to adjust the body shape, size, and head of the figure model, and it would be such a shame if you lost the data, especially if you'd like to use it for a character that appears in your manga several times. Therefore, it's always good to know how to save it. Let's find out how to do that in this section.

Two types of 3D information can be saved to the 3D Material palette: pose information and 3D drawing figures. Pose information can be saved both from the generic male and female figures as well as from the character models. 3D drawing figure (proportion and facial features) information can only be saved from the generic male and female drawing figures. Currently, there is no way to save changes to the character figures as custom materials.

Saving pose information

When you customize the poses of a character or an object, it's always a good idea to save them in case you want to use the same pose again in the future, so you don't need to repeat the same customization process over and over.

Follow these steps to save a character's pose information to the Material palette:

1. Click on the character or drawing figure whose pose you'd like to save.

2. In the command bar below the figure, locate the **Register pose to Material palette** icon, which looks like the screenshot on the right.

Figure 14.33: Register pose to Material palette icon

3. Click on the icon to bring up the **Material property** window. You can also bring up Material property by clicking the up and down triangles next to the human-shaped icon (see *Figure 14.33*), then click the option you want from the drop-down menu: **Register full body pose as material**, **Register left hand pose as material**, or **Register right hand pose as material**. Then, the corresponding **Material property** screen will open, as you can see in the following screenshot:

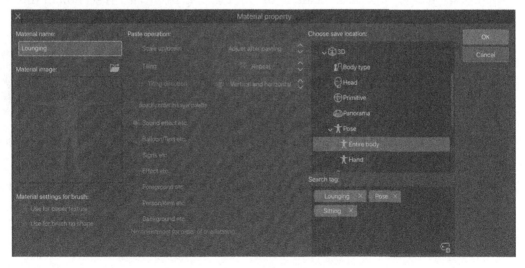

Figure 14.34: Material property window

4. Under **Material name**, enter a catchy name for your pose.

5. In the **Location to save material** section, navigate through the categories until you get to the **3D | Pose | Entire body** folder and select it as the location to save the full-body pose material.

6. Click on the icon in the lower-right corner of the **Search tag** window to bring up the textbox for tag entry. Type in the tag text and press *Enter*. Then, click the icon again to add another tag.

7. Once you have finished naming and tagging your pose, click on the **OK** button to finish saving the pose information.

> **Tip**
>
> I always recommend tagging every material that you save to the Material palette. It's an extra step, but it could save you a lot of time in the long run! In addition to tagging them with terms that describe the material itself, I always use a custom tag for anything that I save to the Material palette so that I can enter that search term and find everything I've saved.

Now you can use this pose information on any figure or character! For instructions on using preset poses, see the *Using preset poses on figure models* section of this chapter.

Let's move on to see how to save 3D drawing figure information.

Saving 3D drawing figure information

These instructions allow you to save any changes to the generic male and female drawing figure proportions that you may have made in the *Customizing figure models* section of this chapter. Follow these steps to save custom proportions to the Material palette:

1. Click on the drawing figure you'd like to save.

2. In the command bar below the figure, locate the **Register 3D drawing figure to Material palette** icon, which looks like the icon on the left; if you are saving facial features on a head model, you need the icon on the right, as shown in the screenshot on the right.

Figure 14.35: Register 3D drawing figure to Material palette icon

3. Click on the **Register 3D drawing figure to Material palette** icon to bring up the **Material property** screen, as shown in the following screenshot:

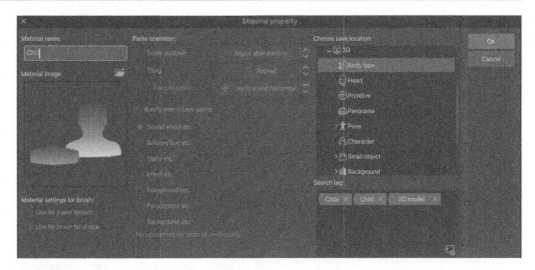

Figure 14.36: Material property screen

4.   Under **Material name**, enter a unique name for your figure.

5.   In the **Choose save location** section, navigate through the categories until you get to the **3D | Body type** folder and select it as the location to save the material for the body type, and the **3D | Head** folder for the facial features.

6.   Click on the icon in the lower-right corner of the **Search tag** section to bring up the textbox for tag entry. Type in a tag and press *Enter*. Then, click the icon again to add another tag.

7.   Once you have finished naming and tagging your figure, click on the **OK** button to finish saving the information.

By collecting favorite poses or character figures, you can save a lot of precious time working on manga.

Did you know that you can also import 3D models from other programs? Read on to see how to do it!

Importing 3D models into Clip Studio Paint

Using the 3D assets in the Material palette is all well and good, but what about importing a unique model from another program? In this section, we are going to look at how to do so, and how to turn it into a line drawing as a finishing touch. But there is a downside to using this function too much, as the characters might look too artificial and generic – it's good to remember to not abuse this tool too much and keep this as a basic template for creating your unique art style.

Although Clip Studio Paint can import 3D information from other programs, there are some limitations. For instance, sometimes, color and texture information for a model from an outside source may not be imported into Clip Studio Paint correctly.

Important note

The file types that can be imported into Clip Studio Paint are the Clip Studio 3D Character format (extension **cs3c**), Clip Studio 3D Object format (extension **cs3o**), Clip Studio 3D Background format (extension **cs3s**), and **fbx**, **6kt**, **6kh**, **lwo**, **lws**, **obj**, and **VRM** files.

Follow these steps to import 3D information into Clip Studio Paint:

1. In the **File** menu, click on **File | Import | 3D Data...**, as shown in the following screenshot:

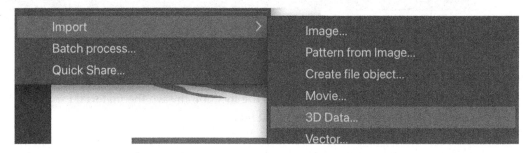

Figure 14.37: Import drop-down menu

2. In the **Open** window, navigate to the location on your computer where the 3D data file is stored. Click on the file that you wish to select, and then click **Open**.

3. It may take a moment for the 3D data to show in the file. Once it does, you will be able to position it and rotate the camera around it as normal.

Once you import a 3D model, you can turn it into a line drawing. If you have the EX version, you can do it by using an image converted to lines and tones. Find out more about conversion in *Chapter 3, Penciling: Layer and Layer Property Palettes.* To access the conversion menu, click on **Layer** in the **File** menu, then click on **Convert to lines and tones** to bring up the settings menu for **Convert to lines and tones.** The screenshot on the right shows our good friend **School Girl B** after the default settings for conversion were used on her:

Don't have the EX version? You can alternatively use the **Convert Layer** option to turn a 3D character into a line drawing!

Figure 14.38: Image converted to lines and tones

To do this, click on **Layer** in the **File** menu, then click on **Convert Layer...** to bring up the **Convert Layer** window, and select **Vector layer** on the **Type** drop-down menu. Then click **Vector settings...** to open the **Vector layer conversion** window, as shown in the following screenshot:

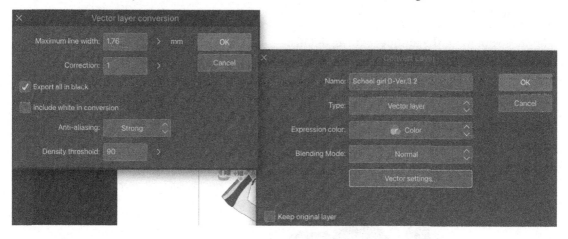

Figure 14.39: Convert Layer window and Vector layer conversion window

I'm afraid there is no preview function for this, but you can try it out several times to get the right look by changing the settings and clicking **OK.** The converted layer with a catgirl becomes the vector layer containing the extracted line drawing, as shown in the following screenshot:

Or, you can simply click on **Layer** in the **File** menu, then click on **Convert Layer...** to bring up the **Convert Layer** window, select **Raster layer** on the **Type** drop-down menu, select **Monochrome** on **Expression color,** and then click **OK.** You will have a raster layer containing a black-and-white drawing, as shown in the following screenshot:

Figure 14.40: 3D character converted to a vector layer

Figure 14.41: 3D character converted to a raster layer

Using the image, add your texture and details, or even customize it to avoid being too generic. In the example on the right, I added my twist to the finished image.

We can see more of the unique texture, details, motion, personality, and attitude of this character.

You can, of course, use the 3D figures and characters just as pose references for your own characters. You can find your own way of using the function!

Figure 14.42: Sample art using converted image

Wow, now you can get control of 3D objects to change poses, figures, and camera angles! And you've even mastered how to load, save, import, and, finally, turn 3D objects into line drawings!

Figure 14.43: 3D character and a drawing based on it

Summary

This chapter took us deep into the third dimension and got us familiar with the 3D assets available in the Material palette. We learned how to add 3D assets to our canvas, as well as how to move them in the 3D space. We learned how to rotate and move our camera to give us a different perspective on 3D models. We also learned how to use saved poses from the Material palette, from picture or photo references, from the Posemaniacs website, and from the camera, as well as how to customize the character models that come with it. Then, we learned how to save our own 3D information as materials that we can use later. Finally, we learned how to import models from other 3D applications and how to turn those models into line drawings using the **Convert to lines and tones** and **Convert layer** options.

These skills will help you draw characters and objects with consistency every time they appear on your manga pages. They'll also expand your range of visual expressions, camera positions, and character poses.

Now, we're going to start getting into coloring your comic! In the next chapter, we will begin by talking about the different ways to make color palettes in Clip Studio Paint, and how to use the eyedropper and **Sub View** palette to select colors.

Join us on Discord!

Read this book alongside other users. Ask questions, provide solutions to other readers, and much more.

Scan the QR code or visit the link to join the community.

`https://packt.link/clipstudiopaint`

15

Color Palette

Just like in painting, we can create color palettes in Clip Studio Paint as well. These palettes are digital values of color that we can save, import, export, and access in different ways to create color schemes and automatically mix colors.

In this chapter, we are going to look at color palette variations, how to use them, and even how to create them. In digital drawing, we can use a palette just like in the traditional way. Having a brilliant line-up of squares set up in front of you, you might feel like it is a serendipity of colors – a chance to encounter interesting color combinations accidentally.

You'll also learn how to import them from Photoshop and pick colors from the **Sub View** palette. It's very useful knowledge to have when you start coloring your art on Clip Studio Paint, and by the end of this chapter, you will be able to handle your desired color combinations with a wide range of techniques. Let's jump into the wonderful world of color!

The following topics will be covered:

- Crafting aesthetics with color palettes
- Understanding color pickers
- Exploring the Color History, Intermediate Color, and Approximate Color, and Colormixing palettes
- Creating color palettes from the Sub View palette
- Importing palettes from Adobe Photoshop

Technical requirements

To get started, you need Clip Studio Paint already installed on your device, and a new canvas opened with a white-colored paper layer. Any size is fine, but I recommend creating a 300 dpi square canvas to go through the content in this chapter.

Creating aesthetics with color palettes

When we use color, we want to have some early ideas of what theme and atmosphere we want to deliver. I will recommend some ideas that we can use immediately for our creation. The first idea is character theme colors. It's great fun to come up with the most suitable theme color for each character. We especially need this when we are creating a color manga as characters need to be distinguishable immediately on a page. This is a particularly good idea because, by the time we get to creating character merchandise, we can have even more fun designing with their theme colors!

Pick a color that describes your character well: should they have an energetic warm color, a cool mysterious color, or a solid dark color? The sample art in *Figure 15.1* shows characters with their theme colors.

Figure 15.1: Sample art of characters with their theme colors

Another idea is overall color combos to deliver the right impression or emotion behind the art-work. For example, we don't use primary colors when we want to create a romantic atmosphere but tend to use them to express danger or thrill instead. The samples in *Figure 15.2* are art with different color combos.

Figure 15.2: Sample art with various color combos

From left to right, we can observe romantic, dangerous, kawaii, fresh, and dreamy aesthetics to express the atmosphere, with each color combo supporting them.

Of course, the preceding images are merely examples. We can edit/create our own. I trained myself by using four or five limited colors to draw a color illustration in one hour with a theme, which helped me tremendously to understand the power of using colors. You can also try it by studying colors from your favorite art/photo and drawing with them on your art. By the way, all the above sample artworks were created using Clip Studio Paint, using its color palettes, which will be introduced later in this chapter.

Understanding color pickers

For traditional painting tools, you need a canvas, brushes, paint colors, and a palette to start. We're going to have a look at paint colors and various palettes in the digital world in this section. In Clip Studio Paint, similar to other digital drawing tools, the palettes come with colors already on them; how handy!

When we pick a color for a specific usage, there are some recommendations I can give when you have doubts about your choice. For shading, I add it with a light purple on the **Multiply** layer blending mode; you will find how to do it in the *Exploring layer blending modes* section in the next chapter of this book. Another tip is that the colors of objects closer to the camera tend to be warmer and more reddish, and those farther away tend to be cooler and blueish.

There are lots of ways to choose colors in Clip Studio Paint, but the three that are most used are the **Color Wheel**, **Color Slider**, and **Color Set** palettes. Each palette gives us a different way to make just about any color we can imagine in our digital illustrations and comics. Let's take a look at each of these palettes and how to use them to pick colors in the following sections.

The Color Wheel palette

The **Color Wheel** palette is probably the most used method for choosing colors in the digital realm. The Color Wheel palette has two modes, **HLS** mode and **HSV** mode:

- **HLS** mode: This stands for **Hue**, **Luminosity**, and **Saturation**. Hue is the degree of variation in the color, luminosity is the brightness of the color, and saturation is how much of the pure color is in the mix (colors get grayer the less saturated they are).
- **HSV** mode: This stands for **Hue**, **Saturation**, and **Value**. Hue is the degree of variation in the color, saturation is how much of the pure color is in the mix (colors get grayer the less saturated they are), and value is how much white or black has been added to the color to make the new color.

Figure 15.3 shows the HLS mode of the Color Wheel palette.

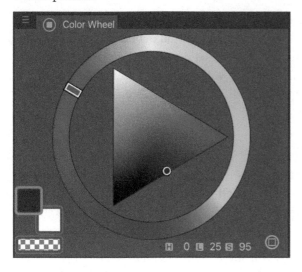

Figure 15.3: HLS mode in the Color Wheel palette

The outer ring of colors controls the hue. The triangle inside of the circle shows the pure hue (chosen from the outer circle). As we move up and to the left, the color becomes lighter and closer to pure white. As we move down and to the left, the color becomes darker and closer to pure black. By clicking inside of the triangle, we can choose any saturation or luminosity of the currently chosen hue.

With this triangle shape, we can see a triad color combination: the three colors pointed to by the triangle are the ones that create a striking impression when used together in art. So, when you want a vivid and intense atmosphere, imagine there is a triangle in the middle of the color circle, and just turn it around, then pick the three colors each corner is pointing to.

In the samples in *Figure 15.4*, we see the triad with other color combinations that work well.

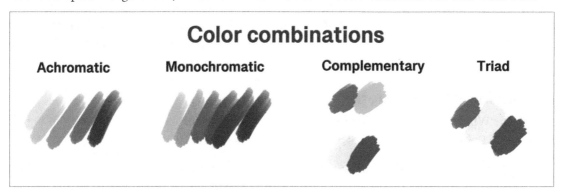

Figure 15.4: Samples of various color combinations

The bottom-left corner of the palette shows our currently selected foreground and background colors, as well as our transparent swatch. We can quickly select to use the foreground or background color from this palette, or in the primary toolbar in the user interface.

Along the bottom edge of the palette, we can see the number values of the currently selected color for hue, luminosity, and saturation, marked **H**, **L**, and **S**, respectively. In the previous screenshot, the hue value is **0**, the luminosity value is **25**, and the saturation value is **95**.

Tip

Knowing these number values can help you match the colors that you use, even if you switch to other graphics software. By clicking on the area with the number values, the options can be changed from hue, luminosity, and saturation to the **Red, Green, and Blue (RGB)** values instead.

The icon at the bottom right of the palette switches our Color Wheel palette to **HSV** mode, which is shown in *Figure 15.5*.

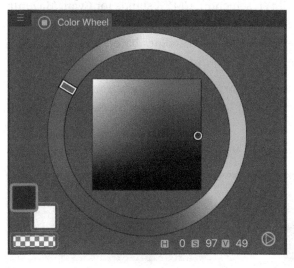

Figure 15.5: HSV mode in the Color Wheel palette

The numbers under the color picker show the **H**, **S**, and **V** values of the currently selected color.

Let's look at the next type of palette.

The Color Slider palette

The next tab in the color palette is the **Color Slider** palette shown in *Figure 15.6*. You can bring it up on the screen by clicking **Window** on the **File** menu and then clicking **Color Slider**.

Like HLS mode, we can choose the hue by clicking along the outer ring in the palette. The upper-right corner of the square shows the pure hue. By moving toward the lower-right corner, the color becomes darker and closer to black. The top-left corner is pure white and choosing a color close to it makes the color lighter in value. Going toward the lower-left corner makes the color less saturated (grayer) and closer to black.

If we look at the rectangle marker at the upper-left of the color wheel, we will find a color directly opposite, which is the complementary color. These samples are shown in the color combinations presented in *Figure 15.4*. If you use only these two colors in art, it creates the highest contrast, and many pop designs use this technique.

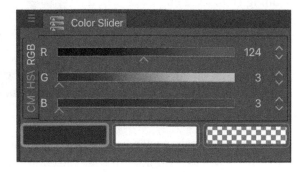

Figure 15.6: Color Slider palette

The tabs along the left edge of the **Color Slider** palette allow us to choose between different ways to select our color. The one shown in the previous screenshot is the RGB mode. Each slider in this mode controls a different amount of color. The top slider controls the amount of red in the current color, the middle slider controls the amount of green, and the bottom slider controls the amount of blue. The swatches along the bottom of the palette window are the current foreground and background colors, as well as our trusty transparent swatch.

The second tab in this palette is the HSV mode, which is the same as the HSV mode from the Color Wheel palette, but instead of a wheel and square, we have sliders to control each aspect of the color selection.

The final tab in the Color Slider palette is the CMYK selection. **CMYK** stands for **Cyan, Magenta, Yellow, and Black** and these are the colors used in printing color images on paper. Although we cannot set our document to be in CMYK mode, we can choose colors based on CMYK values using these color sliders to control the amount of each color present.

The color sliders are very useful when trying to precisely match a color, say from a logo or used in a website design. If you know the number values of the color, you can precisely enter them, using one of the tabs in the Color Slider palette.

Read on to find out about the third palette, **Color Set**. You might find it's easier to use than the previous two.

The Color Set palette

The final color palette we are going to look at is the Color Set palette shown in *Figure 15.7*. Instead of controlling color by using sliders, you can simply pick a color from a set of colors. This can be accessed on the screen by clicking **Window | Color Set** in the **File** menu.

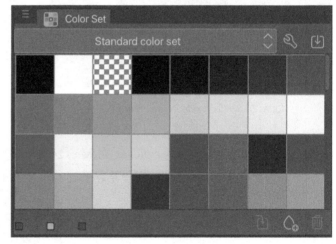

Figure 15.7: Color Set palette

If you are a Photoshop user switching to Clip Studio Paint and you've ever used **Color Swatches**, this palette will look familiar to you. The color sets are pre-made swatches of color that you can click on to select. *Figure 15.8* shows a sample illustration using colors from the standard color set.

Figure 15.8: Illustration created using the standard color set

We can use these to select a color close to what we want and then tweak it to the exact shade we want using the Color Wheel palette or the Color Slider palette, or just use the color sets as they are.

The drop-down menu at the top of the Color Set palette allows us to choose between different sets of colors. The set shown in the preceding screenshot (*Figure 15.8*) is the standard color set. Our own custom color sets can be created as well so that we can save colors we use often, say for the main characters in a comic project. It would boost the efficiency of coloring the same character multiple times if all colors for use on one particular character were collected in the same place, and if a color that you normally use first is at the top of the set.

Follow these steps to create a custom color set:

1. Click on the wrench icon to the right of the drop-down menu at the top of the **Color Set** palette. The window as shown in *Figure 15.9* will appear.

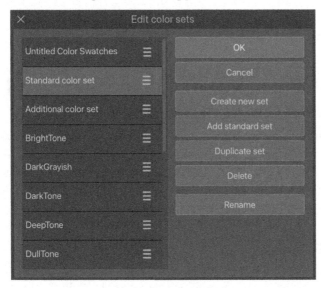

Figure 15.9: Edit color sets window

2. Click on **Create new set** in the **Edit color set** window.

3. Type a name for the new color set and then click on **OK**.

    A new color set made of transparent squares will now show in the **Color Set** palette.

4. In order to add colors to the set, first, click on the transparent square where you'd like to place the new color. Then, use one of the color pickers to set the color to save as the currently active foreground color.

5. In the **Color Set** palette, click on the **Replace color** icon (shown in *Figure 15.10*) in the lower-right corner and then the foreground color will replace the transparent square.

Figure 15.10: Replace color icon

6. To add a color to a new square instead of replacing the currently selected one, click on the **Add color** icon (shown in *Figure 15.11*).

Figure 15.11: Add color icon

Tip

You can create your new color set by picking colors from the canvas with your art to which **Color match** has been applied. The **Color match** function changes the whole color according to the reference image or a color gradient.

You can find it by going to the **File** menu, and clicking **Edit | Tonal Correction | Color Match....** How to use **Color match** is described in the *Using Color Match and filter options* section in *Chapter 16, Using Clip Studio Paint to Color Your Manga*.

Once we use it for brainstorming color coordination, we can pick good colors and create a new color set!

You have seen two different Color Wheel palettes, the Color Slider palette, and finally, the Color Set palette, and now know how to create your own color set. Having solid color sets will give you the security of not losing great color combinations.

Now, let's take a look at some of the other tabs in the color palette and learn how they can help us add color to our illustrations.

Exploring the Color History, Intermediate Color, and Approximate Color, and Color Mixing palettes

Color History, **Intermediate Color**, and **Approximate Color, and Color mixing** are all palettes located within the Clip Studio Paint interface. Color History allows us to keep track of colors that we've already used in our art, and the Intermediate Color and Approximate Color, Color mixing palettes allow us to mix colors in different ways. In this section, we will explore each of these palettes and learn how to use them.

The Color History palette

Have you ever painted and needed a color you were using a while ago, but it's so blended in with the colors around it that it's impossible to get the pure color anymore? The Color History palette is the answer to your prayers, and it's easy to use to boot!

Before opening the Color History palette, open a blank document and select a brush or pen tool. Choose a color and scribble on the open canvas. Do this a few more times with several other colors. Before the Color History palette can show us anything, we need to have some colors used on our page so that we have a history built up. The use of the color can be a simple click of the mouse or a stroke of the stylus, so long as the color was used.

Now that we have used a few colors on the canvas, open the **Color History** palette by clicking on **Window | Color History** in the **File** menu, or by clicking on the **Color History** tab in the color palette. The **Color History** palette should look like *Figure 15.12*.

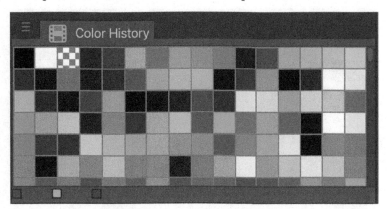

Figure 15.12: Color History palette

The palette will show any colors recently used. Click on the square of the required color to make it active again.

To save the colors from the Color History palette, click on the menu icon in the top-left corner of the palette, then click on **Register to color set palette** to save the color swatches. To clear the color history, click on the icon in the top-left corner and select **Clear color history**. This will reset the palette and start the color history over again.

Color History is such a simple little palette without a lot of options, but for a digital painter, it can be a powerful tool and make it much easier to keep consistent colors across an entire piece.

Next, we are going to see a good palette for picking up in-between colors.

The Intermediate Color palette

The Intermediate Color palette allows us to create a harmonious combination of colors to use in our illustration and manga. By allowing Clip Studio Paint to do the mixing, we can easily create a color scheme that works together.

The steps that we will follow to learn how to use this palette work best if you can see the Intermediate Color palette and the Color Wheel or Color Set palette at the same time. This is impossible when the palettes are nestled together, as they are in the default user interface for Clip Studio Paint. We will need to pop out one of the palettes so that we can see them at the same time.

To pop out the **Intermediate Color** palette, locate it in the tabs nested within the color palette. Click on the tab at the top of the palette where the name of the palette is showing. With the mouse button or stylus still held down, drag the **Intermediate Color** tab out of the color palette. *Figure 15.13* shows the palette in the middle of being dragged out onto the canvas view area.

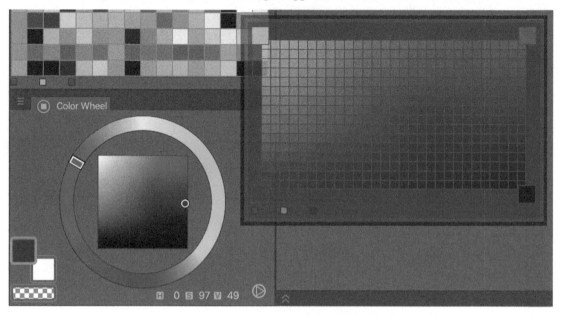

Figure 15.13: Moving the Intermediate Color palette

Once you have moved the Intermediate Color palette out of the main color palette area, release the mouse button. You should now be able to see the Intermediate Color palette and the Color Wheel or Color Set palette side by side, as shown in *Figure 15.14*.

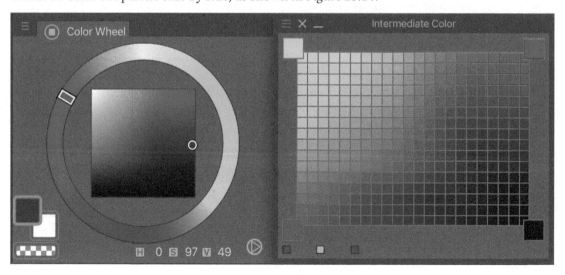

Figure 15.14: Two color palettes located side by side

Once you have these palettes next to each other, follow these steps to create a color scheme that works together using the Intermediate Color palette:

1. Choose a color from the **Color Wheel**, **Color Set**, or **Color Slider** palette windows. This can be any color you wish to use in your color scheme.

2. With your chosen color as the currently active color, move the cursor over the large square at the top left of the **Intermediate Color** palette. The cursor will become a paint bucket icon over the square. Click to add the color to the corner box.

3. Repeat *steps 1 and 2* for any other colors in your color scheme, adding new colors to the other corner boxes. In *Figure 15.15*, we have used green in the upper-left corner, red-orange in the upper-right corner, blue in the lower-left corner, and black in the lower-right corner.

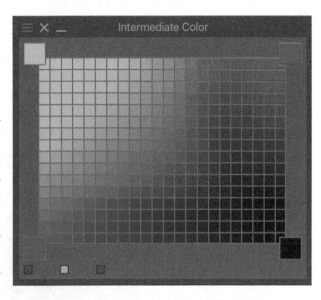

Figure 15.15: Intermediate Color palette with new colors

4. Use the cursor to select colors from the small square color swatches in the center of the **Intermediate Color** palette with which to color your image.

As we add colors to the corners of the Intermediate Color palette, the small squares on the inside of the palette are automatically filled with a blend of those colors. This is an easy way to get mixes of colors the way that we would with paint in the real, physical world, but by using digital tools to do our color mixing for us. It is a great palette to show good shade/light colors instantly! The image in *Figure 15.16* is an example using the Intermediate Color palette:

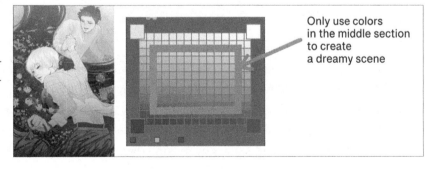

Only use colors in the middle section to create a dreamy scene

Figure 15.16: Example image of using the Intermediate Color palette

It's good to see the intermediate color at a glance when we want to avoid primary colors for drawing. Read on to see a more experimental palette, the Approximate Color palette, which can produce accidentally good color coordination for you!

The Approximate Color palette

The **Approximate Color** palette is a completely different way of mixing colors. This palette requires some experimentation to get used to it with different color mode sliders, but once you play with it, you may just love it! When we want more nuance in the main color we are using, this palette comes in handy. You can search for a slightly more vivid or grayer shade, and then the palette shows a grid of all possible variations! With just a slight tinge of another color, you can use it to express a bounced light from a nearby object's color. The Approximate Color palette is shown in *Figure 15.17*.

Follow these instructions to learn how to use the Approximate Color palette:

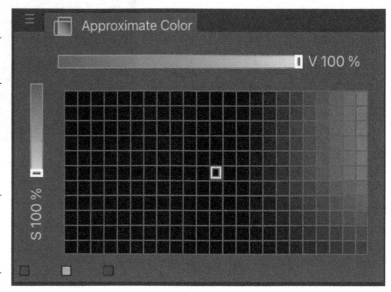

Figure 15.17: Approximate Color palette

1. Open the **Approximate Color** palette by either clicking on the tab in the color palette or by clicking on **Window** in the **File** menu and clicking on **Approximate Color**.

2. Select a color other than black as the active foreground color. The currently selected foreground color will change the results of the blending in the **Approximate Color** palette.

3. Click on the text to the right of the top slider to open the pop-up menu of blending options. These options will be discussed in detail later.

4. Click on the text below the slider on the left side of the **Approximate Color** palette window. Choose an option to blend from this pop-up menu.

5. Adjust the top and left sliders by moving them and seeing how the colors in the palette change.

6. Click on a color square inside of the palette to choose that color as the active foreground color.

The options next to the sliders in this palette are **Hue**, **Saturation**, **Luminosity**, **Luminance**, **Red**, **Green**, and **Blue**.

This list gives details on each of these options:

- **Hue:** The degree of variation of the color.
- **Saturation:** The vividness of the color. Higher values result in more vivid colors.
- **Luminosity:** The value of the color mixed in.
- **Luminance:** The intensity of vivid brightness of the color.
- **Red:** The amount of red mixed in.
- **Green:** The amount of green mixed in.
- **Blue:** The amount of blue mixed in.

The sliders on each axis control how much of the currently selected parameter is being used. For instance, setting both the horizontal and vertical axes to **Hue** and setting both slider values to **100%** produces lots of very saturated colors when a similarly saturated color is the currently active color. *Figure 15.18* shows what the **Approximate Color** palette looks like when a saturated purple color is chosen and the horizontal and vertical axes are set to **Hue**.

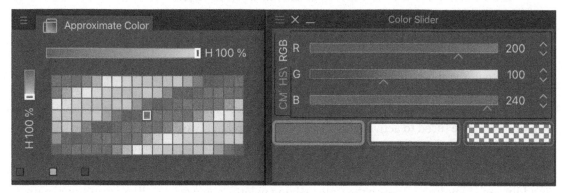

Figure 15.18: Approximate Color and Color Slider palettes

The last palette we will explore is the Color Mixing palette, which offers more visually sensuous way of mixing colors.

The Color Mixing palette

The latest color palette added to Clip Studio Paint is the Color Mixing palette. It recreates the traditional color-mixing experience that traditional painters do. It works best with oil painting brushes. The sample art in *Figure 15.19* is drawn with the Color Mixing palette.

Follow these instructions to use the Color Mixing palette:

1. Click on **Window** in the **File** menu and click on **Color Mixing**.

2. Select a color from the color list on the palette, click the brush shape icon, and select the size of the brush from the drop-down menu in the *Figure 15.19* to make a mark in the

Figure 15.19: Color Mixing palette and art

checkerboard area. Click another color you want to mix from the color list. Select the brush again and then draw on top of the mark you have just made.

3. Select the **Blend color** icon, which is the shape of merging two droplets, then scrub on the area where the two colors are overlapping.

4. Select the **Color picker** icon and click on the area where the color is blended. You will see the color you picked is now the **Foreground** color.

You can add more colors to the color list by clicking the + icon on the far right of the list. Additionally, the **Erase** (used to activate the eraser tool), **Step backward** (used to undo the last action you took), and **Step forward** (used to redo the action that have been undone) icons are located under the color list.

By adding and blending colors on the Color Mixing palette, you work just like a traditional painter, which means you can get more direct feelings just like physical color mixing experiences.

Creating color palettes from the Sub View palette

In addition to all the other wonderful ways we've explored of selecting colors in this chapter, we can select colors from references that we've loaded into the Sub View palette as well. This is easy, convenient, and a real time-saver for those working on comics where the same colors are used for characters or environments over and over.

Follow these steps to import an image into the Sub View palette and then select colors from it:

1. Locate the **Sub View** palette. It is usually nested with the Navigator. If it cannot be located in the interface, go to the **File** menu and click on **Window | Sub View** to bring it up.

2. At the bottom of the palette, click on the **Import** icon, which is circled in *Figure 15.20*.

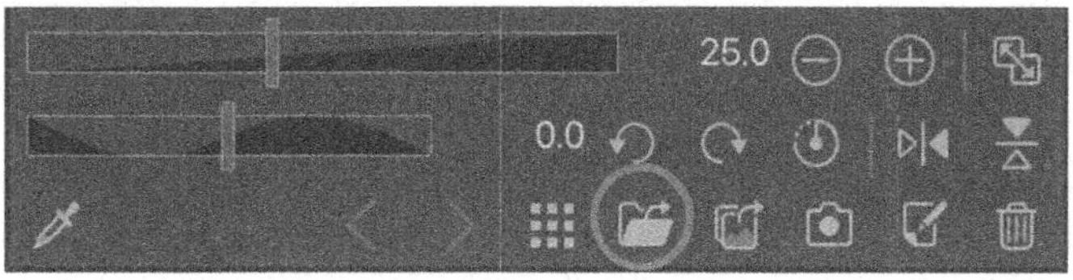

3. Locate your reference image and click on it to select it, then click on the **Open** button to complete the import.

Figure 15.20: Sub View palette

4. Your image will now be visible in the **Sub View** palette.

5. To select colors from the reference image, click on the eyedropper icon circled in *Figure 15.21*.

6. Move the cursor over the image in the Sub View palette and click with the eyedropper to select a color from the reference image. The color will become the currently active color.

Figure 15.21: Sub View palette with an image

The Sub View palette is a great place to keep regularly used references, such as character concept art, environment designs, and anatomy and pose references. Being able to select colors from it means that colored character references become easy-to-use palettes in their own way. We can select the colors directly from the character concept art and then use them to add color to our comics. Additionally, from scenery photos you have taken of the sky with golden clouds or a dark forest, you can, of course, use them as a palette!

For Photoshop users who recently started using Clip Studio Paint, the next section is the one for you!

Importing palettes from Adobe Photoshop

If you are switching from Adobe Photoshop to Clip Studio Paint, there is no reason why you can't take any custom color swatches you may have created with you to your new software! In this section, we will import Photoshop color swatches into the Color Set palette.

Before being able to import your Photoshop swatches, you will need to save them from Photoshop to a **.aco** file. In Photoshop, you will want to go to the **Swatches** palette and click on the menu (it will most likely be in the upper-right corner, depending on your version of Photoshop). Next, click on **Save swatches** in the menu. Save the file to a folder on your computer where you will be able to locate it easily. You can also find **.aco** files for download on the internet with colors such as Copic Marker inks and more.

Follow these steps to import a color swatch set from Adobe Photoshop to Clip Studio Paint:

1. Open the **Color Set** palette by clicking **Window** in the **File** menu, then click **Color Set.**

2. Click on the three-bar shape menu icon in the top-left corner of the **Color Set** palette to see the drop-down menu.

3. Click on **Import color set** in the **Color Set** menu.

4. Navigate to the folder where the **.aco** file is located on your computer's hard drive. Click on the file to select it, as shown in *Figure 15.22*, and then click on **Open.**

Figure 15.22: Color Swatch file in Finder

5. The swatches from the color file will be imported and named automatically, as shown in *Figure 15.23*.

6. To rename the imported color set, click on the wrench icon in the **Color Set** palette. The **Edit color sets** window will open.

Figure 15.23: Imported color swatch

7. Find the imported color set's name in the list to the left. Click on it once to select it, as shown in *Figure 15.24*.

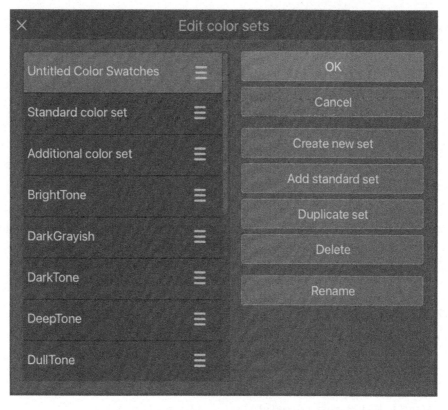

Figure 15.24: Edit color sets window

8. Click on the **Rename** settings. The name on the left will change to a text entry box. Type the new name for the color set and then press *Enter*.

9. The color set's name will be changed, as shown in *Figure 15.25*.

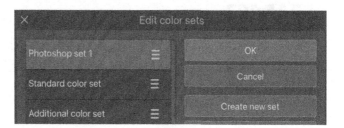

Figure 15.25: Edit color set window with a new name set

10. Click on **OK** to save the changes.

Great, we now imported a color set from Photoshop, which fuels efficiency for everyone working back and forth between Clip Studio Paint and Photoshop.

Summary

In this chapter, we began to explore the wonderful world of color. Color is a complex subject, and many studies can be done on using it effectively, but by using the tools and palettes in Clip Studio Paint, we can make it a little bit easier to handle. We learned how to use the Color Wheel, Color Slider, and Color Set palettes. Then, we learned how to use the Color History, Intermediate Color, and Approximate Color, and Color Mixing palettes to track and mix our colors. Finally, we imported color swatches from Photoshop and learned how to select colors from the Sub View palette and imported color swatches from Photoshop. For certain, these functions will help you color your art in future creations, keep your favorite colors, or build beautiful color combinations.

So, how do we apply these colors to our digital art? In the next chapter, we will learn how to create color flats, use layer blending modes, and color our ink layers, and use Color Match. It's going to be a packed chapter, so let's get going right away!

Join us on Discord!

Read this book alongside other users. Ask questions, provide solutions to other readers, and much more.

Scan the QR code or visit the link to join the community.

`https://packt.link/clipstudiopaint`

16

Using Clip Studio Paint to Color Your Manga

In this chapter, we will take the color-selecting skills that we learned in the previous chapter and use them to start coloring our comics. Here are the topics that we will cover in this chapter:

- Using reference layers
- Creating flats using the fill and pen tools
- Creating colored line art
- Exploring layer blending modes
- Shading with Shading Assist
- Using the Color Match options and filters
- Adding a paper texture
- The Liquify tool adjustment

We are going to look at how to use reference layers and start exploring ways to add colors without having mishaps such as overflooding areas you want to color. Then, we will learn how to change the colors in line art for an organic organic-looking finish. Next, we will learn what layer blending modes are and the benefits of using them, with rich visual references. Then, we will explore the time-saver function, Shading Assist. We will move on to learn how to use color mixing for a realistic way of creating a desired color. Finally, we will look into Color Match options, filters, and the Liquify tool to change the final look of the artwork. By the end of this chapter, you will be able to handle digital coloring easily and effectively, which means you can expand your range of color expressions.

Let's jump into the wonderful world of color!

Technical requirements

To get started, you need Clip Studio Paint already installed on your device, and a new canvas opened with any line art layer and a white-colored paper layer. Any size is fine, but I recommend creating a 300 DPI square canvas to go through the content in this chapter.

Using reference layers

In this section, we are going to look at a basic way, and one of the most useful, to start coloring. Having line art already on your canvas and knowing the great digital coloring benefits really changes your creative life.

Let's have a look at reference layers. **Reference layers** are a game changer for anyone who does digital art. Reference layers allow us to make some aspects of the digital coloring process a lot easier. Many digital art beginners make a mistake when they start adding color to their art. Once they have some nice inks down, they grab the Fill tool in whatever software they're using and start adding color willy-nilly to the same layer that their line art is on. This produces results similar to what's shown in *Figure 16.1.*

Figure 16.1: Image colored by the fill tool

If we look closely at the area between the black lines and the color, we can see a slight line of white and gray pixels that haven't been filled in. This results in an unpolished look, and taking a pen tool and going over the unfilled area takes a lot of time to clean it up.

Each artist is unique and has their own way of working, but it is recommended that you utilize your layers to their full advantage and also to make your process easier. Line art should be on one layer, and coloring should be on another. This is very easy to do if you create your inked lines digitally because, on the layer, you should have just ink lines and the rest of the space is transparent. If you have ink lines from a scanned image, the whole layer is opaque, which means you can't separate layers of ink lines and background color. All you then need to do is create a new layer below the ink layer and then put your colors on that layer, as shown in the layer setup in *Figure 16.2.*

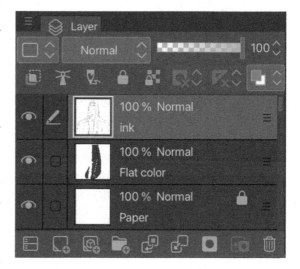

Figure 16.2: Layer palette

Another thing that some digital art beginners do is create their color layer below their lines, then take the pen tool and draw around the outline of each area on the new layer so it can be filled in on the color layer. This also takes a lot of time and effort and can be done much more easily and effectively using the tools and features built into Clip Studio Paint.

Tip

If you draw ink lines on paper and scan them into your computer, you can still digitally color your lines. You will want to set your layer with your scanned lines with the **Multiply** layer mode. This will make your white areas transparent when color is applied to layers underneath, while the black areas will not show color through them.

Before we get into filling in actual colors, let's talk for a moment about reference layers.

Reference layers are layers that have an effect on how tools act on other layers. This setting is turned on and off by clicking on the lighthouse icon at the top of the **Layer** palette. In *Figure 16.3,* this icon is highlighted with a red circle.

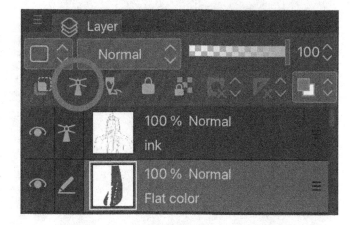

Figure 16.3: Reference layer icon on the Layer palette

Figure 16.3 shows that the **ink** layer has been turned into a reference layer. Now, even if we go to the **Flat color** layer below it, any tools that we set to work will be changed by the contents of the reference layer.

As an example, let's see what happens when we use a pen tool with the reference layer options. In order to do this, we'll open the **Sub Tool Detail** window with **G-pen** selected. We learned how to do this in *Chapter 9, Material Palette and Inking Special Effects*. Then, follow these steps to use the anti-overflow options with the pen tool:

1. Click on the **Anti-overflow** option in the menu of the **Sub Tool Detail** palette.
2. Check the box next to **Do not cross lines of reference layer**.
3. Use the pen on a layer other than the layer set as the reference layer. The pen will only fill inside of the lines where it is clicked. Using the thicker pen, it would be easier to see the effect.

4. If there is still a white outline around the color area, click on the box next to the **Area scaling** option. This option will automatically expand the colored area so that the color goes underneath the line art slightly, eliminating the white pixels.

In *Figure 16.4*, we can see the **Do not cross lines of reference layer** option settings for **Anti-over flow** on the left (pointed to by the arrow), and the **Layer** palette on the right, and we can see that we are coloring on the **Flat color** layer. Even though the line art is on a completely different layer, we can bind the colors to the line art boundaries using this simple combination of settings.

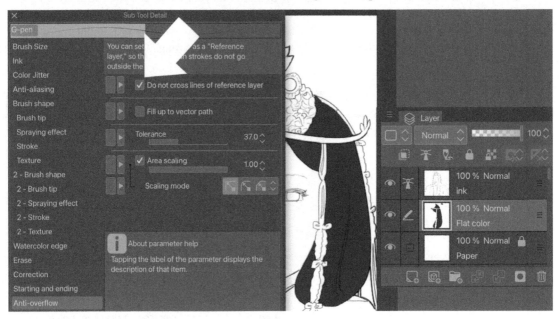

Figure 16.4: Sub Tool Detail and Layer palettes

Now, you know the good way to start coloring with the reference layer and **Anti-overflow** setting on pen tools. Let's explore two ways of making color flats in the next two sections.

Creating flats using the fill and pen tools

In this section, we will use the fill tool, which uses the reference layer as its boundary. *Flats* is a shortened word for *flat-colored layers*; the layer has colors painted without shading or lighting, hence it is flat and two-dimensional looking. Normally, artists create these flats after creating line art layers, which means just painting foundation colors according to the inked line art, then adding patterns, shading, lighting, and special effects later.

To complete this section, we will need a file open that has a set of lines on a layer we have set as a reference layer. Only one layer can be set as the reference layer at a time, but we can use tools that conform to the reference layer on any other layer in the file.

Complete the following steps to create a custom Fill tool that conforms to the reference layer:

1. Select the **Fill** (paint bucket) tool.

2. Select the **Refer other layers** sub tool.

3. In the **Tool property** palette, find the **Refer multiple** option. Select the **reference layer** icon for this option as in *Figure 16.5*.

4. Ensure that the **Area scaling** box is checked.

5. This will automatically expand the boundaries of the color underneath the line art, ensuring a smooth transition from line art to color without any stray white pixels. You may have to adjust this setting for optimal results, depending on how thick or thin your line art is. Use the eraser tool to clean up any overflow that goes into areas where it's not desired.

6. If there are small gaps in your ink lines, check the box next to the **Close gap** option. This will automatically close small gaps and prevent colors from flowing over into other areas. Depending on how large or small the gaps are in your reference layer's lines, you may have to adjust the slider for optimal results. The settings are shown in *Figure 16.5*.

Figure 16.5: screenshot of Refer multiple setting

7. Using the **Fill** tool, click on the areas of the drawing to apply the required colors for that drawing. In *Figure 16.6*, the colors for the hair, skin, eyes, and clothes have been added to the character, but there are still some small white spots that the Fill tool missed because the areas are too small.

8. Use the pen or brush tool to fill in any other stray areas or add details, such as hair decoration or any other areas that need special attention.

Figure 16.6: Image colored with the Fill tool

Tip

Many digital art beginners ask how many layers they should use when creating their pieces. As with almost anything in art, this is really up to the artist. While you can put everything on one layer, it is recommended to separate line art and color layers so that colors can be changed without having to change the line art, and coloring and special effects are made easier. Some artists put all their flat colors on one layer, then have one layer for shadows and another for highlights. Some artists have a separate layer for each and every color used in their pieces. It depends on how you want to work as an artist, and sometimes it is up to the specs of your computer! A computer with less RAM and hard drive space won't be able to handle a file with lots of layers, so keep this in mind.

Now that the flats are done using the Fill and pen tools, we can use the auto-select (magic wand) tool to select the flat colors from the **flats** layer and then add shadows and highlights on another layer using the brush of your choice. Shading is the word we use for adding darker colors to our art to create shadow, and then the art will look three-dimensional, be able to tell the time of the day, and depict a mood. Highlights are for adding a lighter color to create shiny effects on glistening eyes, hair, mechanics, tools, weapons, stars, and wet objects. Both processes are so much fun and creative.

There is also a way that you can add colors and gradients to your black line art, which comes in handy when you want to create art with line drawings appearing to naturally blend in harmony with colored areas. Read on to find out how to do it.

Creating colored line art

It's OK when you draw black-and-white art with a solid black line, but once you start coloring the image, don't you think the black line color can be too harsh on the eyes? We are going to explore how to change the line art color in this section.

Colored line work, or color holds, can be used for a variety of effects. It can highlight an area, make it blend more with the coloring, or make a background element face away to leave the foreground in the spotlight. Colored line art can make an image look much softer by not having harsh black lines in it. This is a very easy technique to use to really add punch to an illustration.

To follow the steps in this section, you will need line art done on a transparent layer, as shown in *Figure 16.7*.

Figure 16.7: Line drawing

The preceding image is an ink drawing scanned from paper, with the white taken out automatically using Clip Studio Paint. You can do this with a scanned image by opening it in Clip Studio Paint. If needed, adjust the brightness and contrast to make the ink lines stand out sharply from the paper color. This will also make the conversion much cleaner. Once this is done, in the **File** menu, click on **Edit** and then **Convert brightness to opacity**. Clip Studio Paint will make the brightest areas transparent and the darkest areas opaque.

Let's add colors to a line drawing with the following steps:

1. On the **Layer** palette, click on the layer with the inked lines to select it.

2. Click on the **lock transparent pixels** icon, located above the list of layers. This icon is circled in *Figure 16.8*.

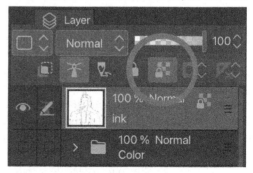

Figure 16.8: Lock transparent pixels icon

3. Select your preferred pen or brush tool.

4. Select the color that you wish to change your line art to.

5. Use the pen or brush over the inked lines to change the color from black to the current color.

6. To change all the lines at the same time, select the color to change the line art to and then click on the **Fill** icon in the command bar at the top of the Clip Studio Paint interface. This will flood all the lines at the same time.

When we lock the transparent pixels of the drawing, we prevent Clip Studio from altering the pixels that are not transparent in that layer. In this case, all ink lines are opaque, so we can only change their colors. In *Figure 16.9*, the pink scribble across the line art was made wildly, but it only shows on the filled-in lines.

This technique allows us to use pens, brushes, or even gradient tools to color our lines. This is good fun to use when you have a new design for merchandise from your manga pages. The drawing in *Figure 16.10* had a **Rainbow** gradient applied to the line layer.

Figure 16.9: Altered line color

Figure 16.10: Rainbow line color

Color holds can also be more subtle and make line work less "in your face," like in the interior of the hair and on the face and lips in *Figure 16.11*.

Let's see another example of changing the color of line works on an umbrella in *Figure 16.12*.

Figure 16.11: Image with a changed line color

Figure 16.12: Image with a changed line color 2

You can use airbrush tools to change the line colors of the ribs of the umbrella to express shade.

Tip

Certainly, you can apply the same method on a flat color layer to change the color instantly to your desired one! But to do so, you need to have each color area as an individual layer. It all depends on your device's RAM allowance. As a guideline, 8 GB is fine, and 16 GB is very usable. With 32 GB, it will be safe to work on 30 or more layers in one image and even have multiple pages open at the same time.

If you can, it's always useful, and even easy, to have a flat skin color, hair color, and clothing color in a different layer, then use layer masks or clipping layers to work on each section. For more on layer masks or clipping layers, go to *Chapter 12, Making Layer Masks and Screentones*. Now, you have total color control of not only filling areas and shading or light effects but also line art!

When you finish your flat coloring on your art, how about giving more three-dimensional effects by adding shading and highlights? Layer blending modes are very useful functions for adding shadows and highlights, which we will explore in the next section.

Exploring layer blending modes

Layer blending modes are functions for colored layers to change how to blend the colors with other layers. You can make colors darker by mixing them with other layers, or lighter, or invert the hue. When you want to add shade, light, light reflections, and color enhancements to your flat color art, layer blending modes will come in handy, because you can add these effects without hiding or ruining the flat color art! We are going to have a look at what layer blending modes are and how you can use them with examples.

At the top of the **Layer** palette is a drop-down menu that controls our layer blending mode. *Figure 16.13* shows the **Layer** palette and some of the blending modes available for us to use in our art.

There are tons of layer blending modes, and each one can give us a different effect. However, in this section, we are going to concentrate on the **Multiply**, **Soft light**, and **Screen** layer blending modes. These are the three modes most used in coloring, though, of course, you may find that other modes fit your style better. Let's look at each of the three modes that we listed and see how we can use them to color our images.

The Multiply mode

The **Multiply** mode is used most often by digital artists. This is because it makes white areas of the layer "transparent" but keeps the black areas opaque. This makes it the ideal selection for something like a scanned ink image. By setting the scanned image to **Multiply**, digital colors can be applied beneath the line art to finish the illustration. **Multiply** also makes

Figure 16.13: Layer blending mode drop-down menu

colors darker by combining them with the colors below them. This makes the **Multiply** mode ideal for shadow layers.

Shading, as we discussed in the *Creating flats using the fill and pen tools* section earlier, is a wonderful skill to have. Compared with observation drawings, manga drawings often have very limited shading, but at the same time, it's very tactical. One obvious place to add a shade is un derneath the face, which instantly lifts the face color and makes it stand out; plus, we can tell the audience that the character's head is a three-dimensional object. Other shading places will be un der eyelids, nose, body, and some parts obviously beneath bigger objects. In *Figure 16.14*, from the left, you can see a flat-colored artwork, a shading part, and a shaded artwork.

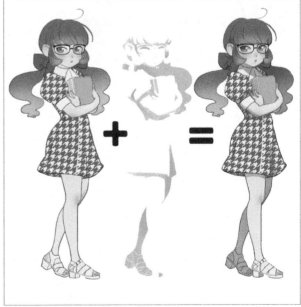

Figure 16.14: Three images with and without shading

The image in the middle shows where exactly the shading is: under the fringe, head, arms, and her left leg. They are limited but effective. We turn this layer of a shading area into the **Multiply** blending layer mode, and it should be placed on top of the flat-colored layers. In the result, which is the image on the right in *Figure 16.14*, we can see the character drawing has more depth in both colors and dimensions.

Light purple is a very popular color to shade with. In *Figure 16.15*, the purple layer is set to the **Normal** blending mode and no mixing is going on with the flat colors beneath.

Figure 16.15: Image with shadows in light purple

Figure 16.16: Image with Multiply shading

Now, we are going to make the light purple color interact with the flat colors below on the **Layer** palette and mix them, making new colors and shades by changing the layer blending modes to **Multiply**. *Figure 16.16* is the artwork with the **Multiply** blending mode layer added with the light purple color.

We can control the contrast between the base color and shadows by adjusting the **opacity** of the **Multiply** mode shadow layer. This is done using the slider to the right of the **Blending mode** drop-down menu. The preceding screenshot has had the shading layer lowered to **90** %, making the shadows much less intense.

Building up multiple layers of shadows can provide greater contrast and deeper shadows. I normally use three different **Multiply** layers for shadows: one for a big mass of shadow to mark the light direction, such as a sunset, a candlelight, or a light coming through between the leaves of the tree shade. Another is for all the object or a character body only using a deep orange **Gradient** tool to create a deeper shadow, which is darker at the bottom, mainly for distinguishing it from the background. The last one is for spot shading, such as in *Figure 16.16*.

Let's look at adding colors or light effects in a subtle way with the **Soft light** layer blending mode.

The Soft light mode

The **Soft light** mode is the best mode when you want to add colors very softly, such as creating rosy cheeks, or the gradient of hair color. First of all, you can select the area you want to add the color to with the **auto-select** magic wand tool and click on the colored area you want to select.

Then, you can only add colors inside the selection boundary without the new color overlapping the old colors. The image in *Figure 16.17* shows the addition of the color pink using the **Soft** airbrush tool with the **Soft light** blending mode only on the cheeks, nose, and fingers on selected skin color areas.

Figure 16.17: Soft light mode used on cheeks

The effect is so gentle that you can have great control of how dense the color you want to add by controlling how much color you will put using the **Soft airbrush** tool. We can always change the **opacity** of the layer if we need an even softer effect. **Soft light** mode is also used to mark the light

zones with the light color as well as the shadow zones with a cold tone. Besides the cheeks, it works very well to add red tones on the articulations (ears, elbows, knees, etc.) due to the blood flow. Read on to find out how to add a lighting effect with the **Screen** layer blending mode.

The Screen mode

The **Screen** mode is useful for creating vivid highlights. You can even use colors that you might not think of using for highlights to create a certain mood in your illustration or comic scene. In *Figure 16.18*, the highlight layer is set to **Normal** to show that we are using a turquoise color on this layer.

Figure 16.18: Image with highlights

Figure 16.19: Image with highlights in the Screen mode

By using our drop-down menu on the **Layer** palette, we can set our highlight layer to **Screen** mode. Using this blending mode, we now get the highlights shown in *Figure 16.19*.

Now, instead of the highlights on the face being turquoise, they are a light color close to white, while the highlights on the clothes still retain the turquoise hue. This mode gives us an effect that's just the opposite of what the **Multiply** mode does – the **Screen** mode makes color on layers underneath lighter, while **Multiply** mode makes them darker.

We have learned how to add shade with the **Multiply** mode, rosy cheeks with the **Soft light** mode, and finally, a light effect with the **Screen** mode. These are just three of the many blending modes available to us. By combining layer modes and opacity in different ways, we can create many different effects. Experimentation is the key here because each artist is different and likes to create a specific look with their art. Changing the layer mode does no damage to the original layer, so play with the layer modes in your art to see what different looks you can create using them and different colors to create shadows and highlights in your art.

With layer blending modes in mind, there is a great time-saving function – Shading Assist.

Shading with Shading Assist

It's totally fine to add shade by yourself, but sometimes it's useful to use a special function that is made for generating shade on your picture, especially when you need to draw tons of characters in a limited timescale. Of course, using **Shading Assist** only assists us by suggesting some different ways of shading and applying specific shading to different artworks, but it's not replaceable for our own unique shading: expressing the environment and mood of art perfectly. It is still an interesting and useful tool, however.

Let's try using it and see how our art will be shaded! Follow these steps:

1. Create an artwork that is divided into a line art layer, flat color layers, and a paper color layer.
2. Set the line art layer as a reference layer, as we learned in the *Using reference layers* section.
3. Create a layer folder that contains all flat color layers, as shown in *Figure 16.20*.

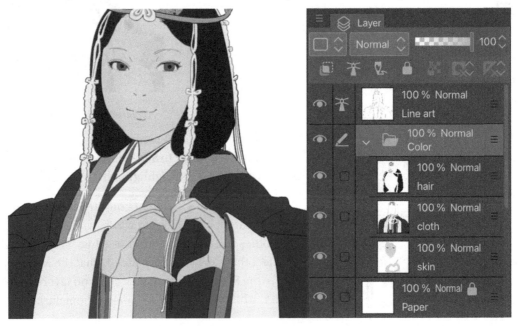

Figure 16.20: Sample art (left), Layer palette (right)

If you are not sure how to create a layer folder and add layers to it, follow the steps in the *Working with layers* section in *Chapter 3, Penciling: Layer and Layer Property Palettes*.

4. Select the **Color** folder in the **Layer** palette, click **Edit** in the **File** menu, and then select **Shading Assist...** from the drop-down menu, as shown in *Figure 16.21*.

Figure 16.21: Edit drop-down menu

5. Selecting **Shading Assist...** brings up a dialog window. As we set the line art layer as a reference layer, turn on the **Refer to lines on reference layer** checkbox, which is pointed to by an arrow in *Figure 16.22*.

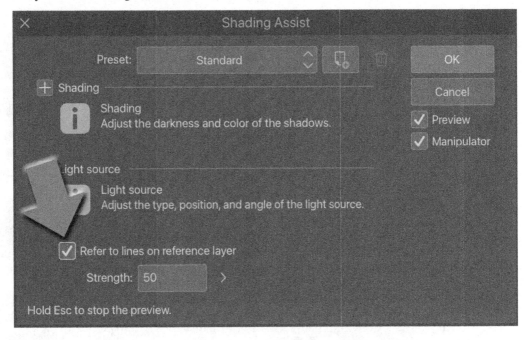

Figure 16.22: Shading Assist dialog window

6. By selecting a different preset shading from the **Preset** drop-down menu, you can see previews of corresponding shading on your art. The drop-down menu and corresponding shadings are shown in *Figures 16.23* and *16.24*.

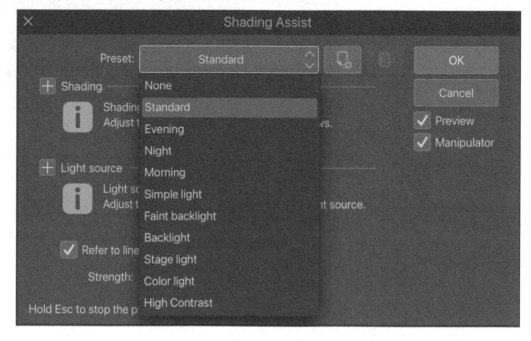

Figure 16.23: Preset shading menu

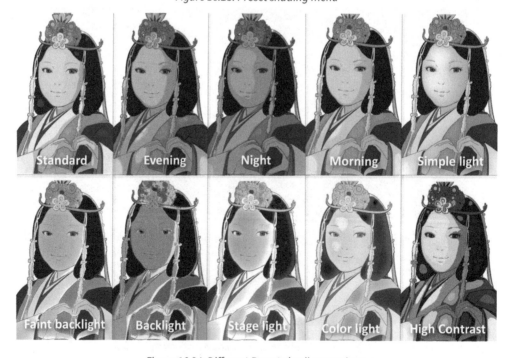

Figure 16.24: Different Preset shading previews

7. As we can see, there are various ways of shading. However, we still need our shading skills as some of them are not quite working well. We can use these results to learn what hue to choose to color in the specific lighting, such as a moody **Evening** shading.

8. On the canvas, move the blue round shape and circle manipulator to adjust the position, size, and intensity of the light. We will see how to control the light source later in this section. The currently selected manipulator turns its color to orange, as seen in *Figure 16.25*.

Figure 16.25: Light manipulator on canvas

Once the light settings are set to what you desire, click **OK** in the dialog to create a shading layer on top of the selected layers in the **Layer** palette, as shown in *Figure 16.26*.

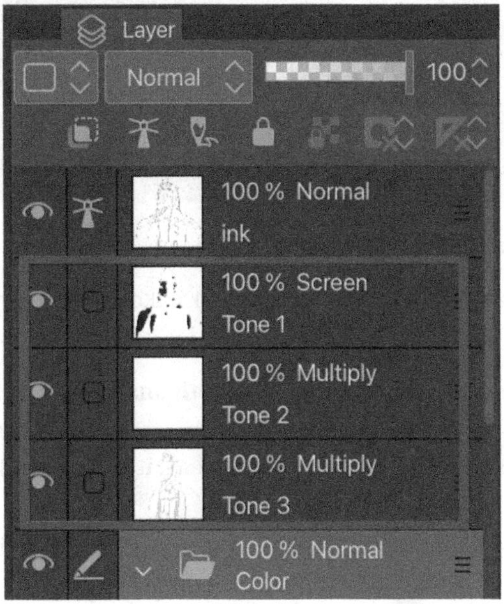

Figure 16.26: New layers in the Layer palette

It's done! Have a look at your artwork with shading now; isn't it quick and easy?

You can, of course, edit the shading by erasing or adding as you wish.

Did you know we can customize how we want the shading and lighting settings?

They are all in the **Shading Assist** dialog window; let's start with the **Shading** settings first. When you click on the + icon next to **Shading** in the dialog window, it opens the menu shown in *Figure 16.27*.

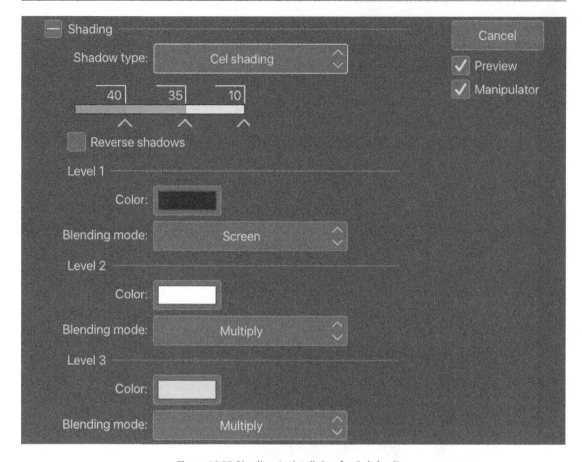

Figure 16.27:Shading Assist dialog for Cel shading

Does it seem a lot to learn? It's actually quite simple! The following breakdown will give you good ideas of what they are:

- **Shadow type:** This gives you two types of shading – **Smooth shading,** which creates a smooth blended transition between shaded and non-shaded areas, and **Cel shading,** which creates a distinct border between shaded and non-shaded areas; it can generate up to four shadows and highlights.
- **Shading bar:** When **Cel shading** is selected in **Shadow type,** the shading bar is displayed, and you can drag the arrow right or left to adjust the shade range.
- **Reverse shadows:** When it's on, shadows and highlights applied to the canvas are inverted.
- **Level 1 Color:** This sets the color of the shade.
- **Blending mode:** This sets the blending mode of the generated layer.

When **Shadow type** is set to **Smooth shading,** you will see different settings, as shown in *Figure 16.28.*

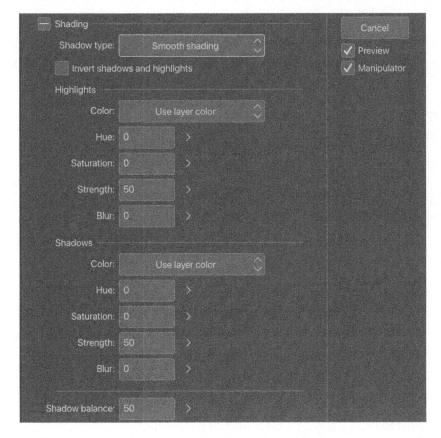

Figure 16.28: Shading Assist dialog for Smooth shading

There are a great number of bars, and the breakdown of each setting is as follows:

- **Invert shadows and highlights:** When it's on, it swaps shadow areas and highlight areas in the image.
- **Highlights Color:** You can select either **Use layer color** or **Use base color**. When **Use layer color** is selected, the selected layer is used for the base color, and the highlights and shadows are generated according to it. When **Use base color** is selected, you can pick a new color for the base color and can set **Blending mode**, **Strength**, **Blur level**, and **Shadow balance**.
- **Hue:** This specifies the amount of hue change relative to the base color, which makes highlights brighter and shadows darker.
- **Saturation:** This specifies the amount of change in saturation relative to the base color, which makes highlights brighter and shadows darker.
- **Strength:** This determines the intensity of highlights and shadows.
- **Blur:** The larger the value, the smoother the highlights and shadows are blended.
- **Shadow balance:** This sets the percentage of shading relative to the total shadows generated. The closer to 100, the larger the shaded area.

Now, you are a master of the **Shading** settings! Let's move on to **Light source** settings, which you can see in *Figure 16.29*.

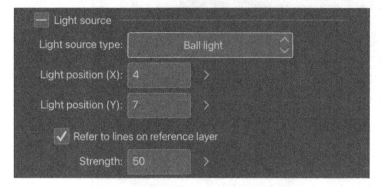

Figure 16.29: Light source settings

Compared with the **Shading** settings, the **Light source** settings are much more compact. Let's have a close look at them:

- **Light source type:** Gives two different types of light source. The **Ball light** type places a light source that can be moved to anywhere on the canvas.

The Directional light type applies light to the entire canvas at the same angle and intensity to generate shading with the angle of your choice.

- **Light position (X) and (Y):** Enabled when the light source type is set to **Ball light**. These set where the light source is placed on the canvas in regards to width and height. You can set any value from -100 to 100; when both **X** and **Y** are set to **50**, the **Ball light** position comes in the middle of the canvas. If we want a light directly above, try **X** for **50** and **Y** as **0**, or directly underneath, try **X** as **50** and **Y** as **100**. When the light source type is set to **Directional light**, you can set a value of the **Light angle**.

- **Refer to lines on reference layer:** When it's on, this refers to lines on the reference layer to generate shading. When off, shading is generated using only the information on the color layer.

- **Strength:** Enabled when **Refer to lines on reference layer** is turned on. This sets the strength at which the line art influences the shading. The higher the value, the more likely it is to generate shading along the lines of the line art.

Great, you can now have control of the **Shading Assist** settings! I'm sure you want to save the settings you have just adjusted to the **Preset** shading. Follow the steps to learn how to save and delete it:

1. Click the **create preset** button next to the **Preset** dropdown menu for registering a preset, which is marked in a red circle in *Figure 16.30*.

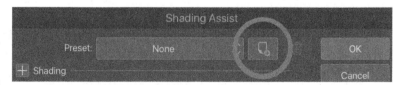

Figure 16.30: Create preset button

2. When the **create preset** dialog pops up, enter a name and save it. To delete a preset you created, select the preset you saved and click the trashcan button icon, which is circled in Figure 16.31.

Figure 16.31: Delete preset button

What a great way of shading and highlighting your image. You might find the brilliant coordination of them totally by chance!

You have inked, colored, changed your line art, and shaded your artwork. Now, do you have fun exploring the complete new color tones by using Color Match and filters using the artwork you just finished? Read on to find out how.

Using Color Match options and filters

Color Match and filters are fun tools to explore new possibilities for changing the final look of your artwork. It will be helpful for game art, especially when we are working with many artists together and use artworks from different artists but still want to have consistency in the game visual. For example, whenever a story takes a thrilling turn, all characters get the same Color Match option and filter, and if we keep this throughout the game, there will be a consistent tone throughout the game. This also helps you to try out different colors on your ordinary choice of color combinations or texture. This might be a good opportunity to step out of your comfort zone.

In this section, we are going to look at the Color Match options first then how to use them, and learn what the filters are and how you can apply them to your art. Read on to explore different tones and textures on the final looks of your art.

The Color Match options

Color Match comes in handy when you are uncertain about the color balance. Yes, you can make a drastic color change to your art by matching colors to those of imported images or gradients.

Let's find out how to use it by following these steps.

First of all, you need to create a layer that contains all the materials you want to apply Color Match to by creating a layer folder and selecting **Merge selected layers.** You can refer to the *Working with layers* section in *Chapter 3, Penciling: Layer and Layer Property Palettes* to see how to do it.

In the **File** menu, click **Edit | Tonal Correction | Color Match...**, as shown in *Figure 16.32*.

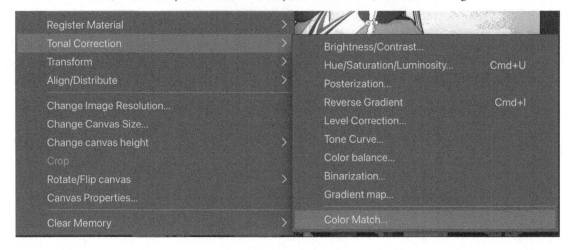

Figure 16.32: Tonal Correction menu

This will bring up a Color Match dialog window. By clicking the image thumbnail, you can see your art change its color accordingly, as in *Figure 16.33*. When you disable **Maintain brightness**, you can totally change the colors.

Figure 16.33: Color Match image dialog window

Use the **Intensity** slider in the dialog in the preceding screenshot to control the strength of the color adjustment. You can also import your images by clicking one of those three icons on the right at the bottom of the window: from your folder, from your photo album, or by taking pictures (this can only be done on tablets and mobile phones). Or, delete images from the gallery by clicking the trashcan icon at the bottom right.

If you prefer using the **Gradient** option, click **Gradient,** and the dialog changes, as shown in *Figure 16.34.*

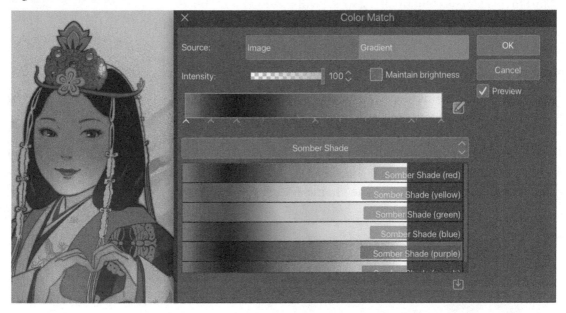

Figure 16.34: Color Match Gradient dialog window

By clicking the default **Somber Shade** gradient set, you can pick any default gradient set from the drop-down menu from **Somber Shade, Sky, Effect,** and **Tool (read-only).** You can find more gradients on **Clip Studio Assets**, which you can learn how to access in *Chapter 18, Exploring the Clip Studio Assets and Animation.* Then, import downloaded gradient sets by clicking the down arrow with the square icon at the bottom.

Once you select the most suitable gradient, adjust it by using the adjustment bar on top by sliding the tiny arrows underneath if you want.

When you are satisfied with the result, click **OK** to close the window.

Tip

Of course, you can apply the Color Match options to your grayscale artwork! Just draw your art in grayscale, use the **Color Match Gradient** option, and see what happens. You might find a brilliant quick way to color your art!

Well done, and what a brilliant way to change the whole mood of your drawing by using the Color Match options!

Filters

Clip Studio Paint has tons of filters, which will come in handy once you know what they are! Just click **Filter** on the **File** menu and you will see a list of filters, as shown in *Figure 16.35*.

Figure 16.35: Filter menu

The options you see in the preceding screenshot are explained here:

- **Blur:** This contains filters for blurring an image. Playing with different blur filters can give our illustrations a photographic effect and depth. After you are finished drawing, apply the **Blur** filter on only the layers containing the parts that need to be blurred. *Figure 16.36* shows samples with blur in the foreground (top), parts of the character (bottom-left), and background (bottom-right).

Figure 16.36: Three sample images with the Blur filter

- **Correction:** This contains filters to adjust line width and remove dust.

- **Distort:** This contains filters to distort an image however you like.

- **Effect:** This contains filters to give more artistic special effects.

- **Render:** This contains filters to give a Perlin noise.

- **Sharpen:** This contains filters to sharpen up an image.

We are particularly looking at two amazing filters: the **Chromatic aberration** filter and the **Noise** filter in the **Effect** filters because they will give you imperfect but nostalgic looks in the artwork in a very fun way. Let's jump into the wonderful usage of the **Effect** filters! Follow these steps:

1. First, create a raster layer that contains the materials you want to add a filter to by combining multiple layers into one (don't forget to duplicate them before combining them).

2. Go to the **File** menu, then click **Filter** | **Effect** | **Chromatic aberration** to bring up the **Chromatic aberration** dialog window, as shown in *Figure 16.37*.

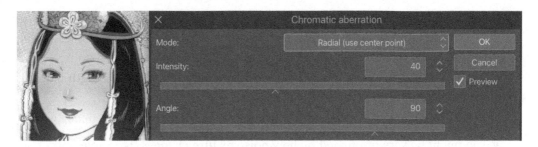

Figure 16.37: Chromatic aberration dialog window

3. Select how you want to apply **Chromatic aberration** from **Radial (use center point**) or **Lateral (use Angle)** by clicking **the Mode** drop-down menu at the top of the preceding screenshot. You can see the way the effects applied changes.

4. Adjust the intensity of the effect by sliding the **Intensity** bar.

5. Adjust the direction of the effect by sliding the **Angle** bar.

6. Once you like the result of the effect, click **OK** to close the dialog window.

Do you see the beauty of the art with the Chromatic aberration effect applied? The coloris now divided into red, green, and blue. Then, each color image was slightly off place, so you can see the image now looks like old printing with the colors not overlapping perfectly.This gives the image a nostalgic beauty. Let's enjoy another wonderful filter: **Noise**.

The **Noise** filter will give you a similar nostalgic impression. It simulates an old magazine image with textured imperfection. Follow these steps to use the **Noise** filter:

1. Create a raster layer with all materials, which you have done in *Step 1* in the preceding guidance.

2. Go to the **File** menu, and then click **Filter | Effect | Noise** to bring up the **Noise** dialog window, as shown in *Figure 16.38*.

Figure 16.38: Noise dialog window

3. Select a **Color Mode** option, either **Color** or **Gray**, from the drop-down menu at the top of the dialog. The noise will be applied in RGB hues in the **Color** mode, and black and white in the **Gray** mode.

4. Increase or decrease the noise particles by sliding the **Noise strength** bar or entering numbers in the box.

5. Once you like how the **Noise** effect is applied, click **OK** to close the dialog window.

Now, you might be very impressed by how noise texture changes the whole impression of the image! Yes, the image now possesses a crafty printed-on-paper feeling. Of course, we can apply multiple filters on one image; keep experimenting and have fun!

Next, we are adding a beautiful paper texture to our art; read on to find out.

Adding a paper texture

There is, of course, no paper texture that really exists in digital drawings since they're not drawn on physical paper, but we can add it as a final touch to our art. We can express a sense of paper texture on a digital drawing using the pencil or watercolor tools to some extent, but it is easier to add it to the entire page by using texture materials and layer blending modes.

Follow these steps to add a rough paper texture to your art:

1. Have your canvas with the art already opened, go to the **File** menu, click **Window | Material**, and then click **Material [Monochromatic pattern]** from the **Material** drop-down menu, as we see in *Figure 16.39*.

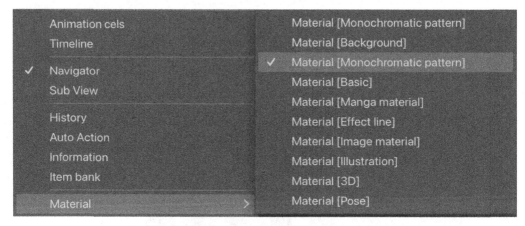

Figure 16.39: Material drop-down menu

2. The Material palette is now opened, showing a list of monochromatic pattern materials with thumbnails. Scroll down the list until you find **Rough textured** and click on it.

3. With the material selected, click the **paste the material to canvas** icon at the bottom of the Material palette, as circled in *Figure 16.40*.

The **Rough textured** texture is now pasted, and we can see the pattern on our canvas, on top of our art. The new layer with the texture is now in the **Layer** palette, as we see in *Figure 16.41*.

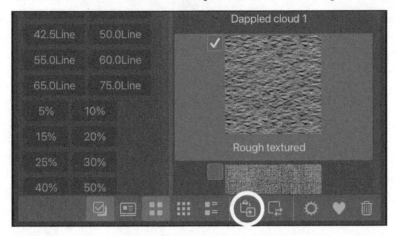

Figure 16.40: Material palette

Figure 16.41: Canvas (left), Layer palette (right)

4. The handle with a square in the middle of the canvas is for changing the angle and size of the pattern by clicking and dragging around. When you finish editing the pattern with the handle, click the **Layer Blending Mode** menu at the top of the **Layer** palette and click **Overlay** from the drop-down menu, as shown in *Figure 16.42*.

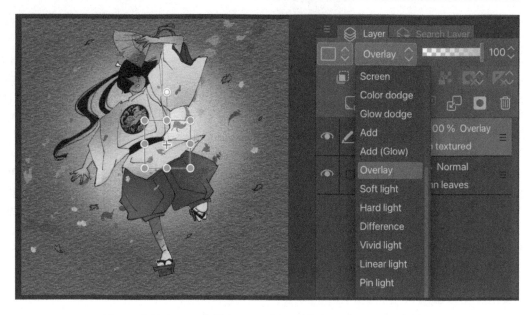

Figure 16.42: Canvas (left), Layer palette with drop-down menu (right)

5. Finally, change the opacity of the texture layer by moving the **Opacity** slider at the top of the **Layer** palette. In this step, change it to **45** %, as shown in *Figure 16.43*.

Figure 16.43: Canvas (left), Layer palette with 45 % texture opacity (right)

It's done! Your image now has a rough paper texture!

If you have a look at the **Textures** category in the **Material** palette, you will find so many textures available, plus you can download new ones from Asset, too! You can try out tons of textures, and you will find your favorite to add to your art to make it truly unique!

The Liquify tool adjustment

This is not a coloring tool, but we might need it for the final touch once the color drawing has been done. The Liquify tool will distort our art however we want by the motion of our stylus. So, let's say we are not satisfied with the face or body balance on our character drawing; we can use the Liquify tool to fix the imperfection!

Follow these steps to retouch your finished art:

1. Select all your layers, go to the **File** menu, and click **Layer | Create folder and insert layer**. Duplicate the **layer** file you have just created, go to the **File** menu, and click **Layer | Merge selected layers**.

2. Select the **Blend** tool from the **Tool** palette and select **Liquify** in the **Sub Tool** palette. In the **Tool property** palette, set **Brush Size** to 30 and select **Push Mode**.

3. Click and slide any part of your art that needs to be amended, as in *Figure 16.44* showing before and after Liquify tool correction.

Figure 16.44: Before and after Liquify correction

Now, your art has got a better facial balance and body proportion!

Summary

In this chapter, we started applying color to our images. We started out by discussing reference layers and how we can use them to make our colored flats easier with anti-overflow brushes and the Fill tools. Then, we explored how to change line art color, and looked at three of the many blending modes available in Clip Studio Paint that can help us shade and highlight our images. We also learned how to shade using Shading Assist, changing the tone of a finished piece of colored art using the Color Match options, and we explored adding the **Chromatic aberration** filter and the **Noise** filter. We explored adding a paper texture to our art. Finally, we learned how to use the Liquify tool to retouch the finished art. You can apply these new coloring skills to both digitally drawn and scanned manga images, for a more polished and professional look.

In the next chapter, we are going to start talking about auto actions. Auto actions are tools that can help you save a lot of time and effort when creating your digital art. Read on to learn how!

Join us on Discord!

Read this book alongside other users. Ask questions, provide solutions to other readers, and much more.

Scan the QR code or visit the link to join the community.

`https://packt.link/clipstudiopaint`

17

Auto Actions and Your Workflow

Auto actions are an amazing feature of digital art. They can simplify your workflow and save you time and effort when creating your drawings. What are auto actions? Auto actions are sets of recorded steps that can be played back, automating a task or tasks and completing them with the press of a button.

What sorts of tasks can be made into an auto action? **Scenario 1:** we have a blank manga page, and to start creating art on it, we need a panel layer folder (we can divide the panel later), a sketch layer named *Sketch*, an ink layer named *Ink* or *Line art*, background layers named *Background 1* and *Background 2*, grayscale layers to add shading named *Gray 1* and *Gray 2*, a highlight layer named *Highlight*, and a sound effect layer named *SE*. Auto action can do all of this in one click. **Scenario 2:** we have a blank canvas on which we want to create a color character drawing. We need a sketch layer named *Sketch*, an ink layer named *Ink*, a skin color layer named *Skin*, a skin details layer named *Skin 2* that has got a clipping mask to the skin layer below, and more... Again, auto action can do all of this in one click. Not only this, though; it can do just about anything that you can dream up!

In this chapter, we will cover the following topics:

- Exploring the Auto Action palette
- Using auto actions
- Creating a custom auto action
- Downloading auto action assets
- Auto action shortcuts

We are going to look at what auto actions are and how to apply them to your workflow. We will learn how to create a new auto action set, download auto action assets, and then finally, create auto action shortcuts in two different ways.

By the end of this chapter, you will be able to save a lot of time by creating and using auto actions to accelerate the speed of a frequently applied set of actions. Let Clip Studio Paint do repetitive actions automatically! It will surely make the creation of a long series of manga or comics less tiring.

Let's get started!

Technical requirements

To get started, you need Clip Studio Paint installed on your device, and a new canvas opened with any line art layer and a white paper layer. Any size is fine, but I recommend creating a 300 dpi square canvas to go through the content in this chapter.

Exploring the Auto Action palette

Let's start by looking at the **Auto Action** palette and what it contains.

Do you have a specific process when you create digital drawings, such as always adding a clipping mask for a clothing color layer of your character or always duplicating a line drawing layer, then adding a blur effect to it? Wouldn't it be a brilliant time saver if you could let Clip Studio Paint do these actions automatically? Your dreams have come true. In this section, you will learn the first step of how to use auto actions: finding the **Auto Action** palette and then opening it.

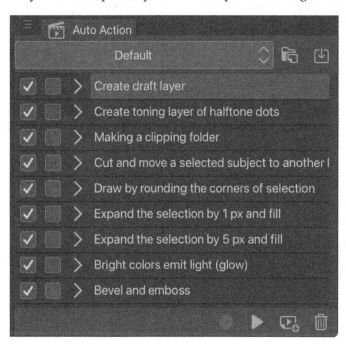

The **Auto Action** palette (*Figure 17.1*) can be found by clicking on the **Window** heading in the **File** menu and then clicking on **Auto Action**. If this menu item is already checked, then the palette is already in the interface somewhere. By default, it is a tab in the **Layer** palette.

Figure 17.1: Auto Action palette (1)

Let's break down the parts of this palette. The drop-down menu at the top of the palette allows us to switch between different sets of auto actions. The set of actions in the preceding screenshot is the **Default** set and comes included in Clip Studio Paint.

The icons to the right of the drop-down menu are **Create New Auto Action Set** and **Add Auto Action Set**. The trashcan icon at the bottom right is the delete button to erase a currently selected step of auto actions. Next to the delete action icon is the **Add New Auto Action Set** button, then to the left of that is the **Play Action** icon, which plays the selected action when you click on it; finally, the far-left round icon is **Record Auto Action**.

For your interest, let's have a look at this **Default** auto action set:

- **Create draft layer:** This creates a new raster layer, names it, and sets it as a draft layer. Basically, it creates a foundation for sketching, shown in *Figure 17.2*.

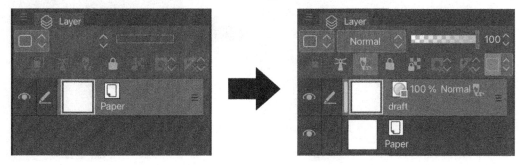

Figure 17.2: Create draft layer result

- **Create toning layer of halftone dots:** This creates a 60.0 LPI dot tone layer. You can find out more about screentones in the *Adding screentones* section of *Chapter 12, Making Layer Masks and Screentones*. You can start adding shade to your black and white manga by creating a new layer and searching for the right screentone.

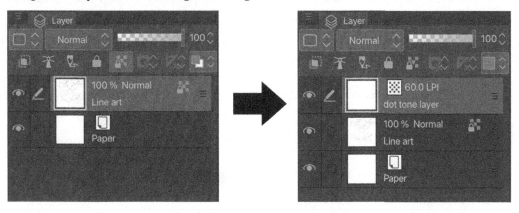

Figure 17.3: Create toning layer result

- **Making a clipping folder:** This creates two clipping layers above the selected layer, creates a folder, and puts the three layers in it. It's a process that gets you ready to add extra colors without flooding a boundary. You can add shade and shine effects safely within the flat color area you have already created. The result will look like *Figure 17.4.*

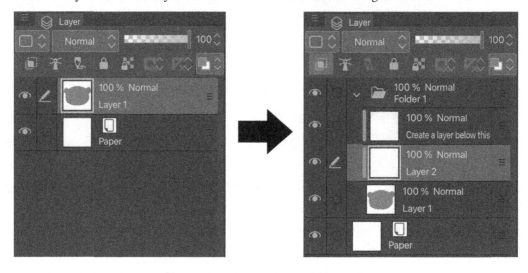

Figure 17.4: Making a clipping folder result

- **Cut and move a selected subject to another layer:** This copies and cuts out the content of the selected area, creates a new layer above the active layer, and pastes the content on the new layer. This is useful when you want to move certain content to a new layer quickly. For instance, you might have several items in one layer but just need to deal with only one item, such as a bunch of hair.

- **Draw by rounding the corners of selection:** This creates a shape with rounded corners of whatever the original shape of the selection area on an active layer was, with a border line of foreground color and filled with the background color. It's a good auto action for whenever you need a rounded corner manga panel! The result will look as shown in *Figure 17.5.*

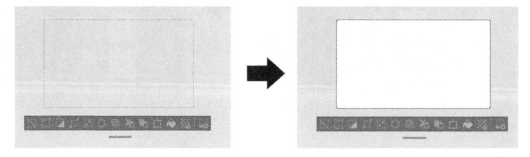

Figure 17.5: Draw by rounding the corners result

- **Expand the selection by 1 px and fill:** This makes the selected colored area expand by 1 px. It's a great solution when you have unnecessary gaps between a color and line drawings.

- **Expand the selection by 5 px and fill:** This does the same thing as the preceding auto action, but it expands the colored area to 5 px wider than the selected area.

- **Bright colors emit light (glow):** This adds a dramatic glow effect to the lighting of your drawing. It duplicates the active layer, adds extra light blurring effects with **Gaussian blur** to one layer, merges the layer with another layer, then turns the layer blending mode to **Add**.

- **Bevel and emboss:** This instantly adds a 3D effect to the drawing in the active layer. This is an easy way to add a lighter area to the top-left corner and a shade to the bottom right. The magic is done by creating a lighter-color copy layer of an original layer and moving it to the upper left slightly, then creating a darker-color copy of the original layer and moving it to the lower right slightly, then finally merging the copies into one layer.

Now you have some ideas of what auto actions are, how to find them, what the **Default** action set is, and what it offers. Let's have a look at how to use auto actions next.

Using auto actions

In this section, we are going to learn how to use auto actions with the eighth auto action in the **Default** set, **Bright colors emit light (glow)**, because it's the easiest action set to see the result of.

In the main window of the **Auto Action** palette are the names of the auto actions we can choose from. The right arrow to the left of the action's name can be clicked on to view the recorded steps that comprise the action. In *Figure 17.6*, the steps under the **Bright colors emit light (glow)** action are shown.

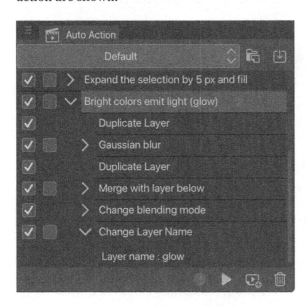

In the preceding screenshot, you can see that there are two rows of checkboxes on the left-hand side of the palette, next to the names of both the auto actions and the steps that they consist of. The first column (the one that has all the boxes checked in the screenshot) controls which steps or which entire actions are able to be played. If the checkbox is empty, then that step or action will not play.

The second column of checkboxes indicates whether a step will produce a dialog box where we must enter information or make a choice.

Figure 17.6: Auto Action palette (2)

In the screenshot of the **Bright colors emit light (glow)** action, for example, if we click on the second column of checkboxes next to the **Gaussian blur** steps, then when these steps come up in the action set when it's played, we will get to set the options ourselves before the action continues.

When we select an action and click on the **Play Action** button at the bottom right of the palette, or double-click the action name, the action steps will play on the currently active layer or selection. In *Figure 17.7*, the white lighting effect layer on the left has had the **Bright colors emit light (glow)** action applied to it, which you can see in the result on the right, making the white lighting effect have a dramatic glow.

Figure 17.7: Before and after an auto action is played (1)

Tip

Some actions require you to have an active selection made for them to work on, instead of just playing on an entire layer. Most actions that require an active selection in the **Default** action set have the *selected area* in the title, so look for this clue when playing actions!

We will look at two more **Default** auto actions to understand the variety of actions you can use.

The fourth option of the **Default** set is named **Cut and move a selected subject to another layer**, which, as was mentioned in the previous section in this chapter, cuts out a selected area from the active layer and pastes it on a new layer. As you can see in *Figure 17.8*, you can move the hair part from the **flats** layer with one click of the **Play Action** button.

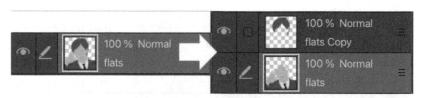

Figure 17.8: Before and after an auto action is played (2)

This will help you work on a particular area separately from other parts, such as adding a different type of shade or lighting effect to part of a character's hair.

Another **Default** auto action is **Bevel and emboss**, which adds an instant 3D effect to a simple shape drawing, as you can see in *Figure 17.9*.

Figure 17.9: Before and after an auto action is played (3)

The auto action added a lighter area to the top-left side and shade to the bottom right instantly!

Now that we know the uses of actions and some of the things we can do with the **Default** actions, let's create a custom action in the next section.

Creating a custom auto action

We're going to create a custom action that will set up a new file with a rough sketch, a final sketch, and ink layers with the press of a button, as I mentioned in the two different scenarios at the beginning of this chapter. You can make almost anything into an auto action, whether it's a few button presses or a longer and more complicated series of steps. By following the instructions in this section, you'll build the foundational knowledge you need to start creating your own actions in the future.

Before making an action of your own, complete the steps of the action a few times to make sure that you know the process and can remove any unnecessary steps or mistakes in its creation. This pre-planning step can help save a lot of troubleshooting later!

Actions are sets of menu commands executed on an existing layer or selection. Some settings and commands, such as setting the brush size, cannot be recorded. If a tool or layer is changed via a palette, this might not be added to the auto action recording.

Follow these steps to complete making this new auto action set and action. You will need to create a new, blank file before completing these steps:

1. In the **Auto Action** palette, click on the **Create new auto action set** icon to the right of the set drop-down menu. (Note that you can add new actions to the **Default** folder, but for the sake of organization you can also put your own actions into a new set.)

2. Name the new set **Custom** when the dialog box appears and click on **OK** to finish creating the new set. The **Create new set** dialog box is shown in *Figure 17.10*.

Figure 17.10: Create new set window

3. While in the new action set, click on the palette menu in the upper-left corner of the palette. In this menu, click on the **Add auto action** option to create the new action.

4. Name the new action by typing a name into the text entry box. For this example, we are naming our action Layer Set Up, as shown in *Figure 17.11*.

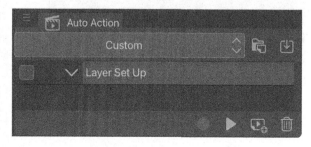

Figure 17.11: Layer Set Up set

Now that you have the new empty action in your **Custom** action set, we can begin recording the action steps!

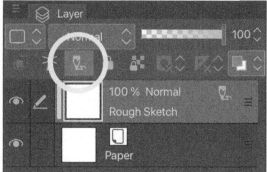

1. Click on the red circle icon at the bottom of the palette, the **Start to record auto action** icon, to begin logging the steps. Once the recording has begun, this circle icon will turn into a square.

2. Create a new raster layer, then rename the layer Rough Sketch. Click on the **Set as draft layer** icon on the **Layer** palette, which is circled in *Figure 17.12*.

Figure 17.12: Set as draft layer icon

3. Create a new raster layer above the one created in *step 2*. Rename this layer Final Sketch.

4. Create a new raster layer above the one created in *step 3*. Rename this layer Inks.

5. Select the **Rough Sketch** layer in the **Layer** palette to make it the active layer.

6. Go back to the **Auto Action** palette and click on the record button again (it is now a square instead of a circle – a square was commonly used in older technology to mark the **stop** button!) to stop the recording. The steps beneath the **Layer Set Up** action should look similar to *Figure 17.13*.

Figure 17.13: Layer Set Up auto actions

7. Open a new canvas and then go to the **Auto Action** palette. Click on the name of the **Layer Set Up** action, then click on the triangular **Start to play auto action** icon in the palette to play the action.

8. If the auto action has been recorded correctly, the **Layer** palette of the new page should look as shown in *Figure 17.14*.

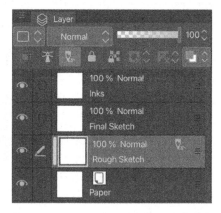

Figure 17.14: Layer Set Up auto action result

How easy it is to create a new auto action and record it! Just click the **Create new auto action set** icon, name it, press the record button to let it memorize all the processes, and then press the stop button.

What steps do you find yourself tediously completing over and over again? Do you get tired of having to manually resize your comic's dimensions before saving it to upload to your website? Do you have a set of steps that you go through a lot to make a special effect? Any process, from the simplest to the most complex, can be made easier with auto actions. Try making some of your own to use in your creation process!

You can also download auto action assets from Clip Studio Assets; read on to find out how.

Downloading auto action assets

There are tons of assets available on Clip Studio Assets to download to use in your art. My favorite auto action asset is **Old Fashioned TV action (Content ID: 1741400)**, which I use in the final stage of coloring art, and this auto action makes your art look like it's on a 1970s TV screen by toning the color, adding a texture, and adding chromatic aberration. You will find out more about Clip Studio Assets features in *Chapter 18, Exploring Clip Studio Assets and Animations*, but for now, let's concentrate on downloading and using auto action assets. Follow these steps:

1. Go to the Clip Studio Start screen by clicking its icon on the Command Bar, as shown circled in *Figure 17.15*.

Figure 17.15: Command Bar

2. If asked, enter your Clip Studio username and password, then click the nine squares icon in the top-right corner to bring up a menu window, as shown in *Figure 17.16*.

Figure 17.16: Clip Studio Start screen

3. When a **Menu** window pops up, click the **Search for materials** icon, as shown in *Figure 17.17*.

4. When you click **Search for materials**, a new screen appears with a search bar and newly uploaded assets in thumbnails underneath it. Type Auto or Autoaction in the search bar and hit the *Enter* button on your keyboard.

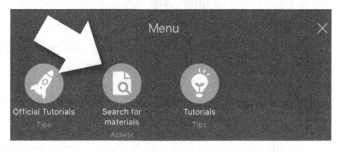

Figure 17.17: Menu window

5. Now you can see the auto action assets in thumbnails lined up. Scroll down to find anything you would like to use in your art. For now, choose an asset that has the word **FREE** under the thumbnail, then click on the thumbnail to see the asset details.

6. If you are fine with the details, click the **Download** button in the upper left-hand corner in red to start downloading the asset.

7. Keep in mind that downloading assets might take a while. After downloading is finished, return to Clip Studio Paint by clicking **DRAW** in the menu on the left.

8. In Clip Studio Paint, in the **File** menu, click **Window**, then click **Material** in the **Window** drop-down menu to bring up the **Material** palette to check whether the asset has been added to your **Material** palette.

9. In the **Material** palette, click on the arrow next to **All materials** if you can't find the **Download** category. If you click **Download**, the most recently downloaded asset will be displayed on the right, as shown in *Figure 17.18*.

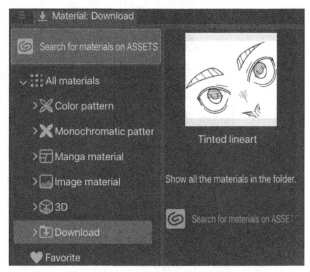

Figure 17.18: Material palette

10. Click the newly downloaded auto action asset thumbnail and click the **Paste material to canvas** icon (*Figure 17.19*) located at the bottom of the **Material** palette.

11. Once you click the **Paste material to canvas** icon, the window shown in *Figure 17.20* will pop up to ask whether you want to add the auto action asset to your **Auto Action** palette; click **OK** to confirm it.

Figure 17.19: Paste material to canvas icon

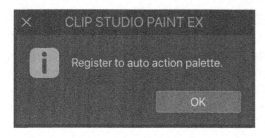

Figure 17.20: Confirmation window

To check whether the asset has been added to your **Auto Action** palette safely, go to the **Auto Action** palette, as we learned in the *Exploring the Auto Action palette section* of this chapter. Then, click the drop-down menu at the top of the palette. You will see the name of the asset there, as shown in *Figure 17.21*.

Now you can use not only the **Default** auto actions and the ones you have created, but also the ones you downloaded! Once you have downloaded auto actions, you can see the workflow in detail, which you can try out by yourself to see if you can apply and arrange them for later creations.

Now that you have two new auto action sets, you can edit and organize them freely following these steps:

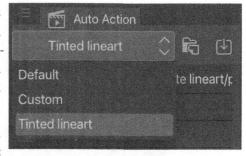

Figure 17.21: Auto Action palette

1. Click the three-bar icon on the **Auto Action** palette to bring up the **Auto Action** drop-down menu.

2. Select **Edit set…** from the drop-down menu and the **Edit set** dialog window will pop up, as shown in *Figure 17.22*.

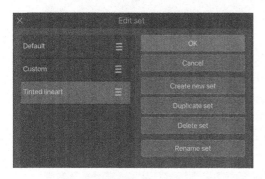

Figure 17.22: Edit set dialog window

3. Click and hold a three-bar icon next to the set name and move up or down to change the order of the set however you want. Click **Create new set** to create a new set. Click **Duplicate set** to duplicate the selected set. Click **Delete set** to delete the selected set. Click **Rename set** to rename the selected set.

4. When you have finished editing the sets, click **OK**.

5. Now your Auto Action sets are neatly stored and ready to use anytime you want them! You can also edit and customize your auto action workflow as you desire. While viewing details in the **Auto Action** palette, you can erase, add, or alter steps.

Let's have a look at the ways to access your favorite auto action quickly!

Auto action shortcuts

If you have auto actions that you use all the time, you can assign them to shortcut keys or even add them to the Command Bar at the top of the Clip Studio Paint interface.

In the next two sections, we are going to take the **Layer Set Up** action we created previously and create two shortcuts for it – one keyboard shortcut and one Command Bar shortcut! This is an easy process and will cut down the amount of time you spend going through palettes, trying to find the commands that you use most often. Let's look at both of these processes to create easy access to our auto actions.

Creating a keyboard shortcut

Follow these steps to create a keyboard shortcut for an auto action:

1. In the **File** menu, click on **CLIP STUDIO PAINT** or its icon and then click on **Shortcut Settings...** in the drop-down menu to open the keyboard shortcut preferences.
2. In the **Category** drop-down menu, select the **Auto actions** option.
3. Click on the arrow to the left of the auto action set name to view the actions under that set name. In *Figure 17.23*, we are looking at the actions in the **Custom** set to find the **Layer Set Up** action we created earlier.

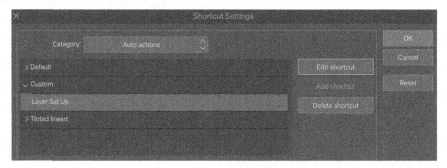

Figure 17.23: Shortcut Settings window (1)

4. Click on the **Layer Set Up** name to select it. Then, click on the **Edit shortcut** button.
5. On the keyboard, press the key or combination of keys you'd like to use for the shortcut. In this set of instructions, we are going to use the *Ctrl + T1* combination of keys to activate our auto action. This shortcut now appears next to the **Layer Set Up** auto action's name, as shown in *Figure 17.24*.

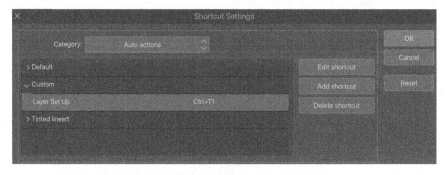

Figure 17.24: Shortcut Settings window (2)

6. To change an existing shortcut to something else, click on **Edit shortcut** and choose a new shortcut. You can also configure these shortcuts on your device.

7. To add another shortcut to the same auto action, click on the **Add shortcut** button and press another key or combination of keys to set a second shortcut.

8. To delete a shortcut, select the shortcut and then click on the **Delete shortcut** button.

9. Once you have finished setting shortcuts, click on the **OK** button to exit **Shortcut Settings**.

Now, when you hold down the *Ctrl* button and press *F1* on the keyboard, your **Layer Set Up** action will play.

Read on to find out about another shortcut you can create!

Creating a command bar shortcut

It's nice to be able to see your frequently used shortcuts on the command bar. To add a shortcut icon to the command bar, follow these steps:

1. In the **File** menu, click on **CLIP STUDIO PAINT** or its icon and then click on **Command Bar Settings...** in its drop-down menu to bring up the **Command Bar Settings** menu.

2. In the drop-down menu at the top of the settings menu, select the **Auto Action** option to view the auto actions.

3. Click on the arrow next to the action set to view the names of the auto actions beneath that set. In *Figure 17.25*, we are looking at the **Custom** set for the **Layer Set Up** action.

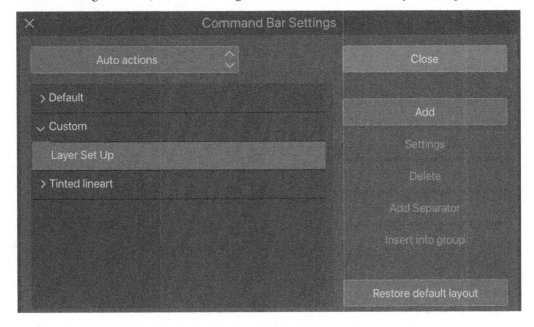

Figure 17.25: Command Bar Settings window

4. With the name of the auto action selected, click on the **Add** button.

5. The shortcut icon will now show in the command bar, as shown in *Figure 17.26*.

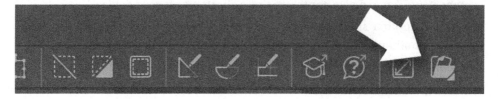

Figure 17.26: Shortcut icon visible on command bar

6. To delete a shortcut, press and hold the shortcut icon to open a drop-down menu, and then click **Delete**.

Wow, how accessible it is to get the auto action done on your layers. You can either press and hold the *Ctrl* key and then press the *F1* key or click on the icon in the command bar to run the **Layer Set Up** action without having to select it from the palette.

Summary

In this chapter, we learned how to make tedious activities more bearable by using recorded auto actions to automate their steps. We looked at the **Auto Action** palette and learned how to play a default action. We learned how to create a new auto action set, how to create a new auto action and record the steps for it, and then how to download an auto action asset. Finally, we learned how to create two different shortcuts to an auto action in order to make accessing it easier.

In the next chapter, we will explore the animation features of Clip Studio Paint and learn how to import materials and other assets from Clip Studio Assets.

Join us on Discord!

Read this book alongside other users. Ask questions, provide solutions to other readers, and much more.

Scan the QR code or visit the link to join the community.

https://packt.link/clipstudiopaint

18

Exploring Clip Studio Assets and Animations

Two of the most exciting Clip Studio Paint features are Clip Studio Assets, which allows the fast and easy downloading of new brushes and other assets, and the ability to create animations in the program. In this chapter, we will explore both options and how to use them.

The following topics will be covered in this chapter:

- Clip Studio Assets
- Creating an account and logging in
- Downloading from Assets
- Creating animations
- Exporting animations

We will start this chapter by looking at what Clip Studio Assets is, then how to create an account and log in to Assets. Then, we are going to learn about the interface of Assets, and how to search for assets you want, even actually downloading a sample asset. We will move on to get to know ways to create an animation in Clip Studio Paint with two example steps, and finally, learn how to export the animation.

By the end of this chapter, you will have useful knowledge of how to get materials to use on your creations, and you'll be able to start creating an animation using an image you have created!

Let's jump right into these amazing features!

Technical requirements

To get started, you need Clip Studio Paint already installed on your device, and a canvas of 1280 x 720 px with 144 dpi with character art and background art in separate layers. You will also need a Clip Studio account to log in.

Downloading from Assets

Clip Studio Assets includes user-created brushes, materials, 3D objects, sound effects, and more that can be downloaded for use in your own works.

In this section, we are going to learn how to use Clip Studio Assets by searching, downloading, and registering materials that are ready to be used!

To access the materials available for download, click on the nine-square icon at the top right of the **CLIP STUDIO START** screen, and click on the **Search for materials - Assets** link in the pop-up menu window. *Figure 18.1* shows the Assets library at the time of writing.

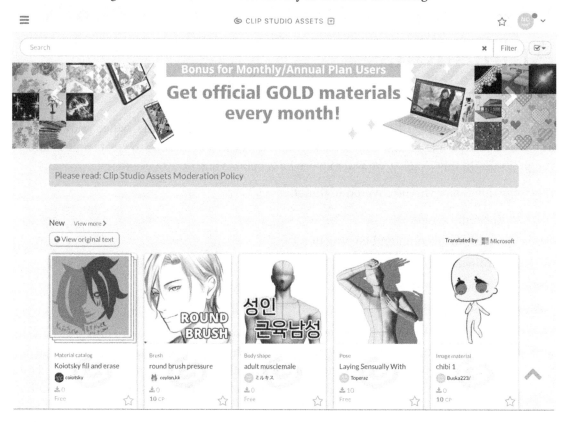

Figure 18.1: Assets library

Each asset has a thumbnail showing us what the asset looks like. Beneath the thumbnail image, we have information about the asset. The first line tells us what type of asset it is (Pose, Workspace, Image material, Brush, and so on). The next line tells us the name of the material. The third line tells us the username of the person who created and uploaded the asset to the online library. The next line tells us how many times that asset has been downloaded, and the final line tells us the cost of the asset.

Important note

Many of the items in the Assets download library are free. However, some assets need special currencies such as Clippy or Gold. You can collect Clippy points by doing some activities on Clip Studio Assets such as uploading materials you made, but Gold costs money. In order to download priced assets, you first have to purchase Gold from Celsys. At the time of writing, 1,000 Gold costs around $10. Gold has an expiration date that is normally one year from the day of purchase, so if you purchase Gold, be sure to use it all before it expires!

To search for a specific asset, type a keyword or keywords into the **Search** bar at the top of the Assets window. Press the *Enter* key on your keyboard to complete the search. The button marked **Filter** to the right of the search bar can be clicked and then used to narrow the search results. For instance, in the following screenshot, we have entered the search keyword **Heart**. If we only want to see Brush assets that match that keyword, click on the **Brush** option under the **Filter** window, as shown in *Figure 18.2*. This will filter the search results accordingly.

Figure 18.2: Search options

There is also a very useful way to pick good assets quickly, which is changing the order of displayed search results, as you can see from the three options in *Figure 18.3*.

You have the option to select **Newest first**, **Oldest first**, or **Popular**. I recommend selecting **Popular** because the most downloaded assets will be displayed first, which means they can be the most useful ones. If you are after very unique ones, then select **Newest first** to see the latest assets. Some old assets can be elementary and not compatible with the latest version of Clip Studio Paint.

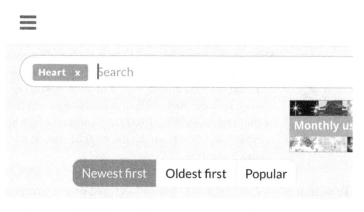

Figure 18.3: Search result order options

So, if you want to browse the most popular free heart-shaped brushes first, you can type **Heart** in the search bar, hit *Enter* on your keyboard, select **Brush** and **Free** from the **Filter** drop-down options, and then click the **Close** button. Finally, click **Popular** from the display order options, and the assets most likely to meet your needs will be displayed at the top!

Important information

As of 2024, Clip Studio Assets now auto-translates material names to English, French, German, Spanish, Korean, Traditional Chinese, or Japanese. When you click on a material, you will see the translated name and the original name in brackets. Materials also now have a unique content ID that users can enter in the search bar to find specific materials. If this doesn't return what you're looking for, then it may be up to you to make that asset and put it out there for others to download! This is a great way to show off your Clip Studio skills, and you can make a little extra money too if you create a paid asset that lots of people download.

Once we locate an asset that we might be interested in downloading, we can click on the thumbnail to view more details about it. The asset in *Figure 18.4* is **Retro Chip Brush**, which looks pretty good.

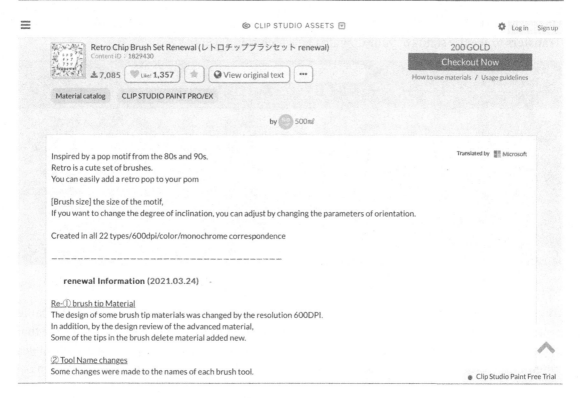

Figure 18.4: Retro Chip Brush asset details

From this detail window, we can add a **Like!** to the asset by clicking on the heart button (and we can see how many likes the asset has, too). We can add the asset to our favorites by clicking on the star-shaped button. Favorites can act as a sort of wish list of paid assets if you like.

Scrolling down further will give us more information about the asset we wish to download. Most users will include more thumbnails and ideas on how to use the asset in an image. Be sure to look at this information before deciding to download an asset.

The Retro Chip Brush asset is a paid asset, so we would need to have Gold in our account to download this brush. In **Free** assets, we will see a **Download** button at the top right of the screen. Clicking on the **Download** button of a free asset, or the **Checkout Now** button on paid assets, will allow you to download them.

Once you've started downloading an asset, click the gear-shaped **Settings** icon, then select **Data Transfers** to see the status of your downloads, which is in *Figure 18.5*.

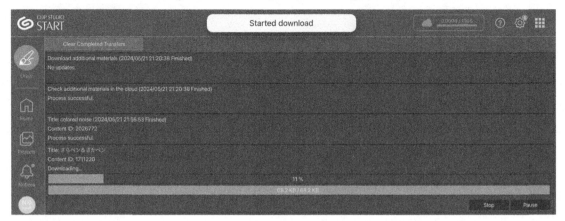

Figure 18.5: Data Transfers window

Any downloading and recently downloaded items will show in this window. We will see the name, content ID, and progress bar for a currently downloading item, the name, date, and time that the download occurred, the status of the download, and the status of the process, which shows whether the process was successful or not, for already downloaded items. Check this to make sure that the download was successful before trying to download the asset again.

Now that we have downloaded an asset, we need to locate it in the Material palette in Clip Studio Paint.

Locating your downloads in Clip Studio Paint

When we download an asset to Clip Studio Paint, it goes into our Material palette. To take a glance and edit your materials, click the **Manage Materials** icon on the left-side menu of the **CLIP STUDIO START** screen. You will see the list of materials with their thumbnails. In Clip Studio Paint, open the **Material** palette and click the arrow next to the words **All materials** if you can't find the **Download** category. If you click **Download**, the most recent downloaded assets will be displayed on the right, as shown in *Figure 18.6*.

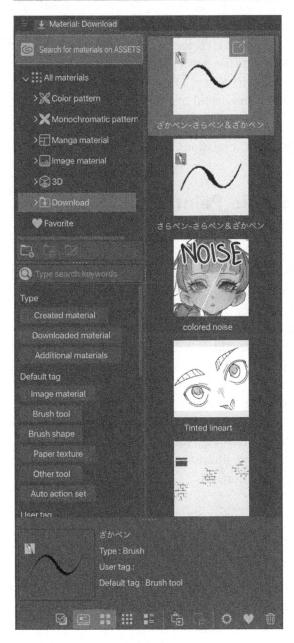

Figure 18.6: Material palette

If the asset you downloaded was an image, pattern, or 3D asset, you will be able to use it right away from the Material palette. If it was a Brush asset, you still need to register that asset to one of the **Sub Tool** palettes. This is a very simple process. To register the Brush material, follow these easy steps:

1. Open the **Sub Tool** palette to show the group of tools to which you wish to register the new Brush asset. We will be registering a new **Pen** asset in this instruction.

2. In the **Download** section of the Material palette, click on the thumbnail of the Brush asset you want to register to Sub Tool.

3. Click and hold the thumbnail and maintain the pressure, then drag it to the **Sub Tool** palette without letting go of it. Once it comes over to the **Sub Tool** palette, you will see a + symbol appear next to the asset you are dragging. Release the pressure now.

4. The new asset will be registered to the **Sub Tool** palette. In *Figure 18.7*, we can see that the brush from the previous screenshot is now in the **Pen Sub Tool** category:

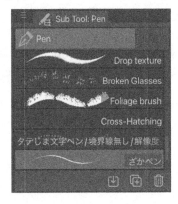

Figure 18.7: Pen Sub Tool palette

Isn't it fantastic to be able to access tons of materials that will help your creations? First, we started with the **CLIP STUDIO ASSETS** screen to learn what it is for and what it offers. Then, we moved on to learn how to create an account and log in to use Assets, and how to search for asset materials. And finally, we learned how to download and register a Brush material. To be honest, I could spend all day searching and collecting fancy and useful materials because it's so much fun and inspiring.

In the next section, we will have a look at how to create animations in Clip Studio Paint. Read on to explore this great feature!

Creating animations in Clip Studio Paint

In this section, we are going to learn how to create animations using the **Layer** and **Timeline** palettes in Clip Studio Paint with two examples.

Technically, the word *animation* comes from the Latin *animare*, which means "to give life to." Nowadays, it is another way of saying "moving image." It is a very complex art form that requires lots of study and practice to get it right. There are many books and internet resources, such as *The Animator's Survival Kit: A Manual of Methods, Principles and Formulas for Classical, Computer, Games, Stop Motion and Internet Animators*, written by Richard Williams, or the *12 Principles of Animation* video by AlanBeckerTutorials on Youtube. They will inspire you with content about how to animate, the principles of animation, and tips for animating well. These things may be beyond the scope of this book. However, we can explore how to create a Clip Studio file with an animation timeline and then add animation cels to make our pictures have the appearance of motion. Once you are used to the basics of animating, I encourage you to check out these resources and refine your skills. Meanwhile, I just want to teach you how to create a basic animation – how to create an animation timeline and how to add animation cels.

Important note

When working in Clip Studio Paint Pro, your animation frames are limited to only 24 in a timeline. Clip Studio Paint EX can create unlimited animation frames in a timeline.

We will learn two different ways of creating animations from your art. One is by using an image and the other is by using the camera movement feature.

Creating an animation using one image

You can either start a new file just for animation or add animation to an existing piece of artwork. In this section, we will use your existing artwork. Follow these steps to create your first animation:

1. First, create a canvas of **1280 x 720 px** at **144 dpi.** You need your artwork to have character and background drawings in separate layers, as in *Figure 18.8*:

Figure 18.8: Illustration with the Layer palette

2. Create two raster layers and name them **1** and **2**.
3. Draw elements you want to animate on **layer 1.** I drew pink stars in this example, as you can see in *Figure 18.9*:

Figure 18.9: Added elements (1)

4. Change the opacity of **layer 1** to around **30 %** by moving the slider bar at the top of the **Layer** palette and draw the variation of the image in **layer 2** with the half-translucent **layer 1** as a reference.

Figure 18.10: Added elements (2)

5. Don't forget to change the opacity of **layer 1** back to **100%** after you have finished drawing on **layer 2**.

6. In the **File** menu, click **Animation**, then **New animation layer**, and finally, **Animation folder** to create an animation folder named **Folder 1 : 0** in the **Layer** palette, as shown in *Figure 18.11*.

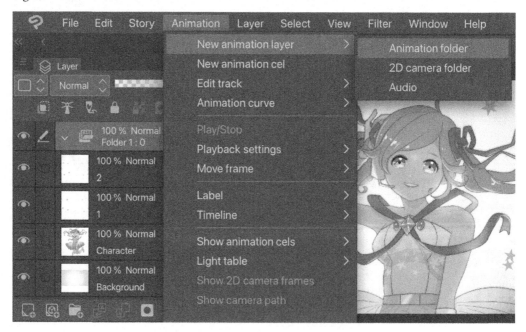

Figure 18.11: Animation drop-down menus and Layer palette

7. On the **Layer** palette, select both **layer 1** and **layer 2**, and click then hold to drag them and release them in **Folder 1 : 0**.

8. Once the two layers are safely stored in **Folder 1**, make the folder hidden by clicking the eye-shaped icon of the folder.

9. Click **Window** from the **File** menu, and click **Timeline** from the drop-down menu to open the **Timeline** palette, as shown in *Figure 18.12*.

10. Now you have a blank **Timeline** palette. In the **Timeline** palette, click on the **New timeline** icon, which is circled in *Figure 18.13*, to open the **New timeline** dialog box.

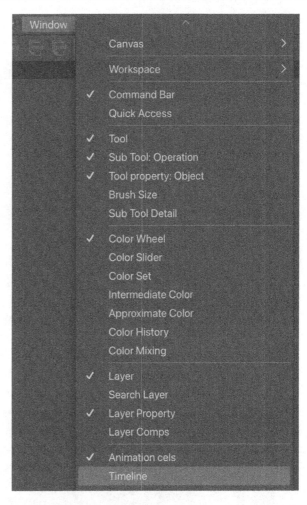

Figure 18.12: Window drop-down menu

Figure 18.13: Timeline palette

11. In the **New timeline** dialog box, set **Frame rate** to **8** and **Playback time** to **8**, then click **OK** as shown in *Figure 18.14*:

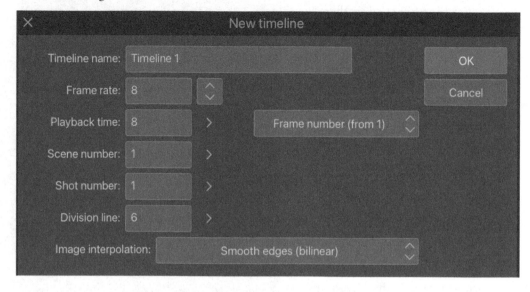

Figure 18.14: New timeline dialog box

12. Your current **Timeline** palette should look like *Figure 18.15*, with a timeline named **1**. Right-click the first frame, which is the area highlighted in red, to bring up a right-click menu:

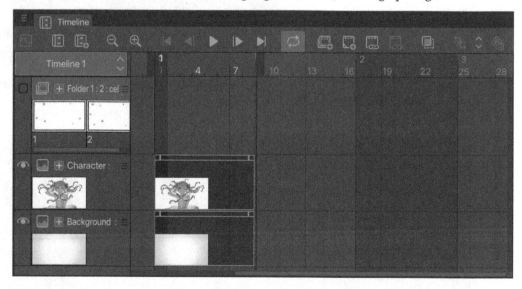

Figure 18.15: Timeline palette

13. Select **layer 1** from the following menu to insert the image into a target frame in **Timeline 1**:

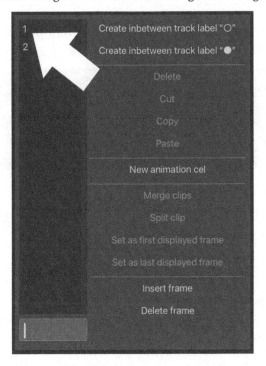

Figure 18.16: Right-click menu

14. Right-click on frame **4** (since we set 8 frames per second, frame 4 comes on half a second) of **Timeline 1**, and select **layer 2** from the right-click menu, then you will see a result that looks like this:

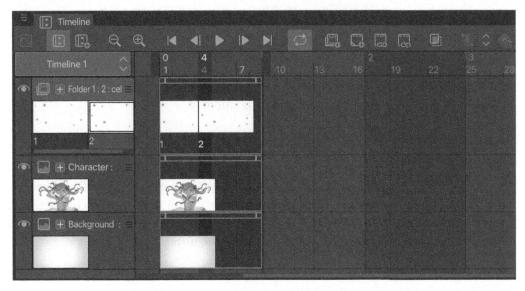

Figure 18.17: Timeline palette with an eight-frame animation

15. Your animation is now complete! Click the checkbox next to **Folder 1 : 2** to make it visible again.

16. To play the animation, click the triangular **Play/Stop** icon on the **Timeline** palette. You can also play it in a loop by clicking the **Play in loop** icon, which is circled in *Figure 18.18*:

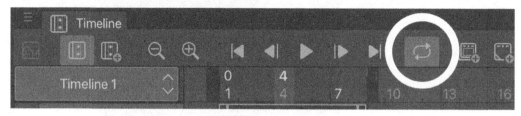

Figure 18.18: Timeline palette

When the animation is played in a loop, it gives the illusion of the stars around the character dancing around by changing their sizes and angles!

> **Tip**
>
> We can display a currently showing animation cel with before and after cels together on the canvas by using the **Onion skin** function! Click **Animation** from the **File** menu, then select **Show animation cels** | **Onion skin settings**. Or click the **Onion skin** icon on the **Timeline** palette, as circled in Figure 18.19.
>
>
>
> *Figure 18.19: Onion skin icon on the Timeline palette*
>
> You can edit the settings such as display color and number of cels by clicking **Animation** | **Show animation cels** | **Onion skin settings**.

Isn't it great to see your art now has some motion? Before we find out how to export the animation, let's learn just one more way of creating an animation.

Creating an animation using one image with the Camera Movement feature

There are animations that you can create by moving the camera position rather than the characters. We need to add something called keyframes, which indicate from which timepoint to start adding an effect such as camera movement, and the timepoint for it to end. Follow these steps to create an animation using the camera movement feature:

1. First of all, create a canvas of **1280 x 720 px** with **144 dpi**, with your artwork with character and background drawings in separate layers, as shown in *Figure 18.20*.

Figure 18.20: Artwork and the Layer palette

2. Click **Window** from the **File** menu and click on **Timeline** from the drop-down menu to open the **Timeline** palette.

3. On the **Timeline** palette, click on the **New timeline** icon, which is circled in *Figure 18.21*, to open the **New timeline** dialog box.

Figure 18.21: New timeline icon on the Timeline palette

4. In *Figure 18.22* of the **New timeline** dialog box, set **Frame rate** to **8** and **Playback time** to **8**, then click **OK.**

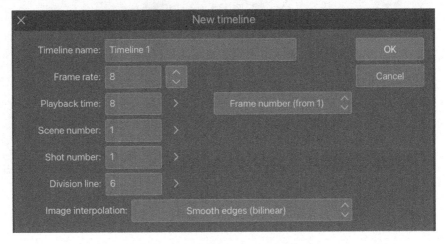

Figure 18.22: New timeline dialog box

5. On the **Timeline** palette, click the **Enable keyframes on this layer** icon, which is circled in *Figure 18.23*.

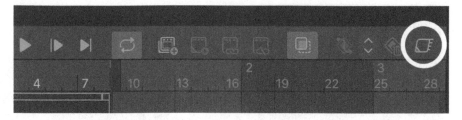

Figure 18.23: Timeline palette

6. Click the first frame, which is highlighted in red *Figure 18.24*.

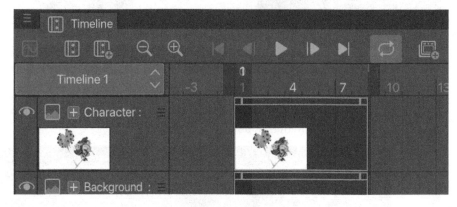

Figure 18.24: Timeline palette 2

7. Click the **Operation** tool on the **Tool** palette, then select the **Object** sub tool. You will then see a square with a handle on the canvas, as shown in *Figure 18.25*.

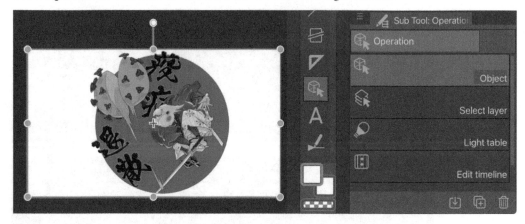

Figure 18.25: Sub Tool palette and canvas

8. Click and drag to rotate with the top control point and change the scale with the handles at the corners. When you transform a layer (make sure the layer you want to move is selected on the **Layer** palette), a keyframe is created in the first frame on the **Timeline** palette, which is a diamond-shaped mark, as shown in *Figure 18.26*.

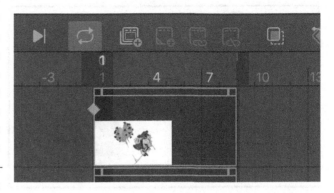

Figure 18.26: Timeline palette

9. Click the fifth frame on the **Timeline** palette and transform the artwork to your desired scale on the canvas using the **Object** sub tool. When you transform it, a keyframe is created on the **Timeline** palette. The diamond-shaped keyframe mark can be clicked and dragged to move it to other frames. Now, you can see two diamond-shaped keyframe marks in *Figure 18.27*.

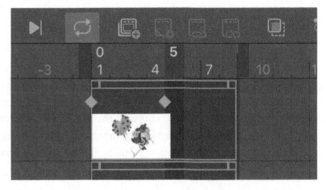

Figure 18.27: Timeline palette with keyframes

10. Click the keyframe mark you added the first time, then right-click and select **Copy** from the menu.

11. Select the final **eighth** frame on the timeline, right-click to bring up the menu, and select **Paste**. The keyframe is now pasted on the eighth frame.

12. Click **Animation | Edit track | Copy** for copying the selected keyframe, and **Animation | Edit track | Paste** for pasting the copied keyframe onto a new place for tablets and mobile users. We can also transform the art on the canvas in the same way as we did the first time:

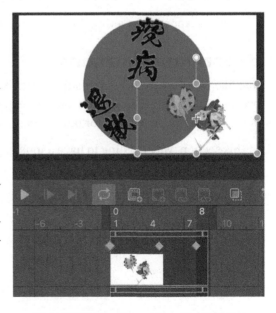

Figure 18.28: Timeline palette with keyframes

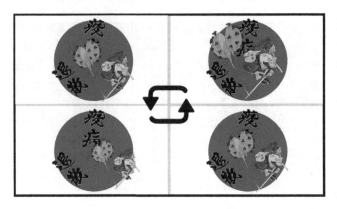

Figure 18.29: Frames of the animation

You have finished creating an animation using the camera movement feature! Let's check that it really works by clicking the **Play** icon.

When the animation is played in a loop, it shows the characters growing bigger and then smaller as if they are about to pop out from the background, as shown in the following screenshot of the frames:

Tip

You can create animation images in one folder, but when doing more complex animation, such as characters moving and interacting with one another, you may have more success by roughing out the animation in one animation folder and then refining the motion in another folder. This way, the original sketches are preserved, and you can adjust anything as needed. This is similar to traditional animation: roughing out the motion in pencil sketches and then painting the finished animation onto transparent celluloids.

You have now created two types of animation: one using one art image and drawing elements you want to move in new layers and the other using the camera movement feature by adding keyframes.

It's time to export those animations to share them with others – read on to find out how.

Exporting animations

Just like when we exported our still images, we can export our animations too. This is a simple process, but there are several formats for export that we need to explore in order to know which is the correct one to choose for our purposes.

In this section, we are going to have a look at each method of exporting animations.

In the **File** menu, you will see the **Export animation** option, and under that option are the different ways we can export animations. These are shown in *Figure 18.30*.

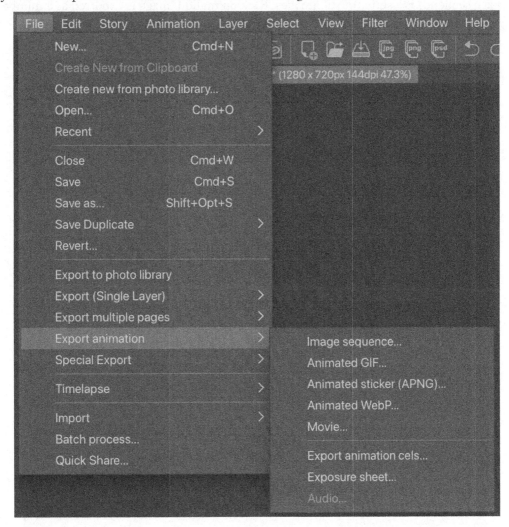

Figure 18.30: Export animation options

We will discuss each of these options next.

Image sequences

An image sequence is a series of still images. Each animation image is exported as a numbered image that can then be imported into other software for further editing. The **Image sequence export settings** window is shown here:

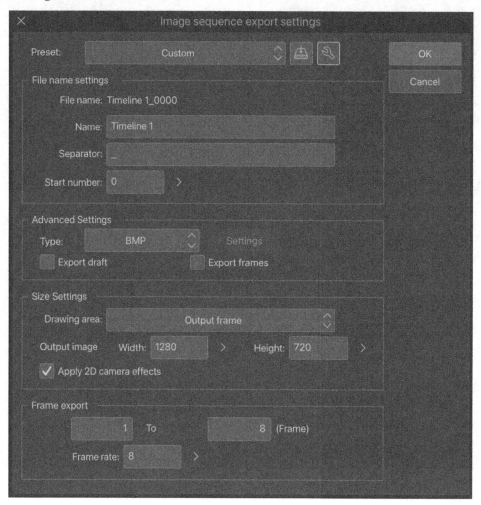

Figure 18.31: Image sequence export settings window

The top part is a drop-down menu for **Preset** exporting information. You can create, edit, and import this information. The text entered in the **Name** field will be the filename for each image. The character entered in the **Separator** field will separate the name from the numbers in the final filenames. By changing the entry for **Start number**, we can adjust what number our image sequence will begin with.

Under **Advanced Settings**, we can set the file format of the images from the drop-down menu. You are also given the choice of either exporting a draft image sequence or already-created frames by checking the corresponding boxes.

Size Settings can be used to select how big a **Drawing area** you want to export: either **Output frame**, **Overflow frame**, or **Entire canvas**. We can also resize the exported image's **Width** and **Height** by setting the values on **Output image**. You can also check the **Apply 2D camera effects** box if you want to export a camera movement that you created with an image sequence.

The **Frame export** settings can be used to specify a section of frames to export, or all frames can be exported. The **Frame rate** option can be used to change the frame rate.

Read on to the next exporting option, **Animated GIFs**.

Animated GIFs

An animated GIF is one of the most common ways to share animation on the internet. You've undoubtedly seen animated GIFs on countless websites and social media posts as internet memes. To export your animation as a GIF, select the **Animated GIF...** option from the **Export animation** menu option.

First, name the file to be saved. Then, the **Animated GIF export settings** will appear, as shown in *Figure 18.32*.

Figure 18.32: Animated GIF export dialog box

There is no other choice in the drop-down menu. Click on **OK** and a new window pops up for you to edit the export settings, as shown here:

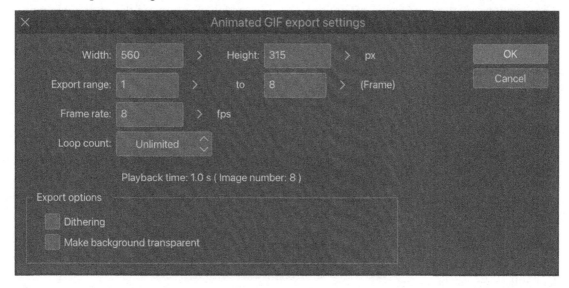

Figure 18.33: Animated GIF export settings dialog box

There are boxes in which you can enter the **Width** and **Height** values of the frame; generally, 720 x 480 for a lower resolution, 960 x 540 for a medium resolution, and 1280 x 720 would be considered a high-resolution animation. Under that option, we can set how many frames to export, the frame rate, and how many times to loop the animation. The standard frame rate for animated videos is often 24 frames per second (fps), but it can vary depending on the style. For a GIF animation, 8 fps is good to go. At the bottom of the screen, there are two options. You can turn **Dithering** on to make the GIF look more naturally higher quality, and there is also a checkbox if you want to **make the background transparent**. When you press **OK**, a save location window will pop up. Navigate to the location you want to export the animated GIF to. Mac and PC versions of Clip Studio Paint might skip the dialog box and go straight to the **Export location** dialog box.

Let's see the next exporting option, **Animated sticker (APNG)**!

Animated stickers (APNG)

An animated sticker, or APNG, is an animated image with the qualities of a **.png** file instead of a **.gif** file, often used for animated stickers in messaging apps. The APNG export options are shown in *Figure 18.34*.

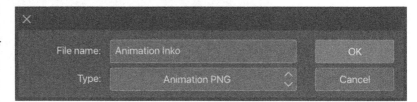

Figure 18.34: Animated Sticker (APNG) export dialog box

These options are the same as the **.gif** options; there are no other options on the drop-down menu. Again, this dialog box might be skipped on the Mac and PC versions of Clip Studio Paint and you might see the Export settings dialog box similar to the Animated GIF export setting straight away, then the **Export location** dialog box.

Let's look at the last exporting option, **Movie…**.

Movie files

Movie files can be uploaded to YouTube or imported into video editing software to add sound or other effects. When you select the **Movie…** option, you will be prompted to add a filename and select a file type, as shown in *Figure 18.35*.

Figure 18.35: Movie export dialog box

As a point of interest, the MP4 file type is much lighter and is used more widely on platforms than the QuickTime Movie file type, but QuickTime Movie beats MP4 for image and audio quality. Once you add a file name, select the file type, and then click **OK**, the following window will appear:

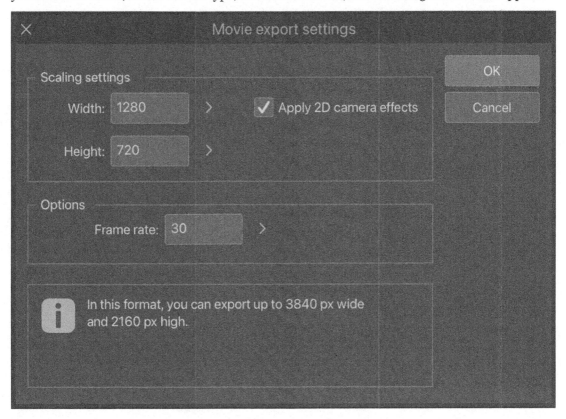

Figure 18.36: Movie export settings window

At the top of the window, we have **Scaling settings.** By using the **Width** and **Height** settings, we can resize the dimensions of our final file. If you check the box labeled **Apply 2D camera effects**, a camera movement you have created will be exported too. The **Frame rate** option controls the frame rate of playback.

Now you know how to use Clip Studio Assets and quick ways to start creating animations and then export them from Clip Studio Paint!

Summary

In this chapter, we started by getting to know what Clip Studio Assets is, and how to register to log in to start using it. We moved on to learn about ways to search for our desired materials, then download them, and finally, register a brush material. Then, we had a quick look at how to bring life to our illustrations with animation using two different methods, and different ways to export them for different uses. Now you can download and use new assets, and create and export animations for GIFs, stickers, and YouTube movies!

In the next chapter, we are going to learn how to export, print, and upload your manga. You can get a better idea of what a finished manga will look like, and also a deeper understanding of how to set up pages as seen in *Chapter 5*, *Pages and Panels to Shape Manga*, if you read it again. We will discuss the many ways we can export our work for display on the web and in print. With physical manga books or webtoons, you will see the many possibilities for how to present your creations.

Join us on Discord!

Read this book alongside other users. Ask questions, provide solutions to other readers, and much more.

Scan the QR code or visit the link to join the community.

`https://packt.link/clipstudiopaint`

19

Exporting, Printing, and Uploading Your Manga

Now that we have our comics or illustrations sketched, inked, and colored, it's time to get them out of Clip Studio Paint and to the print shop or onto our social media or website. This last chapter will teach you about the exporting option in the software, including how to resize pages and adjust the resolution during exporting.

We will start this chapter by learning how to make your manga file ready for homemade printing by adjusting the print settings and moving on to render a file in a printer-shop-friendly format, learning about the uniqueness of each file format. We will look closely at how to adjust image quality and file size, and how to resize the final image. Finally, we will learn how to export manga files for web uploads with an additional two useful EX version-only functions.

The following topics will be covered in this chapter:

- Printing at home
- Exporting for print
- Adjusting image quality and file size
- Resizing an image while exporting
- Exporting for a web display
- Exporting webtoons (EX only)
- Exporting batches of pages (EX only)
- Exporting to Clip Studio SHARE

By the end of this chapter, you will be able to understand how to handle your manga in terms of publishing both on the internet and in physically bound manga books. This will give you a great idea of what your manga will finally look like so that when you create a new manga, you can have the best choice in terms of canvas size and resolution!

Let's get ready to share our work with the world!

Technical requirements

To get started, you need Clip Studio Paint already installed on your device, and in order to create at least three pages of manga, I recommend creating an A5 portrait canvas with 300 dpi per page to go through the content in this chapter.

Printing at home

It takes a great amount of work in terms of getting ready to print, and then doing the actual printing and binding everything together by yourself, but the artwork will give you a wonderful crafty feeling! In this section, we are going to learn how to make your manga creation ready for home printing.

Over the past few years, home printers have become more affordable and more powerful. Just a decade ago, most home printers were only able to produce decent prints from digital photographs. Now, we have home printers that can print beautiful, high-quality images without breaking the bank. Some printers are even "artist-grade" now and can print in wide formats, on fabric, and more.

There are so many home printers now that we obviously can't give a rundown of all of them in this book. It is best to do your own research before buying a printer and think about how you will use the printer. If you are mainly doing black and white prints, you can probably get away with a slightly less expensive printer or even a laser printer that uses toner instead of ink cartridges. If you are going to print lots of large prints, you may want to consider getting a wide-format printer. Printers can be set up with continuous ink systems to save on color ink costs for those who print lots of high-quality photographs or paintings. Read reviews online and compare the features of different printers before purchasing one. I recommend Canon or Epson printers for their fantastic art printing results! My favorite is the Canon PIXMA series for its quality and color expression.

Tip

If you do a lot of printing at home, make sure that you keep ink cartridges handy. Ink always runs out at the most inconvenient times! And it's always safer to buy genuine cartridges, instead of compatible cheaper ones, because this extends your printer's life.

You will also want some high-quality paper. I like photo paper, cardstock, or presentation paper for my art prints, but thinner paper will work as well. Make sure that you don't go too thin, however, because if we saturate a thin piece of paper with lots of ink, it will become wrinkled and warped, and the back of the page will be see-through!

Most inkjet printers will print fine from a file that is set up in RGB color mode, so when we have finished creating our manga, we don't need to convert our Clip Studio file at all to print from it. Ensure that your printer drivers are up to date, as this will solve most printer problems.

Follow these steps to print an image from Clip Studio Paint:

1. Open the file that you wish to print in Clip Studio Paint. Whether it's a color or a black-and-white file is up to you.

2. In the **File** menu, click on **File | Print settings** to review the **Print Settings** dialog box. The **Print Settings** dialog box is shown here:

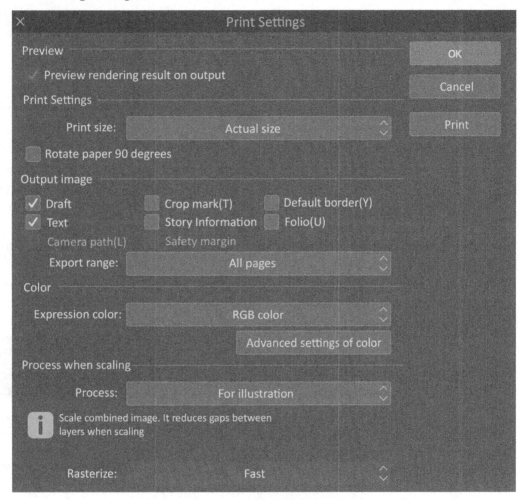

Figure 19.1 – Print Settings dialog box

3. Under **Preview**, check the box next to **Preview rendering result on output**. This option allows us to see what our page will look like before the print begins and will allow us to stop the printing process if something is wrong.

4. Choose the correct **Print size** settings from the drop-down menu.

We will now examine the remainder of the options in the **Print Settings** dialog box:

- **Print Settings:** Most print jobs should be able to use the **Actual size** or **Scale according to paper size** options. The **Actual size** setting prints according to the size the file is set up as. The **Scale according to paper size** option will resize the print contents to the size of the paper in the printer, as the following printing examples demonstrate:

- Other **Print Settings** options are **Pixel size, Dual page (EX only)**, and **Spread (EX only)**. With **Pixel size**, the size for printing is adjusted so that the relationship between the image pixel and screen pixel is 1 to 1. With **Dual page (EX only)**, the page layout for printing is set to dual page. Two pages are printed on one sheet of paper. The margin on the front side becomes the outer

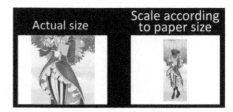

Figure 19.2 – Screenshot of the Actual size and Scale according to paper size option results

side, as the binding margin will be on the outer side of the paper. Finally, with **Spread (EX only)**, the page layout for printing is set to a two-page spread. Two pages are printed on one sheet of paper. The margin will be on the outer side of the paper.

- **Output image:** This option gives us the chance to print or not print some parts of our image. Usually, any layers set as a **Draft** layer will not print or export, but we can choose to print draft layers by checking the box next to **Draft**. We can also choose to print or not print text, story information, and more. Under **Export range (EX only)** are the **All pages, To offset of crop mark**, or **To inside of crop mark** options. If we have artwork that extends outside of any crop marks (the bleed area of the art), but we want it to be printed, we should select the **All pages** option. The other two options will stop the printing at the crop marks or inside of the crop marks. The results of the various options are indicated in the following screenshot:

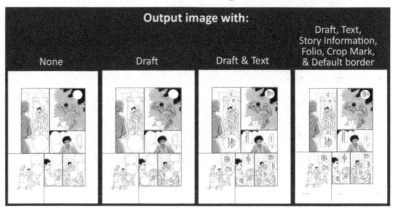

Figure 19.3 – Screenshot of the Output image option results

- **Color:** Under the **Expression color** settings, we have another drop-down menu with several options. The first one is **Auto detect appropriate color depth**, which allows Clip Studio Paint to automatically set the color depth depending on the file being printed.

There are two **Duotone** options, one called **Threshold** and one called **Toning**. Both options print in pure black and white, with no gray tones. The **Threshold** option takes any gray or color tones and automatically converts them into black or white. The **Toning** option still prints in pure black and white with no gray, but it converts any gray or color areas into areas of black dots that mimic shading. The **Gray** option prints in grayscale and the **RGB color** setting prints the image with the RGB values that the printer translates into its own ink colors:

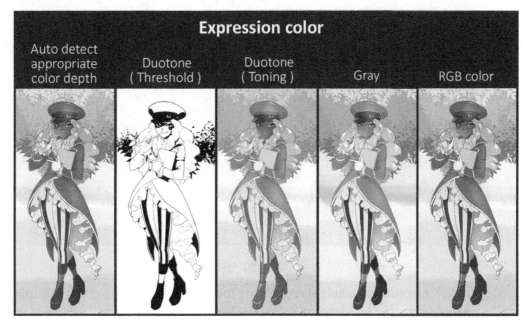

Figure 19.4 – Screenshot of the Expression color option results

- Choose the **Expression color** setting that best matches the image you are printing. The following screenshot shows all the color options:

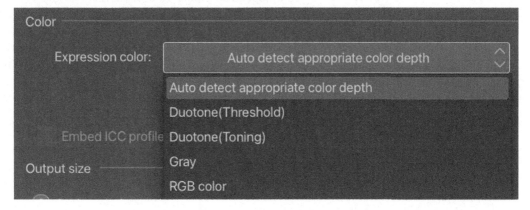

Figure 19.5 – Screenshot of the Expression color options

- The **Advanced settings of color** options do not actually provide us with advanced color options, but instead options for printing out the crop marks and tones. Here is a screenshot of the **Advanced settings of color** dialog box:

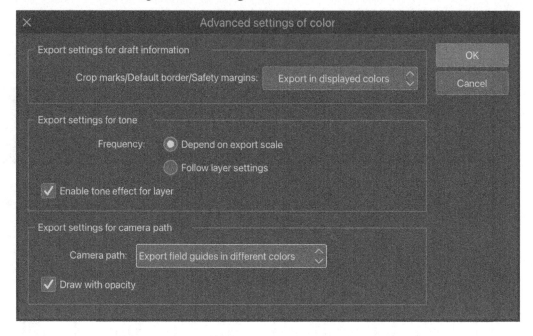

Figure 19.6 – Screenshot of the Advanced settings of color dialog box

- In the **Crop marks/Default border/Safety margins** option, we can set it to **Export in displayed colors** (prints in the color that the borders are set to in the preferences). We can also set it to **Export in black** and **Export in cyan**, which are both pretty self-explanatory!

 Under the **Export settings for tone** settings, we can resize screentones depending on the scale of the print (**Depend on export scale**) or use the settings of the tones in the image itself (**Follow layer settings**). Depending on the scale of the printed image, this can be used to control any moiré patterns that may occur from the screentones. Moiré is a pattern that appears unintentionally on the area where line patterns are overlapped, which sometimes occurs on prints where you used screentones:

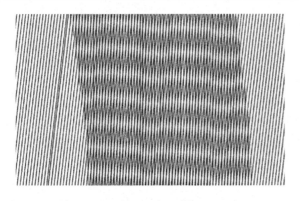

Figure 19.7 – Screenshot of an example
of a moiré pattern

- We can ignore **Export settings for camera path** unless you recorded the camera path with keyframes in animation.

- **Process when scaling:** We can now go back to **Print Settings** to finish adjusting our options. The final print settings section, which is demonstrated in the following screenshot, is the **Process when scaling** options. These are **For illustration** and **For comic**.

These settings change how the image is processed before it is printed. If we don't use lots of tones, then the **For illustration** setting is suitable for our needs. In the **For comic** setting, the tone layers are processed individually before printing so that they are scaled, meaning there's less of a chance of getting a moiré pattern:

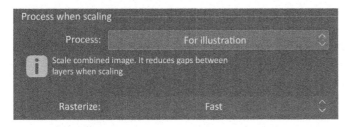

Figure 19.8 – Screenshot of the Process when scaling
settings

Finally, we have a drop-down menu for our **Rasterize** settings. The **Fast** setting is fine if we are printing out a quick copy just to see how our text or layout looks. For a better print, use the **Prefer quality** setting. Well, that's all the explanations for print settings. Now, follow the steps to save the settings you have just adjusted:

1. Click on the **OK** button.

2. To print now, click on the **Print** button. You will be asked to select your printer and any printer settings before seeing the print preview screen. If anything doesn't look right in the preview screen, cancel the print job, adjust the print settings, and then try again.

3. If you did not execute the print from the **Print Settings** window, you can click on **File | Print** to print the image when you are ready.

Even by only focusing on the printing options that Clip Studio Paint has, it's a lot to take in! Be sure to look at any printer-specific options that you may have to adjust, such as the print quality and the number of copies. You may have to adjust things a few times to get the best print from your home printer.

With most home printers, it's not economical to print out multiple copies of our comic to hand out or to sell. It may be perfect for small runs of color prints, but for any larger number of prints, we will want to export our images so that we can send them to a publisher or print shop. Let's find out how in the next section.

Exporting for print

Whether you're making comic books or making pin-up images to sell at a convention, you'll need to know how to print from Clip Studio Paint or how to export the images you create to send to your local print shop, an online printer, or publisher. If you don't know already, you can get your art printed on stickers, badges, mugs, T-shirts, patches, and more!

In this section, we are looking into how to prepare your manga file to be ready to send to a print shop or publisher.

Tip

Even if you are only planning on displaying your work on the internet, you should still think about setting up your file as though you are going to print it. Work in 300 dpi and set up your file dimensions to match whatever paper size you will end up printing on. Even if you are only thinking about the internet now, you may eventually want to start printing your art. Setting it up for print when you create it will save a lot of time, headaches, and redrawing later!

There is a big difference between sending our files to a professional offset printer or to a book publisher that handles small quantities of books on demand or sending them to the copy shop down the street. When sending your files out for printing, make sure that you research what file formats the printer accepts and whether or not they have any restrictions. When taking your files to a local chain office supply store or a copy shop, most file formats will do fine, so it's up to you how you want to format your images.

Tip

If and when possible, find a small, local print shop where you can do large amounts of printing. Not only do they usually have better prices, but they can often work with you on special projects. Also, the staff at these small stores tend to have more knowledge of their equipment and how to get the best quality prints for your art.

In this section, we are going to export high-quality, lossless versions of our images that will look good when printed and can be opened by anyone even if they don't have Clip Studio Paint. Follow these steps to export your images in a format suitable for print:

1. Open the image you wish to export.
2. In the **File** menu, click on **File** and then go down to the **Export (Single Layer)** option.

3. From the list of options under the **Export (Single Layer)** option, choose the file format in which to export the image and then click on it. File formats will be discussed after these steps.

4. Name your file and choose the location to save to in the window that appears.

5. Click **Save** to bring up an export settings dialog window.

6. Choose the parameters to be exported in the window. It should look similar to the **psd export settings window** shown in the following screenshot. Some of these options should look familiar from **Print Settings** in the previous section:

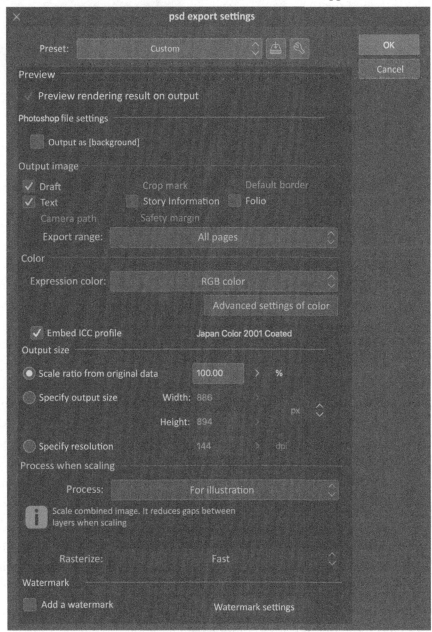

Figure 19.9 – Screenshot of the psd export settings dialog box

7. Click on **OK** to complete the export.

Here is a screenshot of the file format options available under the **Export** settings:

The following list explains each of the file formats:

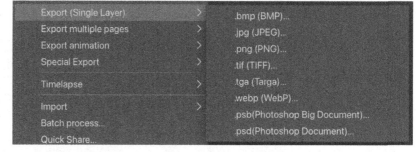

Figure 19.10 – Screenshot of the Export (Single Layer) options

*   **.bmp (BMP):** Bitmap image. Lossless format with no compression. Creates large file sizes.

*   **.jpg (JPEG):** Widely used compressed image format. Suitable for web displays, but sometimes not suitable when printing images.

*   **.png (Portable Network Graphics (PNG)):** Lossless image format capable of preserving transparency in the final output and suitable for color or grayscale. Image file sizes are small but maintain the original quality.

*   **.tif (TIFF):** Lossless file format that can preserve layer information, transparency, and original quality. Not suitable for online displays, but good for storage or editing.

*   **.tga (Truevision Advanced Raster Graphics Adapter (TARGA)):** Bitmap image format not suitable for photographs or images with lots of gradients, but suitable for simple images such as icons, cartoons, and line art.

*   **.webp (WebP):** Google-made file format allows websites to display high-quality images in much smaller sizes than other formats such as PNG and JPEG. Suitable for web displays.

*   **.psb (Photoshop Big Document):** Adobe Photoshop image format suitable for handling large images with lots of color depth, resolution, or large canvas size. Not suitable for web displays.

*   **.psd (Photoshop Document):** Adobe Photoshop document format suitable for images that will be opened and edited further in Photoshop. Not suitable for web displays.

You don't have to memorize all the information pertaining to each file format, but just remember the most suitable one for you, so next time you're exporting a manga file, you know exactly which one to choose. Generally, it's good to know that JPEG is for web display and PNG and PSD are for printing.

You now know about size formats, but what about controlling the image quality and file size? Does this mean that JPEG is a compressed image format and not suitable for printing? We will find that out in the next section.

Adjusting image quality and file size

There are times when you do not need to save a full-resolution image, such as when exporting for the internet or sending proof to a client. This section will explain how to export an image with compression so that the image quality and file size are decreased for easy handling. You will need an open file to export before starting the following steps:

1. In the **File** menu, go to **File | Export (Single Layer) | .jpg (JPEG)**.

2. Name the file and choose the folder to save it in. Click on **Save**.

3. The **JPEG export settings** dialog box will appear. Click on the checkbox next to **Preview rendering result on output** at the top of the window to enable this option.

4. Under **JPEG settings**, find the **Quality** setting. It is marked in the following screenshot:

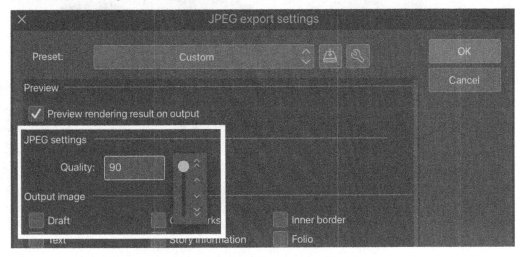

Figure 19.11 – Screenshot of JPEG export settings

5. Adjust the setting using the slider or arrows to change the compression of the file. The smaller the number, the more compressed the file will be. Compression sacrifices image quality to make the final file size smaller.

6. Click on **OK**.

7. The **Export preview** window will now appear. If needed, continue to adjust the quality using the setting in the bottom-right corner of the preview window.

8. Click on **OK** to complete the export.

The quality setting controls the amount of compression in the final file. Compression lowers image quality to make the overall file size smaller, making images load faster on the internet.

In the following screenshot, the **Quality** option is set to **90.** Note the large file size at the bottom right of the window, at 601.97 KB:

Figure 19.12 – Screenshot of Export preview with 90% quality

We can make the final file size smaller by lowering the quality. By doing this, the quality of the image is reduced. Note how much the file size has gone down in the following screenshot, but also note how pixelated the image has become because of the low quality, especially around the gradients and the black lines:

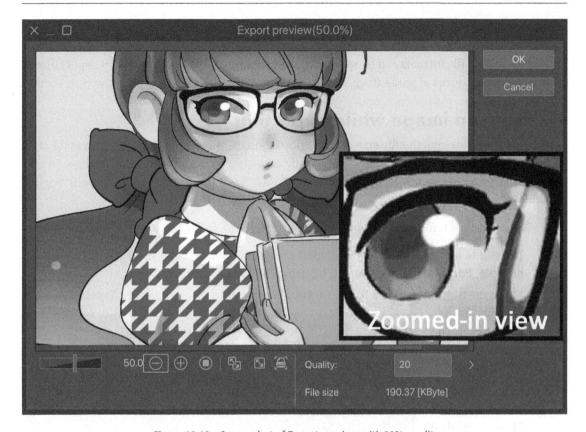

Figure 19.13 – Screenshot of Export preview with 20% quality

We reduced the image quality, so the file size is much lighter and easy to handle! This is perfect for an image that can be used as a thumbnail on the internet. Obviously, we cannot use it for printing because of the low quality and pixelated noise in the image. I would recommend using **.jpg** image files only for internet use.

Important note

The image quality can only be adjusted when exporting to `.jpg` and `.webp` file formats. Other formats are lossless and cannot be compressed.

Now, you know how to adjust the quality of the image, and what will happen if you reduce the image quality to a lower resolution. However, `.jpg` and `.webp` are the only formats for adjusting quality; the other file formats can be resized while maintaining file quality. We can export files to match the size in terms of percentage, width, or resolution, which is covered in the next section.

Resizing an image while exporting

Another way of changing the file size of the exported image is by changing the width and height of the image during the process. This can be done on the fly without making any changes to your original file, ensuring that you'll never accidentally save a 600-pixel-wide version of your original drawing ever again.

You will need an open file to export in order to complete the following steps:

1. In the **File** menu, go to **Export (Single Layer)** and choose the desired file format for the new file. For this example, we will be using the **.png** file format.

2. Name the file and choose a folder on your computer to save it. Click on **Save**. The export settings for the file format you chose in *Step 1* will appear.

3. Locate the **Output size** options. They are marked in this screenshot:

4. Select the ratio button next to **Scale ratio from original data** to scale the image by percentage. In the *Figure19.15*, the scale ratio has been set to **50.00%**. Note that **Width** and **Height** change as the ratio changes:

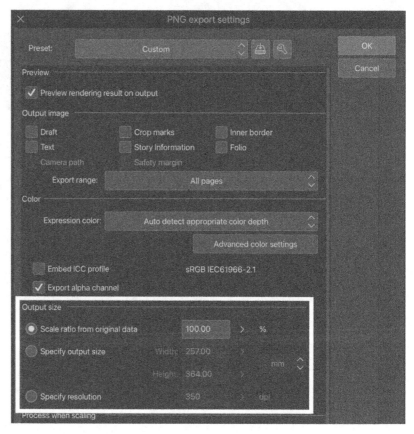

Figure 19.14 – Screenshot of the PNG export settings dialog box

Figure 19.15 – Screenshot of the Output size options

es automatically when we enter a new **Width** measurement:

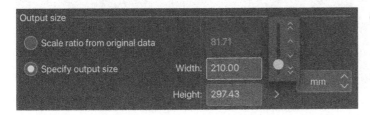

Figure 19.16 – Screenshot of the Output size options (2)

5. Select the ratio button next to **Specify output size** to enter an exact **Width** or **Height** measurement. You can change the measurement scale from the drop-down menu to **cm**, **mm**, **in**, **px**, and **pt**. In the following screenshot, we entered a width of **210 mm**. **Height** changes automatically when we enter a new **Width** measurement:

6. Click on **OK** to complete the export.

Great! Now we know how to change the export image quality and size. Let's see what we need to do specifically when we upload images to the internet in the next section.

Exporting for a web display

In addition to getting your work printed, one of the best ways to get known as an artist is to post your work on the internet. Whether you have your own website, an account on a host, or are posting to social media, the web is a great way to connect with other artists and share your art and stories with the entire world.

Let's export a comic page with internet-friendly settings. You will need an image open to export. It can be of any width, height, and resolution. We will be adjusting these parameters as we complete the export process.

Follow these steps to complete this process:

1. Execute the **Export (Single Layer)** command as detailed in the previous sections of this chapter and choose a format that is friendly for web display. **JPEG** is recommended because of its small file sizes and ability to control the compression, and most social media platforms accept it.

2. Name your file and choose a folder to save it in on your computer. Click on **Save**.

3. In the **export settings** window that then appears, ensure that the **Preview rendering result on output** option is checked.

4. If you are using the `.jpg` format, adjust the **Quality** option as explained in the previous section. In this screenshot, we have set the **Quality** option to **70**:

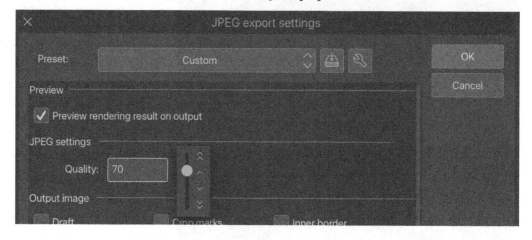

Figure 19.17 – Screenshot of the JPEG Quality option

5. Adjust the **Output size** options to dimensions that are web friendly. Usually, this is **1000** pixels or less in width, but this might change depending on the format of your image or the website that the image will be uploaded to. For example, a horizontal comic strip may need to be wider than this to be legible. In the following screenshot, we have used the **Specify output size** option to set the image width to **1000** pixels:

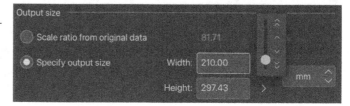

Figure 19.18 – Screenshot of the JPEG Output size options

6. At the bottom of the export settings dialog box, we have the **Process when scaling** options. If you are exporting a colored image or an image that doesn't use screentones, select the **For illustration** option. If the export image is a comic with screentones, choose the **For comic** option instead to cut down on the number of moiré patterns in the exported image.

7. Click on **OK**.

The **Export preview** window will be displayed once the image has been rendered. Use this preview to review the dimensions and the quality of the final exported file. Make any changes to the file quality by using the option in the bottom-right corner of the preview window. This allows us to change the compression before the final export so that we can ensure that we have a good-looking image with a reasonable file size.

In the following screenshot, we adjusted the quality from the initial **70** to **80** to achieve better image quality while keeping the file size small:

Figure 19.19 – Screenshot of the Export preview window

8. Click on **OK** to complete the export.

Done! You are now ready to upload your creation to the internet!

For people who already have or are thinking of switching to the EX version of Clip Studio Paint, which is more expensive and has more functions for expert use than the Pro version, I'd like to tell you that there is a very useful function for creating webtoons. Webtoons are becoming a bigger phenomenon nowadays in scroll-reading style manga and comic websites. Read on to find out how to export a file as a webtoon.

Exporting webtoons (EX only)

A webtoon is a spindle belt-shaped manga or comic, just like a film reel, for readers to scroll through to read the manga or comic. You can create a very long webtoon, which readers can scroll through and read to enjoy without clicking to see the next page. It works wonderfully for a platform such as X, where only a limited number of images can be attached to one post.

The following screenshot shows a style difference between an analog story manga and a webtoon:

Figure 19.20 – Screenshot of the style difference

However, if it's getting too long, it also becomes difficult to handle. You can't check the contents in thumbnails, and it is not easy to jump to a specific spot to edit. The best way is to create a B5-size manga page and then put a few pages together to make a belt shape.

In this section, we will learn how to export files as webtoons easily with the help of Clip Studio Paint EX.

You can do this by following these steps:

1. Create a manga that contains more than two pages.
2. In the **File** menu, select **Special Export | Export webtoon...** to bring up an **Export webtoon** dialog box, which looks like the following screenshot:
3. There are selections for exporting file formats, which are **.png (PNG) or .jpg (JPEG)**, from the **File format** drop-down menu. Select **.jpg (JPEG)** for a safe option because it's widely used on most websites and social media platforms. Also, change the name of the exporting file to something of your choosing.
4. In the **Output size** settings, you can scale up or down by changing the number for the percentage. You can also

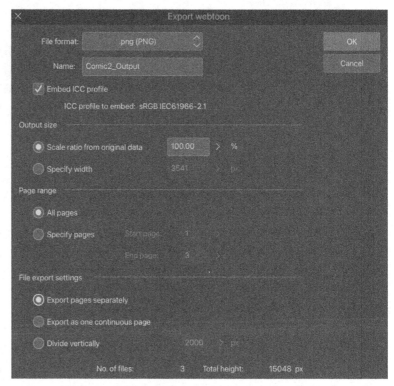

Figure 19.21 – Screenshot of the Export webtoon dialog box

choose **Specify width** by typing the desired width in pixels. This is very useful for some social media platforms or websites where they limit the width of the image to upload.

5. In the **Page range** settings, you can choose what page to export. Selecting **All pages** exports all pages, and by selecting **Specify pages**, you can type the start and end page numbers.

6. In the **File export** settings, selecting **Export pages separately** exports pages as individual images. Selecting **Export as one continuous page** exports one image in which all the selected pages are connected vertically like a film reel. By selecting **Divide vertically**, you can also divide pages into two vertically at the point or length of the pixel you typed. At the bottom of the dialog box, you can see the number of files and the total height in pixels.

7. Once you have finalized all the settings, click **OK** to export. Please be patient; it may take a few minutes to complete.

In the following screenshot, there are samples of how files look when exported with the **Export as one continuous page** and **Divide vertically** options:

Export as
one continuous
page

Divide vertically

Figure 19.22 – Screenshot of the two exported files

You have now mastered how to create a webtoon for sharing on your social media or website!

Now, we are going to look at another great function that Clip Studio EX possesses, which is exporting pages as a batch, meaning you don't need to resize or change the image quality one by one! What a time saver! Read on to find out how to do this.

Exporting batches of pages (EX only)

In this section, we are going to learn how to export manga pages as a batch.

There is no need to export your entire manga one page at a time so long as you have Clip Studio Paint EX. Because we can create story files in the EX version of the software, we can also export all or part of those story files all at once. They can even all be resized and compressed at the same time too, thereby saving you lots of time and effort in finishing up a project.

Follow these steps to export an entire chapter's worth of pages at once:

1. In the **File** menu, go to **Export multiple pages** and then click on **Batch export....** This menu is shown in the following screenshot:

Figure 19.23 – Screenshot of the Export multiple pages option

2. The **Batch export** dialog box will appear, as shown in the following screenshot:

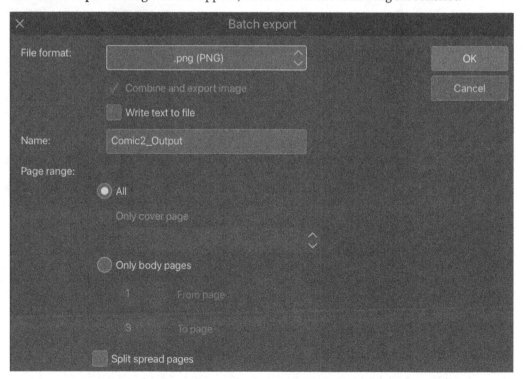

Figure 19.24 – Screenshot of the Batch export dialog box

3. Use the drop-down menu to choose the file format for the exported images.

4. If desired, click on the box next to **Write text to file** to make a file of the text used in the story file.

5. In the **Name** box, type a name, which will be the beginning of the filename for each exported image.

6. Select **Page range**. The **All** option will export all images in the story file. The **Only cover page** option will allow us to export just the front cover, just the back cover, or all cover pages. The **Only body pages** option allows us to select a range of interior pages to export.

7. To export each page of a two-page spread as a separate image, check the box next to **Split spread pages.**

8. Click on **OK**.

    Clip Studio Paint will now load the file and prepare it for export. This may take several minutes, depending on your computer's specifications and the size of your file. Be patient!

9. Once the file has loaded, the export settings for the chosen file format will be shown. Adjust them as detailed in the other sections of this chapter.

10. Click on **OK** when all the settings have been adjusted to complete the export.

I am certain that this will save you so much time if you are creating a long story manga. But did you know that there is a manga-sharing function in Clip Studio Start screen? It's one of the great places to share your creations, which will create a 3D viewer virtual manga book for you. Then, you can use the link to the page to put on your social media! Let's find this out in the next section.

Exporting to Clip Studio SHARE

In this section, we're exploring the Clip Studio SHARE function in Clip Studio Start, where you can create a showcase of your work.

When you are uploading manga that is more than four pages long, it's tough to show everything in order in divided posts on X, Instagram, Facebook, Tumblr, or other social media platforms.

Using Clip Studio SHARE helps to upload a manga that is more than 4 pages in length in the correct order by creating a special link for easy browsing, which you can paste on your social media! Clip Studio SHARE even creates a virtual 3D manga book for you with a cover and a spine of your design.

Fir1st. of all, you need to have a manga that contains more than three pages and then follow these steps to create your manga on display using Clip Studio SHARE:

1. Click on the **CLIP STUDIO** icon on your Command Bar to go to the Clip STudio Start screen. The icon looks like the the one pointed in the far left in the following screenshot:

Figure 19.25 – Screenshot of the command bar

2. Click on the nine-square icon at the top right of the Clip Studio Start screen, as shown in the following screenshot:

3. The Clip Studio Start **Menu** window will pop up. Click the **Showcase your work** icon, as pointed to in the following screenshot:

Figure 19.26 – Screenshot of the Clip Studio Start menu icon

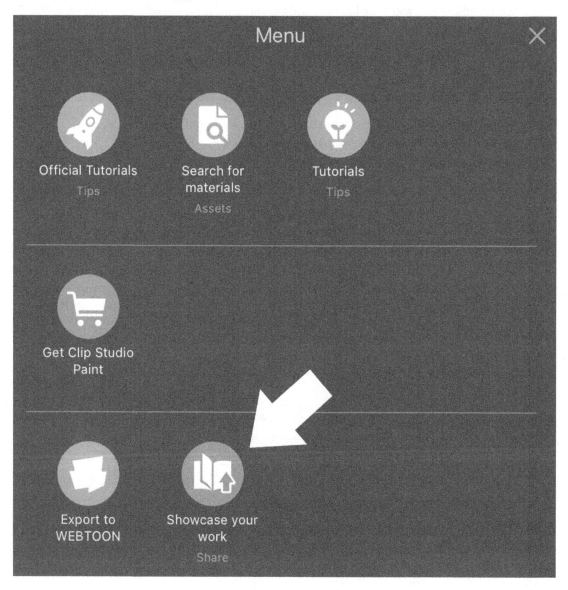

Figure 19.27 – Screenshot of the Clip Studio Assets menu window

4. On the **Clip Studio SHARE** screen, click the **Publish your story** button, as displayed in the following screenshot:

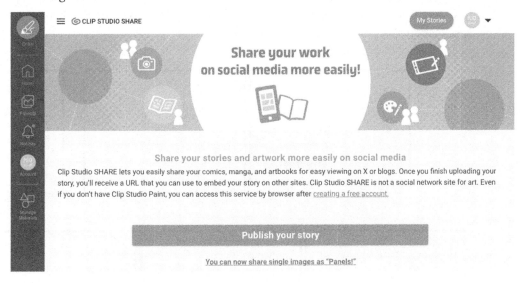

Figure 19.28 – Screenshot of the Clip Studio SHARE screen

5. There are two options – **Upload from browser** and **Upload from Clip Studio**. Clicking the **Upload from browser** option will let you select images from your computer browser, while **Upload from Clip Studio** will take you to the **Your work** list to select the story (the only option with the EX version) or images from the list. Selecting **Upload from browser** takes you to the **Reading direction** settings screen, where you can select the preferred direction. The screen looks like the following screenshot:

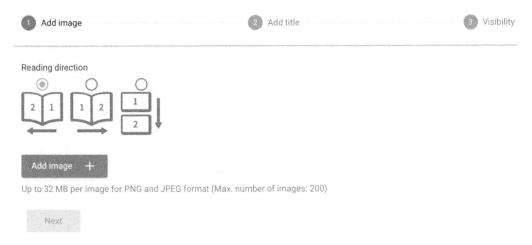

Figure 19.29 – Screenshot of the Reading direction settings screen

6. After selecting the reading direction, click **Add image** + to select images in order on your computer browser, and then click **Add**. The screen will show you a list of the images you have selected and the order in which they will be displayed, which looks like the following screenshot:

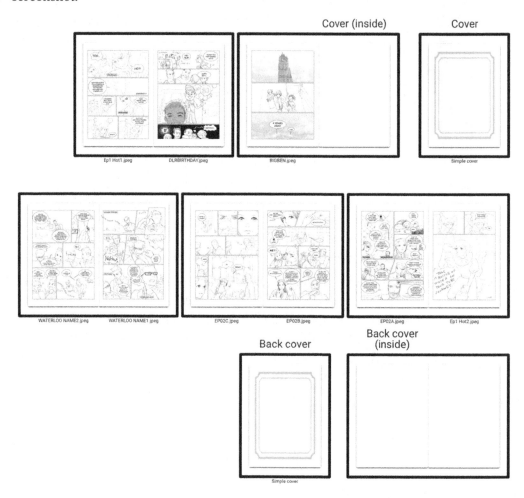

Figure 19.30 – Screenshot of a mock-up page list

7. If everything appears fine to you, click the **Next** button. If you selected **Upload from Clip Studio** in *Step 5*, the reading direction options will appear. Selecting one will take you to the **Select works** list, to select the manga work you want to upload. If you have the Clip Studio EX version, you can select **Stories (horizontal reading direction)**. If not, you can only select one other option, **Webtoons (vertical reading direction)**. After selecting the artwork, a confirmation window will appear. Then, click **OK** in the window.

8. Once you have uploaded images from a browser or Clip Studio, you will see a screen for entering key information, including the title, thumbnail image, summarizing your manga in 200 characters, a thumbnail for social media sharing, a 3D viewer book size to pick from – A4, B5, or B6 – choosing whether the images will be aligned to the book size, cover stiffness, cover texture/finish, page texture, and a spine image.

9. After entering the preceding key information, click the **CREATE PREVIEW** button near the bottom of the screen to see the preview of your manga before displaying it in public. The 3D viewer will look like the following screenshot:

Figure 19.31 – Screenshot of a sample 3D viewer

10. You can edit the contents and click the **SHOW PREVIEW** button until the preview looks fine for you. Once you're satisfied with the preview, click the **Next** button at the bottom of the screen to bring up the **Visibility** settings screen, which looks like the following screenshot:

1 Add image ---------------------------- 2 Add title ---------------------------- 3 Visibility

Visibility(required)

◉ Public   ○ Lock with a secret phrase

☐ Add adult content rating

Please check this box if your story includes content inappropriate for people under 18 (such as nudity, sexual content, extreme violence, or other graphic content). Refer to the Rating Standards for further guidance.

Advice

• If you turn this option on, the thumbnail and story information will not be visible when the story is published.

Comments

◉ Turn on commenting   ○ Turn off commenting

Comiket Web Catalog

○ Link   ◉ Don't link

Select "Link" to link this story to the circle profile or web catalog on Comiket Web Catalog. (Japanese)
To link your story, select the circle you'd like to link from Portal site for Circle.ms, then follow the instructions to link the story.

Advice

• It may take up to 24 hours until changes are reflected.
• You can change these settings even after you have published your work from "My Stories".

Publish

Back

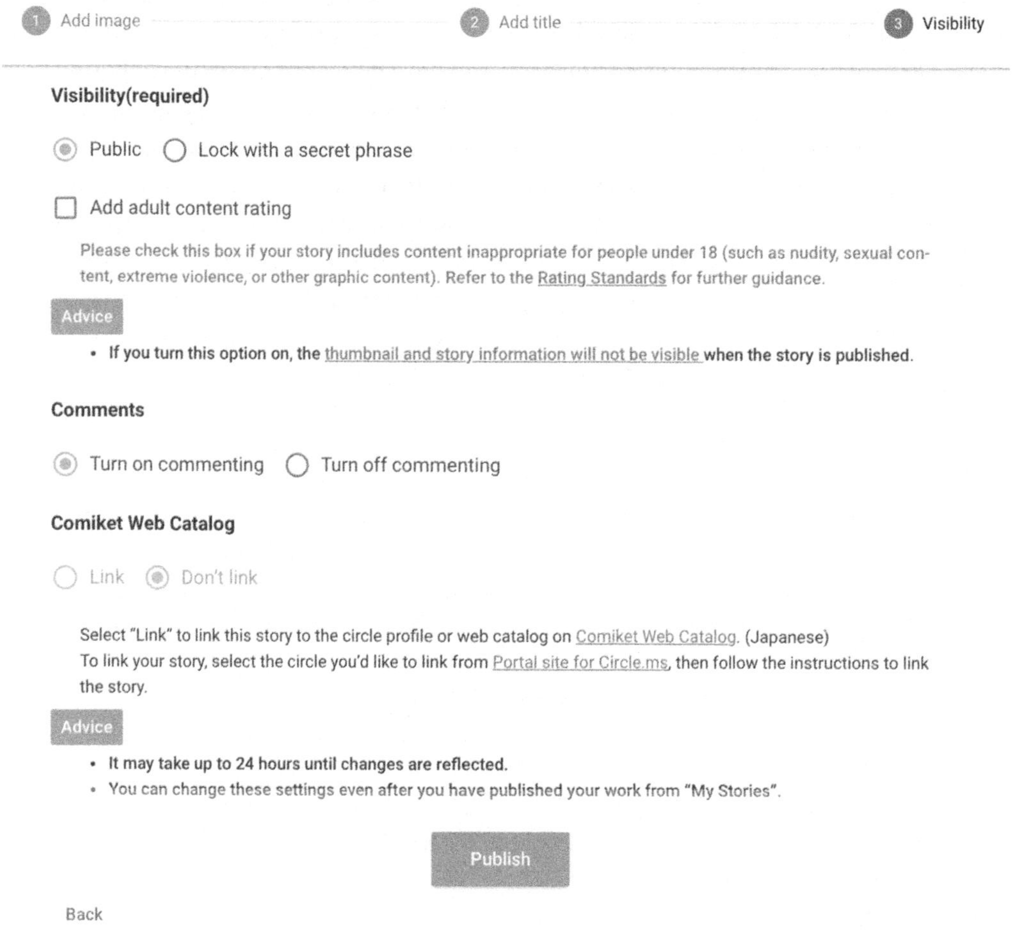

Figure 19.32 – Screenshot of the Visibility settings screen

11. On the **Visibility** settings screen, you can choose to publish your manga either by selecting **Public** (visible for anyone) or **Lock with a secret phrase** (visible only for people who know the secret phrase).

12. If you select **Lock with a secret phrase**, a textbox will appear for you to type in a secret phrase. Check the box next to **Add adult content rating** if the manga is not appropriate for a younger audience. Finally, select whether you want people to comment on your manga, and then click the **Publish** button. Then, the successful upload screen will appear, as per the following screenshot:

Your story has been posted successfully!

Why not add a link to a highlighted area of your choosing?

Add link

You can read your story at the following link.

https://share.clip-studio.com/en-us/contents/view?code=eabb98bc-4fd5-4e4b-ae38-

795327b6e194&at=1716925295   Copy URL

X f URL

HTML embed code

<iframe width='485' height='686' src='https://sh

Go to My Stories

Figure 19.33 – Screenshot of a successful upload screen

13. You can add a link, copy a URL, copy HTML embedded code, or jump to X and Facebook to post the link. If you want to edit or delete the manga, you can go to a screen with a list of your uploaded manga by clicking the **Go to My Stories** button.

Although this is virtual, it is great to see your manga book bound and displayed with a cover and spine, which you can flip through just like a physical book! Now, you have a place for your own online manga showcase, with a function where people can leave comments. So, let's share it with the world.

Summary

In this chapter, we have learned how to take our art from Clip Studio Paint and change it into files that we can share with the world. First, we learned how to print our images from Clip Studio to our home printer. Then, we learned how to export our images to be sent to a print shop, copy shop, or publisher. We learned how to adjust the image quality and the dimensions, and how to export our images so that they display well on the internet. Then, we learned what a webtoon is and how to export this in the EX version, and we also learned about another great EX privilege – exporting batches of pages. Finally, we learned about a great Clip Studio Start service, Clip Studio SHARE, where you can create a virtual showcase of your manga.

This is the last chapter of this book. It has been a long and fun journey learning how to use Clip Studio Paint for our creations, and now it has come to an end. I hope all these skills and tips will be helpful and inspiring to your creative life.

Learning how to draw manga, of course, never really ends. With that in mind, I'd like to suggest two more resources that you might find valuable. If you've got the desire to keep exploring, I'd recommend:

- *Manga in Theory and Practice: The Craft of Creating Manga*, written by Hirohiko Araki, the creator of Jojo's Bizarre Adventure. This book is great for tips on how to write stories and understand the Shonen manga genre.

- *Deep Blizzard's Art School* (@deepblizzard) on YouTube. This channel gives away the best digital drawing tips, with many Clip-Studio-Paint-specific topics.

If this book helped in any way with your art creation, feel free to tag me, @inko_dokotei, on Instagram, or share your progress with other Clip Studio Paint artists with the #clipstudiopaintart hashtag on social media.

Most of all, have great fun!

Join us on Discord!

Read this book alongside other users. Ask questions, provide solutions to other readers, and much more.

Scan the QR code or visit the link to join the community.

`https://packt.link/clipstudiopaint`

packt.com

Subscribe to our online digital library for full access to over 7,000 books and videos, as well as industry leading tools to help you plan your personal development and advance your career. For more information, please visit our website.

Why subscribe?

- Spend less time learning and more time coding with practical eBooks and Videos from over 4,000 industry professionals
- Improve your learning with Skill Plans built especially for you
- Get a free eBook or video every month
- Fully searchable for easy access to vital information
- Copy and paste, print, and bookmark content

At www.packt.com, you can also read a collection of free technical articles, sign up for a range of free newsletters, and receive exclusive discounts and offers on Packt books and eBooks.

Other Books You May Enjoy

If you enjoyed this book, you may be interested in these other books by Packt:

Mastering Adobe Photoshop Elements - Sixth Edition

Robin Nichols

ISBN: 9781835469385

- Master new features in Photoshop Elements 2024, including AI-powered tools and one-click fixes on mobile
- Create captivating photo collages, digital paintings, and graphic designs
- Efficiently organize your photo collections for easy access and management
- Enhance your social media presence with professionally edited photos and artworks
- Employ advanced layer techniques for more powerful and immersive illustrations
- Gain comprehensive knowledge to become a proficient Photoshop Elements user

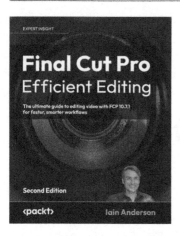

Final Cut Pro Efficient Editing - Second Edition

Iain Anderson

ISBN: 9781837631674

- Organize and manage media from multiple sources
- Edit and manipulate video with an intuitive interface and powerful tools
- Streamline your workflow with customizable workspaces and keyboard shortcuts
- Sync and edit multicam interviews with ease and learn advanced trimming techniques
- Use advanced audio and color grading tools to achieve a professional-quality finish
- Work with other editors using the built-in collaboration tools
- Create stunning visual effects and complex motion graphics titles
- Export video projects in a variety of formats for delivery to multiple platforms and user devices

The Music Producer's Creative Guide to Ableton Live 11 – First Edition

Anna Lakatos

ISBN: 9781801817639

- Understand the concept of Live, the workflow of recording and editing Audio and MIDI, and Warping
- Utilize Groove, MIDI effects, and Live 11 s new workflow enhancements to create innovative music
- Use Audio to MIDI conversion tools to translate and generate ideas quickly
- Dive into Live's automation and modulation capabilities and explore project organization techniques to speed up your workflow
- Utilize MIDI Polyphonic Expression to create evolving sounds and textures
- Adopt useful techniques for production and discover the capabilities of live performance

The Music Producer's Ultimate Guide to FL Studio 21 - Second Edition

Joshua Au-Yeung

ISBN: 9781837631650

- Mix techniques with compressors, equalizers, and stereo width effect plugins
- Record into FL Studio, pitch correct and retime samples, and gain advice for applying effects to vocals
- Create vocal harmonies and learn how to use vocoders to modulate your vocals with an instrument
- Create glitch effects, transform audio samples into playable instruments, and work on sound design with cutting edge effects
- Develop your brand with marketing best practices and tips for creating content to reach a wider audience
- Publish your music online and collect royalty revenues

Packt is searching for authors like you

If you're interested in becoming an author for Packt, please visit authors.packtpub.com and apply today. We have worked with thousands of developers and tech professionals, just like you, to help them share their insight with the global tech community. You can make a general application, apply for a specific hot topic that we are recruiting an author for, or submit your own idea.

Share your thoughts

Now you've finished *Learn Clip Studio Paint, Fourth Edition*, we'd love to hear your thoughts! Scan the QR code below to go straight to the Amazon review page for this book and share your feedback or leave a review on the site that you purchased it from.

https://packt.link/r/1835886590

Your review is important to us and the tech community and will help us make sure we're delivering excellent quality content.

Index

Download a free PDF copy of this book

Thanks for purchasing this book!

Do you like to read on the go but are unable to carry your print books everywhere?

Is your eBook purchase not compatible with the device of your choice?

Don't worry, now with every Packt book you get a DRM-free PDF version of that book at no cost.

Read anywhere, any place, on any device. Search, copy, and paste code from your favorite technical books directly into your application.

The perks don't stop there, you can get exclusive access to discounts, newsletters, and great free content in your inbox daily.

Follow these simple steps to get the benefits:

1. Scan the QR code or visit the link below:

https://packt.link/free-ebook/9781835886588

2. Submit your proof of purchase.
3. That's it! We'll send your free PDF and other benefits to your email directly.